TO

ARNOLD SHIRCLIFFE
STEWARD, GASTRONOMER, AUTHOR AND BIBLIOPHILE
AS THE ACTORS SHAKESPEARE AND MOLIÈRE CREATED
THE BEST DRAMA, SO THE BEST IN GASTRONOMIC
LITERATURE EMANATED FROM WITHIN THE RANKS

THE AUTHOR

SYMPOSION. FROM AN ANCIENT VASE

APICII·LIBRI·X

QVI DICVNTVR DE OBSONIIS ET CONDIMENTIS SIVE ARTE COQVINARIA QVÆ EXTANT

•

NVNC PRIMVM ANGLICE REDDIDIT PROŒMIO
BIBLIOGRAPHICO ATQVE INTERPRETATIONE
DEFENSIT VARIISQVE ANNOTATIONIBVS
INSTRVXIT ITA ET ANTIQVÆ CVLINÆ
VTENSILIARVM EFFIGIIS EXORNAVIT
INDICEM DENIQVE ETYMOLOGICVM ET
TECHNICVM ARTIS MAGIRICÆ ADIECIT

•

IOSEPHVS DOMMERS VEHLING

•

INTRODVXIT FRIDERICVS STARR

APICIUS

COOKERY AND DINING IN IMPERIAL ROME

A Bibliography, Critical Review and Translation of the
Ancient Book known as *Apicius de re Coquinaria*

NOW FOR THE FIRST TIME RENDERED INTO ENGLISH

BY

JOSEPH DOMMERS VEHLING

*With a Dictionary of Technical Terms, Many Notes,
Facsimiles of Originals, and Views and Sketches of
Ancient Culinary Objects Made by the Author*

INTRODUCTION BY PROF. FREDERICK STARR
Formerly of the University of Chicago

DOVER PUBLICATIONS, INC.
NEW YORK

Published in Canada by General Publishing Company, Ltd., 30 Lesmill Road, Don Mills, Toronto, Ontario.

Published in the United Kingdom by Constable and Company, Ltd., 10 Orange Street, London WC2H 7EG.

This Dover edition, first published in 1977, is an unabridged republication of the work originally published by Walter M. Hill, Chicago, 1936, in an edition of 530 copies. Only the list of subscribers has been omitted.

International Standard Book Number:
0-486-23563-7
Library of Congress Catalog Card Number:
77-89410

Manufactured in the United States of America
Dover Publications, Inc.
180 Varick Street
New York, N.Y. 10014

CONTENTS

		PAGE
INTRODUCTION	. . . .	xi
PREFACE	. . . .	xvii

THE BOOK OF APICIUS
A critical review of its times, its authors, and their sources, its
authenticity and practical usefulness in modern times . . .   1

THE RECIPES OF APICIUS AND THE EXCERPTS FROM APICIUS BY VINIDARIUS
Original translation from the most reliable Latin texts, elucidated with notes and comments   41

APICIANA
A bibliography of Apician manuscript books and printed editions   251

DICTIONARY OF CULINARY TERMS AND INDEX . . .   275

ILLUSTRATIONS

A — FACSIMILES

Made from originals and reproductions in the author's collection

		PAGE
1	BREVIS PIMENTORUM, Excerpts of Vinidarius, 8th Century	234
2	INCIPIT CONDITUM PARADOXUM, Vatican MS, 9th Century	253
3	COLOPHON, Signerre Edition, Milan, 1498 . . .	260
4	TITLE PAGE, Tacuinus Edition, Venice, 1503 . . .	262
5	OPENING CHAPTER, same	232
6	TITLE PAGE, Schola Apitiana, Antwerp, 1535 . .	206
7	TITLE PAGE, Torinus Edition, Basel, 1541 . . .	220
8	TITLE PAGE, Torinus Edition, Lyons, 1541 . . .	263
9	TITLE PAGE, Humelbergius Edition, Zürich, 1542 . .	265
10	TITLE PAGE, Lister Edition, London, 1705 . . .	267
11	VERSO of Title Page, Lister Edition, London, 1705 . .	268
12	TITLE PAGE, Lister Edition, Amsterdam, 1709 . .	250
13	FRONTISPIECE, Lister Edition, Amsterdam, 1709 . .	156
14	BANQUET SCENE, from an ancient vase . . .	(opposite)

B — PEN AND INK DRAWINGS BY THE AUTHOR

Sketched from scenes and objects at Pompeii, Naples, Berlin and Chicago. Most of the ancient objects are in the National Museum of Naples with many replicas in the Field Museum, Chicago. The treasure found in 1868 near Hildesheim is in the Kaiser Friedrich Museum in Berlin

PAGE

15 APICII LIBRI X, Latin title of present edition, hand-lettered (facing title)
16 DIAGRAM of Apicius manuscripts and printed editions . . 252
17 GREAT CRATER, Hildesheim Treasure 140
18 THERMOSPODIUM, plain, Naples 90
19 THERMOSPODIUM, elaborate, Naples 72
20 DESSERT or Fruit Dish, Shell, Naples 125
21 DESSERT or Fruit Bowl, fluted 61
22 TABLE, square, adjustable, Naples 138
23 TABLE, round, Naples 122
24 PAN, Frying, round, Naples 155
25 PAN, Frying, oval, Naples 159
26 PAN, Service Saucepan, with decorated handle, Hildesheim . . 73
27 SERVICE DISH, oval, with two handles, Hildesheim Treasure . 43
28 PAN, Saucepan, with handle, Hercules motif, Naples . . . 222
29 PLATTER for Roast, Hildesheim Treasure 219
30 PLATTER, The Great Pallas Athene Dish, Hildesheim . . 158
31 TRIPOD for Crater, Hildesheim Treasure 40
32 EGG SERVICE DISH, Hildesheim Treasure 93
33 WINE DIPPER, Naples 3
34 DIONYSOS CUP, Hildesheim Treasure 141
35 CANTHARUS, Theatrical Decoration, Hildesheim Treasure . 231
36 CANTHARUS, Bacchic Decoration, Hildesheim Treasure . . 274
37 COLANDER, Naples 58
39 WINE PITCHER, Diana handle, Naples 208
39 WINE PRESS, Reconstruction in Naples 92
40 GONG for Slaves, Naples 42
41 WINE STOCK ROOM, Pompeii 124
42 CASA DI FORNO, Pompeii 2
43 SLAVES operating hand mill, reconstruction in Naples . . 60
44 STEW POT, No. 1, Caccabus, Naples 183
45 STEW POT, No. 2, Caccabus, Naples 209
46 STEW POT, No. 3, Caccabus, Naples 223
47 STEW POT, No. 4, Caccabus, Naples 235
48 CRATICULA, combination broiler and stove, Naples . . . 182
49 "LIBRO COMPLETO" . . . . . . (End of Book)

EXPLANATION OF TYPESETTING, ABBREVIATIONS, AND SYSTEM OF NUMBERING

TEXT AND HEADINGS

The original ancient text as presented and rendered in the present translation is printed in capital letters.

Matter in parenthesis ( ) is original. Matter in square brackets [ ] is contributed by the translator.

In most of the early originals the headings or titles of the formulæ are invariably part of the text. In the present translation they are given both in English and in the Latin used by those originals which the translator considered most characteristic titles.

They have been set in prominent type as titles over each formula, whereas in the originals the formulæ of the various chapters run together, in many instances without distinct separation.

NUMBERING OF RECIPES

A system of numbering the recipes has therefore been adopted by the translator, following the example of Schuch, which does not exist in the other originals but the numbers in the present translation do not correspond to those adopted by Schuch for reasons which hereafter become evident.

NOTES AND COMMENTS BY THE TRANSLATOR

The notes, comments and variants added to each recipe by the translator are printed in upper and lower case and in the same type as the other contributions by the translator, the Apiciana, the Critical Review and the Vocabulary and Index.

For the sake of convenience, to facilitate the study of each recipe and for quick reference the notes follow in each and every case such ancient recipe as they have reference to.

ABBREVIATIONS

NY — The New York Codex (formerly Cheltenham), Apiciana, I
Vat. — The Vatican Codex, Apiciana, II.
Vin. — The Codex Salmasianus, Excerpta a Vinidario, Apiciana, III.
B. de V. — Edition by Bernardinus, Venice, n.d., Apiciana, No. 1.
Lan. — Edition by Lancilotus, Milan, 1498, Apiciana, Nos. 2-3.
Tac. — Edition by Tacuinus, Venice, 1503, Apiciana, No. 4.
Tor. — Edition by Torinus, Basel (and Lyons), 1541, Apiciana, Nos. 5-6.

Hum. — Edition by Humelbergius, Zürich, 1542, Apiciana, No. 7.

List. — Edition by Lister, London, 1705, Amst., 1709, Apiciana, Nos. 8-9.

Bern. — Edition by Bernhold, Marktbreit, etc., Apiciana, Nos. 10-11.

Bas. — Edition by Baseggio, Venice, 1852, Apiciana, No. 13.

Sch. — Edition by Schuch, Heidelberg, 1867/74, Apiciana, Nos. 14-15.

Goll. — Edition by Gollmer, Leipzig, 1909, Apiciana, No. 16.

Dann. — Edition by Danneil, Leipzig, 1911, Apiciana, No. 17.

G.-V. — Edition by Giarratano-Vollmer, Leip. 1922, Apiciana, No. 19.

V. — The present translation.

Giarr. — Giarratano; Voll. — F. Vollmer; Bran. — Edward Brandt.

INTRODUCTION

INTRODUCTION

BY

FREDERICK STARR

Formerly Professor of Anthropology at the University of Chicago

NO translation of Apicius into English has yet been published. The book has been printed again and again in Latin and has been translated into Italian and German. It is unnecessary to here give historic details regarding the work as Mr. Vehling goes fully and admirably into the subject. In 1705 the book was printed in Latin at London, with notes by Dr. Martinus Lister. It caused some stir in the England of that time. In a very curious book, The Art of Cookery, in Imitation of Horace's Art of Poetry, with Some Letters to Dr. Lister and Others, Dr. Wm. King says:

> "The other curiosity is the admirable piece of Cœlius Apicius, '*De Op-soniis et condimentis sive arte coquinaria, Libri decem*' being ten books of soups and sauces, and the art of cookery, as it is excellently printed for the doctor, who in this important affair, is not sufficiently communicative. . .
>
> "I some days ago met with an old acquaintance, of whom I inquired if he has seen the book concerning soups and sauces? He told me he had, but that he had but a very slight view of it, the person who was master of it not being willing to part with so valuable a rarity out of his closet. I desired him to give me some account of it. He says that it is a very handsome octavo, for, ever since the days of Ogilvy, good paper and good print, and fine cuts, make a book become ingenious and brighten up an author strangely. That there is a copious index; and at the end a catalogue of all the doctor's works, concerning cockles, English beetles, snails, spiders, that get up into the air and throw us down cobwebs; a monster vomited up by a baker and such like; which if carefully perused, would wonderfully improve us."

More than two hundred years have passed and we now have an edition of this curious work in English. And our edition has nothing to lose by comparison with the old one. For this, too, is a handsome book, with good paper and good print and fine cuts. And the man who produces it can equally bear comparison with Dr. Lister and more earlier commentators and editors whom he quotes — Humelbergius and Caspar Barthius.

The preparation of such a book is no simple task and requires a rare combination of qualities. Mr. Vehling possesses this unusual combination. He was born some forty-five years ago in the small town of Duelken on the German-

Dutch frontier — a town proverbial for the dullness of its inhabitants. There was nothing of dullness about the boy, however, for at the age of fourteen years, he had already four years study of Latin and one of Greek to his credit. Such was his record in Latin that his priest teachers attempted to influence him toward the priesthood. His family, however, had other plans and believing that he had enough schooling, decided that he should be a cook. As he enjoyed good food, had a taste for travel and independence, and was inclined to submit to family direction, he rather willingly entered upon the career planned for him. He learned the business thoroughly and for six years practiced his art in Germany, Belgium, France, England and Scandinavia. Wherever he went, he gave his hours of freedom to reading and study in libraries and museums.

During his first trip through Italy and on a visit to Pompeii he conceived the idea of depicting some day the table of the Romans and of making the present translation. He commenced to gather all the necessary material for this work, which included intensive studies of the ancient arts and languages. Meanwhile, he continued his hotel work also, quite successfully. At the age of twenty-four he was assistant manager of the fashionable Hotel Bristol, Vienna.

However, the necessities of existence prevented his giving that time and study to art, which is necessary if it was to become a real career. In Vienna he found music, drama, languages, history, literature and gastronomy, and met interesting people from all parts of the globe. While the years at Vienna were the happiest of his life, he had a distaste for the "superheated, aristocratic and military atmosphere." It was at that city that he met the man who was responsible for his coming to America. Were we writing Mr. Vehling's biography, we would have ample material for a racy and startling narrative. We desire only to indicate the remarkable preparation for the work before us, which he has had. A Latin scholar of exceptional promise, a professional cook of pronounced success, and an artist competent to illustrate his own work! Could such a combination be anticipated? It is the combination that has made this book possible.

The book has claims even upon our busy and practical generation. Mr. Vehling has himself stated them:

> "The important addition to our knowledge of the ancients — for our popular notions about their table are entirely erroneous and are in need of revision.
> "The practical value of many of the ancient formulæ — for 'In Olde Things There is Newnesse.'
> "The human interest — because of the amazing mentality and the culinary ingenuity of the ancients revealed to us from an altogether new angle.
> "The curious novelty and the linguistic difficulty, the philological interest and the unique nature of the task, requiring unique prerequisites — all these factors prompted us to undertake this translation."

One word as to Mr. Vehling's work in America. He was for five years manager of catering at the Hotel Pfister in Milwaukee; for two and a half years he was inspector and instructor of the Canadian Pacific Railway; he was connected with some of the leading hotels in New York City, and with the Eppley and the Van Orman Hotels chains, in executive capacity. He not only has the practical side of food use and preparation, he is an authority upon the science in his field. His printed articles on food and cookery have been read with extraordinary interest, and his lectures upon culinary matters have been well received. It is to be hoped that both will eventually be published in book form.

There is no financial lure in getting out an English translation of Apicius. It is a labor of love — but worth the doing. We have claimed that Mr. Vehling has exceptional fitness for the task. This will be evident to anyone who reads his book. An interesting feature of his preparation is the fact that Mr. Vehling has subjected many of the formulæ to actual test. As Dr. Lister in the old edition of 1705 increased the value and interest of the work by making additions from various sources, so our editor of today adds much and interesting matter in his supplements, notes and illustrations.

It is hardly expected that many will follow Mr. Vehling in testing the Apician formulæ. Hazlitt in speaking of "The Young Cook's Monitor" which was printed in 1683, says:

> "Some of the ingredients proposed for sauces seem to our ears rather prodigious. In one place a contemporary peruser has inserted an ironical calculation in MS. to the effect that, whereas a cod's head could be bought for fourpence, the condiments recommended for it were not to be had for less than nine shillings."

We shall close with a plagiarism oft repeated. It was a plagiarism as long ago as 1736, when it was admitted such in the preface of Smith's "The Compleat Housewife":

> "It being grown as fashionable for a book now to appear in public without a preface, as for a lady to appear at a ball without a hoop-petticoat, I shall conform to the custom for fashion-sake and not through any necessity. (The subject being both common and universal, needs no argument to introduce it, and being so necessary for the gratification of the appetite, stands in need of no encomiums to allure persons to the practice of it; since there are but a few nowadays who love not good eating and drinking. . ."

Old Apicius and Joseph Dommers Vehling really need no introduction.

FREDERICK STARR

Seattle, Washington, August 3, 1926.

PREFACE

The present first translation into English of the ancient cookery book dating back to Imperial Roman times known as the Apicius book is herewith presented to antiquarians, friends of the Antique as well as to gastronomers, friends of good cheer.

Three of the most ancient manuscript books that exist today bearing the name of Apicius date back to the eighth and ninth century. Ever since the invention of printing Apicius has been edited chiefly in the Latin language. Details of the manuscript books and printed editions will be found under the heading of Apiciana on the following pages.

The present version has been based chiefly upon three principal Latin editions, that of Albanus Torinus, 1541, who had for his authority a codex he found on the island of Megalona, on the editions of Martinus Lister, 1705-9, who based his work upon that of Humelbergius, 1542, and the Giarratano-Vollmer edition, 1922.

We have also scrutinized various other editions forming part of our collection of Apiciana, and as shown by our "family tree of Apicius" have drawn either directly or indirectly upon every known source for our information.

The reasons and raison d'être for this undertaking become sufficiently clear through Dr. Starr's introduction and through the following critical review.

It has been often said that the way to a man's heart is through his stomach; so here is hoping that we may find a better way of knowing old Rome and antique private life through the study of this cookery book — Europe's oldest and Rome's only one in existence today.

J. D. V.

Chicago, in the Spring of 1926.

THANKS

For many helpful hints, for access to works in their libraries and for their kind and sympathetic interest in this work I am especially grateful to Professor Dr. Edward Brandt, of Munich; to Professor Dr. Margaret Barclay Wilson, of Washington, D.C., and New York City; to Mr. Arnold Shircliffe, and Mr. Walter M. Hill, both of Chicago.

J. D. V.

Chicago, in the Summer of 1936.

THE BOOK OF APICIUS

POMPEII: CASA DI FORNO — HOUSE OF THE OVEN

Ancient bakery and flour mill of the year A. D. 79. Four grain grinders to the right. The method of operating these mills is shown in the sketch of the slaves operating a hand-mill. These mills were larger and were driven by donkeys attached to beams stuck in the square holes. The bake house is to the left, with running water to the right of the entrance to the oven. The oven itself was constructed ingeniously with a view of saving fuel and greatest efficiency.

WINE DIPPER

Found in Pompeii. Each end of the long handle takes the form of a bird's head. The one close to the bowl holds in its bill a stout wire which is loosely fastened around the neck of the bowl, the two ends being interlocked. This allows the bowl to tilt sufficiently to hold its full contents when retired from the narrow opening of the amphora. The ancients also had dippers with extension handles to reach down to the bottom of the deep amphora. Ntl. Mus., Naples, 73822; Field M. 24181.

THE BOOK OF APICIUS

A STUDY OF ITS TIMES, ITS AUTHORS AND THEIR SOURCES, ITS AUTHENTICITY AND ITS PRACTICAL USEFULNESS IN MODERN TIMES

ANYONE who would know something worth while about the private and public lives of the ancients should be well acquainted with their table. Then as now the oft quoted maxim stands that man is what he eats.

Much of the ancient life is still shrouded and will forever be hidden by envious forces that have covered up bygone glory and grandeur. Ground into mealy dust under the hoofs of barbarian armies! Re-modeled, re-used a hundred times! Discarded as of no value by clumsy hands! The "Crime of Ignorance" is a factor in league with the forces of destruction. Much is destroyed by blind strokes of fate — fate, eternally pounding this earth in its everlasting enigmatic efforts to shape life into something, the purpose of which we do not understand, the meaning of which we may not even venture to dream of or hope to know.

Whatever there has been preserved by "Providence," by freaks of chance, by virtue of its own inherent strength — whatever has been buried by misers, fondled, treasured by loving hands of collectors and connoisseurs during all these centuries — every speck of ancient dust, every scrap of parchment or papyrus, a corroded piece of metal, a broken piece of stone or glass, so eagerly sought by the archaeologists and historians of the last few generations — all these fragmentary messages from out of the past emphasize the greatness of their time. They show its modernity, its nearness to our own days. They are now hazy reminiscences, as it were, by a middle-aged man of the hopes and the joys of his own youth. These furtive fragments — whatever they are — now tell us a story so full and so rich, they wield so marvelous a power, no man laying claim to possessing any intelligence may pass them without intensely feeling the eternal pathetic appeal to our hearts of these bygone ages that hold us down in an envious manner, begrudging us the warm life-blood of the present, weaving invisible ties around us to make our hearts heavy.

However, we are not here to be impeded by any sentimental considerations.

Thinking of the past, we are not so much concerned with the picture that dead men have placed in our path like ever so many bill boards and posters! We do not care for their "ideals" expounded in contemporary histories and eulogies. We are hardly moved by the "facts" such as they would have loved to see them happen, nor do we cherish the figments of their human, very human, subconsciousness.

To gain a correct picture of the Roman table we will therefore set aside for a while the fragments culled from ancient literature and history that have been misused so indiscriminately and so profusely during the last two thousand years — for various reasons. They have become fixed ideas, making reconstruction difficult for anyone who would gain a picture along rational lines. Barring two exceptions, there is no trustworthy detailed description of the ancient table by an objective contemporary observer. To be sure, there are some sporadic efforts, mere reiterations. The majority of the ancient word pictures are distorted views on our subject by partisan writers, contemporary moralists on the one side, satirists on the other. Neither of them, we venture to say, knew the subject professionally. They were not specialists in the sense of modern writers like Reynière, Rumohr, Vaerst; nor did they approach in technical knowledge medieval writers like Martino, Platina, Torinus.

True there were exceptions. Athenaeus, a most prolific and voluble magiric commentator, quoting many writers and specialists whose names but for him would have never reached posterity. Athenaeus tells about these gastronomers, the greatest of them, Archestratos, men who might have contributed so much to our knowledge of the ancient world, but to us these names remain silent, for the works of these men have perished with the rest of the great library at the disposal of this genial host of Alexandria.

Too, there are Anacharsis and Petronius. They and Athenaeus cannot be overlooked. These three form the bulk of our evidence.

Take on the other hand Plutarch, Seneca, Tertullian, even Pliny, writers who have chiefly contributed to our defective knowledge of the ancient table. They were no gourmets. They were biased, unreliable at best, as regards culinary matters. They deserve our attention merely because they are above the ever present mob of antique reformers and politicians of whom there was legion in Rome alone, under the pagan régime. Their state of mind and their intolerance towards civilized dining did not improve with the advent of Christianity.

The moralists' testimony is substantiated and supplemented rather than refuted by their very antipodes, the satirists, a group headed by Martial, Juvenal and the incomparable Petronius, who really is in a class by himself.

There is one more man worthy of mention in our particular study, Horace, a true poet, the most objective of all writers, man-about-town, pet of society, mundane genius, gifted to look calmly into the innermost heart of his time. His eyes fastened a correct picture on the sensitive diaphragm of a good memory, leaving an impression neither distorted nor "out of focus." His eye did not "pick up," for sundry reasons, the defects of the objects of observation, nor did it work with the uncanny joy of subconscious exaggeration met with so frequently in modern writing, nor did he indulge in that predeliction for ugly detail sported by modern art.

So much for Horatius, poet. Still, he was not a specialist in our line. We cannot enroll him among the gifted gourmets no matter how many meals he enjoyed at the houses of his society friends. We are rather inclined to place him among the host of writers, ancient and modern, who have treated the subject of food with a sort of sovereign contempt, or at least with indifference, because its study presented unsurmountable difficulties, and the subject, *per se*, was a menial one. With this attitude of our potential chief witnesses defined, we have no occasion to further appeal to them here, and we might proceed to real business, to the sifting of the trustworthy material at hand. It is really a relief to know that we have no array of formidable authorities to be considered in our study. We have virgin field before us — i.e., the ruins of ancient greatness grown over by a jungle of two thousand years of hostile posterity.

POMPEII

Pompeii was destroyed in A.D. 79. From its ruins we have obtained in the last half century more information about the intimate domestic and public life of the ancients than from any other single source. What is more important, this vast wealth of information is first hand, unspoiled, undiluted, unabridged, unbiased, uncensored; — in short, untouched by meddlesome human hands.

Though only a provincial town, Pompeii was a prosperous mercantile place, a representative market-place, a favorite resort for fashionable people. The town had hardly recuperated from a preliminary attack by that treacherous mountain, Vesuvius, when a second onslaught succeeded in complete destruction. Suddenly, without warning, this lumbering *force majeur* visited the ill-fated towns in its vicinity with merciless annihilation. The population, just then enjoying the games in the amphitheatre outside of the "downtown" district, had had hardly time to save their belongings. They escaped with their bare lives. Only the aged, the infirm, the prisoners and some faithful dogs were left behind. Today their bodies in plaster casts may be seen, mute witnesses to a frightful disaster. The town was covered with an airtight blanket of ashes, lava and fine pumice stone. There was no prolonged death struggle, no perceivable decay extended over centuries as was the cruel lot of Pompeii's mistress, Rome. There were no agonies to speak of. The great event was consummated within a few hours. The peace of death settled down to reign supreme after the dust had been driven away by the gentle breezes coming in from the bay of Naples. Some courageous citizens returned, searching in the hot ashes for the crashed-in roofs of their villas, to recover this or that. Perhaps they hoped to salvage the strong box in the atrium, or a heirloom from the triclinium. But soon they gave up. Despairing, or hoping for better days to come, they vanished in the mist of time. Pompeii, the fair, the hospitable, the gay city, just like any individual out of luck, was and stayed forgotten. The Pompeians, their joys, sorrows, their work and play, their virtues and vices — everything was arrested with one single stroke, stopped, even as a camera clicks, taking a snapshot.

The city's destruction, it appears, was a formidable opening blow dealt the Roman empire in the prime of its life, in a war of extermination waged by hostile invisible forces. Pompeii makes one believe in "Providence." A great disaster actually moulding, casting a perfect image of the time for future generations! To be exact, it took these generations eighteen centuries to discover and to appreciate the heritage that was theirs, buried at the foot of Vesuvius. During these long dark and dusky centuries charming goat herds had rested unctuous shocks of hair upon mysterious columns that, like young giant asparagus, stuck their magnificent heads out of the ground. Blinking drowsily at yonder villainous mountain, the summit of which is eternally crowned with a halo of thin white smoke, such as we are accustomed to see arising from the stacks of chemical factories, the confident shepherd would lazily implore his patron saint to enjoin that unreliable devilish force within lest the *dolce far niente* of the afternoon be disturbed, for siestas are among the most important functions in the life of that region. Occasionally the more enterprising would arm themselves with pick-axe and shovel, made bold by whispered stories of fabulous wealth, and, defying the evil spirits protecting it, they would set out on an expedition of loot and desecration of the tomb of ancient splendor.

Only about a century and a half ago the archaeological conscience awoke. Only seventy-five years ago energetic moves made possible a fruitful pilgrimage to this shrine of humanity, while today not more than two-thirds but perhaps the most important parts of the city have been opened to our astonished eyes by men who know.

And now: we may see that loaf of bread baked nineteen centuries ago, as found in the bake shop. We may inspect the ingenious bake oven where it was baked. We may see the mills that ground the flour for the bread, and, indeed find unground wheat kernels. We see the oil still preserved in the jugs, the residue of wine still in the amphorae, the figs preserved in jars, the lentils, the barley, the spices in the cupboard; everything awaits our pleasure: the taverns with their "bars"; the ancient guests' opinion of Mine Host scribbled on the wall, the kitchens with their implements, the boudoirs of milady's with the cosmetics and perfumes in the compacts. There are the advertisements on the walls, the foods praised with all the *eclat* of modern advertising, the election notices, the love missives, the bank deposits, the theatre tickets, law records, bills of sale.

Phantom-like yet real there are the good citizens of a good town, parading, hustling, loafing — sturdy patricians, wretched plebeians, stern centurios, boastful soldiers, scheming politicians, crafty law-clerks, timid scribes, chattering barbers, bullying gladiators, haughty actors, dusty travelers, making for Albinus', the famous host at the *Via della Abbondanza* or, would he give preference to Sarinus, the son of Publius, who advertised so cleverly? Or, perhaps, could he afford to stop at the "Fortunata" Hotel, centrally located?

There are, too, the boorish hayseeds from out of town trying to sell their produce, unaccustomed to the fashionable Latin-Greek speech of the city folks, gaping with their mouths wide open, greedily at the steaks of sacrificial meat displayed behind enlarging glasses in the cheap cook shop windows. There they giggle and chuckle, those wily landlords with their blasé habitués and their underlings, the greasy cooks, the roguish "good mixers" at the bar and the winsome if resolute *copæ* — waitresses — all ready to go, to do business. So slippery are the cooks that Plautus calls one *Congrio* — sea eel — so black that another deserves the title *Anthrax* — coal.

There they are, one and all, the characters necessary to make up what we call civilization, chattering agitatedly in a lingo of Latin-Greek-Oscan — as if life were a continuous market day.

It takes no particular scholarship, only a little imagination and human sympathy to see and to hear the ghosts of Pompeii.

There is no pose about this town, no *mise-en-scène*, no stage-setting. No heroic gesture. No theatricals, in short, no lies. There is to be found no shred of that vainglorious cloak which humans will deftly drape about their shoulders whenever they happen to be aware of the camera. There is no "registering" of any kind here.

Pompeii's natural and pleasant disposition, therefore, is ever so much more in evidence. Not a single one of this charming city's movements was intended for posterity. Her life stands before our eyes in clear reality, in naked, unadorned truth. Indeed, there were many things that the good folks would have loved to point to with pride. You have to search for these now. There are, alas and alack, a few things they would have hidden, had they only known what was in store for them. But all these things, good, indifferent and bad, remained in their places; and here they are, unsuspecting, real, natural, charming like Diana and her wood nymphs.

Were it not quite superfluous, we would urgently recommend the study of Pompeii to the students of life in general and to those of Antiquity in particular. Those who would know something about the ancient table cannot do without Pompeii.

Three Ancient Writers: Anacharsis, Apicius, Petronius

To those who lay stress upon documentary evidence or literary testimony, to those trusting implicitly in the honesty and reliability of writers of fiction, we would recommend Petronius Arbiter.

His *cena Trimalchionis*, Trimalchio's dinner, is the sole surviving piece from the pen of a Roman contemporary, giving detailed information on our subject. It is, too, the work of a great writer moving in the best circles, and, therefore, so much more desirable as an expert. Petronius deserves to be quoted in full but his work is too well-known, and our space too short. However, right here we wish to warn the student to bear in mind in perusing Petronius that this writer, in his *cena*, is not depicting a meal but that he is satirizing a man — that makes all the difference in the world as far as we are concerned. Petronius' *cena* is plainly an exaggeration, but even from its distorted contours the student may recognize the true lines of an ancient meal.

There is, not so well-known a beautiful picture of an Athenian dinner party which must not be overlooked, for it contains a wealth of information. Although Greek, we learn from it much of the Roman conditions. Anacharsis' description of a banquet at Athens, dating back to the fourth century B.C. about the time when the Periclean régime flourished, is worth your perusal. A particularly good version of this tale is rendered by Baron Vaerst in his book "Gastrosophie," Leipzig, 1854, who has based his version on the original translation from the Greek, entitled, *Voyage du jeune Anacharsis en Grèce vers le milieu du quatrième siècle avant l'ère vulgaire par J. J. Barthélemy*, Paris, 1824. Vaerst has amplified the excerpts from the young traveler's observations by quotations from other ancient Greek writers upon the subject, thus giving us a most beautiful and authentic ideal description of Greek table manners and habits when Athens had reached the height in culture, refinement and political greatness.

Anacharsis was not a Hellene but a Scythian visitor. By his own admission he is no authority on Grecian cookery, but as a reporter he excels.

This truly Hellenic discussion of the art of eating and living at the table of the cultured Athenians is the most profound discourse we know of, ancient or modern, on eating. The wisdom revealed in this tale is lasting, and, like Greek marble, consummate in external beauty and inner worth.

We thus possess the testimony of two contemporary writers which together with the book of Apicius and with what we learn from Athenaeus should give a fair picture of ancient eating and cookery.

Apicius is our most substantial witness.

Unfortunately, this source has not been spared by meddlesome men, and it has not reached us in its pristine condition. As a matter of fact, Apicius has been badly mauled throughout the centuries. This book has always attracted attention, never has it met with indifference. In the middle ages it became the object of intensive study, interpretation, controversy — in short it has attracted interest that has lasted into modern times.

When, with the advent of the dark ages, it ceased to be a practical cookery book, it became a treasure cherished by the few who preserved the classical literature, and after the invention of printing it became the object of curiosity, even mystery. Some interpreters waxed enthusiastic over it, others who failed to understand it, condemned it as hopeless and worthless.

The pages of our Apiciana plainly show the lasting interest in our ancient book, particularly ever since its presence became a matter of common knowledge during the first century of printing.

The Apicius book is the most ancient of European cookery books. However, Platina's work, *de honesta uolvptate*, is the first cookery book to appear in print. Platina, in 1474, was more up-to-date. His book had a larger circulation. But its vogue stopped after a century while Apicius marched on through centuries to come, tantalizing the scholars, amusing the curious gourmets if not educated cooks to the present day.

APICIUS, THE MAN

Who was Apicius? This is the surname of several renowned gastronomers of old Rome. There are many references and anecdotes in ancient literature to men bearing this name. Two Apicii have definitely been accounted for. The older one, Marcus A. lived at the time of Sulla about 100 B.C. The man we are most interested in, M. Gabius Apicius, lived under Augustus and Tiberius, 80 B.C. to A.D. 40. However, both these men had a reputation for their good table.

ATHENAEUS ON APICIUS

It is worth noting that the well-read Athenaeus, conversant with most authors of Antiquity makes no mention of the Apicius book. This collection of recipes, then, was not in general circulation during Athenaei time (beginning of the third century of our era), that, maybe, it was kept a secret by some Roman cooks. On the other hand it is possible that the Apicius book did not exist during the time of Athenaeus in the form handed down to us and that the monographs on various departments of cookery (most of them of Greek origin, works of which indeed Athenaeus speaks) were collected after the first quarter of the third century and were adorned with the name of Apicius merely because his fame as a gourmet had endured.

What Athenaeus knows about Apicius (one of three known famous eaters bearing that name) is the following:

About the time of Tiberius [42 B.C.-37 A.D.] there lived a man, named Apicius; very rich and luxurious, for whom several kinds of cheesecakes, called Apician, are named [not found in our present A.]. He spent myriads of drachms on his belly, living chiefly at Minturæ, a city of Campania, eating very expensive crawfish, which are found in that place superior in size to those of Smyrna, or even to the crabs of Alexandria. Hearing, too, that they were very large in Africa, he sailed thither, without waiting a single day, and suffered exceedingly on his voyage. But when he came near the coast, before he disembarked (for his arrival made a great stir among the Africans) the fishermen came alongside in their boats and brought him some very fine crawfish; and he, when he saw them, asked if they had any finer; and when they said that there were none finer than those which they had brought, he, recollecting those at Minturnæ ordered the master of the ship to sail back the same way into Italy, without going near the land. . .

When the emperor Trajan [A.D. 52 or 53-117] was in Parthia [a country in Asia, part of Persia?] at a distance of many days from the sea, Apicius sent him fresh oysters, which he had kept so by a clever contrivance of his own; real oysters. . ."

(The instructions given in our Apicius book, Recipe 14, for the keeping of oysters would hardly guarantee their safe arrival on such a journey as described above.)

Athenaeus tells us further that many of the Apician recipes were famous and that many dishes were named after him. This confirms the theory that Apicius was not the author of the present book but that the book was dedicated to him by an unknown author or compiler. Athenaeus also mentions one Apion who wrote a book on luxurious living. Whether this man is identical with the author or patron of our book is problematic. Torinus, in his *epistola dedicatoria* to the 1541 edition expresses the same doubt.

Marcus Gabius (or Gavius) Apicius lived during Rome's most interesting epoch, when the empire had reached its highest point, when the seeds of decline, not yet apparent, were in the ground, when in the quiet villages of that far-off province, Palestine, the Saviour's doctrines fascinated humble audiences — teachings that later reaching the very heart of the world's mistress were destined to tarnish the splendor of that autocrat.

According to the mention by various writers, this man, M. Gabius Apicius, was one of the many ancient gastronomers who took the subject of food seriously. Assuming a scientific attitude towards eating and food they were criticised for paying too much attention to their table. This was considered a superfluous and indeed wicked luxury when frugality was a virtue. These men who knew by intuition the importance of knowing something about nutrition are only now being vindicated by the findings of modern science.

M. Gabius Apicius, this most famous of the celebrated and much maligned bon-vivants, quite naturally took great interest in the preparation of food. He is said to have originated many dishes himself; he collected much material on the subject and he endowed a school for the teaching of cookery and for the promotion of culinary ideas. This very statement by his critics places him high in our esteem, as it shows him up as a scientist and educator. He spent his vast fortune for food, as the stories go, and when he had only a quarter million dollars left (a paltry sum today but a considerable one in those days when gold was scarce and monetary standards in a worse muddle than today) Apicius took his own life, fearing that he might have to starve to death some day.

This story seems absurd on the face of it, yet Seneca and Martial tell it (both with different tendencies) and Suidas, Albino and other writers repeat it without critical analysis. These writers who are unreliable in culinary matters anyway, claim that Apicius spent on hundred million *sestertii* on his appetite — *in gulam*. Finally when the hour of accounting came he found that there were only ten million *sestertii* left, so he concluded that life was not worth living if his gastronomic ideas could no longer be carried out in the accustomed and approved style, and he took poison at a banquet especially arranged for the occasion.

In the light of modern experience with psychology, with economics, depressions, journalism, we focus on this and similar stories, and we find them thoroughly unreliable. We cannot believe this one. It is too melodramatic, too moralistic perhaps to suit our modern taste. The underlying causes for the conduct, life and end of Apicius have not been told. Of course, we have to accept the facts as reported. If only a Petronius had written that story! What a story it might have been! But there is only one Petronius in antiquity. His Trimalchio, former slave, successful profiteer and food speculator, braggard and drunkard, wife-beater — an upstart who arranged extravagant banquets merely to show off, who, by the way, also arranged for his funeral at his banquet (Apician fashion and, indeed, Petronian fashion! for Petronius died in the same manner) and who peacefully "passed out" soundly intoxicated — this man is a figure true to life as it was then, as it is now and as it probably will continue to be. Last but not least: Mrs. Trimalchio, the resolute lady who helped him "make his pile" — these are human characters much more real, much more trustworthy than anything and everything else ever depicted by any ancient pen; they bring out so graphically the modernity of antiquity. Without Petronius and Pompeii the antique world would forever remain at an inexplicably remote distance to our modern conception of life. With him, and with the dead city, the riddles of antiquity are cleared up.

THE BOOK

Many dishes listed in Apicius are named for various celebrities who flourished at a later date than the second Apicius. It is noteworthy, however, that neither such close contemporaries as Heliogabalus and Nero, notorious gluttons, nor Petronius, the arbiter of fashion of the period, are among the persons thus honored. Vitellius, a later glutton, is well represented in the book. It is fair to assume, then, that the author or collector of our present Apicius lived long after the second Apicius, or, at least, that the book was augmented by persons posterior to M. Gabius A. The book in its present state was probably completed about the latter part of the third century. It is almost certain that many recipes were added to a much earlier edition.

PROBABLY OF GREEK PARENTAGE

We may as well add another to the many speculations by saying that it is quite probable for our book to originate in a number of Greek manuals or monographs on specialized subjects or departments of cookery. Such special treatises are mentioned by Athenaeus (cf. Humelbergius, quoted by Lister). The titles of each chapter (or book) are in Greek, the text is full of Greek terminology. While classification under the respective titles is not strictly adhered to at all times, it is significant that certain subjects, that of fish cookery, for instance, appear twice in the book, the same subject showing treatment by widely different hands. Still more significant is the absence in our book of such important departments as desserts — *dulcia* — confections in which the ancients were experts. Bakery, too, even the plainest kind, is conspicuously absent in the Apician books. The latter two trades being particularly well developed, were departmentized to an astonishing degree in ancient Greece and Rome. These indispensible books are simply wanting in our book if it be but a collection of Greek monographs. Roman culture and refinement of living, commencing about 200-250 years before our era was under the complete rule of Hellas. Greek influence included everybody from philosophers, artists, architects, actors, lawmakers to cooks.

"The conquered thus conquered the conquerors."

Humelbergius makes a significant reference to the origin of Apicius. We confess, we have not checked up this worthy editor nor his successor, Dr. Lister, whom he quotes in the preface as to the origin of our book. With reference to Plato's work, Humelbergius says:

"*Que res tota spectat medicinæ partem, quæ diaitetike appelatur, et victu medetur: at in hac tes diaitetikes parte totus est Apicius noster.*"

In our opinion, unfounded of course by positive proof, the Apicius book is somewhat of a gastronomic bible, consisting of ten different books by several authors, originating in Greece and taken over by the Romans along with the rest of Greek culture as spoils of war. These books, or chapters, or fragments thereof, must have been in vogue long before they were collected and assembled in the present form. Editions, or copies of the same must have been numerous, either singly or collectively, at the beginning of our era. As a matter of fact, the Excerpts by Vinidarius, found in the *codex Salmasianus* prove this theory and give rise to the assumption that the Apicius book was a standard work for cookery that existed at one time or other in a far more copious volume and that the present Apicius is but a fragment of a formerly vaster and more complete collection of culinary and medical formulæ.

Thus a fragmentary Apicius has been handed down to us in manuscript form through the centuries, through the revolutionary era of Christian ascendancy, through the dark ages down to the Renaissance. Unknown agencies, mostly medical and monastic, stout custodians of antique learning, reverent lovers of good cheer have preserved it for us until printing made possible the book's wide distribution among the scholars. Just prior to Gutenberg's epoch-making printing press there was a spurt of interest in our book in Italy, as attested to by a dozen of manuscripts, copied in the fourteenth and the fifteenth centuries.

Apicius may justly be called the world's oldest cookery book; the very old Sanscrit book, Vasavarayeyam, unknown to us except by name, is said to be a tract on vegetarian cookery.

The men who have preserved this work for future generations, who have made it accessible to the public (as was Lister's intention) have performed a service to civilization that is not to be underestimated. They have done better than the average archaeologist with one or another find to his credit. The Apicius book is a living thing, capable of creating happiness. Some gastronomic writers have pointed out that the man who discovers a new dish does more for humanity than the man who discovers a new star, because the discovery of a new dish affects the happiness of mankind more pleasantly than the addition of a new planet to an already overcrowded chart of the universe. Viewing Apicius from such a materialistic point of view he should become very popular in this age of ours so keen for utilities of every sort.

CŒLIUS-CÆLIUS

The name of another personality is introduced in connection with the book, namely that of Cœlius or Cælius. This name is mentioned in the title of the first undated edition (ca. 1483-6) as Celius. Torinus, 1541, places "Cælius" before "Apicius"; Humelbergius, 1542, places "Cœlius" after A. Lister approves of this, berating Torinus for his willful methods of editing the book: "*En hominem in conjecturis sane audacissimus!*" If any of them were correct about "Cœlius," Torinus would be the man. (Cf. Schanz, Röm. Lit. Gesch., Müller's Handbuch d. klass. Altertums-Wissenschaft, V III, 112, p. 506.) However, there is no *raison d'être* for Cœlius.

His presence and the unreality thereof has been cleared up by Vollmer, as will be duly shown. The squabble of the medieval savants has also given rise to the story that Apicius is but a joke perpetrated upon the world by a medieval savant. This will be refuted also later on. Our book is a genuine Roman. Medieval savants have made plenty of Roman "fakes," for sundry reasons. A most ingenious hoax was the "completion" of the Petronius fragment by a scholar able to hoodwink his learned contemporaries by an exhibition of Petronian literary style and a fertile imagination. Ever so many other "fakers" were shown up in due time. When this version of Petronius was pronounced genuine by the scientific world, the perpetrator of the "joke" confessed, enjoying a good laugh at the expense of his colleagues. But we shall presently understand how such a "joke" with Apicius would be impossible. Meanwhile, we crave the indulgence of the modern reader with our mention of Cœlius. We desire to do full justice to the ancient work and complete the presentation of its history. The controversies that have raged over it make this course necessary.

Our predecessors have not had the benefit of modern communication, and, therefore, could not know all that is to be known on the subject. We sympathize with Lister yet do not condemn Torinus. If Torinus ever dared making important changes in the old text, they are easily ascertained by collation with other texts. This we have endeavored to do. Explaining the discrepancies, it will be noted that we have not given a full vote of confidence to Lister.

Why should the mysterious Cœlius or Cælius, if such an author or compiler of a tome on cookery existed affix the name of "Apicius" to it? The reason would be commercial gain, prestige accruing from the name of that cookery celebrity. Such business sense would not be extraordinary. Modern cooks pursue the same method. Witness the innumerable à la soandsos. Babies, apartment houses, streets, cities, parks, dogs, race horses, soap, cheese, herring, cigars, hair restorers are thus named today. "Apicius" on the front page of any ancient cookery book would be perfectly consistent with the ancient spirit of advertising. It has been stated, too, that Cœlius had more than one collaborator. Neither can this be proven.

The copyists have made many changes throughout the original text. Misspelling of terms, ignorance of cookery have done much to obscure the meaning. The scribes of the middle ages had much difficulty in this respect since medieval Latin is different from Apician language.

The very language of the original is proof for its authenticity. The desire of Torinus to interpret to his medieval readers the ancient text is pardonable. How much or how little he succeeded is attested to by some of his contemporary readers, former owners of our copies. Scholars plainly confess inability to decipher Apicius by groans inscribed on the fly leaves and title pages in Latin, French and other languages. One French scholar of the 16th century, apparently "kidded" for studying an undecipherable cook book, stoically inscribes the title page of our Lyon, 1541, copy with: "This amuses me. Why make fun of me?" This sort of message, reaching us out of the dim past of bygone centuries is among the most touching reading we have done, and has urged us on with the good though laborious and unprofitable work.

Notwithstanding its drawbacks, our book is a classic both as to form and contents. It has served as a prototype of most ancient and modern books. Its influence is felt to the present day.

The book has often been cited by old writers as proof of the debaucheries and the gluttony of ancient Rome. Nothing could be further from the truth because these writers failed to understand the book.

The Apicius book reflects the true condition (partly so, because it is incomplete) of the kitchen prevailing at the beginning of our era when the mistress of the Old World was in her full regalia, when her ample body had not yet succumbed to that fatty degeneration of the interior so fatal to ever so many individuals, families, cities and nations.

We repeat, our Apicius covers Rome's healthy epoch; hence the importance of the book. The voluptuous concoctions, the fabulous dishes, the proverbial excesses that have made decent people shudder with disgust throughout the ages are not known to Apicius. If they ever existed at all in their traditional ugliness they made their appearance after Apicius' time. We recall, Petronius, describing some of these "stunts" is a contemporary of Nero (whom he satirizes as "Trimalchio"). So is Seneca, noble soul, another victim of Cæsarean insanity; he, too, describes Imperial excesses. These extremely few foolish creations are really at the bottom of the cause for this misunderstanding of true Roman life. Such stupidity has allowed the joy of life which, as Epikuros and Platina believe, may be indulged in with perfect virtue and honesty to become a byword among all good people who are not gastronomers either by birth, by choice or by training.

With due justice to the Roman people may we be permitted to say that proverbial excesses were exceedingly rare occurrences. The follies and the vices of a Nero, a boy Heliogabalus, a Pollio, a Vitellius and a few other notorious wasters are spread sporadically over a period of at least eight hundred years. Between these cases of gastronomic insanity lie wellnigh a thousand years of everyday grind and drudgery of the Roman people. The bulk was miserably fed as compared with modern standards of living. Only a few patricians could afford "high living." Since a prosperous bourgeoisie (usually the economic and gastronomic background of any nation) was practically unknown in Rome, where the so-called middle classes were in reality poor, shiftless and floating freedmen, it is evident that the bulk of the population because of the empire's unsettled economic conditions, its extensive system of slavery (precluding all successful practice of trades by freemen) the continuous military operations, the haphazard financial system, was forced to live niggardly. The contrast between the middle classes and the upper classes seemed very cruel. This condition may account for the many outcries against the "extravagances" of the few privileged ones who could afford decent food and for the exaggerated stories about their table found in the literature of the time.

The seemingly outlandish methods of Apician food preparation become plain and clear in the light of social evolution. "Evolution" is perhaps not the right word to convey our idea of social perpetual motion.

Apicius used practically all the cooking utensils in use today. He only lacked gas, electricity and artificial refrigeration, modern achievements while useful in the kitchen and indispensable in wholesale production and for labor saving, that have no bearing on purely gastronomical problems. There is only one difference between the cooking utensils of yore and the modern products: the old ones are hand-made, more individualistic, more beautiful, more artistic than our machine-made varieties.

Despite his strangeness and remoteness, Apicius is not dead by any means. We have but to inspect (as Gollmer has pointed out) the table of the Southern Europeans to find Apician traditions alive. In the Northern countries, too, are found his traces. To think that Apicius should have survived in the North of Europe, far removed from his native soil, is a rather audacious suggestion. But the keen observer can find him in Great Britain, Scandinavia and the Baltic provinces today. The conquerors and seafarers coming from the South have carried the pollen of gastronomic flowers far into the North where they adjusted themselves to soil and climate. Many a cook of the British isles, of Southern Sweden, Holstein, Denmark, Friesland, Pommerania still observes Apicius rules though he may not be aware of the fact.

We must realize that Apicius is only a book, a frail hand-made record and that, while the record itself might have been forgotten, its principles have become international property, long ago. Thus they live on. Like a living thing — a language, a custom, they themselves may have undergone changes, "improvements," alterations, augmentation, corruption. But the character has been preserved; a couple of thousand years are, after all, but a paltry matter. Our own age is but the grandchild of antiquity. The words we utter, in their roots, are those of our grandfathers. And so do many dishes we eat today resemble those once enjoyed by Apicius and his friends.

Is it necessary to point the tenacity of the spirit of the Antique, reaching deep into the modern age? The latest Apicius edition in the original Latin is dated 1922!

The gastronomic life of Europe was under the complete rule of old Rome until the middle of the seventeenth century. Then came a sudden change for modernity, comparable to the rather abrupt change of languages from the fashionable Latin to the national idioms and vernacular, in England and Germany under the influence of literary giants like Luther, Chaucer, Shakespeare.

All medieval food literature of the continent and indeed the early cookery books of England prior to LaVarenne (Le Cuisinier François, 1654) are deeply influenced by Apicius. The great change in eating, resulting in a new gastronomic order, attained its highest peak of perfection just prior to the French revolution. Temporarily suspended by this social upheaval, it continued to flourish until about the latter part of last century. The last decades of this new order is often referred to as the classical period of gastronomy, with France claiming the laurels for its development. "Classic" for reasons we do not know (Urbain Dubois, outstanding master of this period wrote "La Cuisine classique") except that its precepts appeal as classical to our notion of eating. This may not correspond to the views of posterity, we had therefore better wait a century or two before proclaiming our system of cookery "classical."

Disposing of that old "classic," Apicius, as slowly as a conservative cooking world could afford to do, the present nations set out to cultivate a taste for things that a Roman would have pronounced unfit for a slave. Still, the world moves on. Conquest, discovery of foreign parts, the New World, contributed fine things to the modern table, — old forgotten foods were rediscovered — endless lists of materials and combinations, new daring, preposterous dishes that made the younger generation rejoice while old folks looked on gasping with dismay, despair, contempt.

Be it sufficient to remark that the older practitioners of our own days, educated in "classic" cuisine again are quite apprehensive of their traditions endangered by the spirit of revolt of the young against the old. Again and again we hear of a decline that has set in, and even by the best authorities alarmist notes are spread to the effect that "we have begun our journey back, step by step to our primitive tree and our primitive nuts" (Pennell. Does Spengler consider food in his "Decline of the West?").

It matters not whether we share this pessimism, nor what we may have to say *pro* or *con* this question of "progress" or "retrogression" in eating (or in anything else for that matter). In fact we are not concerned with the question here more than to give it passing attention.

If "classic" cookery is dying nowadays, if it cannot reassert itself that would be a loss to mankind. But this classic cookery system has so far only been the sole and exclusive privilege of a dying aristocracy. It seems quite in order that it should go under in the great *Götterdämmerung* that commenced with the German peasants wars of the sixteenth century, flaring up (as the second act) in the French revolution late in the eighteenth century, the Act III of which drama has been experienced in our own days.

The common people as yet have never had an active part in the enjoyment of the classic art of eating. So far, they always provided the wherewithal, and looked on, holding the bag. Modern hotels, because of their commercial character, have done little to perpetuate it. They merely have commercialized the art. Beyond exercising ordinary salesmanship, our *maîtres d'hôtel* have not educated our *nouveaux riches* in the mysteries and delights of gastronomy. Hotelmen are not supposed to be educators, they merely cater to a demand. And our new aristocracy has been too busy with limousines, golf, divorces and electricity to bemourn the decline of classic cookery.

Most people "get by" without the benefit of classic cookery, subsisting on a medley of edibles, tenaciously clinging to mother's traditions, to things "as she used to make them," and mother's methods still savor of Apicius. Surely, this is no sign of retrogression but of tenacity.

The only fundamental difference between Roman dining and that of our own times may be found in these two indisputable facts —

(First) Devoid of the science of agriculture, without any advanced mechanical means, food was not raised in a very systematic way; if it happened to be abundant, Roma lacked storage and transportation facilities to make good use of it. There never were any food supplies on any large, extensive and scientific scale, hence raw materials, the wherewithal of a "classic" meal, were expensive.

(Second) Skilled labor, so vital for the success of any good dinner, so imperative for the rational preparation of food was cheap to those who held slaves.

Hence, the culinary conditions of ancient Rome were exactly the opposite of today's state of affairs. Then, good food was expensive while good labor was cheap. Now, good food is cheap while skilled labor is at a premium. Somehow, good, intelligent "labor" is reluctant to devote itself to food. That is another story. The chances for a good dinner seemed to be in favor of the Romans — but only for a favored few. Those of us, although unable to command a staff of experts, but able to prepare their own meals rationally and serve them well are indeed fortunate. With a few dimes they may dine in royal fashion. If our much maligned age has achieved anything at all it has at least enabled the working "slave" of the "masses" to dine in a manner that even princes could hardly match in former days, a manner indeed that the princes of our own time could not improve upon. The fly in the ointment is that most modern people do not know how to handle and to appreciate food. This condition, however, may be remedied by instruction and education.

Slowly, the modern masses are learning to emulate their erstwhile masters in the art of eating. They have the advantages of the great improvements in provisioning as compared with former days, thanks chiefly to the great lines of communication established by modern commerce, thanks to scientific agriculture and to the spirit of commercial enterprise and its resulting prosperity.

There are two "Ifs" in the path to humanity's salvation, at least, that of its table. If the commercialization of cookery, i.e., the wholesale production of ready-made foods for the table does not completely enthrall the housewife and if we can succeed to educate the masses to make rational, craftsmanlike use of our wonderful stores of edibles, employing or modifying to this end the rules of classic cookery, there really should be no need for any serious talk about our journey back to the primitive nuts. Even Spengler might be wrong then. Adequate distribution of our foods and rational use thereof seem to be one of the greatest problems today.

THE AUTHENTICITY OF APICIUS

Age-old mysteries surrounding our book have not yet been cleared up. Medieval savants have squabbled in vain. Mrs. Pennell's worries and the fears of the learned Englishmen that Apicius might be a hoax have proven groundless. Still, the mystery of this remarkable book is as perplexing as ever. The authorship will perhaps never be established. But let us forever dispel any doubt about its authenticity.

Modern writers have never doubted the genuineness. To name but a few who believe in Apicius: Thudichum, Vollmer, Brandt, Vicaire, Rumohr, Schuch, Habs, Gollmer.

What matters the identity of the author? Who wrote the Iliad, the Odyssey, the Nibelungen-Lied? Let us be thankful for possessing them!

Apicius is a genuine document of Roman imperial days. There can be no doubt of that!

The unquestionable age of the earliest known manuscripts alone suffices to prove this.

The philologist gives his testimony, too. A medieval scholar could never have manufactured Apicius, imitating his strikingly original terminology. "Faking" a technical treatise requires an intimate knowledge of technical terms and familiarity with the ramifications of an intricate trade. We recommend a comparison of Platina's text with Apicius: the difference of ancient and medieval Latin is convincing. Striking examples of this kind have been especially noted in our dictionary of technical terms.

LATIN SLANG

H. C. Coote, in his commentary on Apicius (cit. Apiciana) in speaking of pan gravy, remarks:

> "Apicius calls this by the singular phrase of *jus de suo sibi*! and sometimes though far less frequently, *succus suus*. This phrase is curious enough in itself to deserve illustration. It is true old fashioned Plautian Latinity, and if other proof were wanting would of itself demonstrate the genuineness of the Apician text."

This scholar goes on quoting from Plautus, *Captivi*, Act I, sc. 2vv 12, 13; *Amphitruo*, Act I, sc. q.v. 116 and *ibid*. v. 174; and from *Asinaria*, Act IV, sc. 2, vv. 16 and 17 to prove this, and he further says:

"The phrase is a rare remnant of the old familiar language of Rome, such as slaves talked so long, that their masters ultimately adopted it — a language of which Plautus gives us glimpses and which the *graffiti* may perhaps help to restore. When Varius was emperor, this phrase of the kitchen was as rife as when Plautus wrote — a proof that occasionally slang has been long lived."

Coote is a very able commentator. He has translated in the article quoted a number of Apician formulæ and betrays an unusual culinary knowledge.

MODERN RESEARCH

Modern means of communication and photography have enabled scientists in widely different parts to study our book from all angles, to scrutinize the earliest records, the Vatican and the New York manuscripts and the codex Salmasianus in Paris.

Friedrich Vollmer, of Munich, in his *Studien* (cit. Apiciana) has treated the manuscripts exhaustively, carrying to completion the research begun by Schuch, Traube, Ihm, Studemund, Giarratano and others with Brandt, his pupil, carrying on the work of Vollmer. More modern scientists deeply interested in the origin of our book! None doubting its genuineness.

Vollmer is of the opinion that there reposed in the monastery of Fulda, Germany, an *Archetypus* which in the ninth century was copied twice: once in a Turonian hand — the manuscript now kept in the Vatican — the other copy written partly in insular, partly in Carolingian minuscle — the Cheltenham *codex*, now in New York. The common source at Fulda of these two manuscripts has been established by Traube. There is another testimony pointing to Fulda as the oldest known source. Pope Nicholas V commissioned Enoche of Ascoli to acquire old manuscripts in Germany. Enoche used as a guide a list of works based upon observations by Poggio in Germany in 1417, listing the Apicius of Fulda. Enoche acquired the Fulda Apicius. He died in October or November, 1457. On December 10th of that year, so we know, Giovanni de'Medici requested Stefano de'Nardini, Governor of Ancona, to procure for him from Enoche's estate either in copy or in the original the book, entitled, *Appicius de re quoquinaria* (cf. No. 3, Apiciana). It is interesting to note that one of the Milanese editions of 1498 bears a title in this particular spelling. Enoche during his life time had lent the book to Giovanni Aurispa.

It stands to reason that Poggio, in 1417, viewed at Fulda the *Archetypus* of our Apicius, father of the Vatican and the New York manuscripts, then already mutilated and wanting books IX and X. Six hundred years before the arrival of Poggio the Fulda book was no longer complete. Already in the ninth century its title page had been damaged which is proven by the title page of the Vatican copy which reads:

INCP
API
CÆ

That's all! The New York copy, it has been noted, has no title page. This book commences in the middle of the list of chapters; the first part of them and the title page are gone. We recall that the New York manuscript was originally bound up with another manuscript, also in the Phillipps library at Cheltenham. The missing page or pages were probably lost in separating the two manuscripts. It is possible that Enoche carried with him to Italy one of the ancient copies, very likely the present New York copy, then already without a title. At any rate, not more than twenty-five years after his book hunting expedition we find both copies in Italy. It is strange, furthermore, that neither of these two ancient copies were used by the fifteenth century copyists to make the various copies distributed by them, but that an inferior copy of the Vatican Ms. became the *vulgata* — the progenitor of this series of medieval copies. One must bear in mind how assiduously medieval scribes copied everything that appeared to be of any importance to them, and how each new copy by virtue of human fallability or self-sufficiency must have suffered in the making, and it is only by very careful comparison of the various manuscripts that the original text may be rehabilitated.

This, to a large extent, Vollmer and Giarratano have accomplished. Vollmer, too, rejects the idea invented by the humanists, that Apicius had a collaborator, editor or commentator in the person of Cœlius or Cælius. This name, so Vollmer claims, has been added to the book by medieval scholars without any reason except conjecture for such action. They have been misled by the mutilated title: Api. . . Cæ. . .; Vollmer reconstructs this title as follows:

API[cii artis magiri- (or) opsartyti-]
CÆ[libri X]

Remember, it is the title page only that is thus mutilated. The ten books or chapters bear the full name of Apicius, never at any time does the name of Cœlius appear in the text, or at the head of the chapters.

The *Archetypus*, with the book and the chapters carefully indexed and numbered as they were, with each article neatly titled, the captions and capital letters rubricated — heightened by red color, and with its proper spacing of the articles and chapters must once have been a representative example of the art of book making as it flourished towards the end of the period that sealed the fate of the Roman empire, when books of a technical nature, law books, almanacs, army lists had been developed to a high point of perfection. Luxurious finish, elaborate illumination point to the fact that our book (the Vatican copy) was intended for the use in some aristocratic household.

THE EXCERPTS OF VINIDARIUS

And now, from a source totally different than the two important manuscripts so much discussed here, we receive additional proof of the authenticity of

Apicius. In the *codex Salmasianus* (cf. III, Apiciana) we find some thirty formulæ attributed to Apicius, entitled: *Apici excerpta a Vinidario vir. inl.* They have been accepted as genuine by Salmasius and other early scholars. Schuch incorporated the *excerpta* with his Apicius, placing the formulæ in what he believed to be the proper order. This course, for obvious reasons, is not to be recommended. To be sure, the *excerpta* are Apician enough in character, though only a few correspond to, or are actual duplicates of, the Apician precepts. They are additions to the stock of authentic Apician recipes. As such, they may not be included but be appended to the traditional text. The *excerpta* encourage the belief that at the time of Vinidarius (got. Vinithaharjis) about the fifth century there must have been in circulation an Apicius (collection of recipes) much more complete than the one handed down to us through Fulda. It is furthermore interesting to note that the *excerpta*, too, are silent about Cœlius.

We may safely join Vollmer in his belief that M. Gabius Apicius, celebrated gourmet living during the reign of Tiberius was the real author, or collector, or sponsor of this collection of recipes, or at least of the major part thereof — the formulæ bearing the names of posterior gourmets having been added from time to time. This theory also applies to the two instances where the name of Varro is mentioned in connection with the preparation of beets and onions (bulbs). It is hardly possible that the author of the book made these references to Varro. It is more probable that some well-versed posterior reader, perusing the said articles, added to his copy: "And Varro prepared beets this way, and onions that way. . ." (cf. Book III, [70]) Still, there is no certainty in this theory either. There were many persons by the names of Commodus, Trajanus, Frontinianus, such as are appearing in our text, who were contemporaries of Apicius.

With our mind at ease as regards the genuineness of our book we now may view it at a closer range.

OBSCURE TERMINOLOGY

Apicius contains technical terms that have been the subject of much speculation and discussion. *Liquamen, laser, muria, garum,* etc., belong to these. They will be found in our little dictionary. But we cannot refrain from discussing some at present to make intelligible the most essential part of the ancient text.

Take *liquamen* for instance. It may stand for broth, sauce, stock, gravy, drippings, even for *court bouillon* — in fact for any liquid appertaining to or derived from a certain dish or food material. Now, if Apicius prescribes *liquamen* for the preparation of a meat or a vegetable, it is by no means clear to the uninitiated what he has in mind. In fact, in each case the term *liquamen* is subject to the interpretation of the experienced practitioner. Others than he would at once be confronted with an unsurmountable difficulty. Scientists may not agree with us, but such is kitchen practice. Hence the many fruitless controversies at the expense of the original, at the disappointment of science.

Garum is another word, one upon which much contemptuous witticism and serious energy has been spent. *Garum* simply is a generic name for fish essences. True, *garus* is a certain and a distinct kind of Mediterranean fish, originally used in the manufacture of *garum*; but this product, in the course of time, has been altered, modified, adulterated, — in short, has been changed and the term has naturally been applied to all varieties and variations of fish essences, without distinction, and it has thus become a collective term, covering all varieties of fish sauces. Indeed, the corruption and degeneration of this term, *garum*, had so advanced at the time of Vinidarius in the fifth century as to lose even its association with any kind of fish. Terms like *garatum* (prepared with g.) have been derived from it. Prepared with the addition of wine it becomes *œnogarum*, — wine sauce — and dishes prepared with such wine sauce receive the adjective of *œnogaratum*, and so forth.

The original *garum* was no doubt akin to our modern anchovy sauce, at least the best quality of the ancient sauce. The principles of manufacture surely are alike. *Garum*, like our anchovy sauce, is the *purée* of a small fish, named *garus*, as yet unidentified. The fish, intestines and all, was spiced, pounded, fermented, salt, strained and bottled for future use. The finest *garum* was made of the livers of the fish only, exposed to the sun, fermented, somehow preserved. It was an expensive article in old Rome, famed for its medicinal properties. Its mode of manufacture has given rise to much criticism and scorn on the part of medieval and modern commentators and interpreters who could not comprehend the "perverse taste" of the ancients in placing any value on the "essence from putrified intestines of fish."

However, *garum* has been vindicated, confirmed, endorsed, reiterated, rediscovered, if you please, by modern science! What, pray, is the difference in principle between *garum* (the exact nature of which is unknown) and the oil of the liver of cod (or less expensive fish) exposed to the beneficial rays of ultraviolet light — artificial sunlight — to imbue the oil with an extra large and uniform dose of vitamin D? The ancients, it appears, knew "vitamin D" to exist. Maybe they had a different name for "vitamins," maybe none at all. The name does not matter. The thing which they knew, does. They knew the nutritive value of liver, proven by many formulæ. Pollio, one of the vicious characters of antiquity, fed murenas·(sea-eel) with slaves he threw into the *piscina*, the fish pond, and later enjoyed the liver of the fish.

Some "modern" preparations are astonishingly ancient, and *vice versa*. Our anchovy sauce is used freely to season fish, to mix with butter, to be made into solid anchovy or fish paste. There are sardine pastes, lobster pastes, fish forcemeats found in the larder of every good kitchen — preparations of Apician character. A real platter of *hors d'oeuvres*, an *antipasto* is not complete unless made according to certain Apician precepts.

Muria is salt water, brine, yet it may stand for a fluid in which fish or meat, fruits or vegetables have been pickled.

The difficulties of the translator of Apicius who takes him literally, are unconsciously but neatly demonstrated by the work of Danneil. Even he, seasoned practitioner, condemns *garum, muria, asa fœtida,* because professors before him have done so, because he forgets that these very materials still form a vital part of some of his own sauces only in a different shape, form or under a different name. Danneil calls some Apician recipes "incredibly absurd," "fabulous," "exaggerated," but he thinks nothing of the serving of similar combinations in his own establishment every day in the year.

Danneil would take pride in serving a Veal Cutlet à la Holstein. (What have we learned of Apicius in the Northern countries?). The ancient Holsteiner was not satisfied unless his piece of veal was covered with a nice fat herring. That "barbarity" had to be modified by us moderns into a veal cutlet, turned in milk and flour, eggs and bread crumbs, fried, covered with fried eggs, garnished with anchovies or bits of herring, red beets, capers, and lemon in order to qualify for a restaurant favorite and "best seller." Apicius hardly has a dish more characteristic and more bewildering.

What of combinations of fish and meat?

De gustibus non est disputandum. It all goes into the same stomach. May it be an sturdy one, and let its owner beware. What of our turkey and oyster dressing? Of our broiled fish and bacon? Of our clam chowder, our divine *Bouillabaisse*? If the ingredients and component parts of such dishes were enumerated in the laconic and careless Apician style, if they were stated without explicit instructions and details (supposed to be known to any good practitioner) we would have recipes just as mysterious as any of the Apician formulæ.

Danneil, like ever so many interpreters, plainly shared the traditional belief, the egregious errors of popular history. People still are under the spell of the fantastic and fanciful descriptions of Roman conviviality and gastronomic eccentricities. Indeed, we rather believe in the insanity of these descriptions than in the insane conduct of the average Roman gourmet. It is absurd of course to assume and to make the world believe that a Roman patrician made a meal of *garum, laserpitium,* and the like. They used these condiments judiciously; any other use thereof is physically impossible. They economized their spices which have caused so much comment, too. As a matter of fact, they used condiments niggardly and sparingly as is plainly described in some formulæ, if only for the one good and sufficient reason that spices and condiments which often came from Asia and Africa were extremely expensive. This very reason, perhaps, caused much of the popular outcry against their use, which, by the way, is merely another form of political propaganda, in which, as we shall see, the mob guided by the rabble of politicians excelled.

We moderns are just as "extravagant" (if not more) in the use of sauces and condiments — Apician sauces, too! Our Worcestershire, catsup, chili, chutney, walnut catsup, A I, Harvey's, Punch, Soyer's, Escoffier's, Oscar's (every culinary coryphee endeavors to create one) — our mustards and condiments in their different forms, if not actually dating back to Apicius, are, at least lineal descendants from ancient prototypes.

To readers little experienced in kitchen practice such phrases (often repeated by Apicius) as, "crush pepper, lovage, marjoram," etc., etc., may appear stereo-typed and monotonous. They have not survived in modern kitchen parlance, because the practice of using spices, flavors and aromas has changed. There are now in the market compounds, extracts, mixtures not used in the old days. Many modern spices come to us ready ground or mixed, or compounded ready for kitchen use. This has the disadvantage in that volatile properties deteriorate more rapidly and that the goods may be easily adulterated. The Bavarians, under Duke Albrecht, in 1553 prohibited the grinding of spices for that very reason! Ground spices are time and labor savers, however. Modern kitchen methods have put the old mortar practically out of existence, at the expense of quality of the finished product.

THE "LABOR ITEM"

The enviable Apicius cared naught for either time or labor. He gave these two important factors in modern life not a single thought. His culinary procedures required a prodiguous amount of labor and effort on the part of the cooks and their helpers. The labor item never worried any ancient employer. It was either very cheap or entirely free of charge.

The selfish gourmet (which gourmet is not selfish?) almost wonders whether the abolition of slavery was a well-advised measure in modern social and eco-nomic life. Few people appreciate the labor cost in excellent cookery and few have any conception of the cost of good food service today. Yet all demand both, when "dining out," at least. Who, on the other hand, but a brute would care to dine well, "taking it out of the hide of others?"

Hence we moderns with a craving for *gourmandise* but minus appropriations for skilled labor would do well to follow the example of Alexandre Dumas who cheerfully and successfully attended to his own cuisine. Despite an extensive fiction practice he found time to edit "Le Grand Dictionnaire de Cuisine" and was not above writing mustard advertisements, either.

SUMPTUARY LAWS

The appetite of the ancients was at times successfully curbed by sumptuary laws, cropping out at fairly regular intervals. These laws, usually given under the pretext of safeguarding the morals of the people and accompanied by similar euphonious phrases were, like modern prohibitions, vicious and virulent effusions of the predatory instinct in mankind. We cannot give a chronological list of them here, and are citing them merely to illustrate the difficulty confronting the prospective ancient host.

During the reign of Cæsar and Augustus severe laws were passed, fixing the sums to be spent for public and private dinners and specifying the edibles to be consumed. These laws classified gastronomic functions with an ingenious eye for system, professing all the time to protect the public's morals and health; but they were primarily designed to replenish the ever-vanishing contents of the Imperial exchequer and to provide soft jobs for hordes of enforcers. The amounts allowed to be spent for various social functions were so ridiculously small in our own modern estimation that we may well wonder how a Roman host could have ever made a decent showing at a banquet. However, he and the cooks managed somehow. Imperial spies and informers were omnipresent. The market places were policed, the purchases by prospective hosts carefully noted, dealers selling supplies and cooks (the more skillful kind usually) hired for the occasion were bribed to reveal the "menu." Dining room windows had to be located conveniently to allow free inspection from the street of the dainties served; the passing Imperial food inspector did not like to intrude upon the sanctity of the host's home. The pitiable host of those days, his unenviable guests and the bewildered cooks, however, contrived and conspired somehow to get up a banquet that was a trifle better than a Chicago quick lunch.

How did they do it?

In the light of modern experience gained by modern governments dillydallying with sumptuary legislation that has been discarded as a bad job some two thousand years ago, the question seems superfluous.

Difficile est satyram non scribere! To make a long story short: The Roman host just broke the law, that's all. Indeed, those who made the laws were first to break them. The minions, appointed to uphold the law, were easily accounted for. Any food inspector too arduous in the pursuit of his duty was disposed of by dispatching him to the rear entrance of the festive hall, and was delivered to the tender care of the chief cook.

Such was the case during the times of Apicius. Indeed, the Roman idea of good cheer during earlier epochs was provincial enough. It was simply barbaric before the Greeks showed the Romans a thing or two in cookery. The methods of fattening fowl introduced from Greece was something unheard-of! It was outrageous, sacrilegious! Senators, orators and other self-appointed saviors of humanity thundered against the vile methods of tickling the human palate, deftly employing all the picturesque tam-tam and *élan* still the stock in trade of ever so many modern colleagues in any civilized parliament. The speeches, to be sure, passed into oblivion, the fat capons, however, stayed in the barnyards until they had acquired the saturation point of tender luscious calories to be enjoyed by those who could afford them. How the capon was "invented" is told in a note on the subject.

Many other so-called luxuries, sausage from Epirus, cherries from the Pontus, oysters from England, were greeted with a studied hostility by those who profited from the business of making laws and public opinion.

Evidently, the time and the place was not very propitious for gastronomic over-indulgence. Only when the ice was broken, when the disregard for law and order had become general through the continuous practice of contempt for an unpopular sumptuary law, when corruption had become wellnigh universal chiefly thanks to the examples set by the higher-ups, it was then that the torrent of human passion and folly ran riot, exceeding natural bounds, tearing every-thing with them, all that is beautiful and decent, thus swamping the great empire beyond the hopes for any recovery.

Apicius the Writer

Most of the Apician directions are vague, hastily jotted down, carelessly edited. One of the chief reasons for the eternal misunderstandings! Often the author fails to state the quantities to be used. He has a mania for giving undue prom-inence to expensive spices and other (quite often irrelevant) ingredients. Plain-ly, Apicius was no writer, no editor. He was a cook. He took it for granted that spices be used within the bounds of reason, but he could not afford to forget them in his formulæ.

Apicius surely pursues the correct culinary principle of incorporating the flavoring agents during the process of cooking, contrary to many moderns who, vigorously protesting against "highly seasoned" and "rich" food, and who, craving for "something plain" proceed to inundate perfectly good, plain roast or boiled dishes with a deluge of any of the afore-mentioned commercial "sauces" that have absolutely no relation to the dish and that have no mission other than to grant relief from the deadening monotony of "plain" food. Chicken or mutton, beef or venison, finnan haddie or brook trout, eggs or oysters thus "sauced," taste all alike — sauce! To use such ready-made sauces with dishes cooked à l'anglaise is logical, excusable, almost advisable. Even the most ascetic of men cannot resist the insiduousness of spicy delights, nor can he for any length of time endure the insipidity of plain food sans sauce. Hence the popu-larity of such sauces amongst people who do not observe the correct culinary principle of seasoning food judiciously, befitting its character, without spoiling but rather in enhancing its characteristics and in bringing out its flavor at the right time, namely during coction to give the kindred aromas a chance to blend well.

Continental nations, adhering to this important principle of cookery (in-herited from Apicius) would not dream of using ready-made (English) sauces.

We have witnessed real crimes being perpetrated upon perfectly seasoned and delicately flavored entrées. We have watched ill-advised people maltreat good things, cooked to perfection, even before they tasted them, sprinkling them as a matter of habit, with quantities of salt and pepper, paprika, cayenne, daubing them with mustards of every variety or swamping them with one or several of the commercial sauce preparations. "Temperamental" chefs, men who know their art, usually explode at the sight of such wantonness. Which painter would care to see his canvas varnished with all the hues in the rainbow by a patron afflicted with such a taste?

Perhaps the craving for excessive flavoring is an olfactory delirium, a patho-logical case, as yet unfathomed like the excessive craving for liquor, and, being a problem for the medical fraternity, it is only of secondary importance to gastronomy.

To say that the Romans were afflicted on a national scale with a strange spice mania (as some interpreters want us to believe) would be equivalent to the assertion that all wine-growing nations were nations of drunkards. As a matter of fact, the reverse is the truth.

Apicius surely would be surprised at some things we enjoy. *Voilà*, a recipe, "modern," not older than half a century, given by us in the Apician style or writing: Take liquamen, pepper, cayenne, eggs, lemon, olive oil, vinegar, white wine, anchovies, onions, tarragon, pickled cucumbers, parsley, chervil, hard-boiled eggs, capers, green peppers, mustard, chop, mix well, and serve.

Do you recognize it? This formula sounds as phantastic, as "weird" and as "vile" as any of the Apician concoctions, confusing even a well-trained cook because we stated neither the title of this preparation nor the mode of making it, nor did we name the ingredients in their proper sequence. This mystery was conceived with an illustrative purpose which will be explained later, which may and may not have to do with the mystery of Apicius. Consider, for a moment, this mysterious creation No. 2: Take bananas, oranges, cherries, flavored with bitter almonds, fresh pineapple, lettuce, fresh peaches, plums, figs, grapes, apples, nuts, cream cheese, olive oil, eggs, white wine, vinegar, cayenne, lemon, salt, white pepper, dry mustard, tarragon, rich sour cream, chop, mix, whip well.

Worse yet! Instead of having our appetite aroused the very perusal of this quasi-Apician *mixtum compositum* repels every desire to partake of it. We are justly tempted to condemn it as being utterly impossible. Yet every day hundreds of thousand portions of it are sold under the name of special fruit salad with *mayonnaise mousseuse*. The above mystery No. 1 is the justly popular tartar sauce.

Thus we could go on analyzing modern preparations and make them appear as outlandish things. Yet we relish them every day. The ingredients, obnoxious in great quantities, are employed with common sense. We are not mystified seeing them in print; they are usually given in clear logical order. This is not the style of Apicius, however.

LATIN CUNNING

We can hardly judge Apicius by what he has revealed but we rather should try to discover what he — purposely or otherwise — has concealed if we would get a good idea of the ancient kitchen. This thought occurred to us at the eleventh hour, after years of study of the text and after almost despairing of a plausible solution of its mysteries. And it seems surprising that Apicius has never been suspected before of withholding information essential to the successful practice of his rather hypothetical and empirical formulæ. The more we scrutinize them, the more we become convinced that the author has omitted vital directions — same as we did purposely with the two modern examples above. Many of the Apician recipes are dry enumerations of ingredients supposed to belong to a given dish or sauce. It is well-known that in chemistry (cookery is but applied chemistry) the knowledge of the rules governing the quantities and the sequence of the ingredients, their manipulation, either separately or jointly, either successively or simultaneously, is a very important matter, and that violation or ignorance of the process may spell failure at any stage of the experiment. In the kitchen this is particularly true of baking and soup and sauce making, the most intricate of culinary operations.

There may have been two chief reasons for concealing necessary information. Apicius, or more likely the professional collectors of the recipes, may have considered technical elaboration of the formulæ quite superfluous on the assumption that the formulæ were for professional use only. Every good practitioner knows, with ingredients or components given, what manipulations are required, what effects are desired. Even in the absence of detailed specifications, the experienced practitioner will be able to devine correct proportions, by intuition. As a matter of fact, in cookery the mention in the right place of a single ingredient, like in poetry the right word, often suffices to conjure up before the gourmet's mental eye vistas of delight. Call it inspiration, association of ideas or what you please, a single word may often prove a guide, a savior.

Let us remember that in Apicii days paper (parchment, papyrus) and writing materials were expensive and that, moreover, the ability of correct logical and literary expression was necessarily limited in the case of a practising cook who, after all, must have been the collector of the Apician formulæ. This is sufficiently proven by the *lingua coquinaria*, the vulgar Latin of our old work. In our opinion, the ancient author did not consider it worth his while to give anything but the most indispensable information in the tersest form. This he certainly did. A comparison of his literary performance with that of the artistic and accomplished writer of the Renaissance, Platina, will at once show up Apicius as a hard-working practical cook, a man who knew his business but who could not tell what he knew.

Like ever so many of his successors, he could not refrain from beginning and concluding many of his articles with such superfluities as "take this" and "And serve," etc., all of which shows him up as a genuine cook. These articles, written in the most laconic language possible — the language of a very busy, very harassed, very hurried man, are the literary product of a cook, or several of them.

The other chief motive for condensing or obscuring his text has a more subtle foundation. Indeed, we are surprised that we should possess so great a collection of recipes, representing to him who could use them certain commercial and social value. The preservation of Apicius seems entirely accidental. Experienced cooks were in demand in Apicii times; the valuation of their ministrations increased proportionately to the progress in gastronomy and to the prosperity of the nation. During Rome's frugal era, up to 200 B.C. the primitive cooks were just slaves and household chattels; but the development of their trade into an art, stimulated by foreign precepts, imported principally from Greece, Sicily and Asia Minor, opened up to the practitioners not only the door to freedom from servitude but it offered even positions of wealth with social and political standing, often arousing the envy, satire, criticism of bona-fide politicians, journalists, moralists, satirists and of the ever-present hordes of parasites and hangers-on. Some cooks became confidants, even friends and advisors of men in high places, emperors, (cf. life of Vitellius) and through their subtle influence upon the mighty they may have contributed in no mean measure to the fate of the nation. But such invisible string-pullers have not been confined to those days alone. (Take Rasputin! Take the valet to William I, reputed to have had more "say" than the mighty Bismarck, who, as it developed, got "the air" while the valet died in his berth.)

Such being the case, what potential power reposed in a greasy cookery manuscript! And, if so, why bare such wonderful secrets to Tom, Dick and Harry?

Weights and measures are given by Apicius in some instances. But just such figures can be used artfully to conceal a trap. Any mediocre cook, gaining possession of a choice collection of detailed and itemized recipes would have been placed in an enviable position. Experimenting for some time (at his master's expense) he would soon reach that perfection when he could demand a handsome compensation for his ministrations. Throughout antique times, throughout the middle ages down to the present day (when patent laws no longer protect a secret) strict secrecy was maintained around many useful and lucrative formulæ, not only by cooks, but also by physicians, alchemists and the various scientists, artisans and craftsmen. Only the favorite apprentice would be made heir to or shareholder in this important stock in trade after his worthiness had been proven to his master's satisfaction, usually by the payment of a goodly sum of money — apprentice's pay. We remember reading in Lanciani (Rodolfo L.: Ancient Rome in the Light of Recent Discoveries) how in the entire history of Rome there is but one voice, that of a solitary, noble-minded physician, complaining about the secrecy that was being maintained by his colleagues as regards their science. To be sure, those fellows had every reason in the world for keeping quiet: so preposterous were their methods in most cases! This secrecy indeed must have carried with it a blessing in disguise. Professional reserve was not its object. The motive was purely commercial.

Seeing where the information given by Apicius is out of reason and unintelligible we are led to believe that such text is by no means to be taken very literally. On the contrary, it is quite probable that weights and measures are not correct: they are quite likely to be of an artful and studied unreliability. A secret private code is often employed, necessitating the elimination or transposition of certain words, figures or letters before the whole will become intelligible and useful. If by any chance an uninitiated hand should attempt to grasp such veiled directions, failure would be certain. We confess to have employed at an early stage of our own career this same strategy and time-honored camouflage to protect a precious lot of recipes. Promptly we lost this unctuous manuscript, as we feared we would; if not deciphered today, the book has long since been discarded as being a record of the ravings of a madman.

The advent of the printing press changed the situation. With Platina, ca.

1474, an avalanche of cookery literature started. The secrets of Scappi, "*cuoco secreto*" to the pope, were "scooped" by an enterprising Venetian printer in 1570. The guilds of French mustard makers and sauce cooks (precursors of modern food firms and manufacturers of ready-made condiments) were a powerful tribe of secret mongers in the middle ages. English gastronomic literature of the 16th, 17th and even the 18th century is crowded with "closets opened," "secrets let out" and other alluring titles purporting to regale the prospective reader with profitable and appetizing secrets of all sorts. Kitchen secrets became commercial articles.

These remarks should suffice to illustrate the assumption that the Apicius book was not created for publication but that it is a collection of abridged formulæ for private use, a treasure chest as it were, of some cook, which after the demise of its owner, collector, originator, a curious world could not resist to play with, although but a few experienced masters held the key, being able to make use of the recipes.

Meat Diet

In perusing Apicius only one or two instances of cruelty to animals have come to our attention (cf. recipes No. 140 and 259). Cruel methods of slaughter were common. Some of the dumb beasts that were to feed man and even had to contribute to his pleasures and enjoyment of life by giving up their own lives often were tortured in cruel, unspeakable ways. The belief existed that such methods might increase the quality, palatability and flavor of the meat. Such beliefs and methods may still be encountered on the highways and byways in Europe and Asia today. Since the topic, strictly speaking does not belong here, we cannot depict it in detail, and in passing make mention of it to refer students interested in the psychology of the ancients to such details as are found in the writings of Plutarch and other ancient writers during the early Christian era. It must be remembered, however, that such writers (including the irreproachable Plutarch) were advocates of vegetarianism. Some passages are inspired by true humane feeling, but much appears to be written in the interest of vegetarianism.

The ancients were not such confirmed meat eaters as the modern Western nations, merely because the meat supply was not so ample. Beef was scarce because of the shortage of large pastures. The cow was sacred, the ox furnished motive power, and, after its usefulness was gone, the muscular old brute had little attraction for the gourmet. Today lives a race of beef eaters. Our beef diet, no doubt is bound to change somewhat. Already the world's grazing grounds are steadily diminishing. The North American prairies are being parcelled off into small farms the working conditions of which make beef raising expensive. The South American pampas and a strip of coastal land in Australia now furnish the bulk of the world's beef supply. Perhaps Northern Asia still holds in store a large future supply of meat but this no doubt will be claimed by

Asia. Already North America is acclimating the Lapland reindeer to offset the waning beef, to utilize its Northern wastes.

With the increasing shortage of beef, with the increasing facilities for raising chicken and pork, a reversion to Apician methods of cookery and diet is not only probably but actually seems inevitable. The ancient bill of fare and the ancient methods of cookery were entirely guided by the supply of raw materials — precisely like ours. They had no great food stores nor very efficient marketing and transportation systems, food cold storage. They knew, however, to take care of what there was. They were good managers.

Such atrocities as the willful destruction of huge quantities of food of every description on the one side and starving multitudes on the other as seen today never occurred in antiquity.

Many of the Apician dishes will not appeal to the beef eaters. It is worthy of note that much criticism was heaped upon Apicius some 200 years ago in England when beef eating became fashionable in that country. The art of Apicius requires practitioners of superior intellect. Indeed, it requires a superior clientèle to appreciate Apician dishes. But practitioners that would pass the requirements of the Apician school are scarce in the kitchens of the beef eaters. We cannot blame meat eaters for rejecting the average *chef d'œuvre* set before them by a mediocre cook who has learned little besides the roasting or broiling of meats. Once the average man has acquired a taste for the refined compositions made by a talented and experienced cook, say, a composition of meats, vegetables or cereals, properly "balanced" by that intuition that never fails the real artist, the fortunate diner will eventually curtail the preponderant meat diet. A glance at some Chinese and Japanese methods of cookery may perhaps convince us of the probability of these remarks.

Nothing is more perplexing and more alarming than a new dish, but we can see in a reversion to Apician cookery methods only a dietetic benefit accruing to this so-called white race of beef eaters.

Apicius certainly excels in the preparation of vegetable dishes (cf. his cabbage and asparagus) and in the utilization of parts of food materials that are today considered inferior, hardly worth preparing for the table except by the very careful and economical housekeeper. Properly prepared, many of these things are good, often more nutritious than the dearer cuts, and sometimes they are really delicious.

One has but to study the methods of ancient and intelligent people who have suffered for thousands of years under the perennial shortage of food supplies in order to understand and to appreciate Apician methods. Be it far from us to advocate their methods, or to wish upon us the conditions that engendered such methods; for such practices have been pounded into these people by dire necessity. They have graduated from the merciless school of hunger.

Food materials, we repeat, were never as cheap and as abundant as they are today. But who can say that they always will be so in the future?

SCIENCE CONFIRMING ANCIENT METHODS

We must not overlook the remarkable intuition displayed by the ancients in giving preference to foods with body- and blood-building properties. For instance, the use of liver, particularly fish liver already referred to. The correctness of their choice is now being confirmed by scientific re-discoveries. The young science of nutrition is important enough to an individual who would stimulate or preserve his health. But since constitutions are different, the most carefully conceived dietary may apply to one particular individual only, provided, however, that our present knowledge of nutrition be correct and final. This knowledge, as a matter of fact, is being revised and changed constantly.

If dietetics, therefore, were important enough to have any bearing at all upon the well-defined methods of cookery, we might go into detail analyzing ancient methods from that point of view. To call attention to the "economy," the stewardship, or craftsmanship, in ancient methods and to the truly remarkable intuition that guided the ancient cooks is more important. Without these qualities there can be no higher gastronomy. Without high gastronomy no high civilization is possible. The honest and experienced nutrition expert, though perhaps personally opposed to elaborate dining, will discover through close study of the ancient precepts interesting pre-scientific and well-balanced combinations and methods designed to jealously guard the vitamins and dietetic values in dishes that may appear curiously "new" to the layman that would nevertheless receive the unqualified approval of modern science.

We respect the efforts of modern dietitians and food reformers; but we are far removed from the so-called "simple" and "plain" foods advocated by some well-meaning individuals. With the progress of civilization we are farther and farther drifting away from it. Even barbaric and beastly food is not "simple."

This furtive "intuition" in cookery (in the absence of scientific facts because of the inability of cooks to transform empirical traditions into practical rules emanating from understood principles) still prevails today. It guides great chefs, saves time spent in scientific study.

The much criticized "unnatural union of sugar and meats" of the ancients still exists today in many popular examples of cookery: lamb and mint sauce, steak and catsup, mutton and currant jelly, pork and apples (in various forms), oyster cocktail, poultry and compote, goose with apple and raisin dressing, venison and Cumberland sauce, mince pie, plum pudding — typical survivals of ancient traditions. "Intuition" is still preceding exact science, and "unnatural unions" as in social, political and any other form of life, seem to be the rule rather than the exception.

DISGUISING FOODS

Apicius is often blamed for his endeavor to serve one thing under the guise of another. The reasons for such deceptions are various ones. Fashion dictated it. Cooks were not considered "clever" unless they could surprise guests with a commonplace food material so skillfully prepared that identification was difficult or impossible. Another reason was the absence of good refrigeration, making "masking" necessary. Also the ambition of hosts to serve a cheaper food for a more expensive one — veal for chicken, pork for partridge, and so on. But do we not indulge in the same "stunts" today? We either do it with the intention of deceiving or to "show off." Have we not "Mock Turtle Soup," *Mouton à la Chasseur*, mutton prepared to taste like venison, "chicken" salad made of veal or of rabbit? In Europe even today much of the traditional roast hare is caught in the alley, and it belongs to a feline species. "Roof hare."

FOOD ADULTERATIONS

There is positive evidence of downright frauds and vicious food adulteration in the times of Apicius. The old rascal himself is not above giving directions for rose wine without roses, or how to make a spoiled honey marketable, and other similar adulterations. Those of our readers with sensitive gastronomic instinct had better skip the paragraphs discussing the treatment of "birds with a goatish smell." But the old food adulterators are no match for their modern successors.

Too, some of our own shams are liable to misinterpretation. In centuries to come our own modern recipes for "Scotch Woodcock" or "Welsh rabbit" may be interpreted as attempts on our part to hoodwink guests by making game birds and rabbits out of cheese and bread, like Trimalchio's culinary artists are reputed to have made suckling pigs out of dough, partridges of veal, chicken of tunny fish, and *vice versa*. What indeed would a serious-minded research worker a thousand years hence if unfamiliar with our culinary practice and traditions make of such terms as *pette de nonne* as found in many old French cookery books, or of the famous *suttelties* (subtleties) — the confections once so popular at medieval weddings?

The ramifications of the *lingua coquinaria* in any country are manifold, and the culinary wonderland is full of pitfalls even for the experienced gourmet.

REACHING THE LIMIT

Like in all other branches of ancient endeavor, cookery had reached a state of perfection around the time of Apicius when the only chance for successful continuation of the art lay in the conquest of new fields, i.e., in expansion, generalization, elaboration and in influence from foreign sources. We have witnessed this in French cookery which for the last hundred years has successfully expanded and has virtually captured the civilized parts of the globe, subject however, always to regional and territorial modifications.

This desirable expansion of antique cookery did not take place. It was violently and rather suddenly checked principally by political and economic events during the centuries following Apicius, perhaps principally by the forces that caused the great migration (the very quest of food!). Suspension ensued instead. The heirs to the ancient culture were not yet ready for their marvelous heritage. Besides their cultural unpreparedness, the cookery of the ancients, like their humor, did not readily appeal to the "Nordic" heirs. Both are so subtle and they depend so much upon the psychology and the economic conditions of a people, and they thus presented almost unsurmountable obstacles to the invaders. Still lo! already in the fifth century, the Goth Vinithaharjis, started to collect the Apician precepts.

OUR PREDECESSORS

The usefulness in our days of Apicius as a practical cookery book has been questioned, but we leave this to our readers to decide after the perusal of this translation.

If not useful in the kitchen, if we cannot grasp its moral, what, then, is Apicius? Merely a curio?

The existing manuscripts cannot be bought; the old printed editions are highly priced by collectors, and they are rare. Still, the few persons able to read the messages therein cannot use them: they are not practitioners in cookery.

None of the Apician editors (except Danneil and the writer) were experienced practising gastronomers. Humelbergius, Lister, Bernhold were medical men. Two serious students, Schuch and Wuestemann, gave up academic positions to devote a year to the study of modern cookery in order to be able to interpret Apicius. These enthusiasts overlooked, however, two facts: Apicius cannot be understood by inquiring into modern average cookery methods, nor can complete mastery of cookery, practical as well as theoretical, including the historical and physiological aspects of gastronomy be acquired in one year. Richard Gollmer, another Apicius editor, declares that the results of this course in gastronomy were negative. We might add here that Schuch's edition of Apicius, apart from the unwarranted inclusion of the *excerpta* of Vinidarius is the least reliable of all editions.

Gollmer published a free version of Apicius in German in 1909. If he did not render the original very faithfully and literally, it must be said in all fairness that his methods of procedure were correct. Gollmer attempted to interpret the ancient text for the modern reader. Unfortunately he based his work upon that of Schuch and Wuestemann and Lister. A year or so later Eduard Danneil published a version of his own, also based on Schuch. This editor is a practising *chef*, — *Hof-Traiteur* or caterer to the court of one of the then reigning princes of Germany. Danneil's preface is dated 1897, though the date of publication is 1911. In view of the fact that Gollmer had covered the ground and that Danneil added nothing new to Apician lore, his publication seems superfluous. Danneil's translation differs in that the translator adhered literally to the questionable Schuch version whereas Gollmer aspired to a free and readable version for an educated public.

A comparison reveals that the one author is not a cook while the other is not a savant.

Like the scholars who tried their hand at cookery, there are a number of worthy and ambitious practitioners of cookery who have endeavored to reach the heights of scholarship, among them Carême and Soyer, men of great calibre. Unfortunately, the span of human life is short, the capacity of the human mind is limited. Fruitful achievements in widely different fields of endeavor by one man are rare. This is merely to illustrate the extreme difficulty encountered by anyone bent on a venturesome exploration of our subject and the very narrow chances of success to extricate himself with grace from the two-thousand year old labyrinth of philosophical, historical, linguistical and gastronomical technicalities.

This task will become comparatively easy, however, and surely interesting and with a foreboding of many delights and surprises if we penetrate the jungle aided by the experience of predecessors, steadfastly relying on the "theory of evolution" as a guide, and armed with the indispensable equipment for gastronomical research, i.e., the practical and technical knowledge of cookery, mastery of languages, augmented by practical experience gathered by observations and travel in many lands, and last but not least, if we are obsessed with the fixed idea that so menial a subject is worth all the bother.

We have purposely refrained from presenting here a treatise in the customary scientific style. We know, there are repetitions, digressions, excursions into adjacent fields that may be open to criticism. We really do not aim to make this critical review an exhibition of scholarly attainments with all the necessary brevity, clarity, scientific restraint and etiquette. Such style would be entirely out of our line. Any bookish flavor attaching itself to our work would soon replace a natural fragrance we aim to preserve, namely our close contact with the subject. Those interested in the scholarly work that has been contributed to this cause are referred to modern men like Vollmer, Giarratano, Brandt and others named in the bibliography. Of the older scientists there is Martinus Lister, a man whose knowledge of the subject is very respectable and whose devotion to it is unbounded, whose integrity as a scientist is above reproach. His notes and commentaries together with those of Humelbergius, the editor-physician of Zürich, will be enjoyed and read with profit by every antiquary. The labors of Bernhold and Schuch are meritorious also, the work, time, and *esprit* these men have devoted to the subject is enormous. As for Torinus, the opinions are divided. Humelbergius ignores him, Gryphius pirates him, Lister scorns him, we like him. Lister praises his brother physician, Humelbergius: *Doctus quidem vir et modestus*! So he is! The notes by Humelbergius alone and his word: *Nihil immutare ausi summus*! entitles him to all the praise Lister can bestow. Unfortunately, the sources of his information are unknown.

Lacking these, we have of course no means of ascertaining whether he always lived up to his word that he is not privileged to change. Humelbergius and Lister may have made contributions of value from a philological point of view but their work appears to have less merit gastronomically than that of Torinus. To us the Basel editor often seems surprisingly correct in cases where the gastronomical character of a formula is in doubt.

In rendering the ancient text into English we, too, have endeavored to follow

Humelbergii example; hence the almost literal translation of the originals before us, namely, Torinus, Humelbergius, Lister, Bernhold, Schuch and the latest, Giarratano-Vollmer which reached us in 1925 in time for collating. We have wavered often and long whether or not to place alongside this English version the original Latin text, but due to the divergencies we have finally abandoned the idea, for practical reasons alone.

In translating we have endeavored to clear up mysteries and errors; this interpretation is a work quite apart and independent of that of the translation. It is merely the sum and substance of our practical experience in gastronomy. It is not to be taken as an attempt to change the original but is presented in good faith, to be taken on its face value. This interpretation appears in the form of notes directly under each article, for quick reference and it is our wish that it be of some practical service in contributing to the general understanding and appreciation of our ancient book.

For the sake of expediency we have numbered and placed a title (in English) on each ancient recipe, following the example of Schuch. This procedure may be counted against us as a liberty taken with the text. The text has remained inviolate. We have merely aimed at a rational and legible presentation — work within the province and the duty of an editor-translator and technical expert.

We do not claim credit for any other work connected with the task of making this most unique book accessible to the English speaking public and for the competition for scholastic laurels we wish to stay *hors de combat*. We feel we are not privileged to pass final judgment upon the excellent work done by sympathetic and erudite admirers of our ancient book throughout the better part of four centuries, and we cannot side with one or the other in questions philological, historical, or of any other nature, except gastronomical. We are deeply indebted to all of our predecessors and through conversations and extensive correspondence with other modern researchers, Dr. Edward Brandt and Dr. Margaret B. Wilson, we are enabled to predict new developments in Apician research. The debates of the scientists, it appears, are not yet closed.

As a matter of fact, the various differences of opinion in minor questions are of little import to us as compared with the delightful fact that we here possess an Apicius, not only a genuine Roman, but an "honest-to-goodness" human being besides. A jolly fellow is Apicius with a basketful of happy messages for a hungry world. We therefore want to make this work of ours the entertainment and instruction the subject deserves to be. If we succeed in proving that Apicius is not a mummyfied, bone-dry classic but that he has "the goods," namely some real human merit we shall have accomplished more than the savants to whom this popularization of our hero has been denied so far.

After all, we live in a practical age, and it is the practical value, the matter-of-fact contribution to our happiness and well-being by the work of any man, ancient or modern, which counts in these days of materialism.

So let us tell the truth, and let us sum up in a few words:

We do not know who Apicius is. We do not know who wrote the book bearing

his name. We do not know when it was written, or whether it is of Greek or
of Roman origin. Furthermore, we do not understand many of its precepts!

We do know, however, that it is the oldest work dealing with the food and
the cookery of the ancient world's greatest empire, and that, as such, it is of the
utmost interest and importance to us.

In this sense we have endeavored to treat the book.

DINING IN APICIAN STYLE

Past attempts to dine à l'Apicius invariably have ended disastrously. Eager
gourmets, ever on the look-out for something new and curious scholars have
attempted to prepare dishes in the manner prescribed by Apicius. Most of such
experimenters have executed the old precepts literally, instead of trying to enter
into their spirit.

"Das Land der Griechen mit der Seele suchen!" says Goethe. The friends of
Apicius who failed to heed this advice, also failed to comprehend the precepts,
they were cured of their curiosity, and blamed the master for their own short-
comings. Christina, queen of Sweden, was made ill by an attempt of this kind to
regale her majesty with a rare Apician morsel while in Italy as the guest of
some noble. But history is dark on this point. Here perhaps Apicius is blamed
for a dastardly attempt on the royal lady's life for this daughter of the Protestant
Gustavus Adolphus was in those days not the only crowned head in danger of
being dispatched by means of some tempting morsel smilingly proffered by some
titled rogue. A deadly dish under the disguise of "Apicius" must have been
particularly convenient in those days for such sinister purposes. The sacred
obligations imposed upon "barbarians" by the virtue of hospitality had been
often forgotten by the super-refined hosts of the Renaissance.

But Apicius continued to prove unhealthful to a number of later amateurs.
Lister, with his perfectly sincere endeavor to popularize Apicius, achieved precisely the opposite. The publication of his work in London, 1705, was the signal
for a number of people, scholars and others, to crack jokes, not at the expense
of Apicius, as they imagined, but to expose their own ignorance. Smollet, Dr.
W. King ("Poor starving wit" — Swift), Dr. Hunter and others. More recently,
a party of English dandies, chaperoned, if we remember correctly, by the pon-
derous George Augustus Sala, fared likewise badly in their attempt to stage a
Roman feast, being under the impression that the days of Tiberius and the mid-
Victorian era may be joined with impunity, *à la minute*, as it were.

Even later, in one of the (alas! not so many) good books on gastronomy,
"Kettner's Book of the Table," London, 1877, the excellent author dismisses
Roman cookery with a few lines of "warning." Kettner, admirer of Sala, evidently was still under the baneful influence. Twenty years later, Danneil, colleague of Kettner's, joined the chorus of "irreverent critics." They all based
their judgment on mere idle conversation, resulting from disappointments in
ill-fated attempts to cook in the Apician style. Even the best experts, it appears,
may fall victims to the mysterious spell surrounding, protecting things of sacred

antiquity, hovering like an avenging angel over them, to ward off all "irreverent critics" and curious intruders.

THE PROOF OF THE PUDDING

After all, the proof of the pudding is in the eating. This homely solid wisdom is literally true of our good old Apicius. We have tested many of his precepts, and have found them practical, good, even delightful. A few, we will say, are of the rarest beauty and of consummate perfection in the realm of gastronomy, while some others again are totally unintelligible for reasons sufficiently explained. Always remembering Humelbergius, we have "laid off" of these torsos, recommending them to some more competent commentator. Many of the ancient formula tried have our unqualified gastronomic approval.

If our work has not differed from that of our predecessors, if it shows the same human frailties and foibles, we have at least one mark of distinction among the editors in that we have subjected the original to severe practical tests as much as this is possible with our modern food materials. We experienced difficulty in securing certain spices long out of use. Nevertheless, the experience of actually sampling Apician dishes and the sensation of dining in the manners of the Cæsars are worth the trouble we took with Apicius. This is a feeling of partaking of an entirely new dish, met with both expectancy and with suspicion, accentuated by the hallowed traditions surrounding it which has rewarded us for the time and expense devoted to the subject. Ever since we have often dined in the classical fashion of the ancients who, after all, were but "folks" like ourselves.

If you care not for the carnal pleasures in Apician gastronomy — for *gulam* —, if you don't give a fig for philology, there still is something healthy, something infinitely soothing and comforting — "educational" — in the perusal of the old book and in similar records.

When we see Apicius, the famous "epicure" descending to the very level of a common food "fakir," giving directions for making Liburnian oil that has never seen that country. . .

When we note, with a gentle shudder, that the grafters of Naples, defying even the mighty Augustus, leveled the "White Earth Hill" near Puteoli because an admixture of plaster paris is exceedingly profitable to the milling profession. . .

When Apicius — celebrated glutton — resorts to the comparatively harmless "stunt" of keeping fresh vegetables green by boiling them in a copper kettle with soda. . .

When we behold hordes of ancient legislators, posing as dervishes of moderation, secretly and openly breaking the prohibition laws of their own making. . .

When we turn away from such familiar sights and, in a more jovial mood, heartily laugh at the jokes of that former mill slave, Plautus (who could not pay his bills) and when we wonder why his wise cracks sound so familiar we remember that we have heard their modern versions only yesterday at the Tivoli on State Street. . .

When, finally, in the company of our respected Horatius we hear him say in the slang of his day: *Ab ovo usque ad mala*, and compare this bright saying with our own dear "From Soup to Nuts." . .

Then we arrive at the comforting conclusion that we moderns are either very ancient and backward or that indeed the ancients are very modern and progressive; and it is our only regret that we cannot decide this perplexing situation to our lasting satisfaction.

Very true, there may be nothing new under the sun, yet nature goes on eternally fashioning new things from old materials. Eternally demolishing old models in a manner of an economical sculptor, nature uses the same old clay to create new specimens. Sometimes nature slightly alters the patterns, discarding what is unfit for her momentary enigmatic purposes, retaining and favoring that which pleases her whimsical fancy for the time being.

Cookery deals exclusively with nature's works. Books on cookery are essentially books on nature's actions and reactions.

In the perpetual search for perfection, life has accomplished one remarkable thing: the development of man, the animal which cooks. Gradually nature has revealed herself to man principally through the food he takes, cooks and prepares for the enjoyment of himself and his fellow men.

THE COOKING ANIMAL

The gastronomer is the highest development of the cooking animal.

He — artist, philosopher, metaphysician, religionist — stands with his head bared before nature: overawed, contemplating her gifts, feasting his eyes on beauteous forms and colors, inhaling intoxicating fragrances aromas, odors, matching them all artistically, partaking only of what he needs for his own subsistence — eternally marveling at nature's inexhaustible resources and inventiveness, at her everlasting bounty born of everlasting fierce struggles.

The gastronomer is grateful for the privilege of holding the custodianship of such precious things, and he guards it like an office of a sacred rite — ever gratefully, reverently adoring, cherishing the things before him . . . ever marveling . . . ever alone, alone with nature.

As for the overwhelming majority of the cooking animals, they behave much more "naturally." They are a merry crowd, ever anticipating a good time, ever jolly, eager, greedy. Or, they are cranky, hungry, starved, miserable, and they turn savage now and then. Some are gluttonous. Many contract indigestion — nature's most subtle punishment.

If they were told that they must kill before they may cook — that might spoil the appetite and dinner joy of many a tender-hearted devourer of fellow-creatures.

Heaven forbid! Being real children of nature, and behaving naturally, nature likes them, and we, too, certainly are well pleased with the majority.

The only fly in the ointment of life is that we don't know what it is all about, and probably never will know.

PROŒMII FINIS

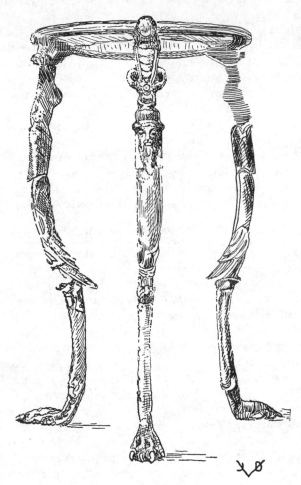

TRIPOD FOR THE GREAT CRATER
Hildesheim Treasure

THE RECIPES OF APICIUS
AND
THE EXCERPTS FROM APICIUS BY VINIDARIUS

ORIGINAL TRANSLATION FROM THE TEXTS
OF TORINUS, HUMELBERGIUS, LISTER
AND GIARRATANO-VOLLMER
WITH NOTES AND COMMENTS

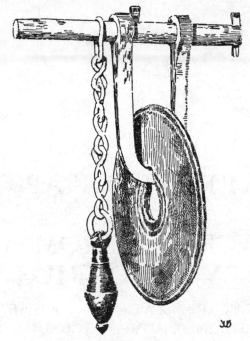

"DINNER GONG"

Heavy bronze disk and substantial "knocker" to signal slaves. Found in Pompeii. "Hurry, fellows, the cakes are piping hot!" — Plautus. Ntl. Mus., Naples, 78622; Field M., 24133.

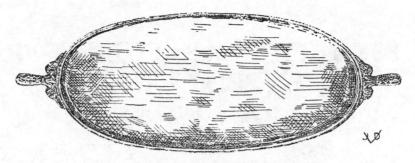

OVAL SERVICE DISH
With two decorated handles. Hildesheim Treas.

THE TEN BOOKS OF APICIUS

I. THE CAREFUL EXPERIENCED COOK. II. MINCES. III. THE GARDENER. IV. MISCELLANEOUS DISHES. V. LEGUMES. VI. POULTRY. VII. FANCY DISHES. VIII. QUADRUPEDS. IX. SEA FOOD. X. FISH SAUCES. THE EXCERPTS OF VINIDARIUS.

[V. The Greek titles of the ten books point to a common Greek origin, indicating that Apicius is a collection of Greek monographs on various branches of cookery, specialization such as highly developed civilizations would produce. Both the literary style and the contents of the books point to different authors, as may be seen from the very repetitions of and similarities in subjects as in VI and VIII, and in IX and X. The absence of books on bread and cake baking, dessert cookery indicates that the present Apicius is not complete.]

BOOK I. THE CAREFUL EXPERI-ENCED COOK

Lib. I. Epimeles

CHAP.   I. FINE SPICED WINE. HONEY REFRESHER FOR TRAVELERS.

CHAP.   II. ROMAN VERMOUTH.

CHAP.   III. ROSE WINE. VIOLET WINE. ROSE WINE WITHOUT ROSES.

CHAP.   IV. LIBURNIAN OIL.

CHAP.   V. TO CLARIFY MUDDY WINE.

CHAP.   VI. TO IMPROVE A BROTH WITH A BAD ODOR.

CHAP. VII. TO KEEP MEATS FRESH WITHOUT SALT. TO KEEP COOKED SIDES OF PORK.

CHAP. VIII. TO MAKE SALT MEATS SWEET.

CHAP.   IX. TO KEEP FRIED FISH. TO KEEP OYSTERS.

CHAP.   X. TO MAKE LASER GO A LONG WAY.

CHAP.   XI. TO MAKE HONEY CAKES LAST. TO MAKE SPOILED HONEY GOOD. TO TEST SPOILED HONEY.

CHAP. XII. TO KEEP GRAPES. TO KEEP POMEGRANATES. TO KEEP QUINCES. TO PRESERVE FRESH FIGS. TO KEEP CITRON. TO KEEP MULBERRIES. TO KEEP POT HERBS. TO PRESERVE SORREL. TO KEEP TRUFFLES. TO KEEP HARD-SKINNED PEACHES.

CHAP. XIII. SPICED SALTS FOR MANY ILLS.

CHAP. XIV. TO KEEP GREEN OLIVES.

CHAP. XV. CUMIN SAUCE FOR SHELLFISH. ANOTHER.

CHAP. XVI. LASER FLAVOR. ANOTHER.

CHAP. XVII. WINE SAUCE FOR TRUFFLES. ANOTHER.

CHAP. XVIII. OXYPORUM.

CHAP. XIX. HYPOTRIMA.

CHAP. XX. OXYGARUM, DIGESTIVE. ANOTHER.

CHAP. XXI. MORTARIA.

I

[1]   FINE SPICED WINE   *CONDITUM PARADOXUM*

T HE COMPOSITION OF [this] EXCELLENT SPICED WINE
     [is as follows]. INTO A COPPER BOWL PUT 6 SEXTARII [1]
OF HONEY AND 2 SEXTARII OF WINE; HEAT ON A SLOW
FIRE, CONSTANTLY STIRRING THE MIXTURE WITH A WHIP.
AT THE BOILING POINT ADD A DASH OF COLD WINE, RE-
TIRE FROM STOVE AND SKIM. REPEAT THIS TWICE OR
THREE TIMES, LET IT REST TILL THE NEXT DAY, AND SKIM
AGAIN. THEN ADD 4 OZS. OF CRUSHED PEPPER [2], 3 SCRU-
PLES OF MASTICH, A DRACHM EACH OF [nard or laurel]
LEAVES AND SAFFRON, 5 DRACHMS OF ROASTED DATE
STONES CRUSHED AND PREVIOUSLY SOAKED IN WINE TO
SOFTEN THEM. WHEN THIS IS PROPERLY DONE ADD 18 SEX-
TARII OF LIGHT WINE. TO CLARIFY IT PERFECTLY, ADD
[crushed] CHARCOAL [3] TWICE OR AS OFTEN AS NECESSARY
WHICH WILL DRAW [the residue] TOGETHER [and carefully
strain or filter through the charcoal].

   [1] *Sextarii.* Tor. *partes* XV; G.-V. *pondo* XV; List. *partes* XV . . . *pondo
lib. . . . qui continent sextarios sex.* One sextarius (a "sixth") equals about 1½
pint English.
   [2] Pepper. *Piperis uncias* IV — ordinarily our black or white pepper
grains, but in connection with honey, sweets, and so forth, the term "pepper"
may just as well stand for our allspice, or even for any spicing in general.
   [3] Charcoal. Still a favorite filterer for liquors.
   List. Apicius is correct in starting his book with this formula, as all meals
were started with this sort of mixed drink.
   Tor. deviates from the other texts in that he elaborates on the cooking process.

[2]   HONEY REFRESHER FOR TRAVELERS
      CONDITUM MELIZOMUM [1] *VIATORIUM*

   THE WAYFARER'S HONEY REFRESHER (SO CALLED BE-
CAUSE IT GIVES ENDURANCE AND STRENGTH TO PEDES-
TRIANS) [2] WITH WHICH TRAVELERS ARE REFRESHED BY
THE WAYSIDE IS MADE IN THIS MANNER: FLAVOR HONEY
WITH GROUND PEPPER AND SKIM. IN THE MOMENT OF
SERVING PUT HONEY IN A CUP, AS MUCH AS IS DESIRED TO
OBTAIN THE RIGHT DEGREE OF SWEETNESS, AND MIX
WITH SPICED WINE NOT MORE THAN A NEEDED QUAN-

TITY; ALSO ADD SOME WINE TO THE SPICED HONEY TO
FACILITATE ITS FLOW AND THE MIXING.

[1] Tor. *Melirhomum; non extat.* G.-V. M. *perpetuum,* i.e., having good
keeping qualities.

[2] Tor. reads thus whereas others apply "endurance" to the honey itself.
The honey could not be preserved (*perpetuum*) by the addition of pepper. Any
addition, as a matter of fact, would hasten its deterioration unless the honey
were boiled and sealed tight, which the original takes for granted.

II

[3] ROMAN VERMOUTH
ABSINTHIUM ROMANUM [1]

ROMAN VERMOUTH [or Absinth] IS MADE THUS: ACCORD-
ING TO THE RECIPE OF CAMERINUM [2] YOU NEED
WORMWOOD FROM SANTO [3] FOR ROMAN VERMOUTH
OR, AS A SUBSTITUTE, WORMWOOD FROM THE PONTUS [4]
CLEANED AND CRUSHED, 1 THEBAN OUNCE [5] OF IT, 6
SCRUPLES OF MASTICH, 3 EACH OF [nard] LEAVES, COST-
MARY [6] AND SAFFRON AND 18 QUARTS OF ANY KIND OF
MILD WINE. [Filter cold] CHARCOAL IS NOT REQUIRED BE-
CAUSE OF THE BITTERNESS.

[1] G.-V. *Apsinthium.*
[2] The mention of a name in a recipe is very infrequent. Camerinum is a
town in Umbria.
[3] Now Saintonge, Southern France.
[4] Black Sea Region.
[5] Weight of indefinite volume, from Thebæ, one of the several ancient
cities by that name. List. thinks it is an Egyptian ounce, and that the author of
the recipe must be an African.
[6] Wanting in Tor.; G.-V. *costi scripulos senos.*

III

[4] ROSE WINE [1]   *ROSATUM*

MAKE ROSE WINE IN THIS MANNER: ROSE PETALS, THE
LOWER WHITE PART REMOVED, SEWED INTO A LINEN BAG
AND IMMERSED IN WINE FOR SEVEN DAYS. THEREUPON
ADD A SACK OF NEW PETALS WHICH ALLOW TO DRAW FOR
ANOTHER SEVEN DAYS. AGAIN REMOVE THE OLD PETALS
AND REPLACE THEM BY FRESH ONES FOR ANOTHER WEEK;

THEN STRAIN THE WINE THROUGH THE COLANDER. BE-
FORE SERVING, ADD HONEY SWEETENING TO TASTE. TAKE
CARE THAT ONLY THE BEST PETALS FREE FROM DEW BE
USED FOR SOAKING.

[1] Used principally as a laxative medicine. List. These wines compounded
of roses and violets move the bowels strongly.

[5]   VIOLET WINE   *VIOLATIUM*

IN A SIMILAR WAY AS ABOVE LIKE THE ROSE WINE VIO-
LET WINE IS MADE OF FRESH VIOLETS, AND TEMPERED
WITH HONEY, AS DIRECTED.

[6]   ROSE WINE WITHOUT [1] ROSES
ROSATUM SINE ROSA

ROSE WINE WITHOUT ROSES IS MADE IN THIS FASHION:
A PALM LEAF BASKET FULL OF FRESH CITRUS LEAVES IS IM-
MERSED IN THE VAT OF NEW WINE BEFORE FERMENTA-
TION HAS SET IN. AFTER FORTY DAYS RETIRE THE LEAVES,
AND, AS OCCASION ARISES, SWEETEN THE WINE WITH
HONEY, AND PASS IT UP FOR ROSE WINE.

[1]   A substitute.

IV

[7]   LIBURNIAN OIL   *OLEUM LIBURNICUM*

IN ORDER TO MAKE AN OIL SIMILAR TO THE LIBURNIAN
OIL PROCEED AS FOLLOWS: IN SPANISH OIL PUT [the follow-
ing mixture of] ELECAMPANE, CYPRIAN RUSH AND GREEN
LAUREL LEAVES THAT ARE NOT TOO OLD, ALL OF IT
CRUSHED AND MACERATED AND REDUCED TO A FINE
POWDER. SIFT THIS IN AND ADD FINELY GROUND SALT
AND STIR INDUSTRIOUSLY FOR THREE DAYS OR MORE.
THEN ALLOW TO SETTLE. EVERYBODY WILL TAKE THIS
FOR LIBURNIAN OIL. [1]

[1] Like the above a flagrant case of food adulteration.

V

[8]   TO CLARIFY MUDDY WINE
VINUM EX ATRO CANDIDUM FACIES

PUT BEAN MEAL AND THE WHITES OF THREE EGGS IN A
MIXING BOWL. MIX THOROUGHLY WITH A WHIP AND ADD

TO THE WINE, STIRRING FOR A LONG TIME. THE NEXT DAY THE WINE WILL BE CLEAR [1]. ASHES OF VINES HAVE THE SAME EFFECT.

[1] Ex Lister whose version we prefer. He says, *Alias die erit candidum* while Tor. adds white salt, saying, *sal si adieceris candidum*, same as Tac. This is unusual, although the ancients have at times treated wine with sea water.

VI

[9] TO IMPROVE A BROTH [1]
DE LIQUAMINE EMENDANDO [2]

IF BROTH HAS CONTRACTED A BAD ODOR, PLACE A VESSEL UPSIDE DOWN AND FUMIGATE IT WITH LAUREL AND CYPRESS AND BEFORE VENTILATING [3] IT, POUR THE BROTH IN THIS VESSEL. IF THIS DOES NOT HELP MATTERS [4] AND IF THE TASTE IS TOO PRONOUNCED, ADD HONEY AND FRESH SPIKENARD [5] TO IT; THAT WILL IMPROVE IT. ALSO NEW MUST SHOULD BE LIKEWISE EFFECTIVE [6].

[1] List. *Liquamen, id est, garum.* Goll. Fish sauce.

[2] Tor. *Qui liquamen corruptum corrigatur.*

[3] Dann. Ventilate it. Goll. Whip the sauce in fresh air.

[4] List., G.-V. *si salsum fuerit* — if this makes it too salty — Tor. *si hoc nihil effecerit.*

[5] Tor. *novem spicam immittas*; List. *Move spica*; Goll.-Dann. stir with a whip.

[6] A classic example of Apician confusion when one interpreter reads "s" for "f" and "*novem*" for "*move*" and another reads something else. Tor. is more correct than the others, but this formula is beyond redemption. Fate has decreed that ill-smelling broths shall be discarded.

VII

[10] TO KEEP MEATS FRESH WITHOUT SALT FOR ANY LENGTH OF TIME
UT CARNES SINE SALE QUOVIS TEMPORE RE-CENTES SINT

COVER FRESH MEAT WITH HONEY, SUSPEND IT IN A VESSEL. USE AS NEEDED; IN WINTER IT WILL KEEP BUT IN SUMMER IT WILL LAST ONLY A FEW DAYS. COOKED MEAT MAY BE TREATED LIKEWISE.

[11] TO KEEP COOKED SIDES OF PORK OR BEEF OR
       TENDERLOINS
       *CALLUM PORCINUM VEL BUBULUM ET UNGUEL-
       LÆ COCTÆ UT DIU DURENT*

PLACE THEM IN A PICKLE OF MUSTARD, VINEGAR, SALT
AND HONEY, COVERING MEAT ENTIRELY. AND WHEN
READY TO USE YOU'LL BE SURPRISED.

V. Method still popular today for pickling raw meats. The originals treat of
cooked meats (Tor. *nucula elixa*; G.-V. *unguellæ coctæ*; Tac. *nucella cocta*).
Dispensing with the honey, we use more spices, whole pepper, cloves, bay leaves,
also onions and root vegetables. Sometimes a little sugar and wine is added to
this preparation which the French call *marinade* and the Germans *Sauerbraten-
Einlage*.

VIII

[12] TO MAKE SALT MEAT SWEET
       UT CARNEM SALSAM DULCEM FACIAS

YOU CAN MAKE SALT MEATS SWEET BY FIRST BOILING
THEM IN MILK AND THEN FINISHING THEM IN WATER.

V. Method still in practice today. Salt mackerel, finnan haddie, etc., are parboiled in milk prior to being boiled in water or broiled or fried.

IX

[13] TO KEEP FRIED FISH
       UT PISCES FRICTI DIU DURENT

IMMEDIATELY AFTER THEY ARE FRIED POUR HOT VINE-
GAR OVER THEM.

Dann. Exactly as we today with fried herring and river lamprey.

[14] TO KEEP OYSTERS   *OSTREA UT DIU DURENT*

FUMIGATE A VINEGAR BARREL WITH PITCH [1], WASH
IT OUT WITH VINEGAR AND STACK THE OYSTERS IN IT [2]

[1] Tor. *vas ascernum*, corrected on margin, *ab aceto*. List. *vas ab aceto*,
which is correct. G.-V. *lavas ab aceto*; V. the oysters? unthinkable! Besides it
would do no good.

[2] Goll. Take oysters out of the shell, place in vinegar barrel, sprinkle with
laurel berries, fine salt, close tight. V. Goll's. authority for this version is not
found in our originals.

V. There is no way to keep live oysters fresh except in their natural habitat
— salt water. Today we pack them in barrels, feed them with oatmeal, put
weights on them — of no avail. The only way English oysters could have arrived
fresh in Imperial Rome was in specially constructed bottoms of the galleys.

X

[15]   MAKING A LITTLE LASER GO A LONG WAY
       UT NUCIA [1] *LASERIS TOTO TEMPORE UTARIS*

PUT THE LASER [2] IN A SPACIOUS GLASS VESSEL; IM-
MERSE ABOUT 20 PINE KERNELS [pignolia nuts]

IF YOU NEED LASER FLAVOR, TAKE SOME NUTS, CRUSH
THEM; THEY WILL IMPART TO YOUR DISH AN ADMIRABLE
FLAVOR. REPLACE THE USED NUTS WITH A LIKE NUMBER
OF FRESH ONES [3]

[1] List. and G.-V. *uncia* — ounce. Making an ounce of laser go a long
way. Tor. *nucea*; Tac. *nucia*. Lister, fond of hair-splitting, is irreconcilably opposed to Tor., and berates Caspar Barthius for defending Tor. List. *Quam fu-
tilis sit in multis labor C. Barthii ut menda Torini passim sustineat, vel ex hoc
loco intelligere licet: Et enim lege modo uncia pro nucea cum Humelbergio, &
ista omnia glossemata vana sunt.*

V. both readings, *uncia* or *nucia* are permissible, and make very little difference. We side with Tor. and Tac. because it takes more than an ounce of laser
to carry out this experiment.

[2] *Laser, laserpitium,* cf. dictionary

[3] V. This article illustrates how sparingly the ancients used the strong and
pungent laser flavor [by some believed to be *asa foetida*] because it was very expensive, but principally because the Roman cooks worked economically and
knew how to treat spices and flavors judiciously. This article alone should dis-
perse for all time all stories of ancient Rome's extravagance in flavoring and
seasoning dishes. It reminds of the methods used by European cooks to get the
utmost use out of the expensive vanilla bean: they bury the bean in a can of
powdered sugar. They will use the sugar only which has soon acquired a delicate
vanilla perfume, and will replace the used sugar by a fresh supply. This is by far
a superior method to using the often rank and adulterated "vanilla extract" readily bottled. It is more gastronomical and more economical. Most commercial
extracts are synthetic, some injurious. To believe that any of them impart to the
dishes the true flavor desired is of course ridiculous. The enormous consumption
of such extracts however, is characteristic of our industrialized barbarism which
is so utterly indifferent to the fine points in food. Today it is indeed hard for the
public to obtain a real vanilla bean.

Cf. also notes regarding flavoring to Nos. 276-7, 345 and 385.

XI

[16]   TO MAKE HONEY CAKES LAST
       UT DULCIA DE MELLE DIU DURENT

TO MAKE HONEY CAKES THAT WILL KEEP TAKE WHAT
THE GREEKS CALL YEAST [1] AND MIX IT WITH THE FLOUR

AND THE HONEY AT THE TIME WHEN MAKING THE COOKY DOUGH.

[1] Tor. and Tac. *nechon*; G.-V. *cnecon*; Dann. *penion*.

[17] SPOILED HONEY MADE GOOD
UT MEL MALUM BONUM FACIAS

HOW BAD HONEY MAY BE TURNED INTO A SALEABLE ARTICLE IS TO MIX ONE PART OF THE SPOILED HONEY WITH TWO PARTS OF GOOD HONEY.

List. *indigna fraus*! V. We all agree with Lister that this is contemptible business. This casts another light on the ancients' methods of food adulteration.

[18] TO TEST SPOILED HONEY
MEL CORRUPTUM UT PROBES

IMMERSE ELENCAMPANE IN HONEY AND LIGHT IT; IF GOOD, IT WILL BURN BRIGHTLY.

XII

[19] TO KEEP GRAPES   UVÆ UT DIU SERVENTUR

TAKE PERFECT GRAPES FROM THE VINES, PLACE THEM IN A VESSEL AND POUR RAIN WATER OVER THEM THAT HAS BEEN BOILED DOWN ONE THIRD OF ITS VOLUME. THE VESSEL MUST BE PITCHED AND SEALED WITH PLASTER, AND MUST BE KEPT IN A COOL PLACE TO WHICH THE SUN HAS NO ACCESS. TREATED IN THIS MANNER, THE GRAPES WILL BE FRESH WHENEVER YOU NEED THEM. YOU CAN ALSO SERVE THIS WATER AS HONEY MEAD TO THE SICK.

ALSO, IF YOU COVER THE GRAPES WITH BARLEY [bran] YOU WILL FIND THEM SOUND AND UNINJURED.

V. We keep grapes in cork shavings, bran and saw dust.

[20] TO KEEP POMEGRANATES
UT MALA GRANATA DIU DURENT [1]

STEEP THEM INTO HOT [sea] WATER, TAKE THEM OUT IMMEDIATELY AND HANG THEM UP. [Tor.] THEY WILL KEEP.

[1] Tor. *conditura malorum Punicorum*; Tac. *mala granata*; G.-V. *mala et mala granata*.

[21] TO KEEP QUINCES
UT MALA CYDONIA DIU SERVENTUR

PICK OUT PERFECT QUINCES WITH STEMS [1] AND
LEAVES. PLACE THEM IN A VESSEL, POUR OVER HONEY
AND DEFRUTUM [2] AND YOU'LL PRESERVE THEM FOR A
LONG TIME [3].

[1] V. Excellent idea, for the stems, if removed, would leave a wound in the
fruit for the air to penetrate and to start fermentation. Cf. also the next formula.

[2] G.-V. *defritum*, from *defervitum*; *defrutum* is new wine, spiced, boiled
down to one half of its volume.

[3] This precept would not keep the fruit very long unless protected by a
closefitting cover and sterilization. Cf. No. 24.

[22] TO PRESERVE FRESH FIGS, APPLES, PLUMS, PEARS
AND CHERRIES
FICUM RECENTEM, MALA, PRUNA, PIRA, CERA-SIA UT DIU SERVES

SELECT THEM ALL VERY CAREFULLY WITH THE STEMS
ON [1] AND PLACE THEM IN HONEY SO THEY DO NOT
TOUCH EACH OTHER.

[1] See the preceding formula.

[23] TO KEEP CITRON *CITRIA UT DIU DURENT* [1]

PLACE THEM IN A GLASS (2) VESSEL WHICH IS SEALED
WITH PLASTER AND SUSPENDED.

[1] Tor. *conditura malorum Medicorum quæ et citria dicuntur*. V. Not quite
identified. Fruit coming from Asia Minor, Media or Persia, one of the many
varieties of citrus fruit. Probably citron because of their size. Goll. Lemon-ap-
ples; Dann. lemons (oranges). List. *Scilicet mala, quæ Dioscorides Persica quoque
& Medica, & citromala, Plinius item Assyria appellari dicit.*

[2] G.-V. *vas vitreum*; Tac. and Tor. *vas citrum*; V. a glass vessel could not
be successfully sealed with plaster paris, and the experiment would fail; cf. note
3 to No. 21.

[24] TO KEEP MULBERRIES *MORA UT DIU DURENT*

MULBERRIES, IN ORDER TO KEEP THEM, MUST BE LAID
INTO THEIR OWN JUICE MIXED WITH NEW WINE [boiled
down to one half] IN A GLASS VESSEL AND MUST BE WATCHED
ALL THE TIME [so that they do not spoil].

V. This and the foregoing formulæ illustrate the ancients' attempts at preserving foods, and they betray their ignorance of "processing" by heating them

in hermetically sealed vessels, the principle of which was not discovered until 1810 by Appert which started the now gigantic industry of canning.

[25] TO KEEP POT HERBS
[H]OLERA UT DIU SERVENTUR

PLACE SELECTED POT HERBS, NOT TOO MATURE, IN A PITCHED VESSEL.

[26] TO PRESERVE SORREL OR SOUR DOCK
LAPÆ [1] UT DIU SERVENTUR

TRIM AND CLEAN [the vegetable] PLACE THEM TOGETHER SPRINKLE MYRTLE BERRIES BETWEEN, COVER WITH HONEY AND VINEGAR.

ANOTHER WAY: PREPARE MUSTARD HONEY AND VINE-GAR ALSO SALT AND COVER THEM WITH THE SAME.

[1] The kind of vegetable to be treated here has not been sufficiently identi-fied. List. and G.-V. *rapæ* — turnips — from *rapus*, seldom *rapa*, — a rape, turnip, navew. Tac. and Tor. *Lapæ* (*lapathum*), kind of sorrel, monk's rhubarb, dock. Tor. explaining at length: *conditura Rumicis quod lapathon Græci, Latini Lapam quoque dicunt.*

V. Tor. is correct, or nearly so. Turnips, in the first place, are not in need of any special method of preservation. They keep very well in a cool, well-venti-lated place; in fact they would hardly keep very long if treated in the above manner. These directions are better applied to vegetables like dock or monk's rhubarb. Lister, taking Humelbergii word for it, accepts "turnips" as the only truth; but he has little occasion to assail Torinus as he does: *Torinus lapam legit, & nullibi temeritatem suam atque inscientiam magis ostendit.*

Now, if Torinus, according to Lister, "nowhere displays more nerve and ig-norance" we can well afford to trust Torinus in cases such as this.

[27] TO KEEP TRUFFLES
TUBERA UT DIU SERVENTUR

THE TRUFFLES WHICH MUST NOT BE TOUCHED BY WATER ARE PLACED ALTERNATELY IN DRY SAWDUST; SEAL THE VESSEL WITH PLASTER AND DEPOSIT IT IN A COOL PLACE.

Dann. Clean [peel] the truffles . . . in another vessel place the peelings, seal the vessels . . . V. this would be the ruin of the truffles, unless they were "pro-cessed" in the modern way. Our originals have nothing that would warrant this interpretation.

[28] TO KEEP HARD-SKINNED PEACHES
DURACINA PERSICA UT DIU DURENT

SELECT THE BEST AND PUT THEM IN BRINE. THE NEXT DAY REMOVE THEM AND RINSING THEM CAREFULLY SET THEM IN PLACE IN A VESSEL, SPRINKLE WITH SALT AND SATURY AND IMMERSE IN VINEGAR.

XIII

[29] SALTS FOR MANY [ILLS]
SALES CONDITOS AD MULTA

THESE SPICED SALTS ARE USED AGAINST INDIGESTION, TO MOVE THE BOWELS, AGAINST ALL ILLNESS, AGAINST PESTILENCE AS WELL AS FOR THE PREVENTION OF COLDS. THEY ARE VERY GENTLE INDEED AND MORE HEALTHFUL THAN YOU WOULD EXPECT. [TOR. MAKE THEM IN THIS MANNER]: 1 LB. OF COMMON SALT GROUND, 2 LBS. OF AMMONIAC SALT, GROUND [LIST. AND G.-V. 3 OZS. WHITE PEPPER, 2 OZS GINGER] 1 OZ. [TOR. 1½ OZ.] OF AMINEAN BRYONY, 1 OF THYME SEED AND 1 OF CELERY SEED [TOR. 1½ OZ.] IF YOU DON'T WANT TO USE CELERY SEED TAKE INSTEAD 3 OZS. OF PARSLEY [SEED] 3 OZS. OF ORIGANY, 1 OZ. OF SAFFRON [List. and G.-V. ROCKET] 3 OZS. OF BLACK PEPPER [1] 1½ OZS. ROCKET SEED, 2 OZS. OF MARJORAM [List. and G.-V. CRETAN HYSSOP] 2 OZS. OF NARD LEAVES, 2 OZS. OF PARSLEY [SEED] AND 2 OZS. OF ANISE SEED.

[1] In view of the white pepper as directed above, this seems superfluous. White pepper and ginger omitted by Tor.

This is one of the few medical formulæ found in Apicius.

Edward Brandt, *op. cit.*, Apiciana No. 29, points out the similarity of this formula with that of the physician, Marcellus, who lived at Rome under Nero, Marcell. med. 30, 51.

XIV

[30] TO KEEP GREEN OLIVES
OLIVAS VIRIDES SERVARE

TO KEEP OLIVES, FRESH FROM THE TREE, IN A MANNER ENABLING YOU TO MAKE OIL FROM THEM ANY TIME YOU DESIRE JUST PLACE THEM [in brine]. [1] HAVING BEEN KEPT THUS FOR SOME TIME THE OLIVES MAY BE USED AS IF THEY

HAD JUST COME OFF THE TREE FRESH IF YOU DESIRE TO MAKE GREEN OIL OF THEM.

[1] The original does not state the liquid in which the olives are to be placed. Hum. *in illud, legendum puto, in muriam.*

Hum. is correct. Olives are preserved in brine to this day.

Schuch's version of this formula (his No. 27) follows our No. 28, together with his own No. 28, To Keep Damascene Plums [etc.] which is wanting in List., G.-V., and all the earlier editions because it is from the codex Salmasianus and will be found among the Excerpts of Vinidarius at the end of the Apician recipes.

XV

[CUMINATUM. Hum., List. and G.-V. — Tac. and Tor. at the end of Book I.]

XVI

[31]   LASER FLAVOR   *LASERATUM*

[Tor.] LASER IS PREPARED IN THIS MANNER: LASER (WHICH IS ALSO CALLED LASERPITIUM BY THE ROMANS, WHILE THE GREEKS CALL IT SILPHION) FROM CYRENE [1] OR FROM PARTHIA [2] IS DISSOLVED IN LUKEWARM MODERATELY ACID BROTH; OR PEPPER, PARSLEY, DRY MINT, LASER ROOT, HONEY, VINEGAR AND BROTH [are ground, compounded and dissolved together].

[1] Cyrene, a province in Africa, reputed for its fine flavored laser.
[2] Parthia, Asiatic country, still supplying *asa fœtida.*
The African root furnishing laser was exterminated by the demand for it. Cf. Laser in Index.

[32]   ANOTHER [LASER]   *ALITER*

[ANOTHER LASER FLAVOR WHICH TAKES] PEPPER, CARRAWAY, ANISE, PARSLEY, DRY MINT, THE LEAVES [1] OF SILPHIUM, MALOBATHRUM [2] INDIAN SPIKENARD, A LITTLE COSTMARY, HONEY, VINEGAR AND BROTH.

[1] Tor. *Silphij folium;* List. *Sylphium, folium;* G.-V. *Silfi, folium,* the latter two interpretations meaning *silphium* (laser) *and leaves* (either nard or bay leaves) while both Tor. and Tac. (*silfii folium*) mean the leaves of *silphium* plant.

[2] *Malobathrum, malobatrum, malabathrum* — leaves of an Indian tree, wild cinnamon.

XVII

[33] WINE SAUCE FOR TRUFFLES
ŒNOGARUM [1] *IN TUBERA*

PEPPER, LOVAGE, CORIANDER, RUE, BROTH, HONEY AND
A LITTLE OIL.

ANOTHER WAY: THYME, SATURY, PEPPER, LOVAGE,
HONEY, BROTH AND OIL.

[1] Also *Elæogarum*.

V. Directions wanting whether the above ingredients are to be added to the already prepared *garum*, which see in dictionary. Gollmer gives the following direction for *garum*: Boil a *sextarium* of anchovies and 3 *sextarii* of good wine until it is thick *purée*. Strain this through a hair sieve and keep it in glass flask for future use. This formula, according to Goll. should have followed our No. 9; but we find no authority for it in the original.

Oenogarum proper would be a *garum* prepared with wine, but in this instance it is the broth in which the truffles were cooked that is to be flavored with the above ingredients. There is no need and no mention of *garum* proper. Thus prepared it might turn out to be a sensible sauce for truffles in the hands of a good practitioner.

Note the etymology of the word "garum," now serving as a generic name for "sauce" which originally stood for a compound of the fish *garus*.

Cf. *Garum* in index.

XVIII

[34] OXYPORUM   *OXYPORUM*

[Tor. OXYPORUM (WHICH SIGNIFIES "EASY PASSAGE") SO
NAMED BECAUSE OF ITS EFFECT, TAKES] 2 OZS. OF CUMIN,
1 OZ. OF GINGER [List. 1 OZ. OF GREEN RUE] 6 SCRUPLES OF
SALTPETER, A DOZEN SCRUPLES OF PLUMP DATES, 1 OZ. OF
PEPPER AND 11 [List. 9] OZS. OF HONEY. THE CUMIN MAY
BE EITHER ÆTHIOPIAN, SYRIAN OR LYBIAN, MUST BE FIRST
SOAKED IN VINEGAR, BOILED DOWN DRY AND POUNDED.
AFTERWARDS ADD YOUR HONEY. THIS COMPOUND, AS
NEEDED, IS USED AS OXYPORUM.

Cf. No. 111, A Harmless Salad.

Bran. *op. cit.*, p. 25-6, of Greek origin.

XIX

[35] HYPOTRIMA [1]   *HYPOTRIMA*

[Tor. HYPOTRIMA, MEANING IN LATIN A PERFECT MESS
OF POTAGE, REQUIRES THIS]: PEPPER, LOVAGE, DRY MINT,

PIGNOLIA NUTS, RAISINS, DATE WINE, SWEET CHEESE, HONEY, VINEGAR, BROTH, WINE, OIL, MUST OR REDUCED MUST [2]

[1] List. and G.-V. *Hypotrimma*.

V. This formula, lacking detailed instructions, is of course perfectly obscure, and it would be useless to debate over it.

[2] Tor. and Tac. *cariotam*; Sch. *cariotum*; List and G.-V. *carœnum*. This (*carenum*) is new wine boiled down one half of its volume. *Cariotum* is a palm wine or date wine.

XX

[36]   OXYGARUM, AN AID TO DIGESTION
        OXYGARUM DIGESTIBILE

[Tor. OXYGARUM (WHICH IS SIMILAR TO GARUM OR RATHER AN ACID SAUCE) IS DIGESTIBLE AND IS COMPOSED OF]: ½ OZ. OF PEPPER, 3 SCRUPLES OF GALLIC SILPHIUM, 6 SCRUPLES OF CARDAMOM, 6 OF CUMIN, 1 SCRUPLE OF LEAVES, 6 SCRUPLES OF DRY MINT. THESE [ingredients] ARE BROKEN SINGLY AND CRUSHED AND [made into a paste] BOUND BY HONEY. WHEN THIS WORK IS DONE [or whenever you desire] ADD BROTH AND VINEGAR [to taste].

Cf. Note to No. 33.

[37]   ANOTHER [OXYGARUM] [1]   *ALITER*

1 OZ. EACH OF PEPPER, PARSLEY, CARRAWAY, LOVAGE, MIX WITH HONEY. WHEN DONE ADD BROTH AND VINEGAR.

[1] Wanting in Torinus.

XXI

[38]   MORTARIA [1]   *MORTARIA*

MORTARIA ARE PREPARATIONS MADE IN THE MORTAR. PLACE IN THE MORTAR [Tor.] MINT, RUE, CORIANDER AND FENNEL, ALL FRESH AND GREEN AND CRUSH THEM FINE. LOVAGE, PEPPER, HONEY AND BROTH [2] AND VINEGAR [3] TO BE ADDED WHEN THE WORK IS DONE.

Ex Tor. first sentence wanting in other texts.

[1] List. and G.-V. *moretaria*, from *moretum*.

[2] Dann. calls this "*Kalte Schale*" which as a rule is a drink or a cold refreshing soup, popular on the Continent in hot weather. Not a bad interpretation if instead of the broth the original called for wine or fruit juices.

V. *Mortaria* are ingredients crushed in the mortar, ready to be used in several combinations, similar to the ground fine herbs, *remoulade*, in French cuisine that may be used for various purposes, principally for cold green sauces.

[3] Wanting in Tor.

[XV]
[39] CUMIN SAUCE FOR SHELLFISH
CUMINATUM IN OSTREA ET CONCHYLIA

[Tor. CUMIN SAUCE (SO CALLED BECAUSE CUMIN IS ITS CHIEF INGREDIENT) FOR OYSTERS AND CLAMS IS MADE OF] PEPPER, LOVAGE, PARSLEY, DRY MINT, MALABAR LEAVES, QUITE SOME CUMIN, HONEY, VINEGAR, AND BROTH.

[40] ANOTHER [CUMIN SAUCE] [1]   *ALITER*

PEPPER, LOVAGE, PARSLEY, DRY MINT, PLENTY OF CUMIN, HONEY, VINEGAR AND BROTH.

[1] wanting in List.

The cumin sauce formulæ are under chap. XV in G.-V., following our No. 30.

END OF BOOK I
EXPLICIT APICII EPIMLES LIBER PRIMUS [Tac.]

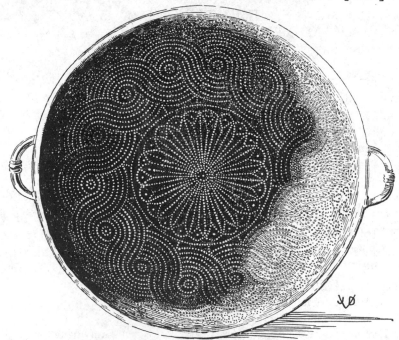

COLANDER FOR STRAINING WINE

The intricate design of the perforation denotes that this strainer was used for straining wine. Various other strainers of simpler design, with and without handles, were used in the kitchen and bakery. Ntl. Mus., Naples, 77602; Field M., 24307.

APICIUS
Book II

SLAVES OPERATING A HAND-MILL
Reconstruction in Naples, in the new section of the National Museum.

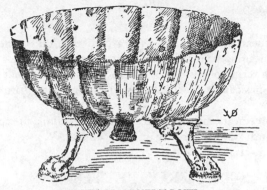

FRUIT OR DESSERT BOWL
Round bowl, fluted symmetrically, with three claw feet, resting on molded bases.
Ntl. Mus., Naples, 74000; Field M., 24028.

BOOK II. MINCES
Lib. II. Sarcoptes [1]

CHAP. I. FORCEMEATS, SAUSAGE, MEAT PUDDINGS, MEAT LOAVES.
CHAP. II. HYDROGARUM, SPELT PUDDING AND ROUX [2].
CHAP. III. SOW'S MATRIX, BLOOD SAUSAGE.
CHAP. IV. LUCANIAN SAUSAGE.
CHAP. V. SAUSAGE.

[1] Tor. *Artoptes*; Tac. *Artoptus*. This may have been derived from *artopta* —a vessel in which bread and pudding are baked. However, Sarcoptes is the better word, which is Greek, meaning "chopped meats."

[2] Tac. *Ambolatum*, and so in Tor. p. 15, *De Ambolato*. Cap. IIII. cf. our note following No. 58.

I

[41] MINCED DISHES   ISICIA

THERE ARE MANY KINDS OF MINCED DISHES [1] SEA-FOOD MINCES [2] ARE MADE OF SEA-ONION, OR SEA CRAB-FISH, LOBSTER, CUTTLE-FISH, INK FISH, SPINY LOBSTER, SCALLOPS AND OYSTERS [3]. THE FORCEMEAT IS SEASONED WITH LOVAGE [4], PEPPER, CUMIN AND LASER ROOT.

[1] Tor. Sentence wanting in other texts. V. Forcemeats, minced meats, sausage. Tor. *Hysitia*, from *Isicia*. This term is derived from *insicium*, from *salsicium*, from *salsum insicium*, cut salt meat; old French *salcisse*, *saulcisse*, modern

French *saucisse*, meaning sausage. This is a confirmation of the meaning of the word *salsum* — meaning primarily salt meat, bacon in particular. It has survived in modern French terminology in *salés* more specially *petits salés* — small rashers of bacon. *Salsum* has caused much confusion in some later formulæ. Cf. notes to Nos. 148, 150, 152.

[2] V. fish forcemeats, fish balls, fish cakes and similar preparations.

[3] Scallops and oysters wanting in List. and G.-V.

[4] Wanting in List.

[42] CUTTLE-FISH CROQUETTES
ISICIA DE LOLLIGINE [1]

THE MEAT IS SEPARATED FROM BONES, SKIN [and refuse] CHOPPED FINE AND POUNDED IN THE MORTAR. SHAPE THE FORCEMEAT INTO NEAT CROQUETTES [2] AND COOK THEM IN LIQUAMEN [3].

THEY ARE DISPLAYED NICELY ON A LARGE DISH.

V. This formula plainly calls for fish balls braised or stewed in broth. Ordinarily we would boil the fish first and then separate the meat from the bones, shred or chop it fine, bind with cream sauce, flour and eggs; some add potatoes as a binder, and fry.

[1] G.-V. *lolligine*; Tor. *loligine*, which is correctly spelled.

[2] Tac. and Tor. *in pulmento tundes*. G.-V. *fulmento* which is wrong. *Pulmentum*, abbreviated for *pulpamentum*, from *pulpa*. It means a fleshy piece of fish or meat, a tid-bit.

[3] The original says *in liquamine fricatur* — fry in l., which is impossible in the sense of the word, frying. Either "frying" here stands for cooking, stewing, braising, poaching, or else the so mysterious *liquamen* must here mean deep fat. Most likely these fish forcemeat balls were fried in olive oil. Cf. ℞ No. 46.

[43] LOBSTER OR CRABMEAT CROQUETTES
ISICIA DE SCILLIS VEL DE CAMMARIS AMPLIS [1]

THE SHELLS OF THE LOBSTERS OR CRABS [which are cooked] ARE BROKEN, THE MEAT EXTRACTED FROM THE HEAD AND POUNDED IN THE MORTAR WITH PEPPER AND THE BEST KIND OF BROTH. THIS PULP [is shaped into neat little cakes which are fried] AND SERVED UP NICELY [2].

[1] *Scilla* or *squilla*, squill, sea-onion, also a crab, *cammarus amplus*, large lobster, langouste, spiny lobster.

[2] The original omits the mode of cooking the fish. A case where it is taken for granted that the shellfish is boiled in water alive. The broth (*liquamen*) is a thick fish sauce in this case, serving as a binder for the meat, conforming to present methods.

Dann. Fill this into sausage casing. There is no authority for this.

[44]   LIVER KROMESKIS   OMENTATA [1]

OMENTATA ARE MADE IN THIS MANNER: [lightly] FRY
PORK LIVER, REMOVE SKIN AND SINEWS FIRST [2]. CRUSH
PEPPER AND RUE IN A MORTAR WITH [a little] BROTH,
THEN ADD THE LIVER, POUND AND MIX. THIS PULP SHAPE
INTO SMALL SAUSAGE, WRAP EACH IN CAUL AND LAUREL
LEAVES AND HANG THEM UP TO BE SMOKED. WHENEVER
YOU WANT AND WHEN READY TO ENJOY THEM TAKE
THEM OUT OF THE SMOKE, FRY THEM AGAIN, AND ADD
GRAVY [3].

[1] From *omentum* — caul, the membrane enclosing the bowels. Hence
"omen." Minced meats wrapped in caul and fried are kromeskis in kitchen terminology.

[2] First — an after thought so characteristic in culinary literature, proof
enough that this formula originated in a kitchen. The *ante tamen* of the original
belongs to this sentence, not to the next, as the editors have it.

[3] Wanting in G.-V. The original continues without interruption to the
next, an entirely new formula.

[45]   [BRAIN SAUSAGE]   [ISICIA DE CEREBELLIS] [1]

PUT IN THE MORTAR PEPPER, LOVAGE AND ORIGANY,
MOISTEN WITH BROTH AND RUB; ADD COOKED BRAINS
AND MIX DILIGENTLY SO THAT THERE BE NO LUMPS. IN-
CORPORATE FIVE EGGS AND CONTINUE MIXING WELL TO
HAVE A GOOD FORCEMEAT WHICH YOU MAY THIN WITH
BROTH. SPREAD THIS OUT IN A METAL PAN, COOK, AND
WHEN COOKED [cold] UNMOULD IT ONTO A CLEAN TABLE.
CUT INTO HANDY SIZE. [Now prepare a sauce] PUT IN THE
MORTAR PEPPER, LOVAGE AND ORIGANY, CRUSH, MIX
WITH BROTH PUT INTO A SAUCE PAN, BOIL, THICKEN AND
STRAIN. HEAT THE PIECES OF BRAIN PUDDING IN THIS
SAUCE THOROUGHLY, DISH THEM UP, SPRINKLED WITH
PEPPER, IN A MUSHROOM DISH [2].

[1] The Original has no title for this dish.

[2] List. and G.-V. here start the next formula, but Tor. continues without
interruption. Cf. Note 2 to No. 46.

[46]   A DISH OF SCALLOPS   ISICIA EX SPONDYLIS [1]

[Lightly] COOK SCALLOPS [or the firm part of oysters] REMOVE
THE HARD AND OBJECTIONABLE PARTS, MINCE THE
MEAT VERY FINE, MIX THIS WITH COOKED SPELT AND

EGGS, SEASON WITH PEPPER, [shape into croquettes and wrap] IN CAUL, FRY, UNDERLAY A RICH FISH SAUCE AND SERVE AS A DELICIOUS ENTRÉE [2].

[1] Sch. *sfondilis*; G.-V. *sphondylis*; List. *spongiolis*. According to Lister, this is a dish of mushrooms, but he is wrong. He directs to remove sinews when mushrooms haven't any, but shellfish have. Torinus is correct. Gollmer makes the same mistake, believing *spondyli* to be identical with *spongioli*. He and Danneil take *elixata* for "choice" when this plainly means "cooked." If one were not sure of either word, the nature of the subject would leave no room for any doubt. Cf. note 1 to Nos. 115-121.

[2] We may find a reason for the combination of these last three distinctly different formulæ into one article in the following explanation. It is possible that these dishes were served together as one course, even on one platter, thus constituting a single dish, as it were. Such a dish would strongly resemble platters of "*fritures*" and "*fritto misto*" (mixed fried foods) esteemed in France and Italy. We, too, have "Shore Dinners" and other "Combination Platters" with lobster, crabs, scallops, shrimps, mushrooms, tomatoes — each article prepared separately, but when served together will form an integral part of ONE dish.

The above formulæ, though somewhat incomplete, are good and gastronomically correct. A combination of these *isicia* such as we here suggest would be entirely feasable and would in fact make a dish of great refinement, taxing the magiric artist's skill to the utmost. We would class them among the *entremets chauds* which are often used on a buffet table or as hot *hors d'œuvres*.

[47] ANOTHER KIND OF KROMESKIS [1]
ALITER ISICIA OMENTATA

FINELY CUT PULP [of pork] IS GROUND WITH THE HEARTS [2] OF WINTER WHEAT AND DILUTED WITH WINE. FLAVOR LIGHTLY WITH PEPPER AND BROTH AND IF YOU LIKE ADD A MODERATE QUANTITY OF [myrtle] BERRIES ALSO CRUSHED, AND AFTER YOU HAVE ADDED CRUSHED NUTS AND PEPPER [3] SHAPE THE FORCEMEAT INTO SMALL ROLLS, WRAP THESE IN CAUL, FRY, AND SERVE WITH WINE GRAVY.

[1] Wanting in Lister.

[2] Fine wheat flour, cream of wheat.

[3] Either pepper corns or allspice.

The original leaves us in doubt as to the kind of meat to be used, if any.

II

[48]   DUMPLINGS OF PHEASANT   *ISICIA PLENA*

[Lightly roast choice] FRESH PHEASANTS [cut them into dice and mix these with a] STIFF FORCEMEAT MADE OF THE FAT AND THE TRIMMINGS OF THE PHEASANT, SEASON WITH PEPPER, BROTH AND REDUCED WINE, SHAPE INTO CRO-QUETTES OR SPOON DUMPLINGS, AND POACH IN HYDRO-GARUM [water seasoned with garum, or even plain salt water].

[49]   DUMPLINGS AND HYDROGARUM
HYDROGARATA ISICIA

CRUSH PEPPER, LOVAGE AND JUST A SUSPICION OF PEL-LITORY, MOISTEN WITH STOCK AND WELL WATER, ALLOW IT TO DRAW, PLACE IT IN A SAUCE PAN, BOIL IT DOWN, AND STRAIN. POACH YOUR LITTLE DUMPLINGS OF FORCE-MEAT IN THIS LIQUOR AND WHEN THEY ARE DONE SERVE IN A DISH FOR ISICIA, TO BE SIPPED AT THE TABLE.

[50]   CHICKEN FORCEMEAT   *ISICIA DE PULLO*

[Raw] CHICKEN MEAT, 1 LB. OF DARNEL [1] MEAL, ONE QUARTER PINT OF STOCK AND ONE HALF OUNCE OF PEP-PER.

[1] Tor. *lolæ floris*; Hum.-List. and G.-V. *olei floris* — virgin olive oil? — first choice flour? Goll. olive (violet?) flowers; Dann. Olive oil.

The suggestion of oil is plausible because of the lack of fat in chicken meat, but the quantity — 1 lb. — is out of question. Moreover, the binder would be lacking. This is found in the Torinus rendering.

His *lolæ floris* should read *lolii* — from *lolium* — darnel rye grass or ray grass which was supposed to have intoxicating qualities, injurious to the eye sight. — Ovid and Plautus. The seeds of this grass were supposed to possess narcotic properties but recent researches have cast doubt upon this theory.

A little butter, fresh cream and eggs are the proper ingredients for chicken forcemeat. Any kind of flour for binding the forcemeat would cheapen the dish. Yet some modern forcemeats (sausage) contain as much as fifty percent of some kind of meal. The most effective is that of the soya bean which is not starchy.

[51]   CHICKEN BROTH ANOTHER STYLE
ALITER DE PULLO

CHICKEN MEAT, 31 PEPPERCORNS CRUSHED, 1 CHOENIX [1] FULL OF THE VERY BEST STOCK, A LIKE AMOUNT OF BOILED MUST AND ELEVEN MEASURES [2] OF WATER. [Put this in a sauce pan] PLACE IT UPON THE FIRE TO SEETH AND EVAPORATE SLOWLY.

[1] V. 2 *sextarii*; Tor. *chœnicem, cenlicem*; List. *calicem*.

[2] *chœnices?* — left in doubt.

This seems to be a chicken broth, or essence for a sauce or perhaps a medicine. Torinus mentions the chicken meat, the others do not.

The original without interruption continues to describe the *isicium simplex* which has nothing to do with the above.

[52]   PLAIN DUMPLING WITH BROTH
ISICIUM SIMPLEX

TO 1 ACETABULUM [1] OF STOCK [2] ADD 7 OF WATER, A LITTLE GREEN CELERY, A LITTLE SPOONFUL OF GROUND PEPPER, AND BOIL THIS WITH THE SAUSAGE MEAT OR DUMPLINGS. IF YOU INTEND TAKING THIS TO MOVE THE BOWELS THE SEDIMENT SALTS [3] OF HYDROGARUM HAVE TO BE ADDED [4].

[1] A measure, 15 Attic drachms.

[2] *liquamen*.

[3] Tor. *pectines, alias peces hydrogaro conditi*; List. *sales*; G.-V. *fæces*.

[4] V. The formula is unintelligible, like No. 52 and others, perhaps just another example of medicinal cookery, dishes not only intended to nourish the body but to cure also certain ills. Authors like Hannah Wolley (The Queen-like Closet, London, 1675) and as late as the middle of the 18th century pride themselves in giving such quasi-Apician formulæ.

[53]   [Rank of] DISHES   *ISICIA*

[Entrées of] PEACOCK OCCUPY THE FIRST RANK, PROVID- ED THEY BE DRESSED IN SUCH MANNER THAT THE HARD AND TOUGH PARTS BE TENDER. THE SECOND PLACE [in the estimation of the Gourmets] HAVE DISHES MADE OF RABBIT [1] THIRD SPINY LOBSTER [2] FOURTH COMES CHICKEN AND FIFTH YOUNG PIG.

[1] List. and G.-V. Pheasant.

[2] Wanting in the above. Dann. Crane fourth.

Isicia, like in the foregoing formula, commences to become a generic term for "dishes."

[54]   POTTED ENTRÉES
ISICIA AMULATA AB AHENO [1]

GROUND PEPPER, LOVAGE, ORIGANY, VERY LITTLE SIL- PHIUM, A PINCH OF GINGER AND A TRIFLE OF HONEY AND

A LITTLE STOCK. [Put on the fire, and when boiling] ADD THE ISICIA [sausage, meat balls and so forth] TO THIS BROTH AND COOK THOROUGHLY. FINALLY THICKEN THE GRAVY WITH ROUX [2] BY SOWING IT IN SLOWLY AND STIRRING FROM THE BOTTOM UP [3].

[1] Tor. *multa ab alieno*; Brandt [a]mul[a]ta ab aheno; List. *amylata* — French: *liés. Ab aheno* — out of the pot.

[2] French, for a mixture of wheat or rice flour with fats or liquids to thicken fluids. *Amylum*, or *amulum* which hereafter will occur frequently in the original does not cover the ground as well as the French term *roux*. The quality of the "binder" depends upon the material in hand. Sometimes the fat and flour are parched, sometimes they are used raw. Sometimes the flour is diluted with water and used in that form.

[3] List. and G.-V. *sorbendum*; Tor. *subruendum*.

[55]   ANOTHER [THICK ENTRÉE GRAVY]   *ALITER*

GRIND PEPPER WHICH HAS BEEN SOAKED OVERNIGHT, ADD SOME MORE STOCK AND WORK IT INTO A SMOOTH PASTE; THEREUPON ADD QUINCE-APPLE CIDER, BOILED DOWN ONE HALF, THAT IS WHICH HAS EVAPORATED IN THE HEAT OF THE SUN TO THE CONSISTENCY OF HONEY. IF THIS IS NOT AT HAND, ADD FIG WINE [1] CONCENTRATE WHICH THE ROMANS CALL "COLOR" [2]. NOW THICKEN THE GRAVY WITH ROUX OR WITH SOAKED RICE FLOUR AND FINISH IT ON A GENTLE FIRE.

[1] Tor. *cammarum*, which should read *caricarum* — wine of Carica figs.

[2] V. the Roman equivalent for "*singe*," "monkey," "*Affe*," — (the *vulgo* French is literally translated into and in actual use in other languages) caramel color made of burnt sugar to give gravies a palatable appearance. Cf. No. 73.

The reference by the original to "which the Romans call 'color'" indicates, according to Brandt, that this formula is NOT of ROMAN origin but probably a translation into Latin from a Greek cookery book.

This is an interesting suggestion, and it could be elaborated on to say that the entire Apicius is NOT of Roman origin. But why should the Greeks who in their balmy days were so far in advance of Rome in culinary matters go there for such information?

It is more likely that this reference to Rome comes from the Italian provinces or the colonies, regions which naturally would look to Rome for guidance in such matters.

[56]   ANOTHER AMULATUM   *AMULATUM ALITER*

DISJOINT A CHICKEN AND BONE IT. PLACE THE PIECES IN A STEW PAN WITH LEEKS, DILL AND SALT [water or stock]

WHEN WELL DONE ADD PEPPER AND CELERY SEED, THICK-EN WITH RICE [1] ADD STOCK, A DASH OF RAISIN WINE OR MUST, STIR WELL, SERVE WITH THE ENTRÉES.

[1] G.-V. *oryzam*; Tor. ditto (and on margin) *oridam*; Hum. *oridiam legendum orindam* — a kind of bread. Dann. and Goll. rice flour.

In a general way the ancient formula corresponds exactly to our present chicken fricassée.

[57]   SPELT OR FARINA PUDDING   *APOTHERMUM*

BOIL SPELT WITH [Tor. PIGNOLIA] NUTS AND PEELED AL-MONDS [1] [G.-V. AND] IMMERSED IN [boiling] WATER AND WASHED WITH WHITE CLAY SO THAT THEY APPEAR PER-FECTLY WHITE, ADD RAISINS, [flavor with] CONDENSED WINE OR RAISIN WINE AND SERVE IT IN A ROUND DISH WITH CRUSHED [2] [nuts, fruit, bread or cake crumbs] SPRINKLED OVER IT [3].

[1] V. We peel almonds in the same manner; the white clay treatment is new to us.

G.-V. and — which is confusing.

[2] The original: *confractum* — crushed, but what? G.-V. pepper, for which there is neither authority nor reason. A wine sauce would go well with it or crushed fruit. List. and Goll. Breadcrumbs.

[3] This is a perfectly good pudding — one of the very few desserts in Apicius. With a little sweetening (supplied probably by the condensed wine) and some grated lemon for flavor it is quite acceptable as a dessert.

[58]   DE AMBOLATO CAP. IIII

Ex Torinus, not mentioned by the other editors. The sense of this word is not clear. It must be a recipe or a chapter the existence of which was known to Torinus, for he says: "This entire chapter is wanting in our copy."

III

[59]   A DISH OF SOW'S MATRIX
VULVULÆ BOTELLI [1]

ENTRÉES [2] OF SOW'S MATRIX [3] ARE MADE THUS: CRUSH PEPPER AND CUMIN WITH TWO SMALL HEADS OF LEEK, PEELED, ADD TO THIS PULP RUE, BROTH [and the sow's matrix or fresh pork] CHOP, [or crush in mortar very fine] THEN ADD TO THIS [forcemeat] INCORPORATING WELL PEPPER GRAINS AND [pine] NUTS [4] FILL THE CASING [5] AND

BOIL IN WATER [with] OIL AND BROTH [for seasoning] AND A BUNCH OF LEEKS AND DILL.

[1] G.-V. *Vulvulæ Botelli*; Sch. *Vulvulæ isiciata*; Tor. *De Vulvulis et botellis*. See note No. 3.

[2] V. *"Entrées"* out of respect for the ancients who used them as such; today we would class such dishes among the *"hors d'œuvres chauds."*

[3] V. *Vulvula*, dim. for *vulva*, sow's matrix. Cf. *vulva* in dictionary. Possible, also possible that *volva* is meant — a meat roll, a croquette.

[4] V. Combinations of chopped nuts and pork still in vogue today; we use the green pistachios.

[5] V. The casings which were filled with this forcemeat may have been the sow's matrices, also caul. The original is vague on the point.

[60]   LITTLE SAUSAGE   *BOTELLUM* [1]

BOTELLUM IS MADE OF [2] HARD BOILED YOLKS OF EGG [3] CHOPPED PIGNOLIA NUTS, ONION AND LEEKS, RAW GROUND PINE [4] FINE PEPPER, STUFF IN CASINGS AND COOK IN BROTH AND WINE [5].

[1] V. *Botelli*, or *botuli*, are sausage of various kind; (French, Boudin, English, Pudding). Originally made of raw blood, they are in fact, miniature blood sausage. The absence of meat in the present formula makes me believe that it is not complete, though hard boiled yolk when properly seasoned and mixed with the right amount of fat, make a tasty forcemeat for sausage.

[2] Tor. *Botellum sic facies ex oui*; Sch. and G.-V. *sex ovi* — the number of eggs is immaterial.

[3] Dann. Calf's Sweetbreads.

[4] Goll. *Thus crudum* — raw blood. *Thus* or *tus* is either frankincense or the herb, ground-pine. Dann. Rosemary. Hum. *Thus crudum lege jus crudum* — jus or broth which would make the forcemeat soft. There is no reason for changing *"thus"* into " *jus!"*

[5] G.V. *Adicies liquamen et vinum, et sic coques*. Tor. & *vino decoquas*.

IV

[61]   LUCANIAN SAUSAGE   *LUCANICÆ*

LUCANIAN SAUSAGE [or meat pudding] ARE MADE SIMILAR TO THE ABOVE: CRUSH PEPPER, CUMIN, SAVORY, RUE, PARSLEY, CONDIMENT, LAUREL BERRIES AND BROTH; MIX WITH FINELY CHOPPED [fresh Pork] AND POUND WELL WITH BROTH. TO THIS MIXTURE, BEING RICH, ADD WHOLE PEPPER AND NUTS. WHEN FILLING CASINGS CAREFULLY

PUSH THE MEAT THROUGH. HANG SAUSAGE UP TO SMOKE.

V. Lister's interesting remarks about the makers of these sausages are given in the dictionary. Cf. Longano.

V

[62] SAUSAGE   FARCIMINA

POUND EGGS AND BRAINS [eggs raw, brains cooked] PINE NUTS [chopped fine] PEPPER [whole] BROTH AND A LITTLE LASER WITH WHICH FILL THE CASINGS. FIRST PARBOIL THE SAUSAGE THEN FRY THEM AND SERVE.

V. The directions are vague enough, but one may recognize in them our modern brain sausage.

[63] ANOTHER SAUSAGE   ALITER

WORK COOKED SPELT AND FINELY CHOPPED FRESH PORK TOGETHER, POUND IT WITH PEPPER, BROTH AND PIGNOLIA NUTS. FILL THE CASINGS, PARBOIL AND FRY WITH SALT, SERVE WITH MUSTARD, OR YOU MAY CUT THE SAUSAGE IN SLICES AND SERVE ON A ROUND DISH.

[64] ANOTHER SAUSAGE   ALITER

WASH SPELT AND COOK IT WITH STOCK. CUT THE FAT OF THE INTESTINES OR BELLY VERY FINE WITH LEEKS. MIX THIS WITH CHOPPED BACON AND FINELY CHOPPED FRESH PORK. CRUSH PEPPER, LOVAGE AND THREE EGGS AND MIX ALL IN THE MORTAR WITH PIGNOLIA NUTS AND WHOLE PEPPER, ADD BROTH, FILL CASINGS. PARBOIL SAUSAGE, FRY LIGHTLY, OR SERVE THEM BOILED.

Tor. and Tac. Serve with pheasant gravy. In the early editions the following formula which thus ends is wanting.

[65] ROUND SAUSAGE   CIRELLOS ISICIATOS

FILL THE CASINGS WITH THE BEST MATERIAL [forcemeat] SHAPE THE SAUSAGE INTO SMALL CIRCLES, SMOKE. WHEN THEY HAVE TAKEN ON (VERMILLION) COLOR FRY THEM LIGHTLY. DRESS NICELY GARNISHED ON A PHEASANT WINE GRAVY, FLAVORED, HOWEVER, WITH CUMIN.

V. In Tor. and in the earliest edition this formula has been contracted with the preceding and made one formula.

END OF BOOK II
EXPLICIT LIBER SECUNDUS APICII ARTOPTUS [Tac.]

APICIUS
Book III

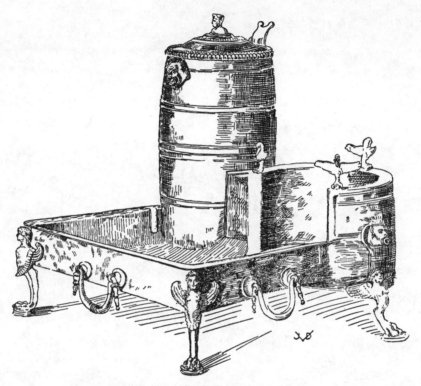

ELABORATE THERMOSPODIUM
A heater for the service of hot foods and drinks in the dining room. Hot drinks were mixed and foods were served from apparatus of this kind. The fuel was charcoal. There were public places, specializing in hot drinks, called Thermopolia. This specimen was found at Stabiæ, one of the ill-fated towns destroyed by eruption of Mt. Vesuvius. Ntl. Mus., Naples, 72986; Field M., 24307.

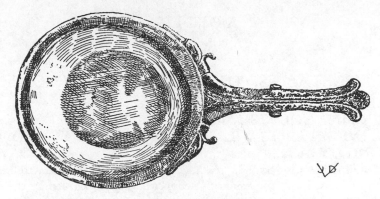

SERVICE PAN

Round, with decorated handle. This and the pan with the Hercules head on handle used in connection with the plain Thermospodium to serve hot foods in the dining room. Hildesheim Treas.

BOOK III. THE GARDENER

Lib. III. Cepuros

CHAP.   I. TO BOIL ALL VEGETABLES GREEN.

CHAP.   II. VEGETABLE DINNER, EASILY DIGESTED.

CHAP.   III. ASPARAGUS.

CHAP.   IV. PUMPKIN, SQUASH.

CHAP.   V. CITRUS FRUIT, CITRON.

CHAP.   VI. CUCUMBERS.

CHAP. VII. MELON GOURD, MELON.

CHAP. VIII. MALLOWS.

CHAP.   IX. YOUNG CABBAGE, SPROUTS, CAULIFLOWER.

CHAP.   X. LEEKS.

CHAP.   XI. BEETS.

CHAP. XII. POT HERBS.

CHAP. XIII. TURNIPS, NAVEWS.

CHAP. XIV. HORSERADISH AND RADISHES.

CHAP.   XV. SOFT CABBAGE.

CHAP. XVI. FIELD HERBS.

CHAP. XVII. NETTLES.

CHAP. XVIII. ENDIVE AND LETTUCE.

CHAP. XIX. CARDOONS.

CHAP.   XX. COW-PARSNIPS.

CHAP. XXI. CARROTS AND PARSNIPS.

I

[66]   VEGETABLES, POT HERBS   *DE HOLERIBUS*

TO KEEP ALL VEGETABLES GREEN.
UT OMNE HOLUS SMARAGDINUM FIAT.
   ALL VEGETABLES WILL REMAIN GREEN IF BOILED WITH
COOKING SODA [1].

   [1] *Nitrium*. Method still in use today, considered injurious to health if
copper vessel is used, but the amount of copper actually absorbed by the vegetable is infinitesimal, imperceptible even by the taste. Copper, to be actually harm-
ful would have to be present in such quantity as to make enjoyment impossible.

II

[67]   VEGETABLE DINNER, EASILY DIGESTED
       PULMENTARIUM AD VENTREM [1]

   ALL GREEN VEGETABLES ARE SUITED FOR THIS PURPOSE
[2] VERY YOUNG [3] BEETS AND WELL MATURED LEEKS
ARE PARBOILED; ARRANGE THEM IN A BAKING DISH,
GRIND PEPPER AND CUMIN, ADD BROTH AND CONDENSED
MUST, OR ANYTHING ELSE TO SWEETEN THEM A LITTLE,
HEAT AND FINISH THEM ON A SLOW FIRE, AND SERVE.

   [1] V. *Ad ventrem*, "for the belly," simple home laxative.
   [2] V. This sentence in Torinus only. Possibly a contraction of the foregoing
formula, No. 66.
   [3] V. *minutas*, "small," i.e., young.

[68]   A SIMILAR DISH   *SIMILITER*

   PARBOIL POLYPODY [1] ROOT SO AS TO SOFTEN THEM,
CUT THEM INTO SMALL PIECES, SEASON WITH GROUND
PEPPER AND CUMIN, ARRANGE IN A BAKING DISH, FINISH
ON THE FIRE AND SERVE [2].

   [1] V. Roots of the fern herb.
   [2] V. Although these instructions for vegetable dinners are rather vague,
they resemble primitive *chartreuses* — fancy vegetable dishes developed by the
Carthusian monks to whom flesh eating was forbidden. Elsewhere in Apicius
we shall find the *chartreuse* developed to a remarkable degree.

[69]   ANOTHER LAXATIVE *ALITER AD VENTREM* [1]

   SCRUB AND WASH BUNDLES OF BEETS BY RUBBING THEM
WITH A LITTLE SODA [2]. TIE THEM IN INDIVIDUAL BUN-
DLES, PUT INTO WATER TO BE COOKED, WHEN DONE, SEA-
SON WITH REDUCED MUST OR RAISIN WINE AND CUMIN,

SPRINKLE WITH PEPPER, ADD A LITTLE OIL, AND WHEN
HOT, CRUSH POLYPODY AND NUTS WITH BROTH, ADD
THIS TO THE RED-HOT PAN, INCORPORATING IT WITH
THE BEETS, TAKE OFF THE FIRE QUICKLY AND SERVE.

[1] This formula wanting in Tor.

[2] V. Ingenious method to skin tender root vegetables, still in vogue today.
We remove the skin of tender young root vegetables, carrots, beets, etc., by placing them in a towel, sprinkling them with rock salt and shaking them energetically. The modern power vegetable peeler is really built on the same principle,
only instead of salt (which soon melts) carborundum or rough concrete surfaces are used, against which surfaces the vegetables are hurled by the rotary
motion; often enough, too much of the skin is removed, however.

[70]   BEETS À LA VARRO   *BETACEOS VARRONIS* [1]

VARRO BEETS, THAT IS, BLACK ONES [2] OF WHICH THE
ROOTS MUST BE CLEANED WELL, COOK THEM WITH MEAD
AND A LITTLE SALT AND OIL; BOIL THEM DOWN IN THIS
LIQUOR SO THAT THE ROOTS ARE SATURATED THEREBY;
THE LIQUID ITSELF IS GOOD DRINKING. IT IS ALSO NICE TO
COOK A CHICKEN IN WITH THEM.

[1] G.-V. *Betacios*; Tor. *B. Varrones*. Probably named for Varro, the writer
on agriculture.

[2] Roots on the order of parsnips, salsify, oysterplant.

[71]   ANOTHER LAXATIVE   *ALITER AD VENTREM*

ANOTHER VEGETABLE DISH, PROMOTING GOOD HEALTH;
WASH CELERY, GREENS AND ROOTS, AND DRY IT IN THE
SUN: THEN ALSO COOK THE TENDER PART AND HEAD OF
LEEKS IN A NEW [1] POT, ALLOWING THE WATER TO BOIL
DOWN ONE THIRD OF ITS VOLUME. THEREUPON GRIND
PEPPER WITH BROTH AND HONEY IN EQUAL AMOUNTS
PROPERLY MEASURED, MIX IT IN THE MORTAR WITH THE
WATER OF THE COOKED CELERY, STRAIN, BOIL AGAIN
AND USE IT TO MASK THE [cooked] CELERY WITH. IF DE-
SIRED, ADD [the sliced root of the] CELERY TO IT [2].

[1] V. "new," i.e., cook leeks in a separate sauce pan; NOT together with
the celery, which, as the original takes for granted, must be cooked also.

[2] V. We would leave the honey out, make a cream sauce from the stock,
or, adding bouillon, tie same with a little flour and butter, and would call the
dish Stewed Celery and Leeks. The ancient method is entirely rational because
the mineral salts of the vegetables are preserved and utilized (invariably observed

by Apicius) which today are often wasted by inexperienced cooks who discard these precious elements with the water in which vegetables are boiled.

III

[72]   ASPARAGUS   *ASPARAGOS*

ASPARAGUS [Tor. IN ORDER TO HAVE IT MOST AGREE-ABLE TO THE PALATE] MUST BE [peeled, washed and] DRIED [1] AND IMMERSED IN BOILING WATER BACKWARDS [2] [3].

[1] V. Must be dried before boiling because the cold water clinging to the stalks is likely to chill the boiling water too much in which the asparagus is to be cooked. Apicius here reveals himself as the consummate cook who is familiar with the finest detail of physical and chemical changes which food undergoes at varying temperatures.

The various editions all agree: *asparagos siccabis*; Schuch, however, says: "For the insane *siccabis* I substitute *siciabis, isiciabis*, prepare with *sicio* [?] and cook." He even goes on to interpret it *cucabis* from the Greek *kouki*, cocoanut milk, and infers that the asparagus was first cooked in cocoanut milk and then put back into water, a method we are tempted to pronounce insane.

[2] V. Backwards! G.-V. *rursum in calidam*; Tac. *rursus in aquam calidam*; Tor. *ac rursus. . .*

This word has caused us some reflection, but the ensuing discovery made it worth while. *Rursus* has escaped the attention of the other commentators. In this case *rursus* means backwards, being a contraction from *revorsum*, h.e. *reversum*. The word is important enough to be observed.

Apicius evidently has the right way of cooking the fine asparagus. The stalks, after being peeled and washed must be bunched together and tied according to sizes, and the bunches must be set into the boiling water "backwards," that is, they must stand upright with the heads protruding from the water. The heads will be made tender above the water line by rising steam and will be done simultaneously with the harder parts of the stalks. We admit, we have never seen a modern cook observe this method. They usually boil the tender heads to death while the lower stalks are still hard.

Though this formula is incomplete (it fails to state the sauce to be served, also that the asparagus must be peeled and bunched, that the water must contain salt, etc.) it is one of the neatest formulæ in Apicius. It is amusing to note how the author herein unconsciously reveals what a poor litérateur but what a fine cook he is. This is characteristic of most good practitioners. One may perfectly master the vast subject of cookery, yet one may not be able to give a definition of even a single term, let alone the ability to exactly describe one of the many processes of cookery. Real poets often are in the same predicament; none of them ever explained the art satisfactorily.

[3] G.-V. add to the formula *callosiores reddes* — give back [eliminate] the

harder ones. This sentence belongs to the next article. And Torinus, similar to Humelbergius, renders this sentence *ut reddas ad gustum calliores* — to render the harder ones palatable — the squash and pumpkin namely — and we are inclined to agree with him.

IV

[73] PUMPKIN, SQUASH   *CUCURBITAS*

TO HAVE THE HARDER ONES PALATABLE, DO THIS: [1] [Cut the fruit into pieces, boil and] SQUEEZE THE WATER OUT OF THE BOILED FRUIT AND ARRANGE [the pieces] IN A BAKING DISH. PUT IN THE MORTAR PEPPER, CUMIN AND SILPHIUM, THAT IS, A VERY LITTLE OF THE LASER ROOT AND A LITTLE RUE, SEASON THIS WITH STOCK, MEASURE A LITTLE VINEGAR AND MIX IN A LITTLE CONDENSED WINE, SO THAT IT CAN BE STRAINED [2] AND POUR THIS LIQUID OVER THE FRUIT IN THE BAKING DISH; LET IT BOIL THREE TIMES, RETIRE FROM THE FIRE AND SPRINKLE WITH VERY LITTLE GROUND PEPPER.

[1] Cf. note 3 to No. 72.

[2] List. *Ut coloretur* — to give it color; Tor. *ut ius coletur* — from *colo* — to strain, to filter.

Cf. also note 2 to No. 55.

[74] PUMPKIN LIKE DASHEENS
      ALITER CUCURBITAS IURE COLOCASIORUM [1]

BOIL THE PUMPKIN IN WATER LIKE COLOCASIA; GRIND PEPPER, CUMIN AND RUE, ADD VINEGAR AND MEASURE OUT THE BROTH IN A SAUCEPAN. THE PUMPKIN PIECES [nicely cut] WATER PRESSED OUT [are arranged] IN A SAUCEPAN WITH THE BROTH AND ARE FINISHED ON THE FIRE WHILE THE JUICE IS BEING TIED WITH A LITTLE ROUX. BEFORE SERVING SPRINKLE WITH PEPPER [2].

[1] V. *Colocasia Antiquorum* belonging to the dasheen or taro family, a valuable tuber, again mentioned in No. 172, 216, 244 and 322. Cf. various notes, principally that to No. 322. Also see U. S. Dept. of Agr. Farmer's Bulletin No. 1396, p. 2. This is a "new" and commercially and gastronomically important root vegetable, the flavor reminding of a combination of chestnuts and potatoes, popularily known as "Chinese potatoes" which has been recently introduced by the U. S. Government from the West Indies where it received the name, Dasheen, derived from *de Chine* — from China.

[2] Tor. continues without interruption into the next formula.

[75]   PUMPKIN, ALEXANDRINE STYLE
       ALITER CUCURBITAS MORE ALEXANDRINO

PRESS THE WATER OUT OF THE BOILED PUMPKIN, PLACE
IN A BAKING DISH, SPRINKLE WITH SALT, GROUND PEPPER,
CUMIN, CORIANDER SEED, GREEN MINT AND A LITTLE
LASER ROOT; SEASON WITH VINEGAR. NOW ADD DATE
WINE AND PIGNOLIA NUTS GROUND WITH HONEY, VINE-
GAR AND BROTH, MEASURE OUT CONDENSED WINE AND
OIL, POUR THIS OVER THE PUMPKIN AND FINISH IN THIS
LIQUOR AND SERVE, SPRINKLE WITH PEPPER BEFORE
SERVING.

[76]   BOILED PUMPKIN
       ALITER CUCURBITAS ELIXATAS

[Boiled Pumpkin] STEWED IN BROTH WITH PURE OIL.

[77]   FRIED PUMPKIN   *ALITER CUCURBITAS FRICTAS*

[Fried pumpkin served with] SIMPLE WINE SAUCE AND PEP-
PER.

[78]   ANOTHER WAY, BOILED AND FRIED
       ALITER CUCURBITAS ELIXATAS ET FRICTAS

BOILED PUMPKIN FRIED IS PLACED IN A BAKING PAN.
SEASON WITH CUMIN WINE, ADD A LITTLE OIL; FINISH ON
THE FIRE AND SERVE.

[79]   ANOTHER WAY, MASHED
       CUCURBITAS FRICTAS TRITAS

FRIED [1] PUMPKIN, SEASONED WITH PEPPER, LOVAGE,
CUMIN, ORIGANY, ONION, WINE BROTH AND OIL: STEW
THE PUMPKIN [in this] IN A BAKING DISH, TIE THE LIQUID
WITH ROUX [mash] AND SERVE IN THE DISH.

[1] V. Baking the fruit reduces the water contents, renders the purée more
substantial. G.-V. *Tritas* — mashed. Tor. connects *tritas* up with pepper, hence
it is doubtful whether this dish of pumpkin is mashed pumpkin.

[80]   PUMPKIN AND CHICKEN
       CUCURBITAS CUM GALLINA

[Stew the pumpkin with a hen, garnish with] HARD-SKINNED
PEACHES, TRUFFLES; PEPPER, CARRAWAY, AND CUMIN, SIL-

PHIUM AND GREEN HERBS, SUCH AS MINT, CELERY, CORI-
ANDER, PENNYROYAL, CRESS, WINE [1] OIL AND VINEGAR.

[1] Tor. *Vinum vel oleum*; List. *vinum, mel, oleum*.

V

[81]   CITRON   *CITRIUM* [1]

FOR THE PREPARATION OF CITRON FRUIT WE TAKE SIL-
ER [2] FROM THE MOUNTAINS, SILPHIUM, DRY MINT, VINE-
GAR AND BROTH.

[1] List. *Citrini* — a lemon or cucumber squash.

[2] Tor. *Silerem*; List. *sil*, which is hartwort, a kind of cumin or mountain
fennel.

VI

[82]   CUCUMBERS   *CUCUMERES*

[Stew the] PEELED CUCUMBERS EITHER IN BROTH [1] OR
IN A WINE SAUCE; [and] YOU WILL FIND THEM TO BE TEN-
DER AND NOT CAUSING INDIGESTION.

[1] Usually cucumbers are parboiled in water and then finished in broth;
most often after being parboiled they are stuffed with forcemeat and then finished in broth.

[83]   CUCUMBERS ANOTHER WAY
       ALITER CUCUMERES RASOS

[Peeled cucumbers are] STEWED WITH BOILED BRAINS, CUM-
IN AND A LITTLE HONEY. ADD SOME CELERY SEED, STOCK
AND OIL, BIND THE GRAVY WITH EGGS [1] SPRINKLE WITH
PEPPER AND SERVE.

[1] Tor. *bis obligabis* — tie twice — for which there is no reason, except in
case the sauce should curdle. List. *oleo elixabis* — fry in oil — obviously wrong,
as the materials for this stew are already cooked. Sch. *ovis obligabis* — bind with
eggs — which is the thing to do in this case.

[84]   ANOTHER CUCUMBER RECIPE
       ALITER CUCUMERES

CUCUMBERS, PEPPER, PENNYROYAL, HONEY OR CON-
DENSED MUST, BROTH AND VINEGAR; ONCE IN A WHILE
ONE ADDS SILPHIUM.

Sounds like a fancy dressing for raw sliced cucumbers, though there are no
directions to this effect.

VII

[85] MELON-GOURD AND MELONS
PEPONES ET MELONES

PEPPER, PENNYROYAL, HONEY OR CONDENSED MUST,
BROTH AND VINEGAR; ONCE IN A WHILE ONE ADDS SIL-
PHIUM.

Same as 84; which confirms above theory. It is quite possible that melons
were eaten raw with this fancy dressing. Many people enjoy melons with pepper
and salt, or, in salad form with oil and vinegar. Gourds, however, to be palatable,
must be boiled and served either hot or cold with this dressing.

VIII

[86] MALLOWS   *MALVAS*

THE SMALLER MALLOWS [are prepared] WITH GARUM [1],
STOCK [2] OIL AND VINEGAR; THE LARGER MALLOWS [pre-
pare] WITH A WINE SAUCE, PEPPER AND STOCK, [adding]
CONDENSED WINE OR RAISIN WINE.

[1] Tor. *Garum*; List. *Oenogarum*.

[2] *Liquamen* — depending upon the mode of serving the mallows, hot or
cold.

IX

[87] YOUNG CABBAGE, SPROUTS [1]
CYMAS ET CAULICULOS [2]

[Boil the] SPROUTS; [1] [season with] CUMIN [3], SALT, WINE
AND OIL; IF YOU LIKE [add] PEPPER, LOVAGE, MINT, RUE,
CORIANDER; THE TENDER LEAVES OF THE STALKS [stew]
IN BROTH; WINE AND OIL BE THE SEASONING.

[1] Including, perhaps, cauliflower and broccoli.

[2] List. *Cimæ & Coliculi. Nunc crudi cum condimentis nunc elixati infe-
rentur.* Served sometimes raw with dressing, sometimes boiled.

[3] Cumin or carraway seed is still used today in the preparation of the delicious "Bavarian" cabbage which also includes wine and other spices.

[88] ANOTHER WAY   *ALITER*

CUT THE STALKS IN HALF AND BOIL THEM. THE LEAVES
ARE MASHED AND SEASONED WITH CORIANDER, ONION,
CUMIN, PEPPER, RAISIN WINE, OR CONDENSED WINE AND
A LITTLE OIL.

Very sensible way of using cabbage stalks that are usually thrown away. Note
the almost scientific procedure: the stalks are separated from the leaves, split to

facilitate cooking; they are cooked separately because they require more time than the tender greens.

Our present method appears barbarous in comparison. We quarter the cabbage head, and either boil it or steam it. As a result either the tender leaves are cooked to death or the stems are still hard. The overcooked parts are not palatable, the underdone ones indigestible. Such being the case, our boiled cabbage is a complete loss, unless prepared the Apician way.

[89] ANOTHER WAY   *ALITER*

THE COOKED [1] STALKS ARE PLACED IN A [baking] DISH; MOISTEN WITH STOCK AND PURE OIL, SEASON WITH CUMIN, SPRINKLE [2] WITH PEPPER, LEEKS, CUMIN, AND GREEN CORIANDER [all] CHOPPED UP.

[1] Tor. *Coliculi assati* — *sauté*, fried; (Remember: *Choux de Bruxelles sauté*) List. *elixati* — boiled. G.-V. *Cauliculi elixati.*

[2] Tor. *Superasperges*; G.-V. *piper asperges.*

Sounds like a salad of cooked cabbage. The original leaves us in doubt as to the temperature of the dish.

[90] ANOTHER WAY   *ALITER*

THE VEGETABLE, SEASONED AND PREPARED IN THE ABOVE WAY IS STEWED WITH PARBOILED LEEKS.

[91] ANOTHER WAY   *ALITER*

TO THE SPROUTS OR STALKS, SEASONED AND PREPARED AS ABOVE, ARE ADDED GREEN OLIVES WHICH ARE HEATED LIKEWISE.

[92] ANOTHER WAY   *ALITER*

PREPARE THE SPROUTS IN THE ABOVE WAY, COVER THEM WITH BOILED SPELT AND PINE NUTS [1] AND SPRINKLE [2] WITH RAISINS.

[1] The nuts should not astonish us. The French today have a delicious dish, *Choux de Bruxelles aux Marrons* — Brussels Sprouts with Chestnuts. Sprouts and chestnuts are, of course, cooked separately; the lightly boiled sprouts are *sauté* in butter; the chestnuts parboiled, peeled, and finished in stock with a little sugar or syrup, tossed in butter and served in the center of the sprouts.

The Apician formula with cereal and raisins added is too exotic to suit our modern taste, but without a question is a nutritious dish and complete from a dietetic point of view.

[2] Tor. *Superasperges*; G.-V. *piper asperges.*

X

[93] LEEKS   *PORROS*

WELL MATURED LEEKS [1] ARE BOILED WITH A PINCH OF
SALT [2] IN [combined] WATER AND OIL [3]. THEY ARE THEN
STEWED IN OIL AND IN THE BEST KIND OF BROTH, AND
SERVED.

[1] Tor. *Poros bene maturos*; G.-V. *maturos fieri*.

[2] One of the rare instances where Apicius mentions salt in cookery, i.e.,
salt in a dry form. *Pugnum salis* — a fist of salt — he prescribes here. Usually
it is *liquamen* — broth, brine — he uses.

[3] Tor. is correct in finishing the sentence here. G.-V. continue *et eximes.*,
which is the opening of the next sentence, and it makes a difference in the
formula.

[94] ANOTHER WAY TO COOK LEEKS
       ALITER PORROS

WRAP THE LEEKS WELL IN CABBAGE LEAVES, HAVING
FIRST COOKED THEM AS DIRECTED ABOVE [1] AND THEN
FINISH THEM IN THE ABOVE WAY.

[1] Tor. *in primis* — first; List., G.-V. *in prunis* — hot embers.

[95] ANOTHER WAY   *ALITER PORROS*

COOK THE LEEKS WITH [laurel] BERRIES [1], [and otherwise
treat them] AND SERVE AS ABOVE.

[1] Tor. *Porros in bacca coctos*; List. *in cacabo* — cooked in a casserole;
Sch. *bafa embama* — steeped, marinated (in oil); G.-V. *in baca coctos*. Another
way to read this: *baca et fabæ* — with beans — is quite within reason. The following formula, 96, is perhaps only a variant of the above.

Brandt: with olives, referring to No. 91 as a precedent.

[96] LEEKS AND BEANS   *ALITER PORROS*

AFTER HAVING BOILED THE LEEKS IN WATER, [green
string] BEANS WHICH HAVE NOT YET BEEN PREPARED OTH-
ERWISE, MAY BE BOILED [in the leek water] [1] PRINCIPALLY
ON ACCOUNT OF THE GOOD TASTE THEY WILL ACQUIRE;
AND MAY THEN BE SERVED WITH THE LEEKS.

[1] Apicius needed no modern science of nutrition to remind him of the
value of the mineral salts in vegetables.

XI

[97]   BEETS   *BETAS*

TO MAKE A DISH OF BEETS THAT WILL APPEAL TO YOUR
TASTE [1] SLICE [the beets, 2, with] LEEKS AND CRUSH CORI-
ANDER AND CUMIN; ADD RAISIN WINE [3], BOIL ALL
DOWN TO PERFECTION: BIND IT, SERVE [the beets] SEPA-
RATE FROM THE BROTH, WITH OIL AND VINEGAR.

[1] Sentence in Tor.; wanting in List. *et al.*

[2] List. No mention of beets is made in this formula; therefore, it may belong to the foregoing leek recipes. V. This is not so. Here the noun is made subject to the first verb, as is practiced frequently. Moreover, the mode of preparation fits beets nicely, except for the flour to which we object in note 3, below.
To cook beets with leeks, spices and wine and serve them (cold) with oil and
vinegar is indeed a method that cannot be improved upon.

[3] Tac., Tor., List., G.-V. *uvam passam, Farinam* — raisins and flour —
for which there is no reason. Sch. *varianam* — raisin wine of the Varianian variety; Bas. *Phariam*. V. inclined to agree with Sch. and Bas.

[98]   ANOTHER WAY   *ALITER BETAS ELIXAS*

COOK THE BEETS WITH MUSTARD [seed] AND SERVE
THEM WELL PICKLED IN A LITTLE OIL AND VINEGAR.

V. Add bay leaves, cloves, pepper grains, sliced onion and a little sugar, and
you have our modern pickled beets.

XII

[99]   GREEN VEGETABLES, POT HERBS   *OLISERA* [1]

[The greens] TIED IN HANDY BUNDLES, COOKED AND
SERVED WITH PURE OIL; ALSO PROPER WITH FRIED FISH.

[1] Tac. *Olisera*; Tor. *Olifera* (*sev mauis olyra*) Tor. is mistaken. Hum.,
List. *Olisatra*; (old Ms. note in our Hum. copy: "*Alessandrina uulgò*") from
olusatrum — *olus* — pot herbs, cabbage, turnips. G.-V. *Holisera*, from *holus*, i.e.
olus and from *olitor* one who raises pot herbs.

XIII

[100]   TURNIPS OR NAVEWS   *RAPAS SIVE NAPOS*

[Turnips are] COOKED [soft, the water is] SQUEEZED [out; then]
CRUSH A GOOD AMOUNT OF CUMIN AND A LITTLE RUE,
ADD PARTHICAN [1] LASER OR [2] VINEGAR, STOCK, CON-
DENSED WINE AND OIL [3] HEAT MODERATELY AND
SERVE.

[1] i.e. Persian laser; List. *laser, Parthicum*; (the comma makes a difference!)
Sch. *particum* — a part.

[2] Tac., Tor. *vel acetum*; List. G.-V. *mel, acetum*. Another comma; and "honey" instead of "or." V. We doubt this: the vinegar is an alternative, for it takes the place of the more expensive Persian *laser* (which was an essence of the *laser* root, often diluted with vinegar).

[3] List., G.-V. *oleum modice: fervere*; Tor. *& oleum, quæ modice fervere facias*. Again note Lister's punctuation here and in the foregoing notes. The misplaced commas and colons raise havoc with the formulæ everywhere. Torinus, who in his preface complains that his authority has no punctuation whatsoever and thereby indicates that it must have been a very ancient copy, (at least prior to the 1503 Tac. ed.) is generally not far from the mark. It is also doubtful that the variants are by him, as is claimed by List. In this instance, indeed, Tor. is again correct.

[101] ANOTHER WAY [1]   *ALITER RAPAS SIVE NAPOS*

[The turnips are] BOILED, SERVED DRESSED WITH OIL, TO WHICH, IF DESIRED, YOU MAY ADD VINEGAR [2].

[1] Tor. *ad delitias* — delightful.
[2] V. Presumably served cold, as a salad; cf. No. 122.

XIV

[102] RADISHES   *RAPHANOS*

PEPPER THE RADISHES WELL; OR, EQUALLY WELL: GRATE IT WITH PEPPER AND BRINE.

Sch., G.-V. *Rafanos; Raphanos agria,* — a kind of horseradish; Plinius: h.e. *raphanus sylvestris.*

XV

[103] SOFT CABBAGE   *OLUS MOLLE*

THE CABBAGE IS COOKED WITH POT HERBS IN SODA WATER; PRESS [the water out] CHOP IT VERY FINE: [now] CRUSH PEPPER, LOVAGE, DRY SATURY WITH DRY ONIONS, ADD STOCK, OIL AND WINE.

[104] ANOTHER MASHED GREEN VEGETABLE
ALTER OLUS MOLLE [EX APIO]

COOK CELERY IN SODA WATER, SQUEEZE [water out] CHOP FINE. IN THE MORTAR CRUSH PEPPER, LOVAGE, ORIGANY, ONION [and mix with] WINE AND STOCK, ADDING SOME OIL.

COOK THIS IN THE BOILER [1] AND MIX THE CELERY WITH THIS PREPARATION.

[1] *in pultario*. The *pultarius* is a pot in which cereals were boiled; from *puls* — porridge, pap.

[105]   ANOTHER MASHED VEGETABLE
        ALITER OLUS MOLLE [*EX LACTUCIS*]

COOK THE LETTUCE LEAVES WITH ONION IN SODA WA-TER, SQUEEZE [the water out] CHOP VERY FINE; IN THE MOR-TAR CRUSH PEPPER, LOVAGE, CELERY SEED, DRY MINT, ONION; ADD STOCK, OIL AND WINE.

[106]   TO PREVENT MASHED VEGETABLES FROM
        TURNING
        OLUS MOLLE NE ARESCAT [1]

IT WILL BE REQUIRED ABOVE ALL TO CLEAN THE VEGE-TABLES WELL, TO CUT OFF ALL DECAYED PARTS AND TO COVER [the cooked vegetables] WITH WORMWOOD WATER.

[1] Tor. *ne . . . exarescat*, the difference in the meaning is immaterial.

XVI

[107]   FIELD HERBS   *HERBÆ RUSTICÆ*

FIELD AND FOREST [1] HERBS ARE PREPARED [2] [either raw] WITH STOCK [3] OIL AND VINEGAR [as a salad, (4)] OR AS A COOKED DISH [5] BY ADDING PEPPER, CUMIN AND MASTICH BERRIES.

[1] Tor. *ac sylvestres*; V. German, *Feldsalat*.
[2] Tor. *parantur*; wanting in other editions.
[3] *Liquamine*, here interpreted as brine.
[4] Tac., Sch., *et al. a manu*; Tor. *vel manu* — because eaten with the hand.
[5] Tor. *vel in patina*.

XVII

[108]   NETTLES   *URTICÆ*

THE FEMALE NETTLES, WHEN THE SUN IS IN THE POSI-TION OF THE ARIES, IS SUPPOSED TO RENDER VALUABLE SERVICES AGAINST AILMENTS OF VARIOUS KINDS [1].

[1] Tac., List., Sch., *et al. adversus ægritudinem.*
Barthius: *Quam ægritudinem?* etc., etc.
Tor. *plurifarias!*
Reinsenius: *ad arcendum morbum*, etc., etc.

Hum. *scilicet quamcunque hoc est* . . . etc., etc., etc.

G.-V. *si voles.*

V. This innocent little superstition about the curative qualities of the female nettle causes the savants to engage in various speculations.

Nettles are occasionally eaten as vegetables on the Continent.

XVIII

[109] ENDIVES AND LETTUCE
INTUBA ET LACTUCÆ

ENDIVES [are dressed] WITH BRINE, A LITTLE OIL AND CHOPPED ONION, INSTEAD OF THE REAL LETTUCE [1] IN WINTER TIME THE ENDIVES ARE TAKEN OUT OF THE PICKLE [2] [and are dressed] WITH HONEY OR VINEGAR.

[1] Hum. *pro lactucis uere*; Tor. *p. l. accipint*; G.-V. *p. l. vero* (separated by period) — all indicating that endives are a substitute for lettuce when this is not available.

[2] Cf. ℞ No. 27, also Nos. 22 and 23.

[110] LETTUCE SALAD, FIELD SALAD
AGRESTES LACTUCÆ [1]

[Dress it] WITH VINEGAR DRESSING AND A LITTLE BRINE STOCK; WHICH HELPS DIGESTION AND IS TAKEN TO COUNTERACT INFLATION [2].

[1] Tor. *sic*; Hum. *agri l.*; Tac. *id.*; Sch. and G.-V. have *acri* as an adjective to vinegar, the last word in the preceding formula.

[2] List. and Hum. continuing: "And this salad will not hurt you"; but Tor., Sch. and G.-V. use this as a heading for the following formula.

[111] A HARMLESS SALAD   *NE LACTUCÆ LÆDANT*

[And in order that the lettuce may not hurt you take (with it or after it) the following preparation] [1] 2 OUNCES OF GINGER, 1 OUNCE OF GREEN RUE, 1 OUNCE OF MEATY DATES, 12 SCRUPLES OF GROUND PEPPER, 1 OUNCE OF GOOD HONEY, AND 8 OUNCES OF EITHER ÆTHIOPIAN OR SYRIAN CUMIN. MAKE AN INFUSION OF THIS IN VINEGAR, THE CUMIN CRUSHED, AND STRAIN. OF THIS LIQUOR USE A SMALL SPOONFUL MIX IT WITH STOCK AND A LITTLE VINEGAR: YOU MAY TAKE A SMALL SPOONFUL AFTER THE MEAL [2].

[1] Tac. and Tor. *Ne lactucæ lædant* [take it] *cum zingiberis uncijs duabus*, etc. Hum., List., G.-V. *cumini unc. II.* They and Sch. read the *cum* of Tac. and Tor. for *cumini*, overlooking the fact that the recipe later calls for Aethiopian or

Syrian cumin as well. This shifts the weights of the various ingredients from the one to the other, completely upsetting the sense of the formula.

[2] Goll. ignores this passage completely.

V. This is another of the medical formulæ that have suffered much by experimentation and interpretation through the ages. It seems to be an aromatic vinegar for a salad dressing, and, as such, a very interesting article, reminding of our present tarragon, etc., vinegars. To be used judiciously in salads.

Again, as might be expected, the medicinal character of the formula inspires the medieval doctors to profound meditation and lively debate.

Cf. ℞ Nos. 34 and 108.

XIX

[112]   CARDOONS   *CARDUI*

CARDOONS [are eaten with a dressing of] BRINY BROTH, OIL, AND CHOPPED [hard] EGGS.

V. Precisely as we do today: French dressing and hard boiled eggs. We do not forget pepper, of course. Perhaps the ancient "briny broth" contained enough of this and of other ingredients, such as fine condiments and spices to make the dressing perfect.

[113]   ANOTHER [Dressing for] CARDOONS
        ALITER CARDUOS

RUE, MINT, CORIANDER, FENNEL — ALL GREEN — FINELY CRUSHED; ADD PEPPER, LOVAGE, AND [1] BRINE AND OIL [2].

[1] Tac. and Tor. *vel.*; List., Sch., G.-V. *mel* — honey — which would spoil this fine *vinaigrette* or cold *fines herbes* dressing. However, even nowadays, sugar is quite frequently added to salad dressings.

[2] Gollmer claims that this dressing is served with cooked cardoons, the recipe for which follows below. This is wanting in Tor.

[114]   BOILED CARDOONS   *ALITER CARDUOS ELIXOS*
        [Are served with] PEPPER, CUMIN, BROTH AND OIL.

XX

[115]   (COW-) PARSNIPS [?]
        SPONDYLI VEL FONDULI [1]

COW-PARSNIPS ARE FRIED [and eaten] WITH A SIMPLE WINE SAUCE.

[1] Tac. *Spondili uel fonduli* and *Sphon* . . .; Tor. as above; Hum. *Spongioli*

uel funguli; List., *id.*; Sch. *Sfondili uel funguli*; G.-V. *Sphondyli uel funduli.*
Cf. note to Nos. 46, 121, 122.

[116] ANOTHER WAY   *ALITER*

BOIL THE PARSNIPS IN SALT WATER [and season them] WITH
PURE OIL [1], CHOPPED GREEN CORIANDER AND WHOLE
PEPPER.

[1] Tac. *Oleo mero*; Other editors: *Oleo, mero.* V. The comma is misplaced.

[117] ANOTHER WAY   *ALITER*

PREPARE THE BOILED PARSNIPS WITH THE FOLLOWING
SAUCE: CELERY SEED, RUE, HONEY, GROUND PEPPER, MIX-
ED WITH RAISIN WINE, STOCK AND A LITTLE OIL; BIND
THIS WITH ROUX [bring to a boiling point, immerse parsnips]
SPRINKLE WITH PEPPER AND SERVE.

[118] ANOTHER WAY [Purée of Parsnips] [1]   *ALITER*

MASH THE PARSNIPS, [add] CUMIN, RUE, STOCK, A LITTLE
CONDENSED WINE, OIL, GREEN CORIANDER [and] LEEKS
AND SERVE; GOES WELL WITH SALT PORK [2].

[1] Again faulty punctuation obscures the text. Carefully compare the following: Tac. and Tor. *Spondylos teres, cuminum*, etc. Hum., List. and G.-V. S.
teres cuminum, i.e. crush the cumin. Sch. S. *tores* — dry, parch!

[2] *Inferes pro salso* — serve with salt pork or bacon. or, instead of —.
Salsum — salt pork. Dann. Well seasoned with salt! Sch. *infares pro salsa.* For
further confirmation of *salsum* cf. ℞ Nos. 148-152.

[119] ANOTHER WAY   *ALITER*

BOIL THE PARSNIPS [sufficiently, if] HARD [1] [then] PUT
THEM IN A SAUCE PAN AND STEW WITH OIL, STOCK, PEP-
PER, RAISIN WINE, STRAIN [2] AND BIND WITH ROUX.

[1] Tor. *præduratos*; List. *prædurabis.* How can they be hardened? It may
perhaps stand for "parboil." We agree with Tor. that the hard ones (*præduratos*) must be cooked soft.

[2] Tor. and Tac. *Colabis* — strain; List. and G.-V. *Colorabis* — color. No
necessity for coloring the gravy, but straining after the binding with roux is
important which proves Tor. correct again. Cf. note 1 to ℞ No. 73 and note 2
to ℞ No. 55.

[120]   ANOTHER WAY   *ALITER* [1]

FINISH [marinate] THE PARSNIPS IN OIL AND BROTH, OR FRY THEM IN OIL, SPRINKLE WITH SALT AND PEPPER, AND SERVE.

[1] Ex G.-V. wanting in Tor. and List. Found in Sch. also. V. Procedure quite in acccordance with modern practice. We envelope the p. in flour or frying batter.

[121]   ANOTHER WAY   *ALITER* [1]

BRUISE THE BOILED PARSNIPS [scallops, muscular part of shell-fish] ELIMINATE THE HARD STRINGS; ADD BOILED SPELT AND CHOPPED HARD EGGS, STOCK AND PEPPER. MAKE CROQUETTES OR SAUSAGE FROM THIS, ADDING PIGNOLIA NUT AND PEPPER, WRAP IN CAUL [or fill in casings] FRY AND SERVE THEM AS AN ENTRÉE DISH IN A WINE SAUCE.

V. This formula is virtually a repetition of ℞ No. 46, all the more bewildering because of the divergence of the term (Cf. ℞ No. 114), which stands for "scallops" or the muscular part of any bivalve, at least in the above formula.

The Græco-Latin word for cow-parsnip is *spondylium, sphondylium, spondylion.* It is almost certain that the preceding parsnips formulæ are in the right place here. They are in direct line with the other vegetables here treated — the shellfish — *spondylus* — would be out of place in this chapter, Book III, The Gardener. All the recipes, with the exception of the above, fit a vegetable like parsnips. Even Lister's and Humelberg's interpretation of the term, who read *spongioli* — mushrooms — could be questioned under this heading, Book III.

It is barely possible that this entire series of formulæ, *Spondyli uel fonduli* (℞ Nos. 114-121) does belong to Book II among the scallop *hysitia,* though we are little inclined to accept this theory.

Cf. ℞ No. 122 which appears to be a confirmation of the view expressed above.

XXI

[122]   CARROTS AND PARSNIPS
        CAROTÆ ET PASTINACÆ

CARROTS OR PARSNIPS ARE FRIED [and served] WITH A WINE SAUCE.

V. Exactly like ℞ No. 115, which may be a confirmation that *spondyli* stands for cow-parsnips.

[123]   ANOTHER WAY   *ALITER*

THE CARROTS [are cooked] SALTED [and served] WITH PURE
OIL AND VINEGAR.

V. As a salad. "Italian Salad" consists of a variety of such cooked vegetables,
nicely dressed with oil and vinegar, or with mayonnaise. Cf. ℞ No. 102.

[124]   ANOTHER WAY   *ALITER*

THE CARROTS [are] BOILED [and] SLICED, STEWED WITH
CUMIN AND A LITTLE OIL AND ARE SERVED. AT THE SAME
TIME [1] [here is your opportunity] MAKE A CUMIN SAUCE [from
the carrot juice] FOR THOSE WHO HAVE THE COLIC [2].

[1] Ex Tor. wanting elsewhere.

[2] Tac. *coliorum*; Tor. *cuminatum colicorum*; List. *c. coloratum* — colored;
G.-V. *c. colorium.*

END OF BOOK III
EXPLICIT APICII CEPURICA DE OLERIBUS LIBER TERTIUS [Tac.]

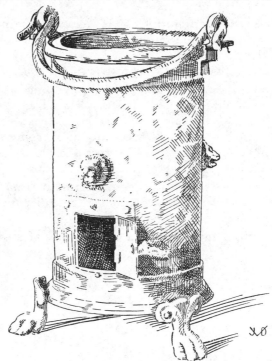

THERMOSPODIUM OF PLAIN DESIGN

Water and food heater for everyday purposes. Charcoal fuel. Foods were kept on top in pans, dishes or
pots, and were thus carried from the kitchen into the dining room. They were also used for food service
in hotel rooms, supplied from adjacent tavern kitchens, as some hotels had no food preparation facilities.
This handy apparatus was designed for general utility, as it also served as a portable stove on chilly days
in living rooms that were not heated from the central heating plant found in larger houses. Ntl. Mus.
Naples, 73882; Field M. 24179.

APICIUS
Book IV

ROMAN WINE PRESS
Reconstruction in Naples, in the new section of the National Museum.

A DISH FOR THE SERVICE OF EGGS
Hildesheim Treasure

BOOK IV. MISCELLANEA

Lib. IV. Pandecter [1]

CHAP. I. BOILED DINNERS.
CHAP. II. DISHES OF FISH, VEGETABLES, FRUITS, AND SO
FORTH.
CHAP. III. FINELY MINCED DISHES, OR *ISICIA*.
CHAP. IV. PORRIDGE, GRUEL.
CHAP. V. APPETIZING DISHES.

I

[125] BOILED DINNER *SALACATTABIA* [2]

PEPPER, FRESH MINT, CELERY, DRY PENNYROYAL, CHEESE [3], PIGNOLIA NUTS, HONEY, VINEGAR, BROTH, YOLKS OF EGG, FRESH WATER, SOAKED BREAD AND THE LIQUID PRESSED OUT, COW'S CHEESE AND CUCUMBERS ARE ARRANGED IN A DISH, ALTERNATELY, WITH THE NUTS; [also add] FINELY CHOPPED CAPERS [4], CHICKEN LIVERS [5]; COVER COMPLETELY WITH [a lukewarm, congealing] BROTH, PLACE ON ICE [and when congealed unmould and] SERVE UP [6].

[1] Read: *Pandectes* — embracing the whole science.
[2] Read: *Salacaccabia* — from *salsa* and *caccabus* — salt meat boiled in the pot. Sch. *Sala cottabia*; G.-V. *cattabia*.
[3] Sch. *casiam* instead of *caseum*.
[4] Sch. *Copadiis porcinis* — small bits of pork; List. *cepas aridas puto* — "shallots, I believe"; Lan. *capparis*; Vat., G.-V. *id.*

[5] Dann. Chicken meat.

[6] This dish if pork were added (cf. Sch. in note 4 above) would resemble our modern "headcheese"; the presence of cheese in this formula and in our word "headcheese" is perhaps not accidental; the cheese has been eliminated in the course of time from dishes of this sort while the name has remained with us. "Cheese" also appears in the German equivalent for custard — *Eierkäse*.

[126]   APICIAN JELLY   *SALACATTABIA APICIANA*

PUT IN THE MORTAR CELERY SEED, DRY PENNYROYAL, DRY MINT, GINGER, FRESH CORIANDER, SEEDLESS RAISINS, HONEY, VINEGAR, OIL AND WINE; CRUSH IT TOGETHER [in order to make a dressing of it]. [Now] PLACE 3 PIECES OF PICENTIAN BREAD IN A MOULD, INTERLINED WITH PIECES OF [cooked] CHICKEN, [cooked] SWEETBREADS OF CALF OR LAMB, CHEESE [1], PIGNOLIA NUTS, CUCUMBERS [pickles] FINELY CHOPPED DRY ONIONS [shallots] COVERING THE WHOLE WITH [jellified] BROTH. BURY THE MOULD IN SNOW UP TO THE RIM; [unmould] SPRINKLE [with the above dressing] AND SERVE [2].

[1] List. *caseum Vestinum* — a certain cheese from the Adriatic coast.

[2] The nature of the first passage of this formula indicates a dressing for a cold dish. The dish was probably unmoulded when firm, and the jelly covered with this dressing, though the original does not state this procedure. In that case it would resemble a highly complicated chicken salad, such as we make today — *mayonnaise de volaille en aspic*, for instance. We recall the artistic molds for puddings and other dishes which the ancients had which were nicely suited for dishes such as the above.

The Picentian bread — made of spelt — was a celebrated product of the bakeries of Picentia, a town of lower Italy, near the Tuscan sea, according to Pliny.

Cf. ℞ No. 141.

[127]   OTHER SALACACCABIA   *ALITER*

HOLLOW OUT AN ALEXANDRINE LOAF OF BREAD, SOAK THE CRUMBS WITH POSCA [a mixture of water, wine, vinegar or lemon juice] AND MAKE A PASTE OF IT. PUT IN THE MORTAR PEPPER, HONEY [1] MINT, GARLIC, FRESH CORIANDER, SALTED COW'S CHEESE, WATER AND OIL. WINE [2] POURED OVER BEFORE SERVING [3].

[1] Wanting in Tor.

[2] G.-V. *insuper nivem* — chilled on snow (like the preceding formula). Tac. *insuper vinum*; Sch. *id*.

[3] A panada as is found in every old cookery book. Today it remains as a dressing for roast fowl, etc. Quoting from "A Collection of Receipts in Cookery, Physick and Surgery," London, 1724:

"Panada for a Sick or Weak Stomach. Put the crumbs of a Penny White-Loaf grated into a Quart of cold Water, set both on the Fire together with a blade of Mace: When 'tis boil'd smooth, take it off the fire and put in a bit of Lemonpeel, the juice of a Lemon, a glass of Sack [Spanish Wine] and Sugar to your Taste. This is very Nourishing and never offends the Stomach. Some season with butter and Sugar, adding Currants which on some occasions are proper; but the first is the most grateful and innocent."

Mrs. Glasse, a quarter century later, in her famous book [The Art of Cookery Made Plain and Easy, London, 1747, 1st ed.] omits the wine, but Mrs. Mason, at about the same time, insists on having it with panada.

The imaginary or real relation between the sciences of cookery and medicine is illustrated here.

II

DISHES OF FISH, VEGETABLES, FRUITS AND SO FORTH
PATINÆ PISCIUM, HOLERUM & POMORUM

[128]   EVERYDAY DISH   PATINA QUOTIDIANA [1]

MAKE A PASTE OF STEWED BRAINS [calf's, pig's, etc.] SEASON WITH PEPPER, CUMIN, LASER, BROTH, THICKENED WINE, MILK AND EGGS [2] POACH IT OVER A WEAK FIRE OR IN A HOT WATER [BATH].

[1] Tac. *quottidiana*; List. *cottidiana*.

[2] List. *ovis* — with eggs, which is correct. Tor. *holus*; Lan. *olus* — herbs, cabbage.

Cf. ℞ No. 142.

[129]   ANOTHER DISH, WHICH CAN BE TURNED
OVER [A Nut Custard]
ALITER PATINA VERSATILIS

THE DISH, CALLED TURN-OVER, IS THUS MADE [1] CRUSH VERY FINE WALNUTS AND HAZELNUTS [2] TOAST THEM AND CRUSH WITH HONEY, MIX IN PEPPER, BROTH, MILK AND EGGS AND A LITTLE OIL [3].

[1] Tor.

[2] List. *torres eas* — toast them (wanting in Tor.) which is the thing to do. Cf. No. 143, practically a repetition of this. Cf. 301.

[3] This laconic formula indicates a custard poached, like in the preceding, in

a mould, which, when cooled off, is unmoulded in the usual way. This *patina versatilis* is in fact the modern *crême renversée*, with nuts.

It is characteristic of Apicius for incompleteness and want of precise directions, without which the experiment in the hands of an inexperienced operator would result in failure.

[130] ANOTHER   *ALITER PATINA*

ANOTHER DISH IS MADE OF THE [1] STRUNKS OF LETTUCE CRUSHED WITH PEPPER, BROTH, THICKENED WINE, [add] WATER AND OIL, AND COOK THIS; BIND WITH EGGS, SPRINKLE WITH PEPPER AND SERVE [2].

[1] Tor.
[2] Very much like a modern soup, purée of lettuce.

[131] VEGETABLE AND BRAIN PUDDING
PATINA FRISILIS [1]

TAKE VEGETABLES, CLEAN AND WASH, SHRED [2] AND COOK THEM [3] COOL THEM OFF AND DRAIN THEM. TAKE 4 [calf's] BRAINS, REMOVE [the skin and] STRINGS AND COOK THEM [4] IN THE MORTAR PUT 6 SCRUPLES OF PEPPER, MOISTEN WITH BROTH AND CRUSH FINE; THEN ADD THE BRAINS, RUB AGAIN AND MEANWHILE ADD THE VEGETABLES, RUBBING ALL THE WHILE, AND MAKE A FINE PASTE OF IT. THEREUPON BREAK AND ADD 8 EGGS. NOW ADD A GLASSFUL [5] OF BROTH, A GLASSFUL OF WINE, A GLASSFUL OF RAISIN WINE, TASTE THIS PREPARATION. OIL THE BAKING DISH THOROUGHLY [put the mixture in the dish] AND PLACE IT IN THE HOT PLATE, (THAT IS ABOVE THE HOT ASHES) [6] AND WHEN IT IS DONE [unmould it] SPRINKLE WITH PEPPER AND SERVE [7].

[1] List. *frictilis*; Vat. Ms. *fusilis*; G.-V. *id.*; Lan. *frisilis*.
Patina frisilis remains unexplained. None of the various readings can be satisfactorily rendered. If the vegetables had remained whole the dish might be compared to a *chartreuse*, those delightful creations by the Carthusians monks who compelled by the strictest rules of vegetarianism evolved a number of fine vegetable dishes. On the other hand, the poached mixture of eggs and brains is akin to our *farces* and *quenelles*; but in modern cookery we have nothing just like this *patina frisilis*.
[2] Wanting in List.
[3] and [4] Wanting in Tor.
[5] *Cyathum*.

[6] Sentence in ( ) ex Tor.

[7] This and some of the following recipes are remarkable for their preciseness and completeness.

[132] ANOTHER COLD ASPARAGUS [and Figpecker] DISH
ALITER PATINA DE ASPARAGIS FRIGIDA

COLD ASPARAGUS PIE IS MADE IN THIS MANNER [1] TAKE WELL CLEANED [cooked] ASPARAGUS, CRUSH IT IN THE MORTAR, DILUTE WITH WATER AND PRESENTLY STRAIN IT THROUGH THE COLANDER. NOW TRIM, PREPARE [i.e. cook or roast] FIGPECKERS [2] [and hold them in readiness]. 3 [3] SCRUPLES OF PEPPER ARE CRUSHED IN THE MORTAR, ADD BROTH, A GLASS OF WINE, PUT THIS IN A SAUCEPAN WITH 3 OUNCES OF OIL, HEAT THOROUGHLY. MEANWHILE OIL YOUR PIE MOULD, AND WITH 6 EGGS, FLAVORED WITH ŒNOGARUM, AND THE ASPARAGUS PREPARATION AS DESCRIBED ABOVE; THICKEN THE MIXTURE ON THE HOT ASHES. THEREUPON ARRANGE THE FIGPECKERS IN THE MOULD, COVER THEM WITH THIS PURÉE, BAKE THE DISH. [When cold, unmould it] SPRINKLE WITH PEPPER AND SERVE.

[1] Tor.

[2] Lan. and Tac. *ficedulas curtas tres*; Tor. *curtas* f. — three figpeckers cut fine. G.-V. *F. curatas. Teres in* . . . (etc.) — Prepared F.

[3] List. six; G.-V. *id.*

[133] ANOTHER ASPARAGUS CUSTARD
ALIA PATINA DE ASPARAGIS

ASPARAGUS PIE IS MADE LIKE THIS [1] PUT IN THE MORTAR ASPARAGUS TIPS [2] CRUSH PEPPER, LOVAGE, GREEN CORIANDER, SAVORY AND ONIONS; CRUSH, DILUTE WITH WINE, BROTH AND OIL. PUT THIS IN A WELL-GREASED PAN, AND, IF YOU LIKE, ADD WHILE ON THE FIRE SOME BEATEN EGGS TO IT TO THICKEN IT, COOK [without boiling the eggs] AND SPRINKLE WITH VERY FINE PEPPER.

[1] Tor.

[2] Reference to wine wanting in Tor. We add that the asparagus should be cooked before crushing.

[134]   A DISH OF FIELD VEGETABLES
PATINA EX RUSTICIS [1]

BY FOLLOWING THE ABOVE INSTRUCTIONS YOU MAY
MAKE [2] A PIE OF FIELD VEGETABLES, OR OF THYME [3] OR
OF GREEN PEPPERS [4] OR OF CUCUMBERS OR OF SMALL
TENDER SPROUTS [5] SAME AS ABOVE, OR, IF YOU LIKE,
MAKE ONE UNDERLAID WITH BONELESS PIECES OF FISH
OR OF CHICKEN [combined with any of the above vegetables] [6].

[1] Tor. *Patina ex oleribus agrestibus.*
[2] Tor. wanting in other texts.
[3] Sch., G.-V. *tamnis* — wild wine; List. *cymis cuminis*; Lan., Tac. *tinis*;
Vat. Ms. *tannis.* Thyme is hardly likely to be the chief ingredient of such a dish;
the chances are it was used for flavoring and that the above enumerated vegetables were combined in one dish.
[4] List., G.-V., Goll. — mustard; Dann. green mustard. Tor. *sive pipere
viridi* — green peppers, which we accept as correct, gastronomically at least.
[5] Goll., Dann. cabbage, the originals have *coliculis* — small tender sprouts
on the order of Brussels sprouts or broccoli, all belonging to the cabbage family.
[6] *Pulpa* — boneless pieces of meat, also fruit purée; *pulpamentum* —
dainty bits of meat.

[135]   ELDERBERRY CUSTARD OR PIE
PATINA DE SAMBUCO [1]

A DISH OF ELDERBERRIES, EITHER HOT OR COLD, IS MADE
IN THIS MANNER [2] TAKE ELDERBERRIES [3] WASH THEM;
COOK IN WATER, SKIM AND STRAIN. PREPARE A DISH IN
WHICH TO COOK THE CUSTARD [4] CRUSH 6 SCRUPLES
OF PEPPER WITH A LITTLE BROTH; ADD THIS TO THE EL-
DERBERRY PULP WITH ANOTHER GLASS OF BROTH, A GLASS
OF WINE, A GLASS OF RAISIN WINE AND AS MUCH AS 4
OUNCES OF OIL. PUT THE DISH IN THE HOT BATH AND
STIR THE CONTENTS. AS SOON AS IT IS GETTING WARM,
QUICKLY BREAK 6 EGGS AND WHIPPING THEM, INCOR-
PORATE THEM, IN ORDER TO THICKEN THE FLUID. WHEN
THICK ENOUGH SPRINKLE WITH PEPPER AND SERVE UP.

[1] G.-V. *Sabuco.*
[2] Tor. wanting in other texts.
[3] Hum. *semen de sambuco* — E. seed.
[4] List. Place the berries in a dish; to their juice add pepper, (etc.).

[136]   ROSE PIE, ROSE CUSTARD OR PUDDING
         PATINA DE ROSIS

TAKE ROSES FRESH FROM THE FLOWER BED, STRIP OFF
THE LEAVES, REMOVE THE WHITE [from the petals and] PUT
THEM IN THE MORTAR; POUR OVER SOME BROTH [and] RUB
FINE. ADD A GLASS OF BROTH AND STRAIN THE JUICE
THROUGH THE COLANDER. [This done] TAKE 4 [cooked
calf's] BRAINS, SKIN THEM AND REMOVE THE NERVES;
CRUSH 8 SCRUPLES OF PEPPER MOISTENED WITH THE
JUICE AND RUB [with the brains]; THEREUPON BREAK 8
EGGS, ADD 1 [1] GLASS OF WINE, 1 GLASS OF RAISIN
WINE AND A LITTLE OIL. MEANWHILE GREASE A PAN,
PLACE IT ON THE HOT ASHES [or in the hot bath] IN WHICH
POUR THE ABOVE DESCRIBED MATERIAL; WHEN THE MIX-
TURE IS COOKED IN THE *BAIN MARIS* [2] SPRINKLE IT WITH
PULVERIZED PEPPER AND SERVE [3].

[1] List., G.-V. 1½ glass.
[2] Hot water bath.
[3] Tor. continues ℞ No. 135 without interruption or caption, and describes
the above recipe. He reads: *De thoris accipies rosas*, but List. insists that *de thoris*
be read *de rosis*; Lan., Tac. *de toris*; V. *de thoris* may be read "fresh from the
flower bed."
    Cf. ℞ Nos. 167 and 171 in which case the "rose" may stand for rosy apple, or
"Roman Beauty" apple. "Rose apple" also is a small pimento, size of a plum.

[137]   PUMPKIN PIE   *PATINA DE CUCURBITIS* [1]

AND PUMPKIN PIE IS MADE THUS [2] STEWED AND
MASHED PUMPKIN IS PLACED IN THE PAN [or pie dish] SEA-
SONED WITH A LITTLE CUMIN ESSENCE. ADD A LITTLE OIL;
HEAT [bake] AND SERVE [3].

[1] Dann. Cucumber Dish.
[2] Tor. Wanting in other texts.
[3] Modern English recipes for stewed pumpkin resemble this Apician precept, but America has made a really palatable dish from pumpkin by the addition of eggs, cinnamon, nutmeg, ginger — spices which the insipid pumpkin
needs. The ancient original may have omitted the eggs because Apicius probably expected his formula to be carried out in accordance with the preceding
formulæ. Perhaps this is proven by the fact that Tor. continues the Rose Pie
recipe with *et cucurbita patina sic fiet*.

[138] SPRATS OR SMELTS AU VIN BLANC
PATINA DE APUA [1]

CLEAN THE SMELTS [or other small fish, filets of sole, etc. of white meat] MARINATE [i.e. impregnate with] IN OIL, PLACE IN A SHALLOW PAN, ADD OIL, BROTH [2] AND WINE. BUNCH [3] [fresh] RUE AND MARJORAM AND COOK WITH THE FISH. WHEN DONE REMOVE THE HERBS, SEASON THE FISH WITH PEPPER AND SERVE [4]

[1] Ex List. and G.-V. wanting in Tor.

[2] *Liquamen*, which in this case corresponds to *court bouillon*, a broth prepared from the trimmings of the fish, herbs, and wine, well-seasoned and reduced.

[3] Our very own *bouquet garni*, a bunch of various aromatic herbs, inserted during coction and retired before serving.

[4] Excellent formula for fish in white wine, resembling our ways of making this fine dish.

This again illustrates the laconic style of the ancient author. He omitted to say that the fish, when cooked, was placed on the service platter and that the juices remaining in the sauce pan were tied with one or two egg yolks, diluted with cream, or wine, or *court bouillon*, strained and poured over the fish at the moment of serving. This is perhaps the best method of preparing fish with white meat of a fine texture. Pink or darker fish do not lend themselves to this method of preparation.

[139] SMELT PIE, OR, SPRAT CUSTARD
PATINA DE ABUA SIVE APUA [1]

BONELESS PIECES OF ANCHOVIES OR [other small] FISH, EITHER ROAST [fried] BOILED, CHOP VERY FINE. FILL A CASSEROLE GENEROUSLY WITH THE SAME [season with] CRUSHED PEPPER AND A LITTLE RUE, ADD SUFFICIENT BROTH AND SOME OIL, AND MIX IN, ALSO ADD ENOUGH RAW EGGS SO THAT THE WHOLE FORMS ONE SOLID MASS. NOW CAREFULLY ADD SOME SEA-NETTLES BUT TAKE PAIN THAT THEY ARE NOT MIXED WITH THE EGGS. NOW PUT THE DISH INTO THE STEAM SO THAT IT MAY CONGEAL [but avoid boiling] [2]. WHEN DONE SPRINKLE WITH GROUND PEPPER AND CARRY INTO THE DINING ROOM. NOBODY WILL BE ABLE TO TELL WHAT HE IS ENJOYING [3].

[1] Tac., Tor. *sic*. List., G.-V. *p. de apua sine apua* — a dish of anchovies (or smelts) without anchovies. Tor. formula bears the title *patina de apua*, and his

article opens with the following sentence: *patin de abua sive apua sic facies*. He is therefore quite emphatic that the dish is to be made with the *abua* or *apua* (an anchovy) and not without *apua*, as List. has it. Lan. calls the dish: *P. de apabadiade*, not identified.

[2] Tor. *impones ad uaporem ut cum ouis meare possint* — warning, get along with the eggs, i.e. beware of boiling them for they will curdle, and the experiment is hopelessly lost. List. however, reads *meare possint* thus: *bullire p.* — boil (!) It is quite plain that Tor. has the correct formula.

[3] *et ex esu nemo agnoscet quid manducet*. Dann. renders this sentence thus: "Nobody can value this dish unless he has partaken of it himself." He is too lenient. We would rather translate it literally as we did above, or say broadly, "And nobody will be any the wiser." List. dwells at length upon this sentence; his erudite commentary upon the *cena dubia*, the doubtful meal, will be found under the heading of *cena* in our vocabulary. List. pp. 126-7. List. undoubtedly made the mistake of reading *sine* for *sive*. He therefore omitted the *apua* from his formula. The above boastful sentence may have induced him to do so.

The above is a fish forcemeat, now seldom used as an integral dish, but still popular as a dressing for fish or as quenelles. The modern fish forcemeat is usually made of raw fish, cream and eggs, with the necessary seasoning. The material is poached or cooked much in the same manner as prescribed by the ancient recipe.

[140]   A RICH ENTRÉE OF FISH, POULTRY AND SAUSAGE IN CREAM   *PATINA EX LACTE*

SOAK [pignolia] NUTS, DRY THEM, AND ALSO HAVE FRESH SEA-URCHINS [1] READY. TAKE A DEEP DISH [casserole] IN WHICH ARRANGE THE FOLLOWING THINGS [in layers]: MEDIUM-SIZED MALLOWS AND BEETS, MATURE LEEKS, CELERY, STEWED TENDER GREEN CABBAGE, AND OTHER BOILED GREEN VEGETABLES [2], A DISJOINTED [3] CHICKEN STEWED IN ITS OWN GRAVY, COOKED [calf's or pig's] BRAINS, LUCANIAN SAUSAGE, HARD BOILED EGGS CUT INTO HALVES, BIG TARENTINIAN SAUSAGE [4] SLICED AND BROILED IN THE ASHES, CHICKEN GIBLETS OR PIECES OF CHICKEN MEAT. BITS OF FRIED FISH, SEA NETTLES, PIECES OF [stewed] OYSTERS AND FRESH CHEESE ARE ALTERNATELY PUT TOGETHER; SPRINKLE IN BETWEEN THE NUTS AND WHOLE PEPPER, AND THE JUICE AS IS COOKED FROM PEPPER, LOVAGE, CELERY SEED AND SILPHIUM. THIS ESSENCE, WHEN DONE, MIX WITH MILK TO WHICH RAW EGGS HAVE BEEN ADDED [pour this over the pieces of food in the dish] SO THAT THE WHOLE IS THOROUGHLY COMBINED, STIFFEN IT [in the hot water bath] AND WHEN DONE [garnish with] FRESH MUSSELS [sea-urchins, poached and chopped fine] SPRINKLE PEPPER OVER AND SERVE.

[1] Sea-urchins, wanting in Tor.

[2] Sentence wanting in G.-V.

[3] *Pullum raptum*, in most texts; G.-V. *p. carptum* — plucked. Of course! Should *raptum* be translated literally? A most atrocious way of killing fowl, to be sure, but anyone familiar with the habits of the ancients, particularly with those of the less educated element, should not wonder at this most bestial fashion, which was supposed to improve the flavor of the meat, a fashion which, as a matter of act still survives in the Orient, particularly in China.

[4] Vat. Ms. *Tarentino farsos*; Tor. cooks the sausage in the ashes — *coctos in cinere*; List. *in cinere legendum jecinora* — chicken giblets. Lister's explanation of the Tarentinian sausage is found in the vocabulary, *v. Longano*.

[141] APICIAN DISH *PATINA APICIANA* [1]

THE APICIAN DISH IS MADE THUS: TAKE SMALL PIECES OF COOKED SOW'S BELLY [with the paps on it] PIECES OF FISH, PIECES OF CHICKEN, THE BREASTS OF FIGPECKERS OR OF THRUSHES [slightly] COOKED, [and] WHICHEVER IS BEST. MINCE ALL THIS VERY CAREFULLY, PARTICULARLY THE FIGPECKERS [the meat of which is very tender]. DISSOLVE IN OIL STRICTLY FRESH EGGS; CRUSH PEPPER AND LOVAGE, POUR OVER SOME BROTH AND RAISIN WINE, PUT IT IN A SAUCE-PAN TO HEAT AND BIND WITH ROUX. AFTER YOU HAVE CUT ALL IN REGULAR PIECES, LET IT COME TO THE BOIL-ING POINT. WHEN DONE, RETIRE [from the fire] WITH ITS JUICE OF WHICH YOU PUT SOME IN ANOTHER DEEP PAN WITH WHOLE PEPPER AND PIGNOLIA NUTS. SPREAD [the ragout] OUT IN SINGLE LAYERS WITH THIN PANCAKES IN BETWEEN; PUT IN AS MANY PANCAKES AND LAYERS OF MEAT AS IS REQUIRED TO FILL THE DISH; PUT A FINAL COVER OF PANCAKE ON TOP AND SPRINKLE WITH PEPPER AFTER THOSE EGGS HAVE BEEN ADDED [which serve] TO TIE THE DISH. NOW PUT THIS [mould or dish] IN A BOILER [steam-er, hot water bath, allow to congeal] AND DISH IT OUT [by un-moulding it]. AN EXPENSIVE SILVER PLATTER WOULD EN-HANCE THE APPEARANCE OF THIS DISH MATERIALLY.

[1] Cf. ℞ No. 126.

[142]   AN EVERY-DAY DISH
         PATINA QUOTIDIANA [1]

PIECES OF COOKED SOW'S UDDER, PIECES OF COOKED
FISH, CHICKEN MEAT AND SIMILAR BITS, MINCE UNIFORM-
LY, SEASON WELL AND CAREFULLY [2]. TAKE A METAL
DISH [for a mould]. BREAK EGGS [in another bowl] AND BEAT
THEM. IN A MORTAR PUT PEPPER, LOVAGE AND ORIGANY
[3], WHICH CRUSH; MOISTEN [this] WITH BROTH, WINE,
RAISIN WINE AND A LITTLE OIL; EMPTY IT INTO THE
BOWL [with the beaten eggs, mix] AND HEAT IT [in the hot water
bath]. THEREUPON WHEN [this is] THICKENED MIX IT WITH
THE PIECES OF MEAT. NOW PREPARE [alternately] LAYERS OF
STEW AND PANCAKES, INTERSPERSED WITH OIL [in the
metal mould reserved for this purpose] UNTIL FULL, COVER WITH
ONE REAL GOOD PANCAKE [4], CUT INTO IT A VENT HOLE
FOR CHIMNEY ON THE SURFACE [bake in hot water bath and
when done] TURN OUT UPSIDE DOWN INTO ANOTHER DISH.
SPRINKLE WITH PEPPER AND SERVE.

[1] List. *cottidiana*; G.-V. *cotidiana*. "Everyday Dish, in contrast to the foregoing Apician dish which is more sumptuous on account of the figpeckers or
thrushes. In the originals these two formulæ are rolled into one. Cf. ℞ No. 128.

[2] G.-V. *Hæc omnia concides*; Tor. *condies*; List. *condies lege concides*
which we dispute. *Condies* — season, flavor — is more correct in this place; *concides* — mince — is a repetition of what has been said already.

[3] Origany wanting in G.-V.

[4] List. *superficie versas in discum insuper in superficium pones*; Sch. *a
superficie versas indusium super focum pones*; G.-V. *in discum*; Tor. *unum verò
laganum fistula percuties à superficie versas in discum in superficiem præterea
pones* — which we have translated literally above, as we believe Tor. to be correct in this important matter of having a chimney on top of such a pie.

[143]   NUT CUSTARD TURN-OVER [1]
         PATINA VERSATILIS VICE DULCIS

PIGNOLIA NUTS, CHOPPED OR BROKEN NUTS [other va-
rieties] ARE CLEANED AND ROASTED AND CRUSHED WITH
HONEY. MIX IN [beat well] PEPPER, BROTH, MILK, EGGS, A
LITTLE HONEY [2] AND OIL. [Thicken slowly on fire without boiling, fill in moulds, taking care that the nuts do not sink to the bottom,
bake in hot water bath, when cold unmould].

[1] Practically the only recipe in Apicius fairly resembling a modern "dessert." This is practically a repetition of ℞ No. 129, which see.

[2] Tor. *modico melle;* List. *m. mero* — pure wine and also pure honey, i.e. thick honey for sweetening. Wine would be out of place here. This is an excellent example of nut custard, if the "pepper" and the "broth" (*liquamen*), of the original, in other words spices and brine, or salt, be used very sparingly. For "pepper" nutmeg or allspice may be substituted, as is used today in such preparations. The oil seems superfluous, but it is taking the place of our butter. This very incomplete formula is characteristic because of the absence of weights and measures and other vital information as to the manipulation of the materials. None but an experienced practitioner could make use of this formula in its original state.

Goll. adds toasted raisins, for which there is no authority.

The text now proceeds without interruption to the next formula.

[144] TYROTARICA [1]
PATELLA THIROTARICA [2]

TAKE ANY KIND OF SALT FISH [3] COOK [fry or broil it] IN OIL, TAKE THE BONES OUT, SHRED IT [and add] PIECES OF COOKED BRAINS, PIECES OF [other, fresh (?)] FISH, MINCED CHICKEN LIVERS [4] AND [cover with] HOT SOFT [i.e. liquefied] CHEESE. HEAT ALL THIS IN A DISH; [meanwhile] GRIND PEPPER, LOVAGE, ORIGANY, SEEDS OF RUE WITH WINE, HONEY WINE AND OIL; COOK ALL ON A SLOW FIRE; BIND [this sauce] WITH RAW EGGS; ARRANGE [the fish, etc.]. PROPERLY [incorporate with the sauce] SPRINKLE WITH CRUSHED CUMIN AND SERVE [5].

[1] G.-V., List., Vat. ms. *Thyrotarnica;* cf. notes to ℞ Nos. 427, 428.

[2] Tor.

[3] Tor. Wanting in other texts.

[4] List., G.-V. here add hard boiled eggs, which is permissible, gastronomically.

[5] Modern fish *au gratin* is made in a similar way. Instead of this wine sauce a spiced cream sauce and grated cheese are mixed with the bits of cooked fish, which is then baked in the dish.

Brains, chicken, etc., too, are served *au gratin*, but a combination of the three in one dish is no longer practiced. However, the Italian method of baking fish, etc., *au gratin à l'Italienne* contains even more herbs and wine reduction than the above formula.

[145] SALT FISH BALLS IN WINE SAUCE [1]
       PATELLA ARIDA [2]

DRY PIECES OF SALT TURSIO [3] ARE BONED, CLEANED
[soaked in water, cooked] SHREDDED FINE AND SEASONED
WITH GROUND PEPPER, LOVAGE, ORIGANY, PARSLEY, COR-
IANDER, CUMIN, RUE SEEDS AND DRY MINT. MAKE FISH
BALLS OUT OF THIS MATERIAL AND POACH THE SAME IN
WINE, BROTH AND OIL; AND WHEN COOKED, ARRANGE
THEM IN A DISH. THEN MAKE A SAUCE [utilizing the broth, the
court bouillon in which the balls were cooked] SEASON WITH PEP-
PER, LOVAGE, SATURY, ONIONS AND WINE AND VINEGAR,
ALSO ADD BROTH AND OIL AS NEEDED, BIND WITH ROUX
[4] [pour over the balls] SPRINKLE WITH THYME AND
GROUND PEPPER [5].

[1] Reminding us of the Norwegian *fiske boller* in wine sauce, a popular
commercial article found canned in delicatessen stores.

[2] List. *patella sicca* — dry, perhaps because made of dried fish.

[3] List. *isicia de Tursione*; G.-V. *Thursione*. Probably a common sturgeon,
or porpoise, or dolphin. List. describes it as "a kind of salt fish from the Black
Sea; a malicious fish with a mouth similar to a rabbit"; Dann. thinks it is a
sturgeon, but in Goll. it appears as tunny. The ancients called the sturgeon
acipenser; but this name was gradually changed into *styrio*, *stirio* and *sturio*,
which is similar to *tursio* (cf. *styrio* in the vocabulary). The fish in question
therefore may have been sturgeon for which the Black Sea is famous.

[4] List., G.-V. *ovis obligabis* — tie with eggs — certainly preferable to the
Tor. version.

[5] Tor. thyme.

The above is an excellent way of making fish balls, it being taken for granted,
of course, that the salt fish be thoroughly soaked and cooked in milk before
shaping into balls. The many spices should be used very moderately, some to be
omitted entirely. We read between the lines of the old formula that the *Tursio*
had a long journey from Pontus to Rome; fish however dry acquires a notorious
flavor upon such journeys which must be offset by herbs and spices.

It is quite possible that the ancients made a *réduction* of the herbs and spices
mentioned in this formula; in fact, the presence of vinegar leads us to believe
this, in which case this formula would be nothing but a very modern sauce. The
herbs and spices in a *réduction* are crushed and boiled down in vinegar and wine,
and strained off, they leave their finest flavor in the sauce.

[146] VEGETABLE DINNER
       PATELLA EX OLISATRO [1]

[Any kind of vegetables or herbs] BLANCHED OFF IN WATER

WITH [a little] SODA; SQUEEZE [out the water] ARRANGE IN A SAUCEPAN. GRIND PEPPER, LOVAGE, CORIANDER, SATURY, ONION WITH WINE, BROTH, VINEGAR AND OIL; ADD [this] TO THE VEGETABLES, STEW [all until nearly done] AND TIE WITH ROUX. SPRINKLE WITH THYME, FINELY GROUND PEPPER AND SERVE. ANY KIND OF VEGETABLE [2] MAY BE PREPARED IN THE ABOVE MANNER, IF YOU WISH.

[1] Wanting in Tac. and Tor. G.-V. *patellam ex holisatro.*

[2] It is worth noting that Tor. and Tac. omit this recipe entirely and that Tor. concludes the preceding formula with the last sentence of the above formula, except for the difference in one word. Tor. *et de quacunque libra* [List. *et al. herba*] *si volueris facies ut demonstratum est suprà.* This might mean that it is optional (in the preceding formula) to shape the fish into one pound loaves instead of the small fish balls, which is often done in the case of forcemeats, as in veal, beef, ham loaves, or fish pie.

We are inclined to accept the reading of Torinus, for the above way of preparing "any kind of vegetables or herbs" is somewhat farfetched. Furthermore, the vegetable dish would more properly belong in Book III.

Just another example of where readings by various editors are different because of the interpretations of one word. In this case one group reads *libra* whereas the other reads *herba.*

[147]   A DISH OF SARDINES   *PATELLA DE APUA* [1]

SARDINE LOAF (OR OMELETTE) IS MADE IN THIS MANNER [2] CLEAN THE SARDINES [of skin and bones]; BREAK [and beat] EGGS AND MIX WITH [half of the] FISH [3]; ADD TO THIS SOME STOCK, WINE AND OIL, AND FINISH [the composition] BY HEATING IT. WHEN DONE TO A POINT, ADD [the remaining part of the] SARDINES TO IT, LET IT STAND A WHILE [over a slow fire to congeal] CAREFULLY TURN OVER [dish it up] MASK WITH A WARM [4] WINE SAUCE, SPRINKLE WITH PEPPER AND SERVE.

[1] G.-V. *Patina de apua fricta* — same as *aphya,* fried fresh small fish of the kind of anchovies, sardines, sprats.

In experimenting with this formula we would advise to use salt and oil judiciously if any at all. We have no knowledge of the ancient *apua fricta* other than our making of modern sardines which is to fry them in oil as quickly as possible after the fish has left the water, for its meat is very delicate. For an omelette, our modern sardines, including kippered smelts, sprotten, and similar smoked and processed fish, contain sufficient salt and fat to season the eggs of an omelette.

[2] Tor. Sentence wanting in other texts.

[3] Tor. *cum aqua*; List., G.-V. *cum apua*. Perhaps a typographical error in Tor. A little water is used to dilute the eggs of an omelette, but Apicius already prescribes sufficient liquids (stock or brine, wine) for that purpose.

[4] Tor. *et in calore œnogarum perfundes*; List., G.-V. *ut coloret* — to keep the omelette in the pan long enough to give it "color." We prefer the Torinus version because an omelette should have no or very little color from the fire (the eggs thus browned are indigestible) and because hot *œnogarum* (wine-fish sauce, not in List.) is accompanying this dish, to give additional savour and a finishing touch.

[148] FINE RAGOUT OF BRAINS AND BACON
PATINA EX LARIDIS [1] *ET CEREBELLIS*

THE DISH OF BACON AND BRAINS IS MADE IN THIS MAN-NER [2] STRAIN [or chop fine] HARD BOILED EGGS [3] WITH PARBOILED BRAINS [calf's or pig's] THE SKIN AND NERVES OF WHICH HAVE BEEN REMOVED; ALSO COOK CHICKEN GIBLETS, ALL IN PROPORTION TO THE FISH [4] PUT THIS AFORESAID MIXTURE IN A SAUCEPAN, PLACE THE COOKED BACON IN THE CENTER, GRIND PEPPER AND LOVAGE AND TO SWEETEN ADD A DASH OF MEAD, HEAT, WHEN HOT STIR BRISKLY WITH A RUE WHIP AND BIND WITH ROUX.

[1] G.-V. *lagitis*; Tor. *laridis* and *largitis*; Vat. Ms. *lagatis*; List. *pro lagitis . . . legendum Lacertis*. The *lacertus*, according to List., is a much esteemed salt fish; not identified. List. *et al.* seem to be mistaken in their reading of *lacertis* for *laridis*. This work stands for salt pork, from *laridum* and *lardum* (French, *lard*; the English *lard* is applied to the rendered fat of pork in general). Cf. notes to ℞ No. 41.

[2] Tor. sentence wanting in other texts.

[3] *oua dura*; Sch. *o. dua* — two eggs.

[4] This formula would be intelligible and even gastronomically correct were it not for this word "fish." However, we cannot accept Lister's reading *lacertis*. We prefer the reading, *laridis*, bacon. The French have another term for this — *petits salés*. Both this and the Torinus term are in the plural. They are simply small strips of bacon to which Torinus again refers in the above formula, *salsum, coctum in medio pones* — put the bacon, when done, in the center (of the dish). Regarding *salsum* also see note to ℞ No. 41.

The above dish resembles *ragoût fin en coquille*, a popular Continental dish, although its principal ingredients are sweetbreads instead of brains.

[149] BROILED MULLET
PATINA EX PISCIBUS MULLIS [1]

A DISH OF MULLET CONSISTS OF [2] SCALED SALT MUL-
LET PLACED IN A CLEAN PAN WITH ENOUGH OIL [3] AS IS
NECESSARY FOR COOKING; WHEN DONE ADD [a dash of
honey-] WINE OR RAISIN WINE, SPRINKLE WITH PEPPER
AND SERVE.

[1] List., G.-V. *mullorum loco salsi* — salt mullet.

[2] Tor. wanting in other texts.

[3] List. *liquamen* — broth, brine, which would be worse than carrying
owls to Athens. As a matter of fact, the mullet if it be what List. says, *loco
salsi* — salted on the spot, i.e. as caught, near the sea shore, requires soaking to
extract the salt.

[150] A DISH OF ANY KIND OF SALT FISH
PATINA EX PISCIBUS QUIBUSLIBET [1]

ANOTHER FISH DISH IS THUS MADE [2] FRY ANY KIND OF
CURED [3] FISH, CAREFULLY TREATED [soaked and cleaned]
PLACE IN A PAN, COVER WITH SUFFICIENT OIL, LAY [strips
of] COOKED SALT [4] [pork or bacon — *petits salés*] OVER THE
CENTER, KEEP IT HOT, WHEN REAL HOT, ADD A DASH OF
HONEY WINE TO THE GRAVY AND STIR IT UP [5].

[1] Ex Tor.; G.-V. *P. piscium loco salsi.*

[2] Tor.; sentence wanting in other texts.

[3] Tor. *duratos* — hard — no sense here, probably a misprint of the d.
List. *curatos* — carefully treated, "cured," processed.

[4] *Salsum coctum*, cf. notes to ℞ No. 148; Goll., Dann. — sprinkle [the
fish] with salt . . . Like Lister's error in the preceding formula it would be a
great blunder to add salt to a cured fish already saturated with salt to the utmost.
Cf. also note 2 to ℞ Nos. 41, 148.

[5] Virtually a repetition of ℞ No. 149, except for the addition of the pork.

[151] ANOTHER FISH DISH, WITH ONIONS
ALIA PISCIUM PATINA

ANOTHER FISH DISH MAKE AS FOLLOWS [1] CLEAN ANY
KIND OF FISH AND PLACE IT PROPERLY IN A SAUCEPAN
WITH SHREDDED DRY ASCALONIAN ONIONS [shallots] OR
WITH ANY OTHER KIND OF ONIONS, THE FISH ON TOP.
ADD STOCK AND OIL AND COOK. WHEN DONE, PUT BROIL-
ED BACON IN THE CENTER, GIVE IT A DASH OF VINEGAR,

SPRINKLE WITH [finely chopped] SAVORY AND GARNISH WITH [the] ONIONS.

[1] Tor., sentence wanting in other texts.

[152]   A LUCRETIAN DISH *PATINA LUCRETIANA* [1]

CLEAN YOUNG ONIONS, REJECTING THE GREEN TOPS, AND PLACE [2] THEM IN A SAUCEPAN WITH A LITTLE BROTH, SOME OIL AND WATER, AND, TO BE COOKED [with the onions] PLACE SALT PORK [3] IN THE MIDST [of the scallions]. WHEN NEARLY DONE, ADD A SPOON OF HONEY [4] A LITTLE VINEGAR AND REDUCED MUST, TASTE IT, IF INSIPID ADD MORE BRINE [broth] IF TOO SALTY, ADD MORE HONEY, AND SPRINKLE WITH SAVORY [5].

[1] Dann. Named for Lucretius Epicuræus, a contemporary of Cicero. List. *ab authore cui in usu fuit sic appellata.*

[2] G.-V. *concides.* Not necessary.

[3] *salsum crudum* — salt pork, i.e. not smoked or cured bacon. Dann. raw salt; Goll. salt. Impossible, of course! Cf. notes to ℞ Nos. 41, 147, 149.

[4] To glaze the pork, no doubt; reminding us of our own use of sugar to glaze ham or bacon, and of the molasses added to pork (and beans).

[5] G.-V. *coronam bubulam.* In experimenting with this formula omit salt completely. Instead of honey we have also added maple syrup once. To make this a perfect luncheon dish a starch is wanting; we have therefore added sliced raw potatoes and cooked with the rest, to make it a balanced meal, by way of improving upon Lucretius. Since the ancients had no potatoes we have, on a different occasion, created another version by added sliced dasheens (*colocasia,* cf. ℞ Nos. 74, 216, 244, 322). It is surprising that the ancients who used the *colocasium* extensively did not combine it with the above dish.

[153]   STEWED LACERTUS FISH
PATINA DE LACERTIS [1]

CLEAN AND WASH [soak] THE FISH [2] [cook and flake it] BREAK AND BEAT EGGS, MIX THEM WITH THE FISH, ADD BROTH, WINE AND OIL. PLACE THIS ON THE FIRE, WHEN COOKED [scrambled] ADD SIMPLE FISH WINE SAUCE [3] TO IT, SPRINKLE WITH PEPPER AND SERVE [4].

[1] Ex List. wanting in Tor. G.-V. *P. de lagitis;* cf. note to ℞ No. 148.

[2] Remembering that List. reads *lagitis* for *lacertis,* this formula appears to be an antique "Scrambled Eggs and Bacon." Cf. notes to ℞ Nos. 42, 148-150.

[3] *Oenogarum,* cf. ℞ No. 147, the Sardine Omelette.

[4] To cook the eggs as described above would be disastrous. The fish, if such was used, was probably first poached in the broth, wine and oil, and when done, removed from the pan. The *fond,* or remaining juice or gravy, was subsequently

tied with the egg yolks, and this sauce was strained over the fish dressed on the service platter, the *œnogarum* sparingly sprinkled over the finished dish. This would closely resemble our modern *au vin blanc* fish dishes; the *œnogarum* taking the place of our meat glace.

Another interpretation of this vexacious formula is that if fish was used, the cooked fish was incorporated with the raw beaten eggs which were then scrambled in the pan. In that event this formula resembles closely the sardine omelette.

[154] A FISH STEW   *PATINA ZOMORE* [1]

THE ZOMORE FISH DISH IS MADE AS FOLLOWS [2] TAKE RAW GANONAS [3] AND OTHER [fish] WHICHEVER YOU LIKE, PLACE THEM IN A SAUCE PAN, ADDING OIL, BROTH, REDUCED WINE, A BUNCH [4] OF LEEKS AND [green] CORIANDER; WHILE THIS COOKS, CRUSH PEPPER, LOVAGE AND A BUNCH OF ORIGANY WHICH CRUSH BY ITSELF AND DILUTE WITH THE JUICE [5] OF THE FISH. NOW DISSOLVE [break and beat egg yolks for a *liaison*] PREPARE AND TASTE THE DISH, BINDING [the sauce with the yolks] SPRINKLE WITH PEPPER AND SERVE.

[1] List. *Zomoteganite* — "a dish of fish boiled in their own liquor"; G.-V. *zomoteganon*; Lan. *zomoreganonas*; Vat. Ms. *zomonam Ganas.*

[2] Tor. sentence wanting in other texts.

[3] *ganonas crudas* — an unidentified fish.

[4] "Bouquet garni."

[5] *ius de suo sibi* — old Plautian latinity. Cf. H. C. Coote, cit. Apiciana; the proof of the antiquity and the genuineness of Apicius.

[155]   SOLE IN WHITE WINE   *PATINA EX SOLEIS* [1]

A DISH OF SOLE IS THUS MADE [2] BEAT THE SOLE [3] PREPARE [4] AND PLACE THEM IN A [shallow] SAUCE PAN, ADD OIL, BROTH AND WINE, AND POACH THEM THUS; NOW CRUSH PEPPER, LOVAGE, ORIGANY AND ADD OF THE FISH JUICE; THEN BIND THE SAUCE WITH RAW EGGS [yolks] TO MAKE A GOOD CREAMY SAUCE OF IT; STRAIN THIS OVER THE SOLE, HEAT ALL ON A SLOW FIRE [to fill it with live heat] SPRINKLE WITH PEPPER AND SERVE [5].

[1] G.-V. P. *solearum.*

[2] Tor. sentence wanting in other texts.

[3] Beat, to make tender, to be able to remove the skin.

[4] Tor. *curatos* — trim, skin, remove entrails, wash.

[5] One of the best of Apician accomplishments. Exactly like our modern *sole au vin blanc*, one of the most aristocratic of dishes. Cf. ℞ No. 487, Excerpta, XIX.

[155a]   FISH LIQUOR   *PATINA EX PISCIBUS*

A LIQUOR [in which to cook fish] IS MADE BY TAKING [1] ONE OUNCE OF PEPPER, ONE PINT OF REDUCED WINE, ONE PINT OF SPICED WINE AND TWO OUNCES OF OIL.

[1] Tor. sentence wanting in other texts.

[156]   A DISH OF LITTLE FISH
        PATINA DE PISCICULIS [1]

TAKE RAISINS, PEPPER, LOVAGE, ORIGANY, ONIONS, WINE, BROTH AND OIL, PLACE THIS IN A PAN; AFTER THIS HAS COOKED ADD TO IT THE COOKED SMALL FISH, BIND WITH ROUX AND SERVE.

[1] Smelts, anchovies, whitebait.

[157]   A DISH OF TOOTH FISH, DORY OR SEA MULLET
        AND OYSTERS
        PATINA DE PISCIBUS DENTICE, AURATA ET
        MUGILE [1]

TAKE THE FISH, PREPARE [clean, trim, wash] AND HALF BROIL OR FRY THEM; THEREUPON SHRED THEM [in good-sized] PIECES: NEXT PREPARE OYSTERS; PUT IN A MORTAR 6 SCRUPLES OF PEPPER, MOISTEN WITH BROTH AND CRUSH. ADD A SMALL GLASS OF BROTH, ONE OF WINE TO IT; PUT IN A SAUCE PAN 3 OUNCES OF OIL AND THE [shelled] OYSTERS AND LET THEM POACH WITH WINE SAUCE. WHEN THEY ARE DONE, OIL A DISH ON WHICH PLACE THE ABOVE MENTIONED FISH PIECES AND STEWED OYSTERS, HEAT AGAIN, AND WHEN HOT, BREAK 40 [2] EGGS [whip them] AND POUR THEM OVER THE OYSTERS, SO THAT THEY CONGEAL. SPRINKLE WITH PEPPER AND SERVE. [3].

[1] *dentex* — "tooth-fish"; *aurata* — "gilt" — dory, red snapper; *mugilis* — Sea Mullet, according to some.

[2] G.-V. *ova* XI — 11 eggs. Tac. *ova* Xl, which may be read XL — forty.

[3] This dish may be allowed to congeal slowly; if done quickly it may become a dish of scrambled eggs with fish and oysters.

[158]   SEA BASS, OR BARRACUDA
        PATINA DE LUPO [1]

GRIND PEPPER, CUMIN, PARSLEY, RUE, ONIONS, HONEY, BROTH, RAISIN WINE AND DROPS OF OIL [2].

[1] G.-V. *p. de pisce lupo* — wolf, because of its voracity; a sea fish, sea

pike, or sea bass; perhaps akin to our barracuda, wolfish both in appearance and character. Sch. *Perca labrax* Lin.

[2] The cleaned fish is cut into convenient portions or fillets, placed in an oiled pan, the ingredients spread over; it is either poached in the oven or cooked under the open fire.

Schuch here inserts his ℞ Nos. 153 to 166 which more properly belong among the Excerpta of Vinidarius and which are found at the end Book X by Apicius.

[159]   A DISH OF SORB-APPLE, HOT OR COLD
PATINA DE SORBIS CALIDA ET FRIGIDA

TAKE MEDLARS, CLEAN THEM; CRUSH THEM IN THE MORTAR AND STRAIN THROUGH COLANDER. 4 COOK-ED [calf's or pork] BRAINS, SKINNED AND FREED FROM STRINGY PARTS, PUT IN THE MORTAR WITH 8 SCRUPLES OF PEPPER, DILUTE WITH STOCK AND CRUSH, ADDING THE MEDLAR PULP AND COMBINE ALL; NOW BREAK 8 EGGS AND ADD A SMALL GLASS OF BROTH. OIL A CLEAN PAN AND PLACE IT IN THE HOT BATH OR IN THE HOT ASHES; AFTER YOU HAVE FILLED IT WITH THE PREPARATION, MAKE SURE THAT THE PAN GETS ENOUGH HEAT FROM BE-LOW; LET IT CONGEAL, AND WHEN DONE SPRINKLE WITH A LITTLE FINE PEPPER AND SERVE.

Sch. ℞ No. 166.

[160]   A DISH OF PEACHES [1]   *PATINA DE PERSICIS*

CLEAN HARD-SKINNED PEACHES AND SLICE, STEW THEM; ARRANGE IN A DISH, SPRINKLE WITH A LITTLE OIL AND SERVE WITH CUMIN-FLAVORED WINE [2].

[1] Tor. is not sure whether this is a Persian fish or peaches — *persica*.
[2] Dann. Pepper, for which there is no authority.
Sch. ℞ No. 167.

[161]   A DISH OF PEARS   *PATINA DE PIRIS*

A DISH OF PEARS IS MADE THIS WAY: [1] STEW THE PEARS, CLEAN OUT THE CENTER [remove core and seeds] CRUSH THEM WITH PEPPER, CUMIN, HONEY, RAISIN WINE, BROTH AND A LITTLE OIL; MIX WITH EGGS, MAKE A PIE [custard] OF THIS, SPRINKLE WITH PEPPER AND SERVE.

[1] Tor. sentence wanting in other texts.
Sch. ℞ No. 168.

[162]   A DISH OF SEA-NETTLES
          PATINA DE URTICA [1]

A DISH OF SEA-NETTLES, EITHER HOT OR COLD, IS MADE
THUS: [2] TAKE SEA-NETTLES, WASH AND DRAIN THEM ON
THE COLANDER, DRY ON THE TABLE AND CHOP FINE.
CRUSH 10 SCRUPLES OF PEPPER, MOISTEN WITH BROTH,
ADD 2 SMALL GLASSES OF BROTH AND 6 OUNCES OF OIL.
HEAT THIS IN A SAUCE PAN AND WHEN COOKED TAKE IT
OUT AND ALLOW TO COOL OFF. NEXT OIL A CLEAN PAN,
BREAK 8 EGGS AND BEAT THEM; COMBINE THESE WITH
THE ABOVE PREPARATIONS, PLACE THE PAN ON HOT ASH-
ES TO GIVE IT HEAT FROM BELOW, WHEN DONE [congealed]
SPRINKLE WITH PEPPER AND SERVE.

[1] G.-V. *p. urticarum calida et frigida.*
[2] Tor. sentence wanting in other texts.

[163]   A DISH OF QUINCES
          PATINA DE CYDONIIS [1]

A DISH OF QUINCES IS MADE AS FOLLOWS: [2] QUINCES
ARE COOKED WITH LEEKS, HONEY AND BROTH, USING
HOT OIL, OR THEY ARE STEWED IN HONEY [3].

[1] G.-V. *p. de Cydoneis.*
[2] Tor. sentence wanting in other texts.
[3] This latter method would appeal to our modern notion of preparing
fruits of this sort; we use sugar syrup to cook them in and flavor with various
spices, adding perhaps a little wine or brandy.

III

OF FINELY CHOPPED, MINCED MEATS
                                          DE MINUTALIBUS [1]

[164]   A MINCE OF SEA FOOD   *MINUTAL MARINUM*

PLACE THE FISH IN SAUCE PAN, ADD BROTH OIL AND
WINE [and poach it]. ALSO FINELY CHOP LEEK HEADS [the
white part only of leeks] AND [fresh] CORIANDER. [When cool,
mince the fish fine] FORM IT INTO SMALL CAKES [2] ADDING
CAPERS [3] AND SEA-NETTLES WELL CLEANED. THESE FISH
CAKES COOK IN A LIQUOR OF PEPPER, LOVAGE AND ORI-
GANY, CRUSHED, DILUTED WITH BROTH AND THE ABOVE

FISH LIQUOR WHICH SKIM WELL, BIND [with roux or eggs] STIR [strain] OVER THE CAKES, SPRINKLE WITH PEPPER AND SERVE.

[1] G.-V. *minutal de piscibus vel Isiciis.*

[2] Tac. G.-V. *isiciola . . . minuta* — resembling our modern *quenelles de poisson* — tiny fish dumplings.

[3] Tac. *cum caparis*; Tor. *c. capparibus*; Vat. Ms. *concarpis*; List. G.-V. *concerpis.*

[165] TARENTINE MINUTAL
MINUTAL TARENTINUM [1]

FINELY CHOP THE WHITE PART OF LEEKS AND PLACE IN A SAUCE PAN; ADD OIL [fry lightly] AND BROTH; NEXT ADD SMALL SAUSAGE TO BE COOKED LIKEWISE. TO HAVE A GOOD TARENTINE DISH, THEY MUST BE TENDER. THE MAK-ING OF THESE SAUSAGE WILL BE FOUND AMONG THE ISICIA [Nos. 60-66] [2]. ALSO MAKE A SAUCE IN THE FOLLOWING MANNER: CRUSH PEPPER, LOVAGE AND ORIGANY, MOIST-EN WITH BROTH, ADD OF THE ABOVE [sausage] GRAVY, WINE, RAISIN WINE; PUT IN A SAUCE PAN TO BE HEATED, WHEN BOILING, SKIM CAREFULLY, BIND, SPRINKLE WITH PEPPER AND SERVE.

[1] G.-V. *Terentinum*, for which there is no reason. Tarentum, town of lower Italy, now Taranto, celebrated for its wine and luxurious living.

[2] Such references to other parts of the book are very infrequent.

[166] APICIAN MINUTAL   *MINUTAL APICIANUM*

THE APICIAN MINUTAL IS MADE AS FOLLOWS: [1] OIL, BROTH WINE, LEEK HEADS, MINT, SMALL FISH, SMALL TID-BITS [2] COCK'S FRIES OR CAPON'S KIDNEYS [3] AND PORK SWEETBREADS; ALL OF THESE ARE COOKED TOGETHER [4] NOW CRUSH PEPPER, LOVAGE, GREEN CORIANDER, OR SEEDS, MOISTENED WITH BROTH; ADD A LITTLE HONEY, AND OF THE OWN LIQUOR [5] OF THE ABOVE MORSELS, WINE AND HONEY TO TASTE; BRING THIS TO A BOILING POINT SKIM, BIND, STIR WELL [strain, pour over the morsels] SPRINKLE WITH PEPPER AND SERVE [6].

[1] Tor. sentence wanting in other texts.

[2] *isitia* — *quenelles*, dumplings of some kind, mostly fine forcemeats.

[3] *testiculi caponum*; the capon has no *testiculi*, these organs having been

removed by an operation when the cock is young. This operation is said to have been first performed by a Roman surgeon with the intention of beating the *Lex Fannia*, or Fannian law, sponsored by a fanatic named Fannius. It prohibited among other restrictions the serving of any fowl at any time or repast except a hen, and this hen was not to be fattened. Note the cunning of the law: The useful hen and her unlaid eggs could be sacrificed while the unproductive rooster was allowed to thrive to no purpose, immune from the butcher's block. This set the shrewd surgeon to thinking; he transformed a rooster into a capon by his surgical trick. The emasculated bird grew fat without his owner committing any infraction of the Roman law against fattening chickens. Of course the capon, being neither hen nor rooster, was perfectly safe to eat, for he was within the law. Thus he became a huge success as an ancient "bootleg" chicken.

[4] These integral parts must be prepared and poached separately and merely heated together before the final service.

[5] Again the Plautian colloquialism *ius de suo sibi*.

[6] This dish is worthy of Apicius. It is akin to our *Ragoût Financière*, and could pass for *Vol-au-vent à la Financière* if it were served in a large fluffy crust of puff paste.

[167] MINUTAL À LA MATIUS [1]
MINUTAL MATIANUM

PUT IN A SAUCE PAN OIL, BROTH FINELY CHOPPED LEEKS, CORIANDER, SMALL TID-BITS, COOKED PORK SHOULDER, CUT INTO LONG STRIPS INCLUDING THE SKIN, HAVE EVERYTHING EQUALLY HALF DONE. ADD MATIAN APPLES [2] CLEANED, THE CORE REMOVED, SLICED LENGTHWISE AND COOK THEM TOGETHER: MEANWHILE CRUSH PEPPER, CUMIN, GREEN CORIANDER, OR SEEDS, MINT, LASER ROOT, MOISTENED WITH VINEGAR, HONEY AND BROTH AND A LITTLE REDUCED MUST, ADD TO THIS THE BROTH OF THE ABOVE MORSELS, VINEGAR TO TASTE, BOIL, SKIM, BIND [strain over the morsels] SPRINKLE WITH PEPPER AND SERVE.

[1] Named for Matius, ancient author, or because of the Matian apples used in this dish, also named for the same man. Plinius, Nat. Hist. lib. XV, Cap. 14-15, Columella, De re Rustica, lib. XII, Cap. XLIIII.

This is not the first instance where fruits or vegetables were named for famous men. Beets, a certain kind of them were named for Varro, writer on agriculture. Matius, according to Varro, wrote a book on waiters, cooks, cellar men and food service in general, of which there is no trace today. It was already lost during Varro's days.

[2] Cf. note 1, above. This illustrates the age-old connection of pork and apples.

[168]   SWEET MINUTAL   *MINUTAL DULCE* [1]

IN A SAUCE PAN PUT TOGETHER OIL, BROTH, COCTURA
[2] FINELY CUT LEEK HEADS AND GREEN CORIANDER,
COOKED PORK SHOULDER, SMALL TID-BITS. WHILE THIS
IS BEING COOKED, CRUSH PEPPER, CUMIN, CORIANDER OR
[its] SEEDS, GREEN RUE, LASER ROOT, MOISTENED WITH
VINEGAR, REDUCED MUST AND THE GRAVY OF THE ABOVE
MORSELS; ADD VINEGAR TO TASTE: WHEN THIS [sauce] IS
COOKED, HOLLOW OUT CITRON SQUASH [3] CUT IN DICE,
BOIL AND PLACE THEM TOGETHER WITH THE REST IN THE
DISH, SKIM, BIND [strain] THE SAUCE [pour it over the morsels]
SPRINKLE WITH PEPPER AND SERVE.

[1] G.-V. *m. ex citriis.*

[2] At this late point Apicius commences to use the term *coctura* which does
not designate any particular ingredient but rather stands for a certain process
of cookery, depending upon the ingredients used in the dish. We would here
interpret it as the frying of the leeks in oil, etc. In another instance *coctura* may
mean our modern *réduction.*

[3] The fruit to be used here has not been satisfactorily identified. The texts
have *citrium* and *citrum* — a sweet squash or cucumber — perhaps even a
melon, but not the citron, the *mala citrea* as read by List. This specimen is hard
to identify because of the many varieties in the cucumber, squash and the citrus
families. *Citrus,* as a matter of fact, is but a corruption of *cedrus,* the cedar tree.

We are not sure whether this fruit is to be stuffed with the ragout and then
baked, as is often the custom to do with such shells; the texts prescribes distinctly to hollow out the fruit.

The title, implying a "sweet dish" is obviously wrong.

It may be remarked here that Apicius makes no mention of that marvelous
citrus fruit, the lemon, nor of the orange, both of which are indispensible to
modern cookery.

[169]   MINUTAL OF FRUIT
          MINUTAL EX PRÆCOQUIS

IN A SAUCE PAN PUT OIL, BROTH AND WINE, FINELY CUT
SHALLOTS, DICED COOKED PORK SHOULDER. WHEN THIS
IS COOKED, CRUSH PEPPER, CUMIN, DRY MINT, DILL, MOIST-
EN WITH HONEY, BROTH, RAISIN WINE [and] A LITTLE
VINEGAR, SOME OF THE GRAVY OF THE ABOVE MORSELS,
ADD FRUITS THE SEEDS OF WHICH HAVE BEEN TAKEN OUT,
LET BOIL, WHEN THOROUGHLY COOKED, SKIM, BIND,
SPRINKLE WITH PEPPER AND SERVE [1].

[1] This, rather than ℞ No. 168, deserves the title, Sweet Minutal, for it is practically the same, with the addition of the fruit.

[170]   MINUTAL OF HARE'S LIVERS
MINUTAL LEPORINUM

THE WAY TO MAKE A MINUTAL OF HARE'S GIBLETS MAY BE FOUND AMONG THE HARE RECIPES [1].

[170a] IN A SAUCE PAN PUT OIL, BROTH AND WINE, FINE-LY CUT SHALLOTS, DICED COOKED PORK SHOULDER. WHEN THIS IS COOKED, CRUSH PEPPER, CUMIN, DRY MINT, DILL, MOISTEN WITH HONEY, BROTH, RAISIN WINE [and] A LITTLE VINEGAR, SOME OF THE GRAVY OF THE ABOVE MORSELS, ADD SEEDLESS FRUITS, LET BOIL, WHEN THOR-OUGHLY COOKED, SKIM, BIND, SPRINKLE WITH PEPPER AND SERVE.

[1] ℞ No. 386, Book VIII is one of these recipes. This is one of the few in-stances where the ancient original makes any reference to any other part of the Apicius book.* After this bare reference, the original proceeds to repeat the text of the preceding formula verbatim.

* Cf. ℞ No. 166.

Brandt suggests a new title for [170a] ANOTHER SWEET MINUTAL.

The G.-V. version differs but little from ℞ No. 169.

[171]   RED APPLE MINUTAL   *MINUTAL EX ROSIS* [1]

MAKE THIS THE SAME WAY AS DESCRIBED IN THE FORE-GOING, ONLY ADD MORE RAISIN WINE.

[1] List. Roses; Tor. *Rosatium*; this term, medieval Latin, does not exist in the ancient language.

Sch. *mala rosea* — rosy or red apple, most likely to be the correct interpre-tation. Cf. ℞ Nos. 136 and 167.

The above title has led to the belief that the ancients made pies, etc., of roses, an idea that was much ridiculed in England after the publication of Lister's work in 1705.

We concur with Schuch's interpretation that rosy apples were used, remem-bering, however, that the fruit of the rose tree, the hip, dog-briar, eglantine is also made into dainty confections on the Continent today. It is therefore entirely possible that this recipe calls for the fruit of the rose tree.

IV
GRUELS   *TISANAM VEL SUCUM*
[172]   BARLEY BROTH, PAP, PORRIDGE, GRUEL
TISANA SIVE CREMORE [1]

CRUSH BARLEY, SOAKED THE DAY BEFORE, WELL WASH-

ED, PLACE ON THE FIRE TO BE COOKED [in a double boiler]
WHEN HOT ADD ENOUGH OIL, A BUNCH OF DILL, DRY
ONION, SATURY AND COLOCASIUM [2] TO BE COOKED TO-
GETHER BECAUSE FOR THE BETTER JUICE, ADD GREEN
CORIANDER AND A LITTLE SALT; BRING IT TO A BOILING
POINT. WHEN DONE TAKE OUT THE BUNCH [of dill] AND
TRANSFER THE BARLEY INTO ANOTHER KETTLE TO
AVOID STICKING TO THE BOTTOM AND BURNING, MAKE
IT LIQUID [by addition of water, broth, milk] STRAIN INTO A POT,
COVERING THE TOPS OF THE COLOCASIA. NEXT CRUSH
PEPPER, LOVAGE, A LITTLE DRY FLEA-BANE, CUMIN AND
SYLPHIUM [3] STIR IT WELL AND ADD VINEGAR, REDUCED
MUST AND BROTH; PUT IT BACK INTO THE POT, THE RE-
MAINING COLOCASIA FINISH ON A GENTLE FIRE [4].

[1] Tor. *ptisana siue Cremore.*

[2] G.-V. *Colœfium*; Tor. *colœsium* and *colesium* (the different readings
perhaps on account of the similarity of the "long" s with the f. Tor. spells this
word differently every time he is confronted with it. Tac., Lan. *coledium* —
unidentified. List. *colocasium*, which see in notes to ℞ Nos. 74, 200, 216, 244,
and 322, also Sch. p. 95.

[3] List. *sil frictum*; Tor. *silphium f.*

[4] Tor. continuing without interruption. This formula is reported in ℞
No. 200.

[173]   ANOTHER TISANA   *TISANA TARICHA* [1]

THE CEREAL [2] IS SOAKED; CHICKPEAS, LENTILS AND
PEAS ARE CRUSHED AND BOILED WITH IT; WHEN WELL
COOKED, ADD PLENTY OF OIL. NOW CUT GREEN HERBS,
LEEKS, CORIANDER, DILL, FENNEL, BEETS, MALLOWS, CAB-
BAGE STRUNKS, ALL SOFT AND GREEN AND FINELY CUT,
AND PUT IN A POT. THE CABBAGE COOK [separately. Also]
CRUSH FENNEL SEED, ORIGANY, SYLPHIUM AND LOVAGE,
AND WHEN CRUSHED, ADD BROTH TO TASTE, POUR THIS
OVER THE PORRIDGE, STIR IT TOGETHER AND USE SOME
FINELY CHOPPED CABBAGE STEMS TO SPRINKLE ON TOP
[2].

[1] Variants: *barrica, farrica*; List. *legendum, puto, Taricam*; *id. est Salsam.*
Cf. ℞ 144, 149, 426-8. Lan., Tor., G.-V. *barricam*, not identified. Sch. *farrica*
— corn spelt; probably not far from the mark. We would venture to suggest
that our "farina" is the thing here used, or any ordinary corn meal.

[2] This formula is repeated in ℞ No. 201.

V

HORS D'ŒUVRES, APPETIZERS, RELISHES   *GUSTUM*

[174] "MOVEABLE" APPETIZERS
       GUSTUM VERSATILE

THE MOVEABLE [1] APPETIZERS ARE THUS MADE: [2] SMALL WHITE BEETS, MATURE LEEKS, CELERY ROOTS [3] STEWED COCKLES [4] GINGER [5] CHICKEN GIBLETS, SMALL FOWL [6] SMALL MORSELS COOKED IN THEIR OWN LIQUOR [7]. OIL A PAN, LINE IT WITH MALLOW LEAVES AND A COMPOSITION OF DIFFERENT VEGETABLES, AND, IF YOU HAVE ROOM ENOUGH, BULBS, DAMASCUS PLUMS, SNAILS, TID-BITS [8] SHORT LUCANIAN SAUSAGE SLICED; ADD BROTH, OIL, WINE, VINEGAR PUT ON THE FIRE TO HEAT AND SO COOK THEM. MEANWHILE CRUSH PEPPER, LOVAGE, GINGER, A LITTLE TARRAGON, MOISTEN IT AND LET IT COOK. BREAK SEVERAL EGGS IN A DISH, USE THE REMAINING LIQUOR IN THE MORTAR TO MIX IT WITH THE SAUCE IN THE DISH AND TO BIND IT. WHEN THIS IS DONE, MAKE A WINE SAUCE FOR IT AS FOLLOWS: CRUSH PEPPER, LOVAGE, MOISTENED WITH BROTH, RAISIN WINE TO TASTE; IN A SMALL SAUCE PAN PUT A LITTLE OIL [with the other ingredients] HEAT, AND BIND WITH ROUX WHEN HOT. NOW [unmould] UPSET THE DISH ON A PLATTER, REMOVE THE MALLOW LEAVES, POUR OVER THE WINE SAUCE, SPRINKLE WITH PEPPER AND SERVE [9].

[1] Moveable, either because it is one show piece that is carried from one guest to another, or, as here indicated, a dish that is to be unmoulded or turned out of its mould or pan before service.

[2] Tor. sentence wanting in other texts.

[3] Celery roots, i.e. the thick bulbs. G.-V. *apios, bulbos* — celery, onions; note the comma after *apios*.

[4] Periwinkles, also snails.

[5] Tac., Lan. *gingibera*; Tor. *zinziber*; Vat. Ms. *gibera*; G.-V. *Gigeria*; Hum. *id.* — giblets. Wanting in List.

[6] List. *avicellas*; Vat. Ms. *aucellare* and *scellas*; Tac., Lan. *id.*; Tor. *pullorum axillas* — chicken wings (?); G.-V. *ascellas.*

[7] *ex iure.*

[8] *isitia* — quenelles of forcemeat, etc.

[9] An extremely complicated composition of varied morsels, definite instructions lacking, however. It is not clear whether the dish was served hot (in which case the dish would not stand up long) or whether served cold, jellyfied.

Moreover, the title *gustum — hors d'œuvres —* is not consistent either with similar creations by Apicius or with our own notions of such dishes. This title may merely suggest that such a dish was to be served at the beginning of a repast. This recipe presents an instance of the difficulty to render the text and its variants in a manner acceptable to our modern palates.

We are of the opinion that the above recipe is a contraction of two or more formulæ, each of which, separately, might make acceptable hot appetizers.

[175]   VEGETABLE RELISH [1]
         GUSTUM DE OLERIBUS [2]

FOR THIS VEGETABLE DISH BOIL BULBS [3] [in] BROTH, OIL, AND WINE; WHEN DONE [add] LIVER OF SUCKLING PIG [4] CHICKEN LIVERS AND FEET AND SMALL BIRDS [5] CUT IN HALVES, ALL TO BE COOKED WITH THE BULBS. WHEN DONE, CRUSH PEPPER, LOVAGE, MOISTENED WITH BROTH, WINE, RAISIN WINE TO SWEETEN IT. ADD OF THE OWN LIQUOR OF THE MORSELS, RETIRE THE ONIONS, WHEN DONE [group the morsels together in the service dish] BIND [the sauce] WITH ROUX IN THE LAST MOMENT [strain over the morsels] AND SERVE.

[1] An entremet of fowl and livers.
[2] a misnomer, as vegetables play the least part in this dish.
[3] Onions, etc.
[4] *jecinora porcelli*; Sch. *iscinera porcellum.*
[5] Tor. *axillas* and *scellas*; see note 6 to ℞ 174.

[176]   STUFFED PUMPKIN FRITTERS
         GUSTUM DE CUCURBITIS FARSILIBUS

A DISH OF STUFFED PUMPKIN [1] IS MADE THUS: [2] PEEL AND CUT THE PUMPKIN LENGTHWISE INTO OBLONG PIECES WHICH HOLLOW OUT AND PUT IN A COOL PLACE. THE DRESSING FOR THE SAME MAKE IN THIS WAY: CRUSH PEPPER, LOVAGE AND ORIGANY, MOISTENED WITH BROTH; MINCE COOKED BRAINS AND BEAT RAW EGGS AND MIX ALL TOGETHER TO FORM A PASTE; ADD BROTH AS TASTE REQUIRES. STUFF THE ABOVE PREPARED PIECES OF PUMPKIN THAT HAVE NOT BEEN FULLY COOKED WITH THE DRESSING; FIT TWO PIECES TOGETHER AND CLOSE THEM TIGHT [holding them by means of strings or skewers]. [Now poach them and] TAKE THE COOKED ONES OUT AND FRY THEM [3]. [The proper] WINE SAUCE [for this dish] MAKE THUS: CRUSH PEPPER, LOVAGE MOISTENED WITH WINE, RAISIN WINE TO

TASTE, A LITTLE OIL, PLACE IN PAN TO BE COOKED; WHEN DONE BIND WITH ROUX. COVER THE FRIED PUMPKIN WITH THIS SAUCE, SPRINKLE WITH PEPPER AND SERVE [4].

[1] Dann. cucumbers, for which there is no authority. Cucumbers lend themselves equally well for a dish of this kind; they are often stuffed with a forcemeat of finely minced meats, mushrooms, eggs, breadcrumbs, or simply with raw sausage meat, cooked as above, and served as a garnish with *entrées*.

[2] Tor. sentence wanting in other texts.

[3] Presumably in deep fat or oil, a procedure which would require previous breading in bread crumbs or enveloping in frying batter.

[4] Whether you like pumpkin and brains or not — Apicius in this dish reveals himself as the consummate master of his art that he really is — a cook for cooks; Moreover, the lucidity of his diction in this instance is equally remarkable. It stands out in striking contrast to his many other formulæ which are so obscured. Many of them perhaps were precepts of likewise striking originality as this one just cited.

[177]   COMPÔTE OF EARLY FRUIT
GUSTUM DE PRÆCOQUIS

CLEAN HARD-SKINNED EARLY FRUITS [1] REMOVE THE SEEDS AND KEEP THEM COLD IN A PAN. CRUSH PEPPER [2] DRY MINT, MOISTENED WITH BROTH, ADDING HONEY, RAISIN WINE, WINE AND VINEGAR; POUR THIS OVER THE FRUIT IN THE PAN, ADDING A LITTLE OIL. STEW SLOWLY ON A WEAK FIRE, THICKEN [the juice] WITH ROUX [rice flour or other starch diluted with water] SPRINKLE WITH PEPPER [2] AND SERVE [3].

[1] Lister praises the early green fruit and the use thereof, and, as a physician, recommends imitation of the above as follows: *In aliis plurimis locis hujus fructus mentio fit; ususque mirabilis fuit; & certe propter salubritatem, nostram imitationem meretur.*

[2] We do not like the "pepper" in this connection and we venture to suggest that in this case the term probably stands for some other kind of aromatic seed less pungent than the grain known to us as "pepper" and one more acceptable to the fine flavor of fruit, namely pimiento, allspice for instance, or clove, or nutmeg, or a mixture of these. "Pepper" formerly was a generic term for all of these spices but was gradually confined to the grain pepper of black and white varieties.

[3] We concur with Lister's idea of the use of early fruits. The use of early and unripe fruit for this and similar purposes is excellent. The above formula is

a good example of our own "spiced" peaches, pears, etc., usually taken as a relish. Of course, we use sugar instead of honey for sweetening, and brandy instead of wine; but the underlying principles are alike.

This is a good illustrations of and speaks well for the economy and the ingenuity of the ancients.

END OF BOOK IV

EXPLICIT APICII PANDECTER, LIBER QUARTUS [Tac.]

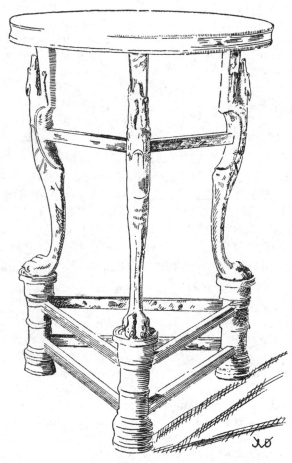

ROUND TABLE

Claw-footed bronze legs on triangular base, consisting of three molded cylindrical supports, connected by cross-bars. Near the top the legs take on a greyhound design, with a three-armed brace connecting them. The round top is of marble. Pompeii. Ntl. Mus., Naples, 78613; Field M., 24281.

APICIUS
Book V

POMPEII: WINE STOCK ROOM OF A TAVERN

Wine was kept in these great jugs, tightly sealed with plaster and pitch, properly dated and labeled, often remaining for many years. Some writers mention wine thus kept for a hundred years; the porosity of the earthen crocks, often holding fifty gallons or more, allowed evaporation, so that the wine in time became as thick as oil or honey, which necessitated diluting with water.

Smaller amphoræ, with various vintages readily mixed, were kept cool in "bars" very similar to our present ice cream cabinets, ready for service for the guests in tavern rooms.

Elaborate dinners (see our illustration) were used to draw the wine from the amphoræ.

FRUIT OR DESSERT DISH, SEA-SHELL SHAPE
The curved handle ends in the head of a griffin. Ntl. Mus., Naples, 76303; Field M. 24298.

BOOK V. LEGUMES

Lib. V. Osprion [*1*]

CHAP.   I. PULSE, MEAL MUSH, PORRIDGE, ETC.
CHAP.   II. LENTILS.
CHAP. III. PEAS.
CHAP. IV. BEANS OR PEAS IN THE POD.
CHAP.   V. BARLEY BROTH.
CHAP. VI. GREEN BEANS, BAIÆAN BEANS.
CHAP. VII. FENUGREEK.
CHAP. VIII. GREEN STRING BEANS AND CHICK-PEAS.

I

MEAL MUSH, MUSH, PULSE, PAP, PORRIDGE, POLENTA
DE PULTIBUS [2]

[178]   JULIAN MEAL MUSH   *PULTES JULIANÆ* [3]

JULIAN PULSES ARE COOKED THUS: SOAK WELL-CLEANED SPELT, PUT IT ON THE FIRE; WHEN COOKED, ADD OIL. IF IT THREATENS TO BECOME THICK, CAREFULLY THIN IT DOWN. TAKE TWO COOKED BRAINS AND HALF A POUND OF MEAT GROUND AS FOR FORCEMEAT, CRUSH THIS WITH THE BRAINS AND PUT IN A POT. CRUSH PEPPER, LOVAGE AND FENNEL SEED, MOISTENED WITH BROTH, A LITTLE

WINE AND PUT IT ON TOP OF THE BRAIN AND MEAT.
WHEN THIS FORCEMEAT IS HEATED SUFFICIENTLY, MIX IT
WITH THE SPELT [finish boiling] TRANSFER INTO SERVICE
DISH, THINNED. THIS MUST HAVE THE CONSISTENCY OF A
HEAVY JUICE [4].

[1] List. *Osprios*; G.-V. *Ospreon* — cookery of leguminous plants.

[2] *Puls* — formerly a simple porridge of various kinds of cereals or legumes,
eaten by the Romans before bread came into use. *Puls* remained in use after the
introduction of bread only as a food of the poor. It was also used at sacrifices.
The *pultes* and *pulticulæ* given by Apicius are illustrations of the ever-present
desire to improve — to glorify, as it were, a thing which once was or still is of
vital importance in the daily life of humans. The *nouveaux-riches* of the ancient
and the modern world cannot find it easy to separate themselves from their
traditions nor are they wont to put up with their plainness, hence the fancy
trimmings. The development of the American pie is a curious analogy in this
respect. We see in this the intricate working of human culture, its eternal strife
for perfection. And perfection is synonymous with decay. The fare of the Carthusian monks, professed, stern vegetarians, underwent the same tortuous evolution.

[3] Named for Didius Julianus, the emperor who was a vegetarian. Of
course, his majesty could not live on a plain porridge, hence the Apician artistry.
The *pultes* were popular with the many professed vegetarians though the oblig-
ing cooks mixed finely ground meat in this and other porridges.

Our various cream soups and legume purées — those most salubrious creations
of modern cookery are no doubt lineal descendants from the Apician *pultes*.
They are so scarce comparatively because they require all the ingenuity and re-
sourcefulness of a gifted cook to be perfect.

[4] Dann. remarks that this formula is wanting in List. Both Lister's first
and second editions have it.

[179] GRUEL AND WINE   *PULTES ŒNOCOCTI*

PORRIDGE AND WINE IS THUS MADE: [1] FLAVOR THE
PULSE WELL WITH WINE [2] AND IMMERSE IN THE JUICE
DAINTY MORSELS [3].

[1] Tor. sentence wanting in other texts.

[2] Tor. *Oenogari*; G.-V. *Oenococti*.

[3] Tor. *cupedias*; *copadia*.

[180] SIMILAR   *SIMILAM* [1]

OR FLAVOR COOKED SPELT WITH THE LIQUOR OF DAIN-
TY PIECES OF PORK, OR CAPON [2] COOKED IN WINE [3].

[1] Tac. *inulam*; Tor. *mulam* — misreading.

[2] Tor.; List. *apponis*.

[3] For practical reasons we have separated the text of ℞ Nos. 179 and 180 which appears as one in the texts.

[181]   MILK TOAST   *PULTES TRACTOGALATÆ* [1]

PUT A PINT OF MILK AND SOME WATER ON THE FIRE IN A NEW [clean] POT; BREAK ROUND BREAD INTO IT [2] DRY, STIR WELL TO PREVENT BURNING; ADD WATER AS NECESSARY [3].

[1] Tor. *pulticula tractogala.*
[2] List. *tres orbiculos tractæ*; Tor. *teres sorbiculos tractæ.*
Tractum is a piece of pastry, a round bread or roll in this case, stale, best suited for this purpose.
[3] The text continues without interruption.

[182]   HONEY PAP   *SIMILITER*

HONEY AND MEAD ARE TREATED SIMILARLY, MIXED WITH MILK, WITH THE ADDITION OF SALT AND A LITTLE OIL.

[178-183]   PULSE   *PULTES* [1]

[1] Tor. *Alia pulticula.*
This is a verbatim repetition of ℞ No. 178.

II

LENTILS   *LENTICULA* [1]

[183]   LENTILS AND COW-PARSNIPS
LENTICULA EX SPONDYLIS SIVE FONDYLIS [2]

PUT THE LENTILS IN A CLEAN SAUCE PAN [and cook with salt]. IN THE MORTAR CRUSH PEPPER, CUMIN, CORIANDER SEED, MINT, RUE, AND FLEA-BANE, MOISTENED WITH VINEGAR, ADD HONEY AND BROTH AND REDUCED MUST, VINEGAR TO TASTE AND PUT THIS IN A SAUCE PAN. THE COOKED COW-PARSNIPS CRUSH, HEAT [mix with the lentils] WHEN THOROUGHLY COOKED, TIE, ADD GREEN [fresh olive] OIL AND SERVE IN AN APPROPRIATE DISH [3].

[1] Tor. *De Lenticula et Castaneis.*
[2] List. again: *ex spongiolis sive fungulis.* See notes to ℞ Nos. 115-120 and 431.
[3] *Boletar* — a "mushroom" dish. G.-V. *in boletari*; Tac. *insuper oleum uiridem mittis*; Tor. *inuolutari* — unidentified.

[184]   LENTILS [1] AND CHESTNUTS
LENTICULAM DE CASTANEIS [2]

TAKE A NEW SAUCE PAN, PLACE THEREIN THE CHEST-
NUTS CAREFULLY CLEANED [3] ADD WATER AND A LIT-
TLE SODA AND PLACE ON THE FIRE TO BE COOKED. THIS
DONE, CRUSH IN THE MORTAR PEPPER, CUMIN, CORIAND-
ER SEED, MINT, RUE, LASER ROOT AND FLEA-BANE MOIST-
ENED WITH VINEGAR, HONEY AND BROTH; ADD VINEGAR
TO TASTE AND POUR THIS OVER THE COOKED CHEST-
NUTS, ADD OIL AND ALLOW TO BOIL. WHEN DONE CRUSH
IT IN THE MORTAR [4]. TASTE TO SEE IF SOMETHING IS
MISSING AND IF SO, PUT IT IN, AND AT LAST ADD GREEN
[fresh virgin] OIL.

[1] Lentils are omitted in this formula; therefore see the following formula.
[2] Thus G.-V.; Tor. Chestnuts.
[3] i.e. peeled and skinned. To do this easily, boil the chestnuts with the skin,
whereupon the outer brown shell and the inner membrane are easily removed.
[4] To make a purée of the chestnuts which strain through the colander.

[184a]   ANOTHER WAY [1]   *ALITER LENTICULAM*

COOK THE LENTILS, SKIM THEM [strain] ADD LEEKS,
GREEN CORIANDER; CRUSH CORIANDER SEED, FLEA-BANE,
LASER ROOT, MINT SEED AND RUE SEED MOISTENED WITH
VINEGAR; ADD HONEY, BROTH, VINEGAR, REDUCED MUST
TO TASTE, THEN OIL, STIRRING [the purée] UNTIL IT IS
DONE, BIND WITH ROUX, ADD GREEN OIL, SPRINKLE WITH
PEPPER AND SERVE.

[1] It is evident that ℞ No. 184 and the above are really one formula, the
former dealing with the cooking of the maroons, the latter describing the lentils.
Presumably the two purées are to be mixed, or to be served as integral parts of
one dish.

III

[185]   PEAS   *DE PISIS*

COOK THE PEAS, WHEN SKIMMED, LAY LEEKS, CORIAND-
ER AND CUMIN ON TOP. CRUSH PEPPER, LOVAGE, CUMIN,
DILL AND GREEN BASILICA, WINE AND BROTH TO TASTE,
MAKE IT BOIL; WHEN DONE STIR WELL, PUT IN WHAT PER-
CHANCE SHOULD BE MISSING AND SERVE [1].

[1] This reminds us of *Petits Pois à la Française*, namely green peas (often

very young ones with the pods) cooked in broth, or *bouillon*, with shredded bacon, lettuce, parsley, onions (or leeks, as above) fresh mint, pepper, salt and other fresh herbs such as chervil. Which is a very delectable way of preparing the tender pea. Some of its refreshing green color is sacrificed by this process, but this loss is amply offset by the savour of the dish.

[186]   PEAS [supreme style]   *PISA FARSILIS* [1]

COOK THE PEAS WITH OIL AND A PIECE OF SOW'S BELLY [2] PUT IN A SAUCE PAN BROTH, LEEK HEADS [the lower white part] GREEN CORIANDER AND PUT ON THE FIRE TO BE COOKED. OF TID-BITS [3] CUT LITTLE DICE. SIMILARLY COOK THRUSHES OR OTHER SMALL [game] BIRDS, OR TAKE SLICED CHICKEN AND DICED BRAIN, PROPERLY COOKED. FURTHER COOK, IN THE AVAILABLE LIQUOR OR BROTH, LUCANIAN SAUSAGE AND BACON; COOK LEEKS IN WATER; CRUSH A PINT OF TOASTED PIGNOLIA NUTS; ALSO CRUSH PEPPER, LOVAGE, ORIGANY AND GINGER, DILUTE WITH THE BROTH OF PORK, TIE [4] TAKE A SQUARE BAKING DISH SUITABLE FOR TURNING OVER WHICH OIL WELL AND LINE WITH CAUL [5] SPRINKLE [on the bottom] A LAYER OF CRUSHED NUTS UPON WHICH PUT SOME PEAS, FULLY COV-ERING THE BOTTOM OF THE SQUASH DISH; ON TOP OF THIS ARRANGE SLICES OF THE BACON [6] LEEKS AND SLICED LUCANIAN SAUSAGE; AGAIN COVER WITH A LAYER OF PEAS AND ALTERNATE ALL THE REST OF THE AVAIL-ABLE EDIBLES IN THE MANNER DESCRIBED UNTIL THE DISH IS FILLED, CONCLUDING AT LAST WITH A LAYER OF PEAS, UTILIZING EVERYTHING. BAKE THIS DISH IN THE OVEN, OR PUT IT INTO A SLOW FIRE [covering it with live coal] SO THAT IT MAY BE BAKED THOROUGHLY. [Next make a sauce of the following] PUT YOLKS OF HARD BOILED EGGS IN THE MORTAR WITH WHITE PEPPER, NUTS, HONEY, WHITE WINE AND A LITTLE BROTH; MIX AND PUT IT INTO A SAUCE PAN TO BE COOKED; WHEN [the sauce is] DONE, TURN OUT THE PEAS INTO A LARGE [silver dish] AND MASK THEM WITH THIS SAUCE WHICH IS CALLED WHITE SAUCE [7].

[1] List. *Pisa farsilis*; Tor. *p. farsilia*; Tac., G.-V. *pisam farsilem* — same as *fartilis*, from *farcio* — fattened, stuffed, or crammed, or as full as it can hold, metaphorically perhaps "supreme style," "most sumptuous," etc.

[2] This meat being fat enough, the oil seems superfluous.

[3] *isicia*, formerly called Greek *hysitia* — any fine forcements, cut into or cooked in tiny dumplings.

[4] *Liaison* wanting in Tor.

[5] Tor. makes no mention of the square dish and its caul lining. Caul is the abdominal membrane.

[6] *petasonis pulpas*; Dann. ham, which is not quite correct. The *petaso* is the shoulder part of pork, either cured or fresh, generally fresh. The cooked pork shoulder here is cut into small pieces. Nothing is said about the utilization of the sow's belly mentioned at the opening of the formula. We assume that the *petaso* can take its place in the dish.

[7] There is nothing just like this dish in the history of gastronomy, considering both the comparatively cheap materials and the refinement of the gastronomic idea which it embodies. The *chartreuses* of Carême are the nearest thing to it. Lister waxes enthusiastic about it.

[187] INDIAN PEAS   *PISAM INDICAM* [1]

COOK PEAS; WHEN SKIMMED, PUT IN THE SAUCE PAN FINELY CHOPPED LEEKS AND CORIANDER TO BE COOKED [with the peas]. TAKE SMALL CUTTLE FISH, MOST DESIRABLE BECAUSE OF THE BLACK LIQUOR AND COOK THEM ALSO. ADD OIL, BROTH AND WINE, A BUNCH OF LEEK AND [green] CORIANDER AND MAKE IT BOIL. WHEN DONE, CRUSH PEPPER, LOVAGE, ORIGANY, A LITTLE WILD CUMIN [2] MOISTEN WITH THE JUICE [of the peas] ADD WINE AND RAISIN WINE TO TASTE; MINCE THE FISH VERY FINE, INCORPORATE IT WITH THE PEAS, AND SPRINKLE WITH PEPPER [3].

[1] Tor. *pisum Indicum.*

[2] Tor., Tac. *casei modicum*; other texts, *carei.*

[3] The texts continues without interruption to the next formula.

[188] ANOTHER WAY   *ALITER*

COOK THE PEAS, WORK WELL [to make a purée] PLACE IN THE COLD, STIRRING UNTIL THEY HAVE COOLED OFF. FINELY CHOP ONIONS AND THE WHITES OF HARD BOILED EGGS, SEASON WITH SALT AND A LITTLE VINEGAR; THE YOLKS PRESS THROUGH A COLANDER INTO AN ENTRÉE DISH, SEASON WITH FRESH OIL AND SERVE [1].

[1] The texts fail to state that the whites, yolks, onions, vinegar and oil must eventually be combined into a dressing very similar to our own modern *vinaigrette*; for decorative and other gastronomic reasons the separate treatment of the whites and the yolks is both ingenious and excellent, and is very often practised in good kitchens today.

[189]   PEAS OR BEANS À LA VITELLIUS
         PISAM VITELLIANAM SIVE FABAM [1]

PEAS OR BEANS WITH YOLKS ARE MADE THUS: [2] COOK
THE PEAS, SMOOTHEN [3] THEM; CRUSH PEPPER, LOVAGE,
GINGER, AND ON THE CONDIMENTS PUT HARD BOILED
YOLKS, 3 OUNCES OF HONEY, ALSO BROTH, WINE AND
VINEGAR; [mix and] PLACE ALL IN A SAUCE PAN; THE
FINELY CHOPPED CONDIMENTS WITH OIL ADDED, PUT ON
THE STOVE TO BE COOKED; WITH THIS FLAVOR THE PEAS
WHICH MUST BE SMOOTH; AND IF THEY BE TOO HARSH
[in taste] ADD HONEY AND SERVE [4].

[1] List. *Pisa Vitelliana* — named for Vitellius, ninth Roman emperor, notorious glutton, according to Hum. who says that V. invented this dish: *ab
auctore Vitellio Imperatore luxui deditissimo*. But Tor. differs; his *pisum uitel-
linum* stands for peas with yolks — *vitellum* — yolk, (also calf) dim. *vitelli-
num*; Tac. *v — am*. Cf. ℞ No. 193.
[2] Tor. sentence wanting in other texts.
[3] *lias* — to make a purée by crushing and straining. Tor. *lævigabis*, from
levigo — meaning the same.
[4] If Vitellius never invented any other dish than this one, his gluttony was
overrated. As a gastronomer he may be safely relegated to the vast multitude of
ill-advised people whose craving for carbohydrates (which is perhaps pathologi-
cal) causes them to accumulate a surplus of fat. This was fatal to Vitellius and
his faithful court baker who is said to have stuck to his master to the last. The
poor emperor's *embonpoint* proved cumbersome when he fled the infuriated
mob. Had he been leaner he might have effected a "getaway." He was dragged
through the streets and murdered, Dec. 21 or 22, A.D. 69.

[190]   ANOTHER WAY   *ALITER PISAM SIVE FABAM*

WHEN [the peas or beans are] SKIMMED MIX BROTH, HONEY,
MUST, CUMIN, RUE, CELERY SEED, OIL AND WINE, STIR [1].
SERVE WITH CRUSHED PEPPER AND SAUSAGE [2].

[1] G.-V. *tudiclabis*; Tor. *misceas*.
[2] *cum isiciis* — bits of forcemeat.

[191]   ANOTHER WAY   *ALITER PISAM SIVE FABAM*

WHEN [the peas or beans are] SKIMMED FLAVOR THEM WITH
CRUSHED PERSIAN [1] LASER, BROTH AND MUST; POUR A
LITTLE OIL OVER AND SERVE.

[1] Parthian, from *Parthia*, a country of Asia.

[192] A TEMPTING DISH OF PEAS
PISAM ADULTERAM [1] VERSATILEM

THIS ADROIT, TEMPTING DISH OF PEAS IS PREPARED IN THIS MANNER: [2] COOK PEAS; BRAINS OR SMALL BIRDS, OR BONED THRUSHES, LUCANIAN SAUSAGE, CHICKEN LIVERS AND GIBLETS — ALL OF WHICH ARE PUT IN A SAUCE PAN; BROTH, OIL AND A BUNCH OF LEEKS, GREEN CORIANDER FINELY CHOPPED, COOK WITH THE BRAINS; CRUSH PEPPER, LOVAGE AND BROTH [3].

[1] Sch., Dann. crafty, i.e. not genuine. *Adulteram* cannot here be used in its most accepted sense, because the peas are genuine, and no attempt is made to adulterate or "fake" this dish in any way, shape or form. Never before have we applied the term "seductive" to any dish, but this is just what *adultera* means. "Tempting" of course is quite common.

[2] Tor. sentence wanting in other texts.

[3] This formula is incomplete or mutilated, the last sentence breaks off in the middle — very likely a description of the sauce or condiments belonging to the peas.

Each and every component of this (really tempting) dish must be cooked separately; they are then composed in a dish, nicely arranged, with the peas in the center, surrounded by the several morsels, with an appropriate gravy made from the natural liquor or juices of the component parts poured over the dish.

[193] PEAS À LA VITELLIUS
PISAM SIVE FABAM VITELLIANAM [1]

PEAS OR BEANS IN THE STYLE OF VITELLIUS PREPARE THUS: [2] [The peas or beans] ARE COOKED, WHEN CAREFULLY SKIMMED, ADD LEEKS, CORIANDER AND MALLOW FLOWERS [3]: WHEN DONE, CRUSH PEPPER, LOVAGE, ORIGANY, AND FENNEL SEED MOISTENED WITH BROTH [and put it] INTO A SAUCE PAN WITH WINE [4], ADDING OIL, HEAT THOROUGHLY AND WHEN BOILING STIR WELL; PUT GREEN OIL ON TOP AND SERVE.

[1] Named for the inventor, Emperor Vitellius; cf. notes to ℞ No. 189. Tor. *Vitellianum*.

[2] Tor. sentence wanting in other texts.

[3] Wanting in Dann.

[4] Tor.

IV

[194]   BEANS IN THE POD   *CONCHICLA* [1]

COOK THE BEANS [2]; MEANWHILE CRUSH PEPPER, LOV-
AGE, CUMIN, GREEN CORIANDER, MOISTENED WITH
BROTH AND WINE, AND ADD [more] BROTH TO TASTE, PUT
INTO THE SAUCE PAN [with the beans] ADDING OIL; HEAT
ON A SLOW FIRE AND SERVE.

[1] Tor. *Concicla* — *conchis* — *conchicula* — young, immature beans,
string or wax, boiled in the shell or pod.

[2] *conchiclam cum faba* — young string beans and (dry, white or kidney)
beans, cooked separately of course and mixed when done, ready for service.

[195]   PEAS IN THE POD APICIAN STYLE
         CONCHICLAM APICIANAM

FOR PEAS IN THE POD [1] APICIAN STYLE TAKE: [2] A
CLEAN EARTHEN POT IN WHICH TO COOK THE PEAS; TO
THE PEAS ADD FINELY CUT LUCANIAN SAUSAGE, LITTLE
PORK CAKES [3], PIECES OF MEAT [4] AND PORK SHOULDER
[5]. CRUSH PEPPER, LOVAGE, ORIGANY, DILL, DRY ONIONS
[6] GREEN CORIANDER MOISTENED WITH BROTH, WINE,
AND ADD [more] BROTH TO TASTE; UNITE THIS WITH THE
PEAS IN THE EARTHEN POT TO WHICH ADD OIL IN SUFFI-
CIENT QUANTITY TO BE ABSORBED BY THE PEAS; FINISH
ON A SLOW FIRE TO GIVE IT LIVE HEAT AND SERVE.

[1] Peas in the pod are likewise called *conchicla*; hence perhaps any legumes
cooked in the shells.

[2] Tor. sentence wanting in other texts.

[3] *isiciola porcina.*

[4] *pulpas* — in this case no specific meat.

[5] *petaso*; Dann. pieces of ham

[6] *cepam siccam* — ordinary dry onions, not shallots.

[196]   SIMPLE DISH OF PEAS IN THE POD
         CONCHICLA DE PISA SIMPLICI [1]

COOK THE PEAS [in the pods] WHEN SKIMMED ADD A
BUNCH [2] OF LEEKS AND GREEN CORIANDER. WHILE BE-
ING COOKED CRUSH PEPPER, LOVAGE, ORIGANY, AND [the
above] BUNCH [of herbs] [3] MOISTEN WITH ITS OWN JUICE,

WINE [4] ENOUGH TO SUIT YOUR TASTE, THEN ADD OIL
AND FINISH ON A SLOW FIRE [5].

[1] Thus G.-V.; Tor. *Concicla Pisorum.*

[2] Sch. *feniculum* instead of *fasciculum.*

[3] G.-V. *de suo sibi fricabis*; Tor. *seorsim f.*

[4] G.-V. wine wanting in Tor.

[5] Brandt, referring to ℞ No. 154, suggests that the things crushed in a
mortar be placed on top of the peas.

[197]   PEAS IN THE POD À LA COMMODUS [1]
CONCHICLA COMMODIANA

MAKE PEAS COMMODIAN STYLE THUS: [2] COOK THE
PEAS, WHEN SKIMMED, CRUSH PEPPER, LOVAGE, DILL,
SHALLOTS MOISTENED WITH BROTH; ADD WINE AND
BROTH TO TASTE: STIR IN A SAUCE PAN [with the peas] TO
COMBINE; FOR EACH SEXTARIUS OF PEAS BEAT 4 EGGS,
AND COMBINE THEM WITH THE PEAS, PLACE ON THE FIRE
TO THICKEN [avoiding ebullition] AND SERVE.

[1] Hum. Named for Commodus, the emperor; List. for Commodus Antonius, son of the philosopher Marcus.

[2] Tor. sentence wanting in other texts.

[198]   ANOTHER STYLE
ALITER CONCHICLAM SIC FACIES [1]

CUT [raw] CHICKEN INTO SMALL PIECES, ADD BROTH,
OIL AND WINE, AND STEW IT. CHOP ONIONS AND CORI-
ANDER FINE AND ADD BRAINS [calf's or pork, parboiled] THE
SKIN AND NERVES REMOVED, TO THE CHICKEN. WHEN
THIS IS COOKED TAKE [the chicken] OUT AND BONE IT. THE
PEAS COOK SEPARATELY, WITHOUT SEASONING, ONLY US-
ING CHOPPED ONIONS AND CORIANDER AND THE BROTH
OF THE CHICKEN; STRAIN [part of] THE PEAS AND AR-
RANGE THEM ALTERNATELY [in a dish with the pieces of chicken,
brains and the unstrained peas] THEN CRUSH PEPPER AND CU-
MIN, MOISTENED WITH CHICKEN BROTH. IN THE MORTAR
BEAT 2 EGGS WITH BROTH TO TASTE, POUR THIS OVER
THE CHICKEN AND PEAS, FINISH ON A SLOW FIRE [1], DISH
OUT ON A HEAP OF PEAS, GARNISH WITH PINE NUTS AND
SERVE.

[1] By congealing in a mould, which is unmoulded on a heap of peas. Danneil
directs to stuff the whole chicken with the pea preparation, brains, etc., and to
poach it in a square pan.

[199]   STUFFED CHICKEN OR SUCKLING PIG
        CONCHICLATUS PULLUS VEL PORCELLUS [1]

BONE [either] CHICKEN [or suckling pig] FROM THE CHICK-
EN REMOVE THE BREAST BONE AND THE [upper joint bones
of the] LEGS; HOLD IT TOGETHER BY MEANS OF WOODEN
SKEWERS, AND MEANWHILE [2] PREPARE [the following
dressing in this manner]: ALTERNATE [inside of the chicken or pig]
PEAS WITH THE PODS [washed and cooked], BRAINS, LU-
CANIAN SAUSAGE, ETC. NOW CRUSH PEPPER, LOVAGE, ORI-
GANY AND GINGER, MOISTENED WITH BROTH, RAISIN
WINE AND WINE TO TASTE, MAKE IT BOIL, WHEN DONE,
USE IT MODERATELY FOR SEASONING AND ALTERNATELY
WITH THE OTHER DRESSING; WRAP [the chicken, or pig] IN
CAUL, PLACE IT IN A BAKING DISH AND PUT IT IN THE
OVEN TO BE COOKED SLOWLY, AND SERVE.

[1] G.-V., Tor. *Concicla farsilis.*
[2] Tor. here splits the formula, using the above title.

V

GRUELS   *TISANAM ET ALICAM* [1]

[200]   BARLEY BROTH
        ALICAM VEL SUCCUM TISANÆ SIC FACIES [2]

CRUSH WELL WASHED BARLEY, SOAKED THE DAY BE-
FORE, PLACE ON THE FIRE TO BE COOKED. WHEN HOT ADD
PLENTY OIL, A SMALL BUNCH OF DILL, DRY ONION, SAT-
URY AND COLOCASIUM, TO BE COOKED TOGETHER BE-
CAUSE THIS GIVES A BETTER JUICE; ADD GREEN CORIAN-
DER AND A LITTLE SALT; BRING IT TO A BOILING POINT.
WHEN WELL HEATED TAKE OUT THE BUNCH [dill] AND
TRANSFER THE BARLEY INTO ANOTHER VESSEL TO AVOID
BURNING ON THE BOTTOM OF THE POT; THIN IT OUT [with
water, broth, milk] AND STRAIN INTO A POT, COVERING THE
TIPS OF THE COLOCASIA [2]. NEXT CRUSH PEPPER, LOVAGE,
A LITTLE DRY FLEA-BANE, CUMIN AND SYLPHIUM, STIR
WELL, ADD VINEGAR, REDUCED MUST AND BROTH; PUT
IT BACK IN THE POT; THE REMAINING COLOCASIA FINISH
ON A GENTLE FIRE.

[1] A repetition of Book IV, Chap. IV, *Tisanam vel sucum*, our ℞ No. 172
[2] Tor. still has difficulties with the vegetable called by Lister *colocasium*.

He reads here *colonium* and *colosium*. G.-V. *colœfium*. Cf. Note 1 to ℞ No. 172 and Note to Nos. 74, 216, 244 and 322.

[201] ANOTHER GRUEL *ALITER TISANAM* [1]

SOAK CHICK-PEAS, LENTILS AND PEAS, CRUSH BARLEY AND COOK WITH THE LEGUMES, WHEN WELL COOKED ADD PLENTY OF OIL. NOW CUT GREENS, LEEKS, CORIANDER, DILL, FENNEL, BEETS, MALLOWS, CABBAGE STRUNKS, ALL SOFT AND GREEN AND VERY FINELY CUT, AND PUT IN A POT. THE CABBAGE COOK [separately; also] CRUSH FENNEL SEED, PLENTY OF IT, ORIGANY, SILPHIUM, AND LOVAGE, AND WHEN GROUND, ADD BROTH TO TASTE, POUR THIS OVER THE PORRIDGE, STIR, AND USE SOME FINELY CHOPPED CABBAGE STEMS TO SPRINKLE ON TOP.

[1] A repetition of ℞ No. 173.

VI

GREEN BEANS *FABACIÆ VIRIDES ET BAIANÆ* [1]

[202] GREEN BEANS *FABACIÆ VIRIDES*

GREEN BEANS ARE COOKED IN BROTH, WITH OIL, GREEN CORIANDER, CUMIN AND CHOPPED LEEKS, AND SERVED.

[1] Beans grown in Baiæ, also called *bajanas* or *bacanas*; beans without skin or pods.

[203] BEANS SAUTÉ *ALITER: FABACIÆ FRICTÆ*

FRIED BEANS ARE SERVED IN BROTH.

[204] MUSTARD BEANS *ALITER: FABACIÆ EX SINAPI*

[The beans previously cooked are seasoned with] CRUSHED MUSTARD SEED, HONEY, NUTS, RUE, CUMIN, AND SERVED WITH VINEGAR.

[205] BAIÆAN BEANS *BAIANAS* [1]

COOKED BEANS FROM BAIÆ ARE CUT FINE [and finished with] RUE, GREEN CELERY, LEEKS, VINEGAR [2] A LITTLE MUST OR RAISIN WINE AND SERVED [3].

[1] Named for Baiæ, a town of Campania, noted for its warm baths; a favorite resort of the Romans.
[2] Wanting in Tor.

[3] These apparently outlandish ways of cooking beans compel us to draw a modern parallel in a cookery book, specializing in Jewish dishes. To prove that Apicius is not dead "by a long shot," we shall quote from Wolf, Rebekka: Kochbuch für Israelitische Frauen, Frankfurt, 1896, 11th edition. As a matter of fact, Rebekka Wolf is outdoing Apicius in strangeness — a case of *Apicium in ipso Apicio*, as Lister sarcastically remarks of Torinus.

Rebekka Wolf: ℞ No. 211 — wash and boil the young beans in fat *bouillon* (Apicius: *oleum et liquamen*) adding a handful of chopped pepperwort (A.: *piper, ligusticum*) and later chopped parsley (A.: *petroselinum*) some sugar (A.: *mel pavo* — little honey) and pepper. Beans later in the season are cooked with potatoes. The young beans are tied with flour dissolved in water, or with roux.

Id. ibid., ℞ No. 212, Beans Sweet-Sour. Boil in water, fat, salt, add vinegar, sugar or syrup, "English aromatics" and spices, lemon peel, and a little pepper; bind with roux.

Id. ibid., ℞ No. 213, Cut Pickled Beans (*Schneidebohnen*) prepare as ℞ No. 212, but if you would have them more delicious, take instead of the roux grated chocolate, sugar, cinnamon, lemon peel and lemon juice, and some claret. If not sour enough, add vinegar, but right here you must add more fat; you may lay on top of this dish a bouquet of sliced apples.

Id. ibid., ℞ No. 214, Beans and Pears. Take cut and pickled beans and prepare as above. To this add peeled fresh pears, cut into quarters; then sugar, lemon peel cut thin, cinnamon, "English" mixed spices, and at last the roux, thinned with broth. This dish must be sweet and very fat.

As for exotic combinations, Apicius surely survives here, is even surpassed by this Jewish cookery book where, no doubt, very ancient traditions have been stored away.

VII

[206]   THE HERB FENUGREEK *FŒNUM GRÆCUM* [1]

FENUGREEK [is prepared] IN BROTH, OIL AND WINE.

[1] Tor. or *fenum*; G.-V. *Fænum*.

VIII

[207]   GREEN STRING BEANS AND CHICK-PEAS *PHASEOLI* [1] *VIRIDES ET CICER*

ARE SERVED WITH SALT, CUMIN, OIL, AND A LITTLE PURE WINE.

[1] Tor. *Faseolus*, the bean with a long, sabre-like pod; a phasel, kidney bean, when ripened.

[208] ANOTHER WAY   *ALITER FASEOLUS ET CICER*

[Beans or chick-peas] ARE COOKED IN A WINE SAUCE AND SEASONED WITH PEPPER [1].

[1] Dann. and Goll.: "roasted" beans.

[209] BOILED, SUMPTUOUSLY
ET ELIXATI, SUMPTO [1]

AND COOK THE BEANS, IN A RICH MANNER, REMOVE THE SEEDS AND SERVE [as a Salad 2], WITH HARD EGGS, GREEN FENNEL, PEPPER, BROTH, A LITTLE REDUCED WINE AND A LITTLE SALT, OR SERVE THEM IN SIMPLER WAYS, AS YOU MAY SEE FIT.

[1] The original continues with the preceding formula.

[2] For a salad we would add finely chopped onion, pepper, and some lemon juice.

The purpose of removing the seeds is obscure. G.-V. reads *semine cum ovis*; Tac. *semie*; Hum. *s. cum lobis*. The passage may mean to sprinkle (sow) with hard boiled (and finely chopped) eggs, which is often done on a salad and other dishes.

END OF BOOK V

EXPLICIT APICII OSPRION LIBER QUINTUS [Tac.]

ADJUSTABLE TABLE

　　Polychrome marble in bronze frame. Four elaborately designed bronze legs, braced and hinged, so that the table may be raised or lowered. The legs end in claw feet resting on a molded base. Above they are encircled with leaves, from which emerge young satyrs, each holding a rabbit under the left arm. The legs below the acanthus leaves are ornamented with elaborate floral patterns, inlaid, with other inlaid patterns on the connecting braces and around the frame of the marble top. Bronze and marble tables that could be folded and taken down after banquets were used by the Babylonians centuries before this table was designed in Pompeii. Ntl. Mus., Naples, 72994; Field M. 24290.

APICIUS
Book VI

THE GREAT CRATER

Found at Hildesheim in 1868. This and a number of other pieces form the collection known as The Hildesheim Treasure, now at the Kaiser Friedrich Museum, Berlin.

This wine crater is entirely of silver, a piece of supreme workmanship of Roman origin. Very delicate decoration, anticipating the Renaissance: Winged griffins and other monsters, half ox, half lion, at the base; aquatic animals, genii angling and spearing fish.

There is a second vessel inside, acting as a liner, to take the weight of the fluid off the decorated bowl. The complete weight is 9451.8 gr., but the inner liner is stamped CVM BASI PONDO XXXXI — 41 pounds with the base. The weight of silver pieces was inscribed as a check on the slaves.

The bowl is 0.36 meter (about 14¼ inches) in height and 0.353 meter in diameter. It stands on the tripod which is depicted separately.

THE DIONYSOS CUP

The Dionysos head in the center and the two satyrs are modeled realistically by a most able artist. Lion and lioness heads on the other side. Hildesheim Treasure.

BOOK VI. FOWL

Lib. VI. Aëropetes [*1*]

CHAP.   I. OSTRICH.

CHAP.   II. CRANE OR DUCK, PARTRIDGE, DOVES, WOOD PIGEON, SQUAB AND DIVERS BIRDS.

CHAP. III. THRUSH [2].

CHAP. IV. FIGPECKER [2].

CHAP.   V. PEACOCK [2].

CHAP. VI. PHEASANT [2].

CHAP. VII. GOOSE.

CHAP. VIII. CHICKEN.

[1] Tac., Tor. *Trophetes*; probably an error in their rendering. List. *Aëroptes*, Greek for Fowl.

[2] The titles of these chapters and the classification is not adhered in the text of Book VI. The chapters are actually inscribed as follows:

Chap. I, Ostrich; II, Crane or Duck, Partridge, Turtle Dove, Wood Pigeon, Squab and divers birds; III, Partridge, Heathcock (Woodcock), Turtle Dove; IV, Wood Pigeon, Squab [Domestic Fattened Fowl, Flamingo]; V, Sauce for divers birds; VI, Flamingo; VII, In Order That Birds May Not Be Spoiled; VIII, Goose; IX, Chicken.

I

OSTRICH   *IN STRUTHIONE*

[210] BOILED OSTRICH   *IN STRUTHIONE ELIXO*

[A stock in which to cook ostrich] PEPPER, MINT, CUMIN, LEEKS [1], CELERY SEED, DATES, HONEY, VINEGAR, RAISIN WINE, BROTH, A LITTLE OIL. BOIL THIS IN THE STOCK KETTLE [with the ostrich, remove the bird when done, strain the liquid] THICKEN WITH ROUX. [To this sauce] ADD THE OSTRICH MEAT CUT IN CONVENIENT PIECES, SPRIN-

KLE WITH PEPPER. IF YOU WISH IT MORE SEASONED OR TASTY, ADD GARLIC [during coction].

[1] G.-V. *Cuminum*; Tor. C., *porrum*, which is more likely.

[211]   ANOTHER OSTRICH STEW
ALITER [in] STRUTHIONE ELIXO

PEPPER, LOVAGE, THYME, ALSO SATURY, HONEY, MUSTARD, VINEGAR, BROTH AND OIL.

II

CRANE, DUCK, PARTRIDGE, DOVE, WOOD PIGEON, SQUAB, AND DIVERS BIRDS
IN GRUE VEL ANATE PERDICE TURTURE PALUMBO COLUMBO ET DIVERSIS AVIBUS

[212]   CRANE OR DUCK   *GRUEM VEL ANATEM*

WASH [the fowl] AND DRESS IT NICELY [1] PUT IN A STEW POT, ADD WATER, SALT AND DILL, PARBOIL [2] SO AS TO HAVE THEM HALF DONE, UNTIL THE MEAT IS HARD, REMOVE THEM, PUT THEM IN A SAUCE PAN [to be finished by braising] WITH OIL, BROTH, A BUNCH OF ORIGANY AND CORIANDER; WHEN NEARLY DONE, ADD A LITTLE REDUCED MUST, TO GIVE IT COLOR. MEANWHILE CRUSH PEPPER, LOVAGE, CUMIN, CORIANDER, LASER ROOT, RUE [moistened with] REDUCED WINE AND SOME HONEY, ADD SOME OF THE FOWL BROTH [3] TO IT AND VINEGAR TO TASTE; EMPTY [the sauce] INTO A SAUCE PAN, HEAT, BIND WITH ROUX, AND [strain] THE SAUCE OVER THE FOWL IN AN ENTRÉE DISH.

[1] *Lavas et ornas*, i.e., singe, empty carcass of intestines, truss or bind it to keep its shape during coction, and, usually, lard it with either strips or slices of fat pork and stuff the carcass with greens, celery leaves, etc.

[2] *Dimidia coctura decoques*. Apicius here pursues the right course for the removable of any disagreeable taste often adhering to aquatic fowl, feeding on fish or food found in the water, by parboiling the meat. Cf. ℞ No. 214.

[3] Again, as so often: *ius de suo sibi*; here the liquor of the braising pan, for stock in which the fowl is parboiled cannot be used for reasons set forth in Note 2.

[213]   ANOTHER WAY OF COOKING CRANE, DUCK
        OR CHICKEN
        ALITER IN GRUE [VEL] IN ANATE VEL IN
        PULLO

PEPPER, SHALLOTS, LOVAGE, CUMIN, CELERY SEED,
PRUNES OR DAMASCUS PLUMS STONES REMOVED, FRESH
MUST, VINEGAR [1] BROTH, REDUCED MUST AND OIL. BOIL
THE CRANE; WHILE COOKING IT TAKE CARE THAT ITS
HEAD IS NOT TOUCHED BY THE WATER BUT THAT IT RE-
MAINS WITHOUT. WHEN THE CRANE IS DONE, WRAP IT IN
A HOT TOWEL, AND PULL THE HEAD OFF SO THAT THE
SINEWS FOLLOW IN A MANNER THAT THE MEAT AND THE
BONES REMAIN; FOR ONE CANNOT ENJOY THE HARD SIN-
EWS [2].

[1] Dann. mead.
[2] Remarkable ingenuity! Try this on your turkey legs. Danneil is of the
opinion that the head and its feathers were to be saved for decorative purposes,
in style during the middle ages when game bird patties were decorated with the
fowl's plumage, a custom which survived to Danneil's time (ca. 1900). But this
is not likely to be the case here, for it would be a simple matter to skin the bird
before cooking it in order to save the plumage for the taxidermist.

[214]   CRANE OR DUCK WITH TURNIPS
        GRUEM VEL ANATEM EX RAPIS [1]

TAKE OUT [remove entrails, 2] CLEAN WASH AND DRESS
[the bird] AND PARBOIL [2] IT IN WATER WITH SALT AND
DILL. NEXT PREPARE TURNIPS AND COOK THEM IN WATER
WHICH IS TO BE SQUEEZED OUT [3]. TAKE THEM OUT OF
THE POT AND WASH THEM AGAIN [4]. AND PUT INTO A
SAUCE PAN THE DUCK WITH OIL, BROTH, A BUNCH OF
LEEKS AND CORIANDER; THE TURNIPS CUT INTO SMALL
PIECES; THESE PUT ON TOP OF THE [duck] IN ORDER TO
FINISH COOKING. WHEN HALF DONE, TO GIVE IT COLOR,
ADD REDUCED MUST. THE SAUCE IS PREPARED SEPARATE-
LY: PEPPER, CUMIN, CORIANDER, LASER ROOT MOISTENED
WITH VINEGAR AND DILUTED WITH ITS OWN BROTH [of
the fowl]; BRING THIS TO A BOILING POINT, THICKEN WITH
ROUX. [In a deep dish arrange the duck] ON TOP OF THE TURNIPS
[strain the sauce over it] SPRINKLE WITH PEPPER AND SERVE.

[1] Duck and Turnips, a dish much esteemed on the Continent today. Only

few prepare it correctly as does Old Apicius; hence it is not popular with the multitude.

[2] Tac., Tor. *excipies*; Hum. *legendum: ex rapis.*

[3] G.-V. *ut exbromari possint*; Tor. *expromi*; Hum. *expromari*; all of which does not mean anything. To cook the turnips so that they can be squeezed out (*exprimo*, from *ex* and *premo*) is the proper thing to do from a culinary standpoint.

[4] The turnips are cooked half, the water removed, and finished with the duck, as prescribed by Apicius. It is really admirable to see how he handles these food materials in order to remove any disagreeable flavor, which may be the case both with the turnips (the small white variety) and the duck. Such careful treatment is little known nowadays even in the best kitchens. Cf. Note 2 to ℞ No. 212.

[215] ANOTHER [SAUCE FOR] CRANE OR DUCK
ALITER IN GRUEM VEL ANATEM ELIXAM

PEPPER, LOVAGE, CUMIN, DRY CORIANDER, MINT, ORIGANY, PINE NUTS, DATES, BROTH, OIL, HONEY, MUSTARD AND WINE [1].

[1] Supposedly the ingredients for a sauce in which the parboiled fowl is braised and served.

[216] ROAST CRANE OR DUCK
ALITER GRUEM VEL ANATEM ASSAM

POUR OVER [the roast bird] THIS GRAVY: CRUSH PEPPER, LOVAGE, ORIGANY WITH BROTH, HONEY, A LITTLE VINEGAR AND OIL; BOIL IT WELL, THICKEN WITH ROUX [strain] IN THIS SAUCE PLACE SMALL PIECES OF PARBOILED PUMPKIN OR COLOCASIUM [1] SO THAT THEY ARE FINISHED IN THE SAUCE; ALSO COOK WITH IT CHICKEN FEET AND GIBLETS (all of which) SERVE IN A CHAFING DISH, SPRINKLE WITH FINE PEPPER AND SERVE.

[1] Cf. ℞ Nos. 74, 216, 244, 322.

[217] BOILED CRANE OR DUCK IN ANOTHER MANNER
ALITER IN GRUE VEL ANATE ELIXA

PEPPER, LOVAGE, CELERY SEED, ROCKET, OR CORIANDER, MINT, DATES, HONEY, VINEGAR, BROTH, REDUCED MUST AND MUSTARD. LIKEWISE USED FOR FOWL ROAST [braised] IN THE POT.

III

WAYS TO PREPARE PARTRIDGE, HEATH-COCK OR WOODCOCK, AND BOILED TURTLE-DOVE
IN PERDICE ET ATTAGENA ET IN TURTURE ELIXIS

[218] PARTRIDGE   *IN PERDICE*

PEPPER, LOVAGE, CELERY SEED, MINT, MYRTLE BERRIES, ALSO RAISINS, HONEY [1] WINE, VINEGAR, BROTH, AND OIL. USE IT COLD [2] THE PARTRIDGE IS SCALDED WITH ITS FEATHERS, AND WHILE WET THE FEATHERS ARE TAKEN OFF; [the hair singed] IT IS THEN COOKED IN ITS OWN JUICE [braised] AND WHEN DONE WILL NOT BE HARD IF CARE IS TAKEN [to baste it]. SHOULD IT REMAIN HARD [if it is old] YOU MUST CONTINUE TO COOK IT UNTIL IT IS TENDER.

[1] Honey wanting in Tor.
[2] G.-V. *Aliter.* This is one formula.

[219]   [SAUCE] FOR PARTRIDGE, HEATH-COCK AND
         TURTLE-DOVE
         IN PERDICE ET ATTAGENA ET IN TURTURE

PEPPER, LOVAGE, MINT, RUE SEED, BROTH, PURE WINE, AND OIL, HEATED.

IV

WOOD PIGEONS, SQUABS, FATTENED FOWL, FLAMINGO
IN PALUMBIS COLUMBIS AVIBUS IN ALTILE ET IN FENICOPTERO

[220]   FOR ROASTS: PEPPER, LOVAGE, CORIANDER, CARRAWAY, SHALLOTS, MINT, YOLKS OF EGG, DATES, HONEY, VINEGAR, BROTH, OIL AND WINE.

[221]   ANOTHER [sauce] FOR BOILED [birds]
         ALITER IN ELIXIS

TO THE BOILED FOWL ADD [1] PEPPER, CARRAWAY, CELERY SEED, PARSLEY, CONDIMENTS, MORTARIA [2] DATES, HONEY, VINEGAR, WINE, OIL AND MUSTARD.

[1] Tor. wanting in other texts.
[2] *Mortaria*: herbs, spices, things pounded in the "mortar." Cf. ℞ No. 38.

[222]   ANOTHER [sauce]   *ALITER*

PEPPER, LOVAGE, PARSLEY, CELERY SEED, RUE, PINE
NUTS, DATES, HONEY, VINEGAR, BROTH, MUSTARD AND
A LITTLE OIL.

[223]   ANOTHER [sauce]   *ALITER*

PEPPER, LOVAGE, LASER, WINE [1] MOISTENED WITH
BROTH. ADD WINE AND BROTH TO TASTE. MASK THE
WOOD PIGEON OR SQUAB WITH IT. SPRINKLE WITH PEP-
PER [2] AND SERVE.

[1] Tac., Tor. *laserum, vinum*; G.-V. *l. vivum*.
[2] Wanting in Tor.

V

[224]   SAUCE FOR DIFFERENT BIRDS
        IUS IN DIVERSIS AVIBUS

PEPPER, DRY CUMIN, CRUSHED. LOVAGE, MINT, SEED-
LESS RAISINS OR DAMASCUS PLUMS, LITTLE HONEY, MYR-
TLE WINE TO TASTE, VINEGAR, BROTH, AND OIL. HEAT
AND WHIP IT WELL WITH CELERY AND SATURY [1].

[1] For centuries sauce whips were made of dry and green twigs, the bark
of which was carefully peeled off.

[225]   ANOTHER SAUCE FOR FOWL
        ALITER IUS IN AVIBUS

PEPPER, LOVAGE, PARSLEY, DRY MINT, FENNEL BLOS-
SOMS [1] MOISTENED WITH WINE; ADD ROASTED NUTS
FROM PONTUS [2] OR ALMONDS, A LITTLE HONEY, WINE,
VINEGAR, AND BROTH TO TASTE. PUT OIL IN A POT, AND
HEAT AND STIR THE SAUCE, ADDING GREEN CELERY SEED,
CAT-MINT; CARVE THE FOWL AND COVER WITH THE
SAUCE [3].

[1] Dann. *Cnecus*.
[2] Turkish hazelnuts.
[3] Tor. continuing without interruption.

[226]   WHITE SAUCE FOR BOILED FOWL
        IUS CANDIDUM IN AVEM ELIXAM

PEPPER, LOVAGE, CUMIN, CELERY SEED, TOASTED NUTS
FROM PONTUS, OR ALMONDS, ALSO SHELLED PINE NUTS,
HONEY [1] A LITTLE BROTH, VINEGAR AND OIL.

[1] Tor. *vel*; List. *mel*.

[227]   GREEN SAUCE FOR FOWL
IUS VIRIDE IN AVIBUS

PEPPER, CARRAWAY, INDIAN SPIKENARD, CUMIN, BAY LEAVES, ALL KINDS OF GREEN HERBS, DATES, HONEY, VINEGAR, WINE, LITTLE BROTH, AND OIL.

[228]   WHITE SAUCE FOR BOILED GOOSE
IUS CANDIDUM IN ANSERE ELIXO

PEPPER, CARRAWAY, CUMIN, CELERY SEED, THYME, ONION, LASER ROOT, TOASTED NUTS, HONEY, VINEGAR, BROTH AND OIL [1]

[1] A "sweet-sour" white sauce with herbs and spices is often served with goose in northern Germany.

[229]   TREATMENT OF STRONG SMELLING BIRDS OF EVERY DESCRIPTION
AD AVES HIRCOSAS [1] *OMNI GENERE*

FOR BIRDS OF ALL KINDS THAT HAVE A GOATISH [1] SMELL [2] PEPPER, LOVAGE, THYME, DRY MINT, SAGE, DATES, HONEY, VINEGAR, WINE, BROTH, OIL, REDUCED MUST, MUSTARD. THE BIRDS WILL BE MORE LUSCIOUS AND NUTRITIOUS, AND THE FAT PRESERVED, IF YOU ENVELOP THEM IN A DOUGH OF FLOUR AND OIL AND BAKE THEM IN THE OVEN [3].

[1] Probably game birds in an advanced stage of *"haut goût"* (as the Germans use the antiquated French term), or *"mortification"* as the French cook says. Possibly also such birds as crows, black birds, buzzards, etc., and fish-feeding fowl. Moreover, it must be borne in mind that the refrigeration facilities of the ancients were not too good and that fresh goods spoiled quickly. Hence, perhaps, excessive seasoning, at least, as compared to our modern methods.

List. *aves piscivoras*; Hum. thinks the birds to be downright spoiled: *olidas, rancidas, & grave olentes.*

[2] Tor. Sentence wanting in other texts.

[3] For birds with a goatish smell Apicius should have repeated his excellent formula in ℞ No. 212, the method of parboiling the birds before final coction, if, indeed, one cannot dispense with such birds altogether. The above recipe does not in the least indicate how to treat smelly birds. Wrapping them in dough would vastly increase the ill-savour.

As for game birds, we agree with most connoisseurs that they should have just a suspicion of *"haut goût"* — a condition of advanced mellowness after the *rigor mortis* has disappeared.

[230] ANOTHER TREATMENT OF ODOR
ALIUD CONTRA UIROSUM ODOREM [1]

[IF THE BIRDS SMELL, 1] STUFF THE INSIDE WITH CRUSH-
ED FRESH OLIVES, SEW UP [the aperture] AND THUS COOK,
THEN RETIRE THE COOKED OLIVES.

[1] Tor.; other texts *aliter avem*, i.e. that the olive treatment is not necessarily confined to ill smelling birds alone.

VI

[231] FOR FLAMINGO [and Parrot]
IN PHŒNICOPTERO

SCALD [1] THE FLAMINGO, WASH AND DRESS IT, PUT IT
IN A POT, ADD WATER, SALT, DILL, AND A LITTLE VINE-
GAR, TO BE PARBOILED. FINISH COOKING WITH A BUNCH
OF LEEKS AND CORIANDER, AND ADD SOME REDUCED
MUST TO GIVE IT COLOR. IN THE MORTAR CRUSH PEPPER,
CUMIN, CORIANDER, LASER ROOT, MINT, RUE, MOISTEN
WITH VINEGAR, ADD DATES, AND THE FOND OF THE BRAIS-
ED BIRD, THICKEN, [strain] COVER THE BIRD WITH THE
SAUCE AND SERVE. PARROT IS PREPARED IN THE SAME
MANNER.

[1] Prior to removing the feathers; also singe the fine feathers and hair.

[232] ANOTHER WAY   *ALITER*

ROAST THE BIRD. CRUSH PEPPER, LOVAGE, CELERY SEED,
SESAM [1] PARSLEY, MINT, SHALLOTS, DATES, HONEY,
WINE, BROTH, VINEGAR, OIL, REDUCED MUST TO TASTE.

[1] Tor. *sesamum, defrutum*; G.-V. s. *frictum*.

VII

[233] TO PREVENT BIRDS FROM SPOILING
AVES OMNES NE LIQUESCANT

SCALDED WITH THE FEATHERS BIRDS WILL NOT ALWAYS
BE JUICY; IT IS BETTER TO FIRST EMPTY THEM THROUGH
THE NECK AND STEAM THEM SUSPENDED OVER A KETTLE
WITH WATER [1].

[1] Dry picking is of course the best method. Apicius is trying to overcome
the evils of scalding fowl with the feathers. This formula is mutilated; the
various texts differ considerably.

VIII

[FOR GOOSE]   [*IN ANSERE*]

[234]   BOILED GOOSE WITH COLD APICIAN SAUCE
  ANSEREM ELIXUM EX IURE APICIANO FRIGIDO

CRUSH PEPPER, LOVAGE, CORIANDER SEED [1] MINT, RUE,
MOISTEN WITH BROTH AND A MODERATE AMOUNT OF
OIL. TAKE THE COOKED GOOSE OUT OF THE POT AND
WHILE HOT WIPE IT CLEAN WITH A TOWEL, POUR THE
SAUCE OVER IT AND SERVE.

[1] G.-V.; Tor. (fresh) coriander, more suited for a cold sauce.

IX

[FOR CHICKEN]   [IN PULLO]

[235]   RAW SAUCE FOR BOILED CHICKEN
  IN PULLO ELIXO IUS CRUDUM

PUT IN THE MORTAR DILL SEED, DRY MINT, LASER ROOT,
MOISTEN WITH VINEGAR, FIG WINE, BROTH, A LITTLE
MUSTARD, OIL AND REDUCED MUST, AND SERVE [1]
[Known as] DILL CHICKEN [2].

[1] This and the preceding cold dressings are more or less variations of our
modern cold dressings that are used for cold dishes of all kinds, especially salads.

[2] Tor. heads the following formula *præparatio pulli anethi* — chicken in
dill sauce, which is the correct description of the above formula. Tac., G.-V.
also commence the next with *pullum anethatum*, which is not correct, as the
following recipe contains no dill.

[236]   ANOTHER CHICKEN *ALITER PULLUS* [1]

A LITTLE HONEY IS MIXED WITH BROTH; THE COOKED
[parboiled] CHICKEN IS CLEANED [skin taken off, sinews, etc., re-
moved] THE CARCASS DRIED WITH A TOWEL, QUARTERED,
THE PIECES IMMERSED IN BROTH [2] SO THAT THE SAVOUR
PENETRATES THOROUGHLY. FRY THE PIECES [in the pan]
POUR OVER THEIR OWN GRAVY, SPRINKLE WITH PEPPER,
SERVE.

[1] Hum., List. cf. Note 2 to ℞ No. 235.

[2] Marinated; but the nature of this marinade is not quite clear; a spicy
marinade of wine and herbs and spices would be appropriate for certain game
birds, but chicken ordinarily requires no marinade except some oil before frying.
It is possible that Apicius left the cooked chicken in the broth to prevent it from
drying out, which is good.

[237] CHICKEN PARTHIAN STYLE
PULLUM PARTHICUM [1]

DRESS THE CHICKEN CAREFULLY [2] AND QUARTER IT. CRUSH PEPPER, LOVAGE AND A LITTLE CARRAWAY [3] MOISTENED WITH BROTH, AND ADD WINE TO TASTE. [After frying] PLACE THE CHICKEN IN AN EARTHEN DISH [4] POUR THE SEASONING OVER IT, ADD LASER AND WINE [5] LET IT ASSIMILATE WITH THE SEASONING AND BRAISE THE CHICKEN TO A POINT. WHEN DONE SPRINKLE WITH PEPPER AND SERVE.

[1] Lister is of the opinion that the *pullus Parthicus* is a kind of chicken that came originally from Asia, Parthia being a country of Asia, the present Persia or northern India, a chicken of small size with feathers on its feet, i.e., a bantam.

[2] Pluck, singe, empty, wash, trim. The texts: *a navi.* Hum. *hoc est, à parte posteriore ventris, qui ut navis cavus & figuræ ejus non dissimile est.* Dan. takes this literally, but *navo* (*navus*) here simply means "to perform diligently."

[3] Tor. *casei modicum*; List. *carei* — more likely than cheese.

[4] *Cumana* — an earthenware casserole, excellent for that purpose.

[5] G.-V. *laser* [*et*] *vivum.*

[238] CHICKEN SOUR *PULLUM OXYZOMUM*

A GOOD-SIZED GLASS OF OIL, A SMALLER GLASS OF BROTH, AND THE SMALLEST MEASURE OF VINEGAR, 6 SCRUPLES OF PEPPER, PARSLEY AND A BUNCH OF LEEKS.

G.-V. [*laseris*] *satis modice.*

These directions are very vague. If the raw chicken is quartered, fried in the oil, and then braised in the broth with a dash of vinegar, the bunch of leeks and parsley, seasoned with pepper and a little salt, we have a dish gastronomically correct. The leeks may be served as a garnish, the gravy, properly reduced and strained over the chicken which like in the previous formula is served in a casserole.

[239] GUINEA HEN *PULLUM NUMIDICUM*

PREPARE [1] THE CHICKEN [as usual; par-] BOIL IT; CLEAN IT [2] SEASONED WITH LASER AND PEPPER, AND FRY [in the pan; next] CRUSH PEPPER, CUMIN, CORIANDER SEED, LASER ROOT, RUE, FIG DATES AND NUTS, MOISTENED WITH VINEGAR, HONEY, BROTH AND OIL TO TASTE [3] WHEN BOILING THICKEN WITH ROUX [strain] POUR OVER THE CHICKEN, SPRINKLE WITH PEPPER AND SERVE.

[1] *Curas.*

[2] Remove skin, tissues, bones, etc., cut in pieces and marinate in the pickle.

[3] Immerse the chicken pieces in this sauce and braise them to a point.

[240] CHICKEN WITH LASER   *PULLUM LASERATUM*

DRESS THE CHICKEN CAREFULLY [1] CLEAN, GARNISH [2] AND PLACE IN AN EARTHEN CASSEROLE. CRUSH PEPPER, LOVAGE, LASER MOISTENED WITH WINE [3] ADD BROTH AND WINE TO TASTE, AND PUT THIS ON THE FIRE; WHEN DONE SERVE WITH PEPPER SPRINKLED OVER.

[1] *a navi.* cf. Note 2 to ℞ No. 237.
[2] G.-V. *lavabis, ornabis,* with vegetables, etc.
[3] G.-V. *laser vivum.*

[241] ROAST CHICKEN   *PULLUM PAROPTUM*

A LITTLE LASER, 6 SCRUPLES OF PEPPER, A GLASS OF OIL, A GLASS OF BROTH, AND A LITTLE PARSLEY.

[1] *Paropsis, parapsis,* from the Greek, a platter, dish.
A most incomplete formula. It does not state whether the ingredients are to be added to the sauce or the dressing. We have an idea that the chicken is pickled in this solution before roasting and that the pickle is used in making the gravy.

[242] BOILED CHICKEN IN ITS OWN BROTH
PULLUM ELIXUM EX IURE SUO

CRUSH PEPPER, CUMIN, A LITTLE THYME, FENNEL SEED, MINT, RUE, LASER ROOT, MOISTENED WITH VINEGAR, ADD FIG DATES [1] WORK WELL AND MAKE IT SAVORY WITH HONEY, VINEGAR, BROTH AND OIL TO TASTE: THE BOILED CHICKEN PROPERLY CLEANED AND DRIED [with the towel] IS MASKED WITH THIS SAUCE [2].

[1] Goll. cloves — *cariophyllus*; the originals have *caryotam* and *careotam*.
[2] Apparently another cold sauce of the vinaigrette type similar to ℞ No. 235.

[243] CHICKEN AND PUMPKIN
PULLUM ELIXUM CUM CUCURBITIS ELIXIS

TO THE ABOVE DESCRIBED DRESSING ADD MUSTARD, POUR OVER [1] AND SERVE.

G.-V. *Perfundes*; Tor. *piper fundes.*
The pumpkin, not mentioned here, is likewise served cold boiled, seasoned with the same dressing. It is perhaps used for stuffing the chicken and cooked simultaneously with the same.

[244] CHICKEN AND DASHEENS [1]
PULLUM ELIXUM CUM COLOCASIIS ELIXIS

THE ABOVE SAUCE IS ALSO USED FOR THIS DISH. STUFF THE CHICKEN WITH [peeled] DASHEENS AND [stoned] GREEN OLIVES, THOUGH NOT TOO MUCH SO THAT THE DRESSING MAY HAVE ROOM FOR EXPANSION, TO PREVENT BURSTING WHILE THE CHICKEN IS BEING COOKED IN THE POT. HOLD IT DOWN WITH A SMALL BASKET, LIFT IT UP FREQUENTLY [2] AND HANDLE CAREFULLY SO THAT THE CHICKEN DOES NOT BURST [3].

[1] Dasheens are the equivalent of the ancient colocasium; at least they are very close relatives. Cf. Notes to ℞ Nos. 74, 216, 244, 322.

[2] For inspection. G.-V. *levas*; Tor. *lavabis*, for which there is no reason.

[3] Dann. and Goll., not knowing the colocasium or dasheen have entirely erroneous versions of this formula. The dasheen is well adapted for the stuffing of fowl. Ordinarily the dasheen is boiled or steamed, mashed, seasoned and then stuffed inside of a raw chicken which is then roasted. Being very starchy, the dasheen readily absorbs the fats and juices of the roast, making a delicious dressing, akin in taste to a combined potato and chestnut purée.

As the above chicken is cooked in *bouillon* or water, the dasheen may be used. in a raw state for filling. We have tried this method. Instead of confining the chicken in a basket, we have tied it in a napkin and boiled slowly until done. Serve cold, with the above dressing.

[245] CHICKEN À LA VARUS [1]
PULLUS VARDANUS

COOK THE CHICKEN IN THIS STOCK: BROTH, OIL, WINE, A BUNCH OF LEEKS, CORIANDER, SATURY; WHEN DONE, CRUSH PEPPER, NUTS WITH 2 GLASSES OF WATER [2] AND THE JUICE OF THE CHICKEN. RETIRE THE BUNCHES OF GREENS, ADD MILK TO TASTE. THE THINGS CRUSHED IN THE MORTAR ADD TO THE CHICKEN AND COOK IT TOGETHER: THICKEN THE SAUCE WITH BEATEN WHITES OF EGG [3] AND POUR THE SAUCE OVER THE CHICKEN. THIS IS CALLED "WHITE SAUCE."

[1] G.-V. *Vardanus*; Tor. *Vardamus*; Hum. *Vardanus legendum, puto, Varianus, portentuosæ luxuriæ Imperator.* Hum. thinks the dish is dedicated to emperor Varianus (?) The word may also be the adjective of Varus, Quintilius V., commander of colonial armies and glutton, under Augustus. Varus committed suicide after his defeat in the Teutoburg Forest by the Germans.

[2] G.-V. broth, own stock — *ius de suo sibi.*

[3] Strain, avoid ebullition after the eggs have been added. Most unusual

liaison; usually the yolks are used for this purpose. The whites are consistent with the name of the sauce.

[246] CHICKEN À LA FRONTO [1]
PULLUM FRONTONIANUM

A HALF-COOKED CHICKEN MARINADED IN A PICKLE OF BROTH, MIXED WITH OIL, TO WHICH IS ADDED A BUNCH OF DILL, LEEKS, SATURY AND GREEN CORIANDER. FINISH IT IN THIS BROTH. WHEN DONE, TAKE THE CHICKEN OUT [2] DRESS IT NICELY ON A DISH, POUR OVER THE [sauce, colored with] REDUCED MUST, SPRINKLE WITH PEPPER AND SERVE.

[1] Named for a Roman by the name of Fronto. There is a sucking pig à la Fronto, too. Cf. ℞ No. 374. M. Cornelius Fronto was orator and author during the reign of Emperor Hadrian. According to Dann. a certain Frontone under Emperor Severus.

[2] List., G.-V. *levabis*; Tor. *lavabis*, for which there is little or no occasion. He may mean to clean, i.e. remove skin, tissues, sinews, small bones, etc.

[247] CREAMED CHICKEN WITH PASTE [1]
PULLUS TRACTOGALATUS [2]

COOK THE CHICKEN [as follows, in] BROTH, OIL, WITH WINE ADDED, TO WHICH ADD A BUNCH OF CORIANDER AND [green] ONIONS. WHEN DONE TAKE IT OUT [3] [strain and save] THE BROTH, AND PUT IT IN A NEW SAUCE PAN, ADD MILK AND A LITTLE SALT, HONEY AND A PINT [4] OF WATER, THAT IS, A THIRD PART: PLACE IT BACK ON A SLOW FIRE TO SIMMER. FINALLY BREAK [the paste, 1] PUT IT LITTLE BY LITTLE INTO [the boiling broth] STIRRING WELL SO IT WILL NOT BURN. PUT THE CHICKEN IN, EITHER WHOLE OR IN PIECES [5] DISH IT OUT IN A DEEP DISH. THIS COVER WITH THE FOLLOWING SAUCE [6] PEPPER, LOVAGE, ORIGANY, MOISTENED WITH HONEY AND A LITTLE REDUCED MUST. ADD SOME OF THE [chicken] BROTH, HEAT IN A SMALL SAUCE PAN AND WHEN IT BOILS THICKEN WITH ROUX [7] AND SERVE.

[1] Spätzle, noodles, macaroni; this dish is the ancient "Chicken Tetrazzini." Dann. Chicken pie or patty.

[2] *tractum* and *gala*, prepared with paste and milk. Cf. *tractomelitus*, from *tractum* and *meli*, paste and honey.

[3] Cf. Note 2 to ℞ Nos. 244 and 246.

[4] List. *minimum*; Tor. *heminam*; Sch. *eminam*. See Measures. The noodle paste should be cooked separately in the water.

[5] List. *vel carptum*, which is correct. Tor. *vel careotam*, out of place here.

[6] This sauce seems to be superfluous. Very likely it is a separate formula for a sauce of some kind.

[7] Seems superfluous, too. The noodle paste in the chicken gravy makes it sufficiently thick.

[248] STUFFED CHICKEN [OR PIG]
PULLUS FARSILIS [1]

EMPTY THE CHICKEN THROUGH THE APERTURE OF THE NECK SO THAT NONE OF THE ENTRAILS REMAIN. CRUSH PEPPER, LOVAGE, GINGER, CUT MEAT [2] COOKED SPELT, BESIDES CRUSH BRAINS COOKED IN THE [chicken] BROTH, BREAK EGGS AND MIX ALL TOGETHER IN ORDER TO MAKE A SOLID DRESSING; ADD BROTH TO TASTE AND A LITTLE OIL, WHOLE PEPPER, PLENTY OF NUTS. WITH THIS DRESS-ING STUFF EITHER A CHICKEN OR A SUCKLING PIG, LEAV-ING ENOUGH ROOM FOR EXPANSION [3].

[1] Tor. *fusilis*.

[2] Preferably raw pork or veal.

[3] A most sumptuous dressing; it compares favorably with our popular stale bread pap usually called "chicken dressing."

[249] STUFFED CAPON LIKEWISE
SIMILITER IN CAPO FACIES [1]

THE CAPON IS STUFFED IN A SIMILAR WAY BUT IS COOK-ED WITH ALL THE BONES REMOVED [2].

[1] Sch. *in capso*. May be interpreted thus: Cooked in an envelope of caul or linen, in which case it would correspond to our modern galantine of chicken.

[2] Tor. *ossibus eiectis*; Hum. *omnibus e.*; i.e. all the entrails, etc., which is not correct. The bones must be removed from the capon in this case.

[250] CHICKEN AND CREAM SAUCE [1]
PULLUS LEUCOZOMUS [2]

TAKE A CHICKEN AND PREPARE IT AS ABOVE. EMPTY IT THROUGH THE APERATURE OF THE NECK SO THAT NONE OF THE ENTRAILS REMAIN. TAKE [a little] WATER [3] AND PLENTY OF SPANISH OIL, STIR, COOK TOGETHER UNTIL ALL MOISTURE IS EVAPORATED [4] WHEN THIS IS DONE TAKE THE CHICKEN OUT, SO THAT THE GREATEST POSSI-

BLE AMOUNT OF OIL REMAINS BEHIND [5] SPRINKLE WITH PEPPER AND SERVE [6].

[1] The ancient version of Chicken à la Maryland, Wiener Backhähndl, etc.

[2] Tor. *Leocozymus*; from the Greek *leucozomos*, prepared with white sauce. The formula for the cream sauce is lacking here. Cf. ℞ No. 245.

[3] The use of water to clarify the oil which is to serve as a deep frying fat is an ingenious idea, little practised today. It surely saves the fat or oil, prevents premature burning or blackening by frequent use, and gives a better tasting *friture*. The above recipe is a mere fragment, but even this reveals the extraordinary knowledge of culinary principles of Apicius who reveals himself to us as a master of well-understood principles of good cookery that are so often ignored today. Cf. Note 5 to ℞ No. 497.

[4] The recipe fails to state that the chicken must be breaded, or that the pieces of chicken be turned in flour, etc., and fried in the oil.

[5] Another vital rule of deep fat frying not stated, or rather stated in the language of the kitchen, namely that the chicken must be crisp, dry, that is, not saturated with oil, which of course every good fry cook knows.

[6] With the cream sauce, prepared separately, spread on the platter, with the fried chicken inside, or the sauce in a separate dish, we have here a very close resemblance to a very popular modern dish.

(Schuch and Danneil insert here Excerpta XXIX, XXX and XXXI.)

END OF BOOK VI

[explicit] *TROPHETES APICII. LIBER SEXTUS* [Tac.]

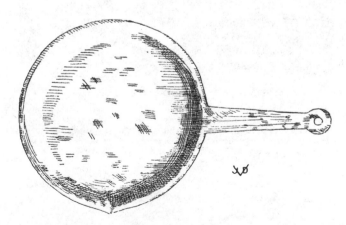

FRYING PAN, ROUND

Provided with a lip to pour our fluids, a convenience which many modern pans lack. The broad flat handle is of one piece with the pan and has a hole for suspension. On some ancient pans these handles were hinged so as to fold over the cavity of the pan, to save room in storing it away, particularly in a soldier's knapsack. Ntl. Mus., Naples, 76571; Field M. 24024.

FRONTISPICE, SECOND LISTER EDITION

purporting to represent the interior of an ancient kitchen. J. Gœree, the artist and engraver, has invented it. The general tidiness differs from contemporary Dutch kitchens and the clothing of the cooks reminds one of Henry VIII, who issued at Eltham in 1526 this order: ". . . provide and sufficiently furnish the kitchens of such scolyons as shall not goe naked or in garments of such vilenesse as they doe . . . nor lie in the nights and dayes in the kitchens . . . by the fire-side. . ." — MS. No. 642, Harleian Library.

APICIUS
Book VII

THE GREAT PALLAS ATHENE DISH

One of the finest show platters in existence. Of Hellenic make. The object in the right hand of Athene has created considerable conjecture but has never been identified.

Hildesheim Treasure.

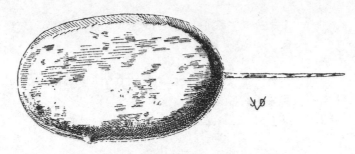

FRYING PAN, OVAL

This oblong pan was no doubt primarily used in fish cookery. An oblong piece of food material fitted snugly into the pan, thus saving fats and other liquids in preparation. Around the slender handle was no doubt one of non-heat-conducting material. The shape and the lip of the pan indicate that it was not used for "sauter." Ntl. Mus., Naples, 76602; Field M. 24038.

BOOK VII. SUMPTUOUS DISHES

Lib. VII. Polyteles

CHAP.   I. SOW'S WOMB, CRACKLINGS, BACON, TENDER-LOIN, TAILS AND FEET.

CHAP.   II. SOW'S BELLY.

CHAP. III. FIG-FED PORK.

CHAP. IV. TID-BITS, CHOPS, STEAKS.

CHAP.   V. ROASTS.

CHAP. VI. BOILED AND STEWED MEATS.

CHAP. VII. PAUNCH.

CHAP. VIII. LOINS AND KIDNEYS.

CHAP. IX. PORK SHOULDER.

CHAP.   X. LIVERS AND LUNGS.

CHAP. XI. HOME-MADE SWEETS.

CHAP. XII. BULBS, TUBERS.

CHAP. XIII. MUSHROOMS.

CHAP. XIV. TRUFFLES.

CHAP. XV. TAROS, DASHEENS.

CHAP. XVI. SNAILS.

CHAP. XVII. EGGS.

[In addition to the above chapters two more are inserted in the text of Book VII, namely Chap. X, Fresh Ham and Chap. XI, To Cook Salt Pork; these being inserted after Chap. IX, Pork Shoulder, making a total of XIX Chapters.]

I

SOW'S WOMB, CRACKLINGS, UDDER, TENDERLOIN,
    TAILS AND FEET
*VULVÆ STERILES, CALLUM LUMBELLI COTICULÆ ET
    UNGELLÆ*

[251]   SPAYED SOW'S WOMB [1]   *VULVÆ STERILES*

STERILE SOW'S WOMB (ALSO UDDER AND BELLY) IS PRE-
PARED IN THIS MANNER: TAKE [2] LASER FROM CYRENE
OR PARTHIA, VINEGAR AND BROTH.

[1] The vulva of a sow was a favorite dish with the ancients, considered a great delicacy. Sows were slaughtered before they had a litter, or were spayed for the purpose of obtaining the sterile womb.

[2] Tor. sentence wanting in other texts.

[252]   ANOTHER WAY   *ALITER*

TAKE PEPPER, CELERY SEED, DRY MINT, LASER ROOT, HONEY, VINEGAR AND BROTH.

[253]   SPAYED SOW'S WOMB   *VULVÆ STERILES*

WITH PEPPER, BROTH AND PARTHIAN LASER.

[254]   ANOTHER WAY   *ALITER*

WITH PEPPER, LOVAGE [1] AND BROTH AND A LITTLE CONDIMENT.

[1] Wanting in Lister.

[255]   CRACKLINGS, PORK SKIN, TENDERLOIN, TAILS
            AND FEET
            CALLUM, LUMBELLI [1] COTICULÆ, UNGELLÆ

SERVE WITH PEPPER, BROTH AND LASER (WHICH THE GREEKS CALL "SILPHION") [2].

[1] Tor., G.-V. *libelli*.

[2] Tor. sentence wanting in other texts.

[256]   GRILLED SOW'S WOMB
            VULVAM UT TOSTAM FACIAS

ENVELOPE IN BRAN, AFTERWARDS [1] PUT IN BRINE AND THEN COOK IT.

[1] We would reverse the process: first pickle the vulva, then coat it with bran (or with bread crumbs) and fry.

II

[257]   SOW'S BELLY   *SUMEN*

SOW'S UDDER OR BELLY WITH THE PAPS ON IT IS PRE-
PARED IN THIS MANNER [1] THE BELLY BOIL, TIE IT TO-
GETHER WITH REEDS, SPRINKLE WITH SALT AND PLACE
IT IN THE OVEN, OR, START ROASTING ON THE GRIDIRON.
CRUSH PEPPER, LOVAGE, WITH BROTH, PURE WINE, ADD-
ING RAISIN WINE TO TASTE, THICKEN [the sauce] WITH
ROUX AND POUR IT OVER THE ROAST.

[1] Tor. sentence wanting in other texts.

[258]   STUFFED SOW'S BELLY   *SUMEN PLENUM*

FULL [1] SOW'S BELLY IS STUFFED WITH [2] CRUSHED
PEPPER, CARRAWAY, SALT MUSSELS; SEW THE BELLY TIGHT
AND ROAST. ENJOY THIS WITH A BRINE SAUCE AND MUS-
TARD.

[1] Full grown, also stuffed with forcemeat.
[2] Tor. sentence wanting in other texts.

III

FIG-FED PORK   *FICATUM* [1]
[1] Tor. *De Sycoto, id est, Ficato.*

[259]   WINE SAUCE FOR FIG-FED PORK
IN FICATO ŒNOGARUM [1]

FIG-FED PORK LIVER (THAT IS, LIVER CRAMMED WITH
FIGS) IS PREPARED IN A WINE SAUCE WITH [2] PEPPER,
THYME, LOVAGE, BROTH, A LITTLE WINE AND OIL [3].

[1] Tor. *Ficatum, iecur suillum.*
[2] Tor. sentence wanting in other texts.
[3] Reinsenius, *ficatum* [or *sicatum*] *projecore.*

According to the invention of Marcus Apicius, pigs were starved, and the
hungry pigs were crammed with dry figs and then suddenly given all the mead
they wanted to drink. The violent expansion of the figs in the stomachs, or the
fermentation caused acute indigestion which killed the pigs. The livers were very
much enlarged, similar to the cramming of geese for the sake of obtaining ab-
normally large livers. This latter method prevailed in the Strassburg District
until recently when it was prohibited by law.

[260]   ANOTHER WAY   *ALITER*

TRIM [the liver] MARINATE IN BROTH, WITH PEPPER, LOV-

AGE, TWO LAUREL BERRIES, WRAP IN CAUL, GRILL ON THE GRIDIRON AND SERVE.

Goll. Stick figs into the liver by making apertures with the knife or with a needle.

It is by no means clear that the liver is meant.

IV

TID BITS, CHOPS, CUTLETS   *OFFELLÆ* [1]

[261] OSTIAN [2] MEAT BALLS   *OFFELLÆ OSTIENSES*
PREPARE THE MEAT IN THIS MANNER [3] CLEAN THE MEAT [of bones, sinews, etc.] SCRAPE IT AS THIN AS A SKIN [and shape it]. CRUSH PEPPER, LOVAGE, CUMIN, CARRAWAY, SILPHIUM, ONE LAUREL BERRY, MOISTENED WITH BROTH; IN A SQUARE DISH PLACE THE MEAT BALLS AND THE SPICES WHERE THEY REMAIN IN PICKLING FOR TWO OR THREE DAYS, COVERED CROSSWISE WITH TWIGS. THEN PLACE THEM IN THE OVEN [to be roasted], WHEN DONE TAKE THE FINISHED MEAT BALLS OUT. CRUSH PEPPER, LOVAGE, WITH THE BROTH, ADD A LITTLE RAISIN WINE TO SWEETEN. COOK IT, THICKEN WITH ROUX, IMMERSE THE BALLS IN THE SAUCE AND SERVE.

[1] G.-V. *Ofellæ*; apparently the old Roman "Hamburger Steak." The term covers different small meat pieces, chops, steaks, etc.

[2] Ostia, town at the mouth of the river Tiber, Rome's harbour.

[3] Tor. sentence wanting in other texts.

[262] APICIAN ROULADES   *OFFELLAS APICIANAS*
BONE THE MEAT FOR THE [roulades — a pork loin, roll it, tie it] OVEN, SHAPE ROUND, COVER WITH OR WRAP IN RUSHES. [Roast] WHEN DONE, RETIRE, ALLOW TO DRIP AND DRY ON THE GRIDIRON BUT SO THAT THE MEAT DOES NOT HARDEN. CRUSH PEPPER, LOVAGE, RUSH [1], CUMIN, ADDING BROTH AND RAISIN WINE TO TASTE. PLACE THE ROULADES WITH THIS SAUCE TOGETHER IN A SAUCE PAN [finish by braising] WHEN DONE, RETIRE THE ROULADES AND DRY THEM. SERVE WITHOUT THE GRAVY SPRINKLED WITH PEPPER. IF TOO FAT REMOVE THE OUTER SKIN [2].

[1] *Cyperis, -os, -um, cypirus*, variants for a sort of rush; probably "Cyprian Grass."

[2] Dann. Dumplings; but this formula appears to deal with boneless pork chops, pork roulades or "*filets mignons*."

[263] PORK CUTLETS, HUNTER STYLE
          OFFELLÆ APRUGNEO [1] *MORE*

IN THE SAME MANNER YOU CAN MAKE TIDBITS OF SOW'S
BELLY [2] PORK CHOPS PREPARED IN A MANNER TO RE-
SEMBLE WILD BOAR ARE [3] PICKLED IN OIL AND BROTH
AND PLACED IN SPICES. WHEN THE CUTLETS ARE DONE
[marinated] THE PICKLE IS PLACED ON THE FIRE AND BOIL-
ED; THE CUTLETS ARE PUT BACK INTO THIS GRAVY AND
ARE FINISHED WITH CRUSHED PEPPER, SPICES, HONEY,
BROTH, AND ROUX. WHEN THIS IS DONE SERVE THE CUT-
LETS WITHOUT THE BROTH AND OIL, SPRINKLED WITH
PEPPER.

[1] G.-V. *Aprugineo*; List. *Offellæ Aprugneæ*, i.e. wild boar chops or cutlets.
Vat. Ms. *aprogneo more*; Tor. *pro genuino more*; Tac. *aprogeneo* — from *aprugnus*, wild boar.

Mutton today is prepared in a similar way, marinated with spices, etc., to resemble venison, and is called *Mouton à la Chasseur*, hunter style.

[2] This sentence, probably belonging to the preceding formula, carried over
by Torinus.

[3] This sentence only in Torinus.

[264]   TIDBITS ANOTHER WAY   *ALITER OFFELLÆ*

THE BALLS OR CUTLETS ARE [1] PROPERLY FRIED IN THE
PAN, NEARLY DONE. [Next prepare the following] ONE WHOLE
[2] GLASS BROTH, A GLASS OF WATER, A GLASS OF VINEGAR
AND A GLASS OF OIL, PROPERLY MIXED; PUT THIS IN AN
EARTHEN BAKING DISH [immerse meat pieces] FINISH ON THE
FIRE AND SERVE.

[1] Tor.
[2] Tor. *Summi*; List. *sumis*, i.e. broth of the pork.

[265]   TIDBITS IN ANOTHER STYLE
          ALITER OFFELLAS

ALSO FRY THE CUTLETS THIS WAY: [1] IN A PAN WITH
PLENTY OF WINE SAUCE, SPRINKLE WITH PEPPER AND
SERVE. [ANOTHER WAY] [2] THE CUTLETS PREVIOUSLY
SALT AND PICKLED IN A BROTH OF CUMIN, ARE PROPERLY
FRIED [3].

[1] Tor. sentence wanting in other texts.
[2] The texts have two formulæ; by the transposition of the two sentences

the formula appears as a whole and one that is intelligible from a culinary point of view.

[3] The texts have: *in aqua recte friguntur*; the *acqua* presumably belongs to the cumin pickle. To fry in water is not possible.

V

CHOICE ROASTS [1]   *ASSATURÆ*

[266] ROASTING, PLAIN *ASSATURAM SIMPLICEM* [2]

SIMPLY PUT THE MEATS TO BE ROASTED IN THE OVEN, GENEROUSLY SPRINKLED WITH SALT, AND SERVE [it glazed] WITH HONEY [3].

[1] Tor. *De assaturæ exquisitæ apparatu.*
[2] Brandt adds "plain."
[3] Corresponding to our present method of roasting; fresh and processed ham is glazed with sugar.

Roasting in the oven is not as desirable as roasting on the spit, universally practised during the middle ages. The spit seems to have been unknown to the Romans. It is seldom used today, although we have improved it by turning it with electrical machinery.

[267] ANOTHER STYLE FOR ROASTS
ALITER ASSATURAS

TAKE 6 SCRUPLES OF PARSLEY, OF LASER [1] JUST AS MANY, 6 OF GINGER, 5 LAUREL BERRIES, 6 SCRUPLES OF PRESERVED LASER ROOT, CYPRIAN RUSH 6, 6 OF ORIGANY, A LITTLE COSTMARY, 3 SCRUPLES OF CHAMOMILE [or pellitory] 6 SCRUPLES OF CELERY SEED, 12 SCRUPLES OF PEPPER, AND BROTH AND OIL AS MUCH AS IT WILL TAKE UP [2].

[1] G.-V. *asareos* [?] *Asarum*, the herb foalbit, wild spikenard.
[2] No directions are given for the making of this compound which are essential to insure success of this formula. Outwardly it resembles some of the commercial sauces made principally in England (Worchestershire, etc.), which are served with every roast.

[268] ANOTHER [Condiment for] ROAST
ALITER ASSATURAS

CRUSH DRY MYRTLE BERRIES WITH CUMIN AND PEPPER, ADDING HONEY ALSO BROTH, REDUCED MUST AND OIL. HEAT AND BIND WITH ROUX. POUR THIS OVER THE ROAST THAT IS MEDIUM DONE, WITH SALT; SPRINKLE WITH PEPPER AND SERVE.

[269]   ANOTHER ROAST [Sauce]   *ALITER ASSATURAS*

6 SCRUPLES PEPPER, 6 SCRUPLES LOVAGE, 6 SCRUPLES PAR-
SLEY, 6 SCRUPLES CELERY SEED, 6 SCRUPLES DILL, 6 SCRUPLES
LASER ROOT, 6 SCRUPLES WILD SPIKENARD [1], 6 SCRUPLES
CYPRIAN RUSH, 6 SCRUPLES CARRAWAY, 6 SCRUPLES CU-
MIN, 6 SCRUPLES GINGER, A PINT OF BROTH AND A SPOON-
FUL OIL.

[1] Tor. *assareos*; cf. note 1 to ℞ No. 267.

[270]   ROAST NECK [1]   *ASSATURAS IN COLLARI*

PUT IN A BRAISIÈRE [2] AND BOIL PEPPER, SPICES, HONEY,
BROTH; AND HEAT THIS WITH THE MEAT IN THE OVEN.
THE NECK PIECE ITSELF, IF YOU LIKE, IS ALSO ROASTED
WITH SPICES AND THE HOT GRAVY IS SIMPLY POURED
OVER AT THE MOMENT OF SERVING [3].

[1] A piece of meat from the neck of a food animal, beef, veal, pork; a muscular hard piece, requiring much care to make it palatable, a "pot roast."

[2] A roasting pan especially adapted for braising tough meats, with closefitting cover to hold the vapors.

[3] Tor. combines this and the foregoing formula. G.-V. *siccum calidum*, for
hot gravy. Perhaps a typographical error for *succum*.

VI

BOILED, STEWED MEATS, AND DAINTY FOOD
IN ELIXAM ET COPADIA

[271]   SAUCE FOR ALL BOILED DISHES
JUS IN ELIXAM OMNEM

PEPPER, LOVAGE, ORIGANY, RUE, SILPHIUM, DRY ONION,
WINE, REDUCED WINE, HONEY, VINEGAR, A LITTLE OIL,
BOILED DOWN, STRAINED THROUGH A CLOTH AND
POURED UNDER THE HOT COOKED MEATS [1].

[1] A very complicated sauce for boiled viands. Most of the ingredients are
found in the Worcestershire Sauce.

[272]   SAUCE FOR BOILED VIANDS   *JUS IN ELIXAM*

MAKE IT THUS: [Tor.] PEPPER, PARSLEY, BROTH, VINEGAR,
FIG-DATES, ONIONS, LITTLE OIL, POURED UNDER VERY
HOT.

[273]   ANOTHER   *JUS IN ELIXAM*

CRUSH PEPPER, DRY RUE, FENNEL SEED, ONION, FIG-DATES, WITH BROTH AND OIL.

[274]   WHITE [bread] [1] SAUCE FOR BOILED VIANDS
        JUS CANDIDUM IN ELIXAM

WHITE SAUCE FOR BOILED DISHES IS MADE THUS: [2] PEPPER, BROTH, WINE, RUE, ONIONS, NUTS, A LITTLE SPICE, BREAD SOAKED TO THE SATURATION POINT, OIL, WHICH IS COOKED AND SPREAD UNDER [the meat].

[1] Our present bread sauce, somewhat simpler, but essentially the same as the Apician sauce, is very popular with roast partridge, pheasant and other game in England.

[2] Tor. sentence wanting in other texts.

[275]   ANOTHER WHITE SAUCE FOR BOILED VIANDS
        ALITER JUS CANDIDUM IN ELIXAM

ANOTHER WHITE SAUCE FOR BOILED DISHES CONTAINS: [1] PEPPER, CARRAWAY, LOVAGE, THYME, ORIGANY, SHALLOTS, DATES, HONEY, VINEGAR, BROTH AND OIL.

[276]   WHITE SAUCE FOR DAINTY FOOD
        IN COPADIIS [1] *JUS ALBUM*

TAKE CUMIN, LOVAGE, RUE SEED, PLUMS FROM DAMASCUS [2] SOAK IN WINE, ADD HONEY MEAD AND VINEGAR, THYME AND ORIGANY TO TASTE [3].

[1] Lacking definite description of the *copadia* it is hard to differentiate between them and the *offellæ.* — *Cupedia* (Plaut. and Gell.), nice dainty dishes, from *cupiditas*, appetite, desire for dainty fare. Hence *cupedinarius* (Terent.) and *cupediarius* (Lamprid.) a seller or maker of dainties, a confectioner.

[2] *Damascena*; they correspond apparently to our present stewed (dried) prunes. It is inconceivable how this sauce can be white in color, but, as a condiment and if taken in small quantity, it has our full approval.

[3] G.-V. *agitabis*, i.e. stir the sauce with a whip of thyme and origany twigs. Cf. note to following.

[277]   ANOTHER WHITE SAUCE FOR APPETIZERS
        ALITER JUS CANDIDUM IN COPADIIS

IS MADE THUS [1] PEPPER, THYME, CUMIN, CELERY SEED, FENNEL, RUE, MINT [2], MYRTLE BERRIES, RAISINS, RAISIN

WINE, AND MEAD TO TASTE; STIR IT WITH A TWIG OF SAT-
URY [3].

[1] Tor.

[2] G.-V., rue wanting.

[3] An ingenious way to impart a very subtle flavor. The sporadic discoveries
of such very subtle and refined methods (cf. notes to ℞ No. 15) should dispell
once and for all time the old theories that the ancients were using spices to ex-
cess. They simply used a greater variety of flavors and aromas than we do today,
but there is no proof that spices were used excessively. The great variety of
flavors at the disposal of the ancients speaks well for the refinement of the olfactory sense and the desire to bring variety into their fare. Cf. ℞ Nos. 345, 369
and 385.

[278] SAUCE FOR TIDBITS *JUS IN COPADIIS*

PEPPER, LOVAGE, CARRAWAY, MINT, LEAVES OF SPIKE-
NARD (WHICH THE GREEKS CALL "NARDOSACHIOM")
[*sic!*] [1] YOLKS, HONEY, MEAD, VINEGAR, BROTH AND OIL.
STIR WELL WITH SATURY AND LEEKS [2] AND TIE WITH
ROUX.

[1] Tor. [*sic!*] *spicam nardi* — sentence wanting in other texts. G.-V. *nardo-
stachyum*, spikenard.

[2] A fagot of satury and leeks! Cf. notes to ℞ Nos. 276 and 277.

[279] WHITE SAUCE FOR TIDBITS
JUS ALBUM IN COPADIIS

IS MADE THUS: [1] PEPPER, LOVAGE, CUMIN, CELERY
SEED, THYME, NUTS, WHICH SOAK AND CLEAN, HONEY,
VINEGAR, BROTH AND OIL TO BE ADDED [2].

[1, 2] First three and last three words in Tor.

[280] SAUCE FOR TIDBITS   *JUS IN COPADIIS*

PEPPER, CELERY SEED, CARRAWAY, SATURY, SAFFRON,
SHALLOTS, TOASTED ALMONDS, FIGDATES, BROTH, OIL
AND A LITTLE MUSTARD; COLOR WITH REDUCED MUST.

[281] SAUCE FOR TIDBITS   *JUS IN COPADIIS*

PEPPER, LOVAGE, PARSLEY, SHALLOTS, TOASTED AL-
MONDS, DATES, HONEY, VINEGAR, BROTH, REDUCED MUST
AND OIL.

[282] SAUCE FOR TIDBITS   *JUS IN COPADIIS*

CHOP HARD EGGS, PEPPER, CUMIN, PARSLEY, COOKED
LEEKS, MYRTLE BERRIES, SOMEWHAT MORE HONEY, VINE-
GAR, BROTH AND OIL.

[283]   RAW DILL SAUCE FOR BOILED DISH
        IN ELIXAM ANETHATUM CRUDUM

PEPPER, DILL SEED, DRY MINT, LASER ROOT, POUR UN-
DER: VINEGAR, DATE WINE, HONEY, BROTH, AND A LIT-
TLE MUSTARD, REDUCED MUST AND OIL TO TASTE; AND
SERVE IT WITH ROAST PORK SHOULDER.

[284]   BRINY SAUCE FOR BOILED DISH
        JUS IN ELIXAM ALLECATUM

PEPPER, LOVAGE, CARRAWAY, CELERY SEED, THYME,
SHALLOTS, DATES, FISH BRINE [1] STRAINED HONEY, AND
WINE TO TASTE; SPRINKLE WITH CHOPPED GREEN CELERY
AND OIL AND SERVE.

[1] G.-V. *allecem*; Tor. *Halecem*.

VII

PAUNCH   *VENTRICULA*

[285]   PIG'S PAUNCH   *VENTREM PORCINUM*

CLEAN THE PAUNCH OF A SUCKLING PIG WELL WITH
SALT AND VINEGAR AND PRESENTLY WASH WITH WATER.
THEN FILL IT WITH THE FOLLOWING DRESSING: PIECES OF
PORK POUNDED IN THE MORTAR, THREE BRAINS — THE
NERVES REMOVED — MIX WITH RAW EGGS, ADD NUTS,
WHOLE PEPPER, AND SAUCE TO TASTE. CRUSH PEPPER,
LOVAGE, SILPHIUM, ANISE, GINGER, A LITTLE RUE; FILL
THE PAUNCH WITH IT, NOT TOO MUCH, THOUGH, LEAV-
ING PLENTY OF ROOM FOR EXPANSION LEST IT BURSTS
WHILE BEING COOKED. PUT IT IN A POT WITH BOILING
WATER, RETIRE AND PRICK WITH A NEEDLE SO THAT IT
DOES NOT BURST. WHEN HALF DONE, TAKE IT OUT AND
HANG IT INTO THE SMOKE TO TAKE ON COLOR; NOW BOIL
IT OVER AGAIN AND FINISH IT LEISURELY. NEXT TAKE
THE BROTH, SOME PURE WINE AND A LITTLE OIL, OPEN
THE PAUNCH WITH A SMALL KNIFE. SPRINKLE WITH THE
BROTH AND LOVAGE; PLACE THE PIG NEAR THE FIRE TO
HEAT IT, TURN IT AROUND IN BRAN [or bread crumbs] IM-
MERSE IN [sprinkle with] BRINE AND FINISH [the outer crust to
a golden brown] [1].

[1] The good old English way of finishing a roast joint called dredging.

Lister has this formula divided into two; Danneil and Schuch make three different formulas out of it.

VIII

LOINS AND KIDNEYS *LUMBI ET RENES*

[286] ROAST LOINS MADE THUS
LUMBULI ASSI ITA FIUNT

SPLIT THEM INTO TWO PARTS SO THAT THEY ARE SPREAD OUT [1] SPRINKLE THE OPENING WITH CRUSHED PEPPER AND [ditto] NUTS, FINELY CHOPPED CORIANDER AND CRUSHED FENNEL SEED. THE TENDERLOINS ARE THEN ROLLED UP TO BE ROASTED; TIE TOGETHER, WRAP IN CAUL, PARBOIL IN OIL [2] AND BROTH, AND THEN ROAST IN THE OVEN OR BROIL ON THE GRIDIRON.

[1] "Frenched," the meat here being pork tenderloin.

[2] G.-V. best broth and a little oil, which is more acceptable.

IX

HAM *PERNA*

[287] [Baked Picnic] HAM [Pork Shoulder, fresh or cured]
PERNAM

THE HAM SHOULD BE BRAISED WITH A GOOD NUMBER OF FIGS AND SOME THREE LAUREL LEAVES; THE SKIN IS THEN PULLED OFF AND CUT INTO SQUARE PIECES; THESE ARE MACERATED WITH HONEY. THEREUPON MAKE DOUGH CRUMBS OF FLOUR AND OIL [1] LAY THE DOUGH OVER OR AROUND THE HAM, STUD THE TOP WITH THE PIECES OF THE SKIN SO THAT THEY WILL BE BAKED WITH THE DOUGH [bake slowly] AND WHEN DONE, RETIRE FROM THE OVEN AND SERVE [2].

[1] Ordinary pie or pastry dough, or perhaps a preparation similar to streusel, unsweetened.

[2] Experimenting with this formula, we have adhered to the instructions as closely as possible, using regular pie dough to envelop the parboiled meat. The figs were retired from the sauce pan long before the meat was done and they were served around the ham as a garnish. As a consequence we partook of a grand dish that no inmate of Olympus would have sneezed at.

In Pompeii an inn-keeper had written the following on the wall of his establishment: *Ubi perna cocta est si convivæ apponitur non gustat pernam linguit ollam aut caccabum.*

When we first beheld this message we took the inn-keeper for a humorist and clever advertiser; but now we are convinced that he was in earnest when he said that his guests would lick the sauce pan in which his hams were cooked.

[288] TO COOK PORK SHOULDER
PERNÆ [1] *COCTURAM*

HAM SIMPLY COOKED IN WATER WITH FIGS IS USUALLY DRESSED ON A PLATTER [baking pan] SPRINKLED WITH CRUMBS AND REDUCED WINE, OR, STILL BETTER, WITH SPICED WINE [and is glazed under the open flame, or with a shovel containing red-hot embers].

[1] *Perna* is usually applied to shoulder of pork, fresh, also cured.
Coxa is the hind leg, or haunch of pork, or fresh ham. Cf. note 1 to ℞ No. 289.

X

[289] FRESH HAM *MUSTEIS* [1] *PETASONEM* [2]

A FRESH HAM IS COOKED WITH 2 POUNDS OF BARLEY AND 25 FIGS. WHEN DONE SKIN, GLAZE THE SURFACE WITH A FIRE SHOVEL FULL OF GLOWING COALS, SPREAD HONEY OVER IT, OR, WHAT'S BETTER: PUT IT IN THE OVEN COVERED WITH HONEY. WHEN IT HAS A NICE COLOR, PUT IN A SAUCE PAN RAISIN WINE, PEPPER, A BUNCH OF RUE AND PURE WINE TO TASTE. WHEN THIS [sauce] IS DONE, POUR HALF OF IT OVER THE HAM AND IN THE OTHER HALF SOAK SPECIALLY MADE GINGER BREAD [3] THE REMNANT OF THE SAUCE AFTER MOST OF IT IS THOROUGHLY SOAKED INTO THE BREAD, ADD TO THE HAM [4].

[1] *Musteus*, fresh, young, new; *vinum mustum*, new wine, must. Properly perhaps, *Petasonem ex mustaceis*; cf. note 3.
[2] Hum. *verum petaso coxa cum crure* [shank] *esse dicitur.* . . .
Plainly, we are dealing here with fresh, uncured ham.
[3] A certain biscuit or cake made of must, spices and pepper, perhaps baked on laurel leaves. *Mustaceus* was a kind of cake, the flour of which had been kneaded with must, cheese, anise, etc., the cake was baked upon laurel leaves.
[4] Tor. continues without interruption. He has the three foregoing formulæ thrown into one.

XI

[290] BACON, SALT PORK *LARIDI* [1] *COCTURA*

COVER WITH WATER AND COOK WITH PLENTY OF DILL; SPRINKLE WITH A LITTLE OIL AND A TRIFLE OF SALT.

[1] Lister, at this point, has forgotten his explanation of *laridum*, and now accepts the word in its proper sense. This rather belated correction by Lister

confirms the correctness of our own earlier observations. Cf. note to ℞ Nos. 41 and 148.

XII

LIVERS AND LUNGS   *JECINORA SIVE PULMONES*

[291]   SHEEP LIVER
JECINORA HŒDINA VEL AGNINA [1]

COOK THUS: MAKE A MIXTURE OF WATER, MEAD, EGGS AND MILK IN WHICH THOROUGHLY SOAK THE SLICED LIVER. STEW THE LIVER IN WINE SAUCE, SPRINKLE WITH PEPPER AND SERVE.

[1] G.-V. *Iecinera hœdina.*

[292]   ANOTHER WAY TO COOK LUNG
ALITER IN PULMONIBUS

LIVER AND LUNG ARE ALSO COOKED THIS WAY: [1] SOAK WELL IN MILK, STRAIN IT OFF IF OFFNSIVE IN TASTE [2] BREAK 2 EGGS AND ADD A LITTLE SALT, MIX IN A SPOONFUL HONEY AND FILL THE LUNG WITH IT, BOIL AND SLICE [3].

[1] Tor.

[2] Lungs of slaughtered animals are little used nowadays. The soaking of livers in milk is quite common; it removes the offensive taste of the gall.

[3] G.-V. continue without interruption.

[293]   A HASH OF LIVER   *ALITER*

CRUSH PEPPER, MOISTEN WITH BROTH, RAISIN WINE, PURE OIL, CHOP THE LIGHTS [1] FINE AND ADD WINE SAUCE [2].

[1] Edible intestines, livers, lung, kidney, etc., are thus named.

[2] List., Tor., G.-V. have both recipes in one. Dann. is in doubt whether to separate them or not.

XIII

HOME-MADE SWEET DISHES AND HONEY SWEET-
     MEATS
DULCIA DOMESTICA [1] *ET MELCÆ*

[294]   HOME-MADE SWEETS   *DULCIA DOMESTICA*

LITTLE HOME CONFECTIONS (WHICH ARE CALLED DUL-CIARIA) ARE MADE THUS: [2] LITTLE PALMS OR (AS THEY

ARE ORDINARILY CALLED) [3] DATES ARE STUFFED — AFTER THE SEEDS HAVE BEEN REMOVED — WITH A NUT OR WITH NUTS AND GROUND PEPPER, SPRINKLED WITH SALT ON THE OUTSIDE AND ARE CANDIED IN HONEY AND SERVED [4].

[1] *Dulcia*, sweetmeats, cates; hence *dulciarius*, a pastry cook or confectioner. The fact that here attention is drawn to home-made sweet dishes may clear up the absence of regular baking and dessert formulæ in Apicius. The trade of the *dulciarius* was so highly developed at that time that the professional bakers and confectioners supplied the entire home market with their wares, making it convenient and unprofitable for the domestic cook to compete with their organized business, a condition which largely exists in our modern highly civilized centers of population today. Cf. "Cooks."

[2 + 3] Tor.

[4] Still being done today in the same manner.

[295]   ANOTHER SWEETMEAT   *ALITER DULCIA*

GRATE [scrape, peel] SOME VERY BEST FRESH APHROS [1] AND IMMERSE IN MILK. WHEN SATURATED PLACE IN THE OVEN TO HEAT BUT NOT TO DRY OUT; WHEN THOROUGHLY HOT RETIRE FROM OVEN, POUR OVER SOME HONEY, STIPPLE [the fruit] SO THAT THE HONEY MAY PENETRATE, SPRINKLE WITH PEPPER [2] AND SERVE.

[1] Tor., Tac., Lan. *musteos aphros*; Vat. Ms., G.-V. *afros*; List. *apios*, i.e. celery, which is farthest from the mark. Goll. interprets this a "cider apple," reminiscent, probably, of *musteos*, which is fresh, new, young, and which has here nothing to do with cider.

Aphros is not identified. Perhaps the term stood for Apricots (Old English: Aphricocks) or some other African fruit or plant; Lister's celery is to be rejected on gastronomical grounds.

The above treatment would correspond to that which is given apricots and peaches today. They are peeled, immersed in cream and sweetened with sugar. Apicius' heating of the fruit in milk is new to us; it sounds good, for it has a tendency to parboil any hard fruit, make it more digestible and reduce the fluid to a creamy consistency.

[2] The "pepper" again, as pointed out in several other places, here is some spice of agreeable taste as are used in desserts today.

[296]   ANOTHER SWEET DISH   *ALITER DULCIA*

BREAK [slice] FINE WHITE BREAD, CRUST REMOVED, INTO RATHER LARGE PIECES WHICH SOAK IN MILK [and beaten eggs] FRY IN OIL, COVER WITH HONEY AND SERVE [1].

[1] "French" Toast, indeed! — *Sapienti sat!*

[297]   ANOTHER SWEET   *ALITER DULCIA*

IN A CHAFING-DISH PUT [1] HONEY, PURE WINE, RAISIN
WINE, RUE, PINE NUTS, NUTS, COOKED SPELT, ADD CRUSH-
ED AND TOASTED HAZELNUTS [2] AND SERVE.

[1] G.-V. *Piperato mittis. Piperatum* is a dish prepared with pepper, any
spicy dish; the term may here be applied to the bowl in which the porridge is
served. Tac. *Dulcia piperata mittis.*
[2] Dann. Almonds.

[298]   ANOTHER SWEET   *ALITER DULCIA*

CRUSH PEPPER, NUTS, HONEY, RUE, AND RAISIN WINE
WITH MILK, AND COOK THE MIXTURE [1] WITH A FEW
EGGS WELL WORKED IN, COVER WITH HONEY, SPRINKLE
WITH [crushed nuts, etc.] AND SERVE.

[1] *Tractam*, probably with a starch added, or else it is a nut custard, practically a repetition of ℞ Nos. 128 and 142.

[299]   ANOTHER SWEET   *ALITER DULCIA*

TAKE A PREPARATION SIMILAR [1] [to the above] AND IN
THE HOT WATER [bath or double boiler] MAKE A VERY HARD
PORRIDGE OF IT. THEREUPON SPREAD IT OUT ON A PAN
AND WHEN COOL CUT IT INTO HANDY PIECES LIKE SMALL
COOKIES. FRY THESE IN THE BEST OIL, TAKE THEM OUT,
DIP INTO [hot] HONEY, SPRINKLE WITH PEPPER [2] AND
SERVE.

[1] This confirms the assumption that some flour or meal is used in ℞ No.
298 also without which this present preparation would not "stand up."
[2] It is freely admitted that the word "pepper" not always stands for the
spice that we know by this name. Cf. note 2 to ℞ No. 295 *et al.*

[300]   A STILL BETTER WAY   *ALITER*
IS TO PREPARE THIS WITH MILK INSTEAD OF WATER.

[301]   CUSTARD   *TYROPATINAM*

ESTIMATE THE AMOUNT OF MILK NECESSARY FOR THIS
DISH AND SWEETEN IT WITH HONEY TO TASTE; TO A PINT
[1] OF FLUID TAKE 5 EGGS; FOR HALF A PINT [2] DIS-
SOLVE 3 EGGS IN MILK AND BEAT WELL TO INCOR-
PORATE THOROUGHLY, STRAIN THROUGH A COLANDER
INTO AN EARTHEN DISH AND COOK ON A SLOW FIRE [in

hot water bath in oven]. WHEN CONGEALED SPRINKLE WITH
PEPPER AND SERVE [3].

[1] *Sextarium.*
[2] *ad heminam.*
[3] Dann. calls this a cheese cake, which is a far-fetched conclusion, although
standard dictionaries say that the *tyropatina* is a kind of cheese cake. It must
be borne in mind, however, that the ancient definition of "custard" is "egg
cheese," probably because of the similarity in appearance and texture.
    Cf. ℞ Nos. 129 and 143.

[302]   OMELETTE SOUFFLÉE [1]
OVA SPHONGIA EX LACTE

FOUR EGGS IN HALF A PINT OF MILK AND AN OUNCE OF
OIL WELL BEATEN, TO MAKE A FLUFFY MIXTURE; IN A PAN
PUT A LITTLE OIL, AND CAREFULLY ADD THE EGG PREPA-
RATION, WITHOUT LETTING IT BOIL [2] HOWEVER. [Place
it in the oven to let it rise] AND WHEN ONE SIDE IS DONE, TURN
IT OUT INTO A SERVICE PLATTER [fold it] POUR OVER
HONEY, SPRINKLE WITH PEPPER [3] AND SERVE [4].

[1] Dann. misled by the title, interprets this dish as "Floating Island"; he,
the chef, has completely misunderstood the ancient formula.
[2] Tor. *sinas bullire* – which is correct. List. *facies ut bulliat* — which is
monstrous.
[3] G.-V.
[4] Tor. continues without interruption.

[303]   CHEESE AND HONEY   *MEL ET CASEUM* [1]

PREPARE [cottage] CHEESE EITHER WITH HONEY AND
BROTH [brine] OR WITH SALT, OIL AND [chopped] CORIAN-
DER [2].

[1] G.-V. *Melca ... stum*; List. *mel castum*, refined honey; Tac. *Mel caseum*;
Tor. *mel, caseum.* Cf. ℞ No. 294.
[2] To season cottage (fresh curd) cheese today we use salt, pepper, cream,
carraway or chopped chives; sometimes a little sugar.

XIV

[304]   BULBS [1]   *BULBOS*

SERVE WITH OIL, BROTH AND VINEGAR, WITH A LITTLE
CUMIN SPRINKLED OVER.

[1] Onions, roots of tulips, narcissus. Served raw sliced, with the above dressing, or cooked. Cf. notes to ℞ No. 307.

[305]   ANOTHER WAY   *ALITER*

SOAK [1] THE BULBS AND PARBOIL THEM IN WATER; THEREUPON FRY THEM IN OIL. THE DRESSING MAKE THUS: TAKE THYME, FLEA-BANE, PEPPER, ORIGANY, HONEY, VINEGAR, REDUCED WINE, DATE WINE, IF YOU LIKE [2] BROTH AND A LITTLE OIL. SPRINKLE WITH PEPPER AND SERVE.

[1] Tor. *tundes*; probably a typographical error, as this should read *fundis*, i.e. *infundis*. Wanting in the other texts.

[306]   ANOTHER WAY   *ALITER*

COOK THE BULBS INTO A THICK PURÉE [1] AND SEASON WITH THYME, ORIGANY, HONEY, VINEGAR, REDUCED WINE, DATE WINE, BROTH AND A LITTLE OIL.

[1] *Tundes*, i.e. mash. Practically a correction of ℞ No. 305, repeated by Tor.

[307]   VARRO SAYS OF BULBS [1]
          VARRO SI QUID DE BULBIS DIXIT

COOKED IN WATER THEY ARE CONDUCIVE TO LOVE [2] AND ARE THEREFORE ALSO SERVED AT WEDDING FEASTS, BUT ALSO SEASONED WITH PIGNOLIA NUT OR WITH THE JUICE OF COLEWORT, OR MUSTARD, AND PEPPER.

[1] The first instance in Apicius where the monotony and business-like recital of recipes is broken by some interesting quotation or remark.
Brandt is of the opinion that this remark was added by a posterior reader.
[2] The texts: *qui Veneris ostium quærunt* — "seek the mouth of Venus."
This favorite superstition of the ancients leads many writers, as might be expected, into fanciful speculations. Humelberg, quoting Martial, says: *Veneram mirè stimulant, unde et salaces à Martiali vocantur.* 1. XIII, Ep. 34:

> *Cum sit anus conjunx, cum sint tibi mortua membra*
> *Nil aliud, bulbis quam satur esse potes.*

We fail to find this quotation from Varro in his works, M. Teren. Varronis De Re Rustica, Lugduni, 1541, but we read in Columella and Pliny that the buds or shoots of reeds were called by some "bulbs," by others "eyes," and, remembering that these shoots make very desirable vegetables when properly cooked, we feel inclined to include these among the term "bulbs." Platina also adds the squill or sea onion to this category. Nonnus, p. 84, Diæteticon, Antwerp, 1645, quotes Columella as saying: *Jam Magaris veniant genitalia semina Bulbi.*

[308]   FRIED BULBS   *BULBOS FRICTOS*

ARE SERVED WITH WINE SAUCE [Oenogarum].

XV

MUSHROOMS OR MORELS [1]

FUNGI FARNEI VEL BOLETI

[309] MORELS [2]   *FUNGI FARNEI*

MORELS ARE COOKED QUICKLY IN GARUM AND PEPPER, TAKEN OUT, ALLOWED TO DRIP; ALSO BROTH WITH CRUSHED PEPPER MAY BE USED [to cook the mushrooms in].

[1] It is noteworthy that the term *spongiolus* which creates so much misunderstanding in Book II is not used here in connection with mushrooms. Cf. ℞ No. 115.

[2] "Ashtree-Mushrooms."

[310] FOR MORELS   *IN FUNGIS FARNEIS*

PEPPER, REDUCED WINE, VINEGAR AND OIL.

[311] ANOTHER WAY OF COOKING MORELS
ALITER FUNGI FARNEI

IN SALT WATER, WITH OIL, PURE WINE, AND SERVE WITH CHOPPED CORIANDER.

[312] MUSHROOMS   *BOLETOS FUNGOS*

FRESH MUSHROOMS ARE STEWED [1] IN REDUCED WINE WITH A BUNCH OF GREEN CORIANDER, WHICH REMOVE BEFORE SERVING.

[1] Tor.

[313] ANOTHER STYLE OF MUSHROOMS
BOLETOS ALITER [1]

MUSHROOM STEMS [or buds, very small mushrooms] ARE COOKED IN BROTH. SERVE SPRINKLED WITH SALT.

[1] Tor. *Boletorum coliculi*; G.-V. *calyculos*.

[314] ANOTHER WAY OF COOKING MUSHROOMS
BOLETOS ALITER

SLICE THE MUSHROOM STEMS [1] [stew them as directed above] AND FINISH BY COVERING THEM WITH EGGS [2] ADDING PEPPER, LOVAGE, A LITTLE HONEY, BROTH AND OIL TO TASTE.

[1] *Thyrsos*.

[2] G.-V. *in patellam novam*; nothing said about eggs. Tor. *concisos in pa-tellam; ovaque perfundes*; Tac. *ova perfundis*.

A mushroom omelette.

XVI

[315]   TRUFFLES   *TUBERA*

SCRAPE [brush] THE TRUFFLES, PARBOIL, SPRINKLE WITH SALT, PUT SEVERAL OF THEM ON A SKEWER, HALF FRY THEM; THEN PLACE THEM IN A SAUCE PAN WITH OIL, BROTH, REDUCED WINE, WINE, PEPPER, AND HONEY. WHEN DONE [retire the truffles] BIND [the liquor] WITH ROUX, DECORATE THE TRUFFLES NICELY AND SERVE [1].

[1] This formula clearly shows up the master Apicius. Truffles, among all earthly things, are the most delicate and most subtle in flavor. Only a master cook is privileged to handle them and to do them justice.

Today, whenever we are fortunate enough to obtain the best fresh truffles, we are pursuing almost the same methods of preparation as described by Apicius.

The commercially canned truffles bear not even a resemblance of their former selves.

[316]   ANOTHER WAY TO PREPARE TRUFFLES
ALITER TUBERA

[Par]BOIL THE TRUFFLES, SPRINKLE WITH SALT AND FASTEN THEM ON SKEWERS, HALF FRY THEM AND THEN PLACE THEM IN A SAUCE PAN WITH BROTH, VIRGIN OIL, REDUCED WINE, A LITTLE PURE WINE [1] CRUSHED PEPPER AND A LITTLE HONEY; ALLOW THEM TO FINISH [gently and well covered] WHEN DONE, BIND THE LIQUOR WITH ROUX, PRICK THE TRUFFLES SO THEY MAY BECOME SATURATED WITH THE JUICE, DRESS THEM NICELY, AND WHEN REAL HOT, SERVE.

[1] Preferably Sherry or Madeira.

[317]   ANOTHER WAY   *ALITER*

IF YOU WISH YOU MAY ALSO WRAP THE TRUFFLES IN CAUL OF PORK, BRAISE AND SO SERVE THEM.

[318]   ANOTHER TRUFFLE   *ALITER TUBERA*

STEW THE TRUFFLES IN WINE SAUCE, WITH PEPPER, LOV-AGE, CORIANDER, RUE, BROTH, HONEY, WINE, AND A LIT-TLE OIL.

[319] ANOTHER WAY FOR TRUFFLES
ALITER TUBERA

BRAISE THE TRUFFLES WITH PEPPER, MINT, RUE, HONEY, OIL, AND A LITTLE WINE. HEAT AND SERVE.

[320] ANOTHER WAY FOR TRUFFLES
ALITER TUBERA [1]

PEPPER, CUMIN, SILPHIUM, MINT, CELERY, RUE, HONEY, VINEGAR, OR WINE, SALT OR BROTH, A LITTLE OIL.

[1] Wanting in G.-V.

[321] ANOTHER WAY FOR TRUFFLES
ALITER TUBERA [1]

COOK THE TRUFFLES WITH LEEKS, SALT, PEPPER, CHOPPED CORIANDER, THE VERY BEST WINE AND A LIT-TLE OIL.

[1] Wanting in Tor.

This, to our notion of eating truffles, is the best formula, save ℞ Nos. 315 and 316.

XVII

TARO, DASHEEN   *IN COLOCASIO*

[322] COLOCASIUM [1] TARO, DASHEEN
COLOCASIUM

FOR THE COLOCASIUM (WHICH IS REALLY THE COLOCA-SIA PLANT, ALSO CALLED "EGYPTIAN BEAN" USE) [2] PEP-PER, CUMIN, RUE, HONEY, OR BROTH, AND A LITTLE OIL; WHEN DONE BIND WITH ROUX [3] COLOCASIUM IS THE ROOT OF THE EGYPTIAN BEAN WHICH IS USED EXCLU-SIVELY [4].

[1] Cf. notes to ℞ Nos. 74, 172, 216, 244; also the copious explanations by Humelberg, fol. 111.

[2] Tor. who is trying hard to explain the *colocasium*. His name, "Egyptian Bean" may be due to the mealiness and bean-like texture of the *colocasium* tuber; otherwise there is no resemblance to a bean, except, perhaps, the seed pod which is not used for food. This simile has led other commentators to believe that the *colocasium* in reality was a bean.

The U. S. Department of Agriculture has in recent years imported various specimens of that taro species (belonging to the *colocasia*), and the plants are now successfully being farmed in the southern parts of the United States, with fair prospects of becoming an important article of daily diet. The Department has favored us repeatedly with samples of the taro, or dasheen, (*Colocasium Antiquorum*) and we have made many different experiments with this agreeable, delightful and important "new" vegetable. It can be prepared in every way like a potato, and possesses advantages over the potato as far as value of nutrition, flavor, culture and keeping qualities are concerned. As a commercial article, it is not any more expensive than any good kind of potato. It grows where the potato will not thrive, and vice versa. It thus saves much in freight to parts where the potato does not grow.

The ancient *colocasium* is no doubt a close relative of the modern dasheen or taro. The Apician *colocasium* was perhaps very similar to the ordinary Elephant-Ear, *colocasium Antiquorum Schott*, often called *caladium esculentum*, or *tanyah*, more recently called the "Dasheen" which is a corruption of the French "de Chine" — from China — indicating the supposed origin of this variety of taro. The dasheen is a broad-leaved member of the *arum* family. The name dasheen originated in the West Indies whence it was imported into the United States around 1910, and the name is now officially adopted.

Mark Catesby, in his Natural History of Carolina, Florida and the Bahama Islands, London, 1781, describes briefly under the name of *arum maximum Aegypticum* a plant which was doubtless one of the tanyahs or taros. He says: "This was a welcome improvement among the negroes and was esteemed a blessing; they being delighted with all their African food, particularly this, which a great part of Africa subsists much on."

Torinus, groping for the right name, calls it variously *colosium, coledium, coloesium,* till he finally gets it right, *colocasium.*

[3] The root or tubers of this plant was used by the ancients as a vegetable. They probably boiled and then peeled and sliced the tubers, seasoning the pieces with the above ingredients, heated them in bouillon stock and thickened the gravy in the usual way. Since the tuber is very starchy, little roux is required for binding.

[4] Afterthought by Tor. printed in italics on the margin of his book.

XVIII

SNAILS *COCHLEAS*

[323] MILK-FED SNAILS *COCHLEAS LACTE PASTAS*

TAKE SNAILS AND SPONGE THEM; PULL THEM OUT OF THE SHELLS BY THE MEMBRANE AND PLACE THEM FOR A DAY IN A VESSEL WITH MILK AND SALT [1] RENEW THE MILK DAILY. HOURLY [2] CLEAN THE SNAILS OF ALL REFUSE, AND WHEN THEY ARE SO FAT THAT THEY CAN NO LONGER RETIRE [to their shells] FRY THEM IN OIL AND SERVE

THEM WITH WINE SAUCE. IN A SIMILAR WAY THEY MAY BE
FED ON A MILK PORRIDGE [3].

[1] Just enough so they do not drown.

[2] Wanting in Tor.

[3] The Romans raised snails for the table in special places called *cochlearia.*
Fluvius Hirpinus is credited with having popularized the snail in Rome a little
before the civil wars between Cæsar and Pompey. If we could believe Varro,
snails grew to enormous proportions. A supper of the younger Pliny consisted
of a head of lettuce, three snails, two eggs, a barley cake, sweet wine, refrig-
erated in snow.

Snails as a food are not sufficiently appreciated by the Germanic races who
do not hesitate to eat similar animals and are very fond of such food as oysters,
clams, mussels, cocles, etc., much of which they even eat in the raw state.

[324] ANOTHER WAY   *ALITER*

THE SNAIL ARE FRIED WITH PURE SALT AND OIL AND [a
sauce of] LASER, BROTH, PEPPER AND OIL IS UNDERLAID; OR
THE FRIED SNAILS ARE FULLY COVERED WITH BROTH, PEP-
PER AND CUMIN.

Tor. divides this into three articles.

[325] ANOTHER WAY FOR SNAILS
ALITER COCHLEAS

THE LIVE SNAILS ARE SPRINKLED WITH MILK MIXED
WITH THE FINEST WHEAT FLOUR, WHEN FAT AND NICE
AND PLUMP THEY ARE COOKED.

XIX

EGGS   *OVA*

[326] FRIED EGGS   *OVA FRIXA*

FRIED EGGS ARE FINISHED IN WINE SAUCE.

[327] BOILED EGGS   *OVA ELIXA*

ARE SEASONED WITH BROTH, OIL, PURE WINE, OR ARE
SERVED WITH BROTH, PEPPER AND LASER.

[328] WITH POACHED EGGS   *IN OVIS HAPALIS*

SERVE PEPPER, LOVAGE, SOAKED NUTS, HONEY, VINEGAR
AND BROTH.

END OF BOOK VII

EXPLICIT APICII POLYTELES: LIBER SEPTIMUS [Tac.]

APICIUS
Book VIII

CRATICULA

Combination broiler and stove; charcoal fuel. The sliding rods are adjustable to the size of food to be cooked thereon. Pans of various sizes would rest on these rods. In the rear two openings to hold the caccabus, or stewpot, of which we have four different illustrations. The craticula usually rested on top of a stationary brick oven or range. The apparatus, being moveable, is very ingenious. The roughness of the surface of this specimen is caused by corrosion and lava adhering to its metal frame. Found in Pompeii. Ntl. Mus., Naples, 121321; Field M., 26145.

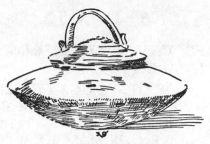

CACCABUS

A stewpot, marmite, kettle. The cover, rising from the circumference to the center in a succession of steps, fits inside the mouth of the kettle. Ntl. Mus., Naples, 72766; Field M., 24178.

BOOK VIII. QUADRUPEDS

Lib. VIII. Tetrapus

CHAP.   I. WILD BOAR.
CHAP.   II. VENISON.
CHAP. III. CHAMOIS, GAZELLE.
CHAP.   IV. WILD SHEEP.
CHAP.   V. BEEF AND VEAL.
CHAP.   VI. KID AND LAMB.
CHAP. VII. PIG.
CHAP. VIII. HARE.
CHAP.   IX. DORMOUSE.

I

[329]   WILD BOAR IS PREPARED THUS
APER ITA CONDITUR

IT IS CLEANED; SPRINKLED WITH SALT AND CRUSHED CUMIN AND THUS LEFT. THE NEXT DAY IT IS PUT INTO THE OVEN; WHEN DONE SEASON WITH CRUSHED PEPPER. A SAUCE FOR BOAR: HONEY [1] BROTH, REDUCED WINE, RAISIN WINE.

[1] Lan., Tor. *vel* instead of *mel*.

[330]   ANOTHER WAY TO PREPARE BOAR
ALITER IN APRO

YOU BOIL THE BOAR IN SEA WATER WITH SPRIGS OF LAUREL; WHEN DONE NICE AND SOFT, REMOVE THE SKIN, SERVE WITH SALT, MUSTARD, VINEGAR.

[331] ANOTHER WAY TO COOK [sauce for] BOAR
       ALITER IN APRO

CRUSH PEPPER, LOVAGE, ORIGANY, SEEDLESS MYRTLE
BERRIES, CORIANDER, ONIONS; ADD HONEY, WINE, BROTH
AND A LITTLE OIL; HEAT AND TIE WITH ROUX. THE BOAR,
ROASTED IN THE OVEN, IS MASKED WITH THIS SAUCE,
WHICH YOU MAY USE FOR ANY KIND OF ROAST GAME [1].

[1] Tor. continues without interruption.

[332] MAKE A HOT SAUCE FOR ROAST BOAR THUS
       JURA FERVENTIA IN APRUM ASSUM FACIES SIC
       [1]

CRUSH PEPPER, CUMIN, CELERY SEED, MINT, THYME, SAT-
URY, SAFFRON, TOASTED NUTS, OR TOASTED ALMONDS,
HONEY, WINE, BROTH, VINEGAR AND A LITTLE OIL.

[1] Tor. *In aprum uerò assum*, indicating, perhaps, that ordinary pork also
was prepared "boar style." Cf. ℞ No. 362.

[333] ANOTHER HOT SAUCE FOR BOAR
       ALITER IN APRUM ASSUM IURA FERVENTIA

PEPPER, LOVAGE, CELERY SEED, MINT, THYME, TOASTED
NUTS, WINE, VINEGAR, BROTH, AND A LITTLE OIL. WHEN
THE SIMPLE BROTH [1] IS BOILING INCORPORATE THE
CRUSHED THINGS AND STIR WITH AN AROMATIC BOU-
QUET OF ONIONS AND RUE. IF YOU DESIRE TO MAKE THIS A
RICHER SAUCE, TIE IT WITH WHITES OF EGG, STIRRING
THE LIQUID EGG IN GENTLY. SPRINKLE WITH A LITTLE
PEPPER AND SERVE.

[1] Presumably the broth or stock in which the meat was roasted or braised.

[334] SAUCE FOR BOILED BOAR
       IUS IN APRUM ELIXUM

REAL SAUCE FOR BOILED BOAR IS COMPOSED IN THIS
MANNER [1] PEPPER, LOVAGE, CUMIN, SILPHIUM, ORI-
GANY, NUTS, FIGDATES, MUSTARD, VINEGAR, BROTH AND
OIL.

[1] Tor. sentence wanting in other texts.

[335] COLD SAUCE FOR BOILED BOAR [1]
       IUS FRIGIDUM IN APRUM ELIXUM

PEPPER, CUMIN, LOVAGE, CRUSHED CORIANDER SEED,

DILL SEED, CELERY SEED, THYME, ORIGANY, LITTLE ON-
ION, HONEY, VINEGAR, MUSTARD, BROTH AND OIL.

[1] ℞ No. 336 precedes this formula in Tor.

[336]   ANOTHER COLD SAUCE FOR BOILED BOAR
ALITER IUS FRIGIDUM IN APRUM ELIXUM

PEPPER, LOVAGE, CUMIN, DILL SEED, THYME, ORIGANY,
LITTLE SILPHIUM, RATHER MORE MUSTARD SEED, ADD
PURE WINE, SOME GREEN HERBS, A LITTLE ONION, CRUSH-
ED NUTS FROM THE PONTUS, OR ALMONDS, DATES, HONEY,
VINEGAR, SOME MORE PURE WINE, COLOR WITH REDUCED
MUST [and add] BROTH AND OIL [1].

[1] Strongly resembling our *vinaigrette*.

[337]   ANOTHER [sauce] FOR BOAR
ALITER [ius] IN APRO

CRUSH PEPPER, LOVAGE, ORIGANY, CELERY SEED, LASER
ROOT, CUMIN, FENNEL SEED, RUE, BROTH, WINE, RAISIN
WINE; HEAT, WHEN DONE TIE WITH ROUX; COVER THE
MEAT WITH THIS SAUCE SO AS TO PENETRATE THE MEAT
AND SERVE.

[338]   SHOULDER OF BOAR IS STUFFED IN THIS MAN-
NER
PERNA APRUNA ITA IMPLETUR [1]

LOOSEN THE MEAT FROM THE BONES BY MEANS OF A
WOODEN STICK IN ORDER TO FILL THE CAVITY LEFT BY
THE BONES WITH DRESSING WHICH IS INTRODUCED
THROUGH A FUNNEL. [The dressing season with] CRUSHED PEP-
PER, LAUREL BERRIES AND RUE; IF YOU LIKE, ADD LASER,
THE BEST KIND OF BROTH, REDUCED MUST AND SPRINKLE
WITH FRESH OIL. WHEN THE FILLING IS DONE, TIE THE
PARTS THUS STUFFED IN LINEN, PLACE THEM IN THE STOCK
POT IN WHICH THEY ARE TO BE COOKED AND BOIL THEM
IN SEA WATER, WITH A SPRIG OF LAUREL AND DILL [2].

[1] G.-V. *Terentina*, referring to a place in the Campus Martius, where the
ludi seculares were celebrated. Tor. *recentia*, fresh.

[2] The dressing consisted principally of pork or veal pounded fine, seasoned
as directed above, and tied with eggs, as is often prescribed by Apicius.

To verify how little high class cookery methods have changed consult one of
the foremost of modern authorities, Auguste Escoffier, of the Carlton and Ritz

hotels, London and Paris, who in his "Guide Culinaire" presents this dish under its ancient Italian name of *Zampino*.

II

VENISON [Stag]   *IN CERVO*

[339]   SAUCE FOR STAG   *IUS IN CERVUM*

CRUSH PEPPER, LOVAGE, CARRAWAY [1] ORIGANY, CEL-ERY SEED, LASER ROOT, FENNEL SEED, MOISTEN WITH BROTH, WINE [2] RAISIN WINE AND A LITTLE OIL. WHEN BOILING BIND WITH ROUX; THE COOKED MEAT IMMERSE IN THIS SAUCE [braise] TO PENETRATE AND TO SOFTEN, AND SERVE. FOR BROAD HORN DEER AS WELL AS FOR OTH-ER VENISON FOLLOW SIMILAR METHODS AND USE THE SAME CONDIMENTS.

[1] Tor. *carenum*; Hum. *legendum: careum*.
[2] Wanting in Tor.

[340]   ANOTHER WAY [1]   *ALITER*

PARBOIL AND BRAISE THE VENISON. CRUSH PEPPER, LOV-AGE, CARRAWAY, CELERY SEED, MOISTEN WITH HONEY, VINEGAR, BROTH AND OIL; HEAT, BIND WITH ROUX AND POUR OVER THE ROAST.

[1] Tor. Another little sauce for venison.

[341]   VENISON SAUCE   *IUS IN CERVO*

MIX PEPPER, LOVAGE, ONION, ORIGANY, NUTS, FIGDATES, HONEY, BROTH, MUSTARD, VINEGAR, OIL [1].

[1] Resembling a *vinaigrette*, except for the nuts and dates.

[342]   PREPARATION OF VENISON
CERVINÆ CONDITURA

PEPPER, CUMIN, CONDIMENTS, PARSLEY, ONION, RUE, HONEY, BROTH, MINT, RAISIN WINE, REDUCED WINE, AND A LITTLE OIL; BIND WITH ROUX WHEN BOILING.

[343]   HOT SAUCE FOR VENISON
IURA FERVENTIA IN CERVO

PEPPER, LOVAGE, PARSLEY, CUMIN, TOASTED NUTS OR ALMONDS, HONEY, VINEGAR, WINE, A LITTLE OIL; ADD BROTH AND STIR WELL.

[344]   MARINADE FOR ROAST VENISON
        EMBAMMA [1] *IN CERVINAM ASSAM*

PEPPER, NARD LEAVES, CELERY SEED, DRY ONIONS, GREEN RUE, HONEY, VINEGAR, BROTH, ADD DATES, RAISINS AND OIL.

[1] Tor. *Intinctus*, same; a *marinade*, a pickle or sauce in which to preserve or to flavor raw meat or fish.

[345]   ANOTHER HOT SAUCE FOR VENISON
        ALITER IN CERVUM ASSUM IURA FERVENTIA

PEPPER, LOVAGE, PARSLEY, STEWED DAMASCUS PRUNES, WINE, HONEY, VINEGAR, BROTH, A LITTLE OIL; STIR WITH A FAGOT OF LEEKS AND SATURY [1].

[1] A fagot of herbs; regarding this method of flavoring. Cf. notes to B No. 277 *seq*.

A sauce resembling our Cumberland, very popular with venison which is sweetened with currant jelly instead of the above prunes.

III

CHAMOIS, GAZELLE   *IN CAPREA*

[346]   SAUCE FOR WILD GOAT   *IUS IN CAPREA*

PEPPER, LOVAGE, CARRAWAY, CUMIN, PARSLEY, RUE SEED, HONEY, MUSTARD, VINEGAR, BROTH AND OIL

[347]   SAUCE FOR ROAST WILD GOAT
        IUS IN CAPREA ASSA

PEPPER, HERBS, RUE, ONION, HONEY, BROTH, RAISIN WINE, A LITTLE OIL, BIND WITH ROUX.

[347, a]   STILL ANOTHER   *ALITER*

AS ABOVE IS MADE WITH PARSLEY AND MARJORAM [1].

[1] Wanting in G.-V.

[347, b]   ANOTHER SAUCE FOR WILD GOAT
           ALITER IUS IN CAPREA

PEPPER, SPICES, PARSLEY, A LITTLE ORIGANY, RUE, BROTH, HONEY, RAISIN WINE, AND A LITTLE OIL; BIND WITH ROUX [1].

[1] Wanting in Tor.

IV

WILD SHEEP
        IN OVIFERO (HOC EST OVIS SILVATICA) [1]

[348]   SAUCE FOR MOUNTAIN SHEEP.
         IUS IN OVIFERO FERVENS

[THAT IS, (ROAST) THE MEAT, PREPARE A SAUCE OF] [2]
PEPPER, LOVAGE, CUMIN, DRY MINT [3], THYME, SILPHIUM,
MOISTEN WITH WINE, ADD STEWED DAMASCUS PRUNES,
HONEY, WINE, BROTH, VINEGAR, RAISIN WINE, — ENOUGH
TO COLOR — AND STIR WITH A WHIP OF ORIGANY AND
DRY MINT [3].

[1] G.-V., List. *in ovi fero*; Dann. "wild eggs," i.e., the eggs of game birds,
and he comes to the conclusion that game birds themselves are meant to be used
in this formula, as no reference to "eggs" is made.

There can be no doubt but what this formula deals with the preparation of
sheep; Torinus says expressly: *oviferum, hoc est, carnem ovis sylvestris* — the
meat of sheep from the woods, mountain sheep. *Ferum* is "wild," "game," but
it also means "pregnant." For this double sense the formula may be interpreted
as dealing with either wild sheep, or with pregnant sheep, or, more probably,
with unborn baby lamb, which in antiquity as today is often killed principally
for its skin.

[2] Tor.

[3] Mint is still associated with lamb; the above sauce appears to be merely
an elaborate Roman ancestor of our modern mint sauce, served with lamb, the
chief ingredients of which are mint, vinegar and sugar, served both hot and cold.

[349]   SAUCE FOR ALL KINDS OF GAME, BOILED OR
             ROAST
         *IUS IN VENATIONIBUS OMNIBUS ELIXIS ET
             ASSIS* [1]

8 SCRUPLES OF PEPPER, RUE, LOVAGE, CELERY SEED, JUNI-
PER, THYME, DRY MINT, 6 SCRUPLES IN WEIGHT [each] 3
SCRUPLES OF FLEA-BANE; REDUCE ALL THIS TO THE FINEST
POWDER, PUT IT TOGETHER IN A VESSEL WITH SUFFICIENT
HONEY AND USE IT WITH VINEGAR AND GARUM.

[1] Tor. *Jusculum omni venationi competens.*

[350]   COLD SAUCE FOR WILD SHEEP
         IUS FRIGIDUM IN OVIFERO [1]

PEPPER, LOVAGE, THYME, CUMIN, CRUSHED TOASTED

NUTS, HONEY, VINEGAR, BROTH, AND OIL; SPRINKLE WITH PEPPER.

[1] List. *omni fero*; which Dann. interprets, "All kind of game." Cf. note 1 to ℞ No. 348.

V

BEEF OR VEAL   *BUBULA SIVE VITELLINA*

[351]   VEAL STEAK   *VITELLINA FRICTA* [1]

[FOR A SAUCE WITH FRIED BEEF OR VEAL TAKE] [2] PEP-PER, LOVAGE, CELERY SEED, CUMIN, ORIGANY, DRY ONION, RAISINS, HONEY, VINEGAR, WINE, BROTH, OIL, AND RE-DUCED MUST.

[1] Evidently a beef or veal steak *sauté*. Beef did not figure very heavily on the dietary of the ancients in contrasts to present modes which make beef the most important meat, culinarily speaking. The above sauce, save for the raisins and the honey, resembles the modern *Bordelaise*, often served with beef steaks *sauté*, in contrast to the grilled steaks which are served with *maître d'hôtel* butter.

[352]   VEAL OR BEEF WITH LEEKS,
         VITULINAM [1] *SIVE BULULAM CUM PORRIS*

[or] WITH QUINCES [2] OR WITH ONIONS, OR WITH DASHEENS [3] [use] BROTH, PEPPER, LASER AND A LITTLE OIL.

[1] G.-V. same as *vitellinam*.
[2] Tor. *cydoniis*; List. *succidaneis*.
[3] Cf. ℞ No. 332 *et al.*

[353]   FRICASSÉE OF VEAL   *IN VITULINAM ELIXAM*

CRUSH PEPPER, LOVAGE, CARRAWAY, CELERY SEED, MOISTEN WITH HONEY, VINEGAR, BROTH AND OIL; HEAT, BIND WITH ROUX AND COVER THE MEAT.

[354]   ANOTHER VEAL FRICASSÉE
         ALITER IN VITULINA EXLIXA

PEPPER, LOVAGE, FENNEL SEED, ORIGANY, NUTS, FIG-DATES, HONEY, VINEGAR, BROTH, MUSTARD AND OIL.

VI

KID OR LAMB   *IN HÆDO VEL AGNO*

[355]   DAINTY DISHES OF KID OR OF LAMB
         COPADIA HÆDINA SIVE AGNINA

COOK WITH PEPPER AND BROTH, ALSO WITH VARIOUS

ORDINARY BEANS [1] BROTH, PEPPER AND LASER, CUMIN, DUMPLINGS [2] AND A LITTLE OIL [3].

[1] *cum faseolis*, green string beans.

[2] Tor. *imbrato*; G.-V. *inbracto*, broken bread, regular dumplings.

[3] Lamb and beans is a favorite combination, as in the French *haricot*, made with white beans, or boiled lamb with fresh string beans, quite a modern dish. Torinus omits the cumin, which is quite characteristic.

[356] ANOTHER LAMB STEW
ALITER HÆDINAM SIVE AGNINAM EXCALDA-TAM

PUT [pieces of] KID OR LAMB IN THE STEW POT WITH CHOPPED ONION AND CORIANDER. CRUSH PEPPER, LOVAGE, CUMIN, AND COOK WITH BROTH OIL AND WINE. PUT IN A DISH AND TIE WITH ROUX [1].

[1] It appears that the binding should be done before the stew is dished out; but this sentence illustrates the consummate art of Apicius. The good cook carefully separates the meat (as it is cooked) from the sauce, eliminates impurities, binds and strains it and puts the meat back into the finished sauce. This is the ideal way of making a stew which evidently was known to Apicius.

[357] ANOTHER LAMB STEW
ALITER HÆDINAM SIVE AGNINAM EXCALDA-TAM

ADD TO THE PARBOILED MEAT THE RAW HERBS THAT HAVE BEEN CRUSHED IN THE MORTAR AND COOK IT. GOAT MEAT IS COOKED LIKEWISE.

[358] BROILED KID OR LAMB STEAK
HÆDUM SIVE AGNUM ASSUM

KID AFTER BEING COOKED IN BROTH AND OIL IS SLICED AND MARINATED [1] WITH CRUSHED PEPPER, LASER, BROTH AND A LITTLE OIL. IT IS THEN GRILLED ON THE BROILER AND SERVED WITH GRAVY. SPRINKLE WITH PEPPER AND SERVE UP.

[1] The marinade is used to make the gravy.

[359] ROAST KID OR LAMB
ALITER HÆDUM SIVE AGNUM ASSUM

[LET US ROAST THE KID OR LAMB, ADDING] [1] HALF AN OUNCE OF PEPPER, 6 SCRUPLES OF FOALBIT [2] A LITTLE

GINGER, 6 SCRUPLES OF PARSLEY, A LITTLE LASER, A PINT OF BEST BROTH AND A SPOONFUL OIL [3].

[1] Tor.

[2] *Asarum*; Tor. *aseros*; List. *asareos* — the herb foalbit, foalfoot, wild spikenard.

[3] Tor. continues without interruption.

[360] STUFFED BONED KID OR LAMB
HÆDUS SIVE AGNUS SYRINGIATUS [1]

MILK-FED [2] KID OR LAMB IS CAREFULLY BONED THROUGH THE THROAT SO AS TO CREATE A PAUNCH OR BAG; THE INTESTINES ARE PRESERVED WHOLE IN A MANNER THAT ONE CAN BLOW OR INFLATE THEM AT THE HEAD IN ORDER TO EXPEL THE EXCREMENTS AT THE OTHER END; THE BODY IS WASHED CAREFULLY AND IS FILLED WITH A LIQUID DRESSING. THEREUPON TIE IT CAREFULLY AT THE SHOULDERS, PUT IT INTO THE ROASTING PAN, BASTE WELL. WHEN DONE, BOIL THE GRAVY WITH MILK AND PEPPER, PREVIOUSLY CRUSHED, AND BROTH, REDUCED WINE, A LITTLE REDUCED MUST AND ALSO OIL; AND TO THE BOILING GRAVY ADD ROUX. TO PLAY SAFE PUT THE ROAST IN A NETTING, BAG OR LITTLE BASKET AND CAREFULLY TIE TOGETHER, ADD A LITTLE SALT TO THE BOILING GRAVY. AFTER THIS HAS BOILED WELL THREE TIMES, TAKE THE MEAT OUT, BOIL THE BROTH OVER AGAIN [to reduce it] INCORPORATE WITH THE ABOVE DESCRIBED LIQUOR, ADDING THE NECESSARY SEASONING.

[1] "Hollowed out like a pipe."

[2] G.-V. *syringiatus* (*id est mammotestus*). Tor. *mammocestis*. We are guessing.

[3] We would call this a galatine of lamb if such a dish were made of lamb today.

This article, like the following appears to be a contraction of two different formulæ.

[361] STUFFED KID OR LAMB ANOTHER WAY
ALITER HÆDUS SIVE AGNUS SYRINGIATUS

KID OR LAMB IS THUS PREPARED AND SEASONED: TAKE [1] 1 PINT MILK, 4 OUNCES HONEY, 1 OUNCE PEPPER, A LITTLE SALT, A LITTLE LASER, GRAVY [of the lamb] 8 OUNCES CRUSHED DATES, A SPOONFUL OIL, A LITTLE BROTH, A

SPOONFUL HONEY [2] A PINT OF GOOD WINE AND A LITTLE ROUX.

[1] Tor.
[2] G.-V.

[362] THE RAW KID OR LAMB [1]
HÆDUS SIVE AGNUS CRUDUS

IS RUBBED WITH OIL AND PEPPER AND SPRINKLED WITH PLENTY OF CLEAN SALT AND CORIANDER SEED, PLACED IN THE OVEN, SERVED ROAST.

[1] It is quite evident that this sentence belongs to the preceding formula; but all the texts make a distinct separation.

[363] KID OR LAMB À LA TARPEIUS [1]
HÆDUM SIVE AGNUM TARPEIANUM

BEFORE COOKING THE LAMB TRUSS IT PROPERLY AND [marinate it in] PEPPER, RUE, SATURY, ONIONS, AND A LITTLE THYME AND BROTH. PLACE THE ROAST IN A PAN WITH OIL, BASTE WELL WHILE IN THE OVEN, WHEN COOKED THOROUGHLY, FILL THE PAN WITH CRUSHED SATURY, ONIONS, RUE, DATES, BROTH, WINE, REDUCED WINE, AND OIL; WHEN THIS GRAVY IS WELL COOKED [strain] PUT IT UP IN A DISH, SPRINKLE WITH PEPPER AND SERVE.

[1] Tor. *Tatarpeianum.* Tarpeius, family name of Romans. Humelberg thinks this dish is named for the people who dwelled on Mount Tarpeius. This was the Tarpeian Rock from which malefactors were thrown.

[364] KID OR LAMB PARTHIAN STYLE
HÆDUM SIVE AGNUM PARTHICUM

PUT [the roast] IN THE OVEN; CRUSH PEPPER, RUE, ONION, SATURY, STONED DAMASCUS PLUMS, A LITTLE LASER, WINE, BROTH AND OIL. HOT WINE IS SERVED ON THE SIDE AND TAKEN WITH VINEGAR.

[365] CREAMED KID FLAVORED WITH LAUREL [1]
HÆDUM LAUREATUM EX LACTE

[The kid] DRESS AND PREPARE, BONE, REMOVE THE INTESTINES WITH THE RENNET AND WASH. PUT IN THE MORTAR PEPPER, LOVAGE, LASER ROOT, 2 LAUREL BERRIES, A LITTLE CHAMOMILE AND 2 OR 3 BRAINS, ALL OF WHICH CRUSH. MOISTEN WITH BROTH AND SEASON

WITH SALT. OVER THIS MIXTURE STRAIN 2 PINTS [2] OF MILK, 2 LITTLE SPOONS OF HONEY. WITH THIS FORCE-MEAT STUFF THE INTESTINES AND WRAP THEM AROUND THE KID. COVER THE ROAST WITH CAUL AND PARCH-MENT PAPER TIGHTENED WITH SKEWERS, AND PLACE IT IN THE ROASTING PAN, ADDING BROTH, OIL AND WINE. WHEN HALF DONE, CRUSH PEPPER, LOVAGE, MOIST-EN WITH THE ROAST'S OWN GRAVY AND A LITTLE RE-DUCED MUST; PUT THIS BACK INTO THE PAN AND WHEN THE ROAST IS DONE COMPLETELY GARNISH IT AND BIND [the gravy] WITH ROUX AND SERVE.

[1] Dan. thinks *laureatus* stands for the best, the prize-winning meat, but the laurel may refer to the flavor used.

List. remarks that cow's milk was very scarce in Italy; likewise was goat's and sheep's milk; hence it is possible that the kid was cooked with it's mother's own milk.

[2] pints — *sextarii.*

VII

PIG   *IN PORCELLO*

[366]   SUCKLING PIG STUFFED TWO WAYS
PORCELLUM FARSILEM DUOBUS GENERIBUS

PREPARE, REMOVE THE ENTRAILS BY THE THROAT BE-FORE THE CARCASS HARDENS [immediately after killing]. MAKE AN OPENING UNDER THE EAR, FILL AN OX BLADDER WITH TARENTINE [1] SAUSAGE MEAT AND ATTACH A TUBE SUCH AS THE BIRD KEEPER USES TO THE NECK OF THE BLADDER AND SQUEEZE THE DRESSING INTO THE EAR AS MUCH AS IT WILL TAKE TO FILL THE BODY. THEN SEAL THE OPENING WITH PARCHMENT, CLOSE SECURELY [with skewers] AND PREPARE [the roast for the oven].

[1] Tor. *impensam Tarentinam*; G.-V. *Terentinam.*
The birdkeeper's tube may be an instrument for the cramming of fowl.

[366, a]   THE OTHER DRESSING IS MADE THUS:

CRUSH PEPPER, LOVAGE, ORIGANY, LASER ROOT, MOIST-EN WITH A LITTLE BROTH, ADD COOKED BRAINS, RAW EGGS, COOKED SPELT, GRAVY OF THE PIG, SMALL BIRDS (IF ANY) NUTS, WHOLE PEPPER, AND SEASON WITH BROTH. STUFF THE PIG, CLOSE THE OPENING WITH PARCHMENT AND SKEWERS AND PUT IT IN THE OVEN. WHEN DONE,

DRESS AND GARNISH VERY NICELY, GLAZE THE BODY AND
SERVE.

[367]   ANOTHER SUCKLING PIG *ALITER PORCELLUM*

SALT, CUMIN, LASER; ADD SAUSAGE MEAT. DILUTE
WITH BROTH [1] REMOVE THE WOMB OF THE PIG SO THAT
NO PART OF IT REMAINS INSIDE. CRUSH PEPPER, LOVAGE,
ORIGANY, MOISTEN WITH BROTH, ADD WINE [2] BRAINS,
MIX IN 2 EGGS, FILL THE [previously] PARBOILED PIG
WITH THIS FORCEMEAT, CLOSE TIGHT, PLACE IN A BASKET
AND IMMERSE IN THE BOILING STOCK POT. WHEN DONE
REMOVE THE SKEWERS BUT IN A MANNER THAT THE
GRAVY REMAINS INSIDE. SPRINKLE WITH PEPPER, SERVE.

[1] G.-V. treats the following as a separate article under the heading of
porcellum liquaminatum.

[2] G.-V. *unum* (one brain) instead of *uinum.*

[368]   STUFFED BOILED SUCKLING PIG
        PORCELLUM ELIXUM FARSILEM

REMOVE THE WOMB OF THE PIG. PARBOIL. CRUSH PEP-
PER, LOVAGE, ORIGANY, MOISTEN WITH BROTH. ADD
COOKED BRAINS, AS MUCH AS IS NEEDED [1] LIKEWISE DIS-
SOLVE EGGS, [add] BROTH TO TASTE, MAKE A SAUSAGE [of
this forcemeat] FILL THE PIG WHICH HAS BEEN PARBOILED
AND RINSED WITH BROTH. TIE THE PIG SECURELY IN A
BASKET, IMMERSE IN THE BOILING STOCK POT. REMOVE
WHEN DONE, WIPE CLEAN CAREFULLY, SERVE WITHOUT
PEPPER.

[1] To have a forcemeat of the right consistency.

[369]   ROAST SUCKLING PIG WITH HONEY
        PORCELLUM ASSUM TRACTOMELINUM [1]

EMPTY THE PIG BY THE NECK, CLEAN AND DRY, CRUSH
ONE OUNCE PEPPER, HONEY AND WINE, PLACE [this in a
sauce pan and] HEAT; NEXT BREAK DRY TOAST [2] AND MIX
WITH THE THINGS IN THE SAUCE PAN; STIR WITH A WHIP
OF FRESH LAUREL TWIGS [3] SO THAT THE PASTE IS NICE
AND SMOOTH UNTIL SUFFICIENTLY COOKED. THIS DRESS-
ING FILL INTO THE PIG, WRAP IN PARCHMENT, PLACE IN
THE OVEN [roast slowly, when done, glaze with honey] GARNISH
NICELY AND SERVE.

[1] treated with honey.

[2] Tor. *tactam siccatam* for *tractam*.

[3] Again this very subtle method of flavoring, so often referred to. This time it is a laurel whip. Cf. ℞ Nos. 277 *seq.*, 345, 369, 385.

[370] MILK-FED PIG, COLD, APICIAN SAUCE
PORCELLUM LACTE PASTUM ELIXUM CALIDUM
IURE FRIGIDO CRUDO APICIANO

SERVE BOILED MILK-FED PIG EITHER HOT OR COLD WITH THIS SAUCE [1] IN A MORTAR, PUT PEPPER, LOVAGE, CORIANDER SEED, MINT, RUE, AND CRUSH IT. MOISTEN WITH BROTH. ADD HONEY, WINE AND BROTH. THE BOILED PIG IS WIPED OFF HOT WITH A CLEAN TOWEL, [cooled off] COVERED WITH THE SAUCE AND SERVED [2].

[1] Tor.

[2] This sentence wanting in Tor.

[371] SUCKLING PIG À LA VITELLIUS [1]
PORCELLUM VITELLIANUM

SUCKLING PIG CALLED VITELLIAN STYLE IS PREPARED THUS [2] GARNISH THE PIG LIKE WILD BOAR [3] SPRINKLE WITH SALT, ROAST IN OVEN. IN THE MORTAR PUT PEPPER, LOVAGE, MOISTEN WITH BROTH, WINE AND RAISIN WINE TO TASTE, PUT THIS IN A SAUCE PAN, ADDING VERY LITTLE OIL, HEAT; THE ROASTING PIG BASTE WITH THIS IN A MANNER SO THAT [the aroma] WILL PENETRATE THE SKIN.

[1] Named for Vitellius, Roman emperor.

[2] Tor. sentence wanting in other texts.

[3] i.e. marinated with raw vegetables, wine, spices, etc. Cf. ℞ Nos. 329-30.

[372] SUCKLING PIG À LA FLACCUS
PORCELLUM FLACCIANUM [1]

THE PIG IS GARNISHED LIKE WILD BOAR [2] SPRINKLE WITH SALT, PLACE IN THE OVEN. WHILE BEING DONE PUT IN THE MORTAR PEPPER, LOVAGE, CARRAWAY, CELERY SEED, LASER ROOT, GREEN RUE, AND CRUSH IT, MOISTEN WITH BROTH, WINE AND RAISIN WINE TO TASTE, PUT THIS IN A SAUCE PAN, ADDING A LITTLE OIL, HEAT, BIND WITH ROUX. THE ROAST PIG, FREE FROM BONES, SPRINKLE WITH POWDERED CELERY SEED AND SERVE.

[1] List. named for Flaccus Hordeonius, (*puto*). Flaccus was a rather common Roman family name.

[2] Cf. note 3 to ℞ No. 371, also ℞ Nos. 329-30. Lister is thoroughly puzzled by this procedure, but the problem is very simple: just treat the pig like wild boar.

[373] SUCKLING PIG, LAUREL FLAVOR
PORCELLUM LAUREATUM

THE PIG IS BONED AND GARNISHED WITH A LITTLE WINE SAUCE [1] PARBOIL WITH GREEN LAUREL IN THE CENTER [2] AND PLACE IT IN THE OVEN TO BE ROASTED SUFFICIENTLY. MEANWHILE PUT IN THE MORTAR PEPPER, LOVAGE, CARRAWAY, CELERY SEED, LASER ROOT, AND LAUREL BERRIES, CRUSH THEM, MOISTEN WITH BROTH, WINE AND RAISIN WINE TO TASTE. [Put this in a sauce pan and heat] BIND [with roux; untie the pig] REMOVE THE LAUREL LEAVES; INCORPORATE THE JUICE OF THE BONES [from which a gravy has been made in the meantime] AND SERVE.

[1] marinate in the ordinary way with œnogarum as the dominant flavor.

[2] It is presumed that the boned pig is rolled and tied, with the leaves in the center.

[374] SUCKLING PIG À LA FRONTO [1]
PORCELLUM FRONTINIANUM

BONE THE PIG, PARBOIL, GARNISH; IN A SAUCE PAN. ADD BROTH, WINE, BIND. WHEN HALF DONE, ADD A BUNCH OF LEEKS AND DILL, SOME REDUCED MUST. WHEN COOKED WIPE THE PIG CLEAN, LET IT DRIP OFF; SPRINKLE WITH PEPPER, SERVE.

[1] List. Probably named for Julius Fronto, prætor urbanus under Vitellius. Cornelius Fronto was an orator and author at the time of emperor Hadrian. Cf. ℞ No. 246. G. V. Frontinianus.

[375] SUCKLING PIG STEWED IN WINE
PORCELLUM ŒNOCOCTUM [1]

SCALD [parboil] THE PIG [and] MARINATE [2] PLACE IN A SAUCE PAN [with] OIL, BROTH, WINE AND WATER, TIE A BUNCH OF LEEKS AND CORIANDER; [cook (in the oven)] WHEN HALF DONE COLOR WITH REDUCED MUST. IN THE MORTAR PUT PEPPER, LOVAGE, CARRAWAY, ORIGANY, CELERY SEED, LASER ROOT AND CRUSH THEM, MOISTEN WITH BROTH, ADD THE PIG'S OWN GRAVY AND RAISIN WINE TO TASTE. ADD THIS [to the meat in the sauce pan] AND

LET IT BOIL. WHEN BOILING BIND WITH ROUX. THE PIG, PLACED ON A PLATTER, MASK [with the sauce] SPRINKLE WITH PEPPER AND SERVE.

[1] Tor. *vino elixatus*; G.-V. *œnococtum*.

[2] It is presumed that the pig is prepared for coction as in the foregoing, namely cleaned, washed, boned, etc. This also applies to the succeeding recipes of pig.

[376] PIG À LA CELSINUS [1]
PORCELLUM CELSINIANUM

PREPARE [as above] INJECT [the following dressing made of] PEPPER, RUE, ONIONS, SATURY, THE PIG'S OWN GRAVY [and] EGGS THROUGH THE EAR [2] AND OF PEPPER, BROTH AND A LITTLE WINE [make a sauce which is served] IN THE SAUCE BOAT [3]; AND ENJOY IT.

[1] Tor. *Cæsianus*; Tac. *cesinianum*; G.-V. *Celsinianum*. Lister goes far out of his way to prove that the man for whom this dish was named was Celsinus. He cites a very amusing bit of ancient humor by Petrus Lambecius, given below.

[2] Really a dressing in a liquid state when raw, a custard syringed into the carcass, which congeals during coction. Eggs must be in proper proportion to the other liquids. The pig thus filled is either steamed, roasted or baked, well protected by buttered or oiled paper — all of which the ancient author failed to state, as a matter of course.

[3] *acetabulum.*

"The Porker's Last Will and Testament"
by Petrus Lambecius
(V. Barnab. Brissonium de Formulis lib. VII, p. 677)
[ex Lister, 1705, p. 196; Lister, 1709, p. 236].

"I, M. Grunter Corocotta Porker, do hereby make my last will and testament. Incapable of writing in my own hand, I have dictated what is to be set down:

"The Chief Cook sayeth: 'Come here, you — who has upset this house, you nuissance, you porker! I'll deprive you of your life this day!'

"Corocotta Porker sayeth: 'What, perchance, have I done? In what way, please, have I sinned? Have I with my feet perhaps smashed your crockery? I beg of you, Mr. Cook, I entreat you, if such be the case, kindly grant the supplicant a reprieve.'

"The Chief Cook sayeth: 'Go over there, boy! Fetch me from the kitchen that slaughtering-knife. I'm just itching to give this porker a blood-bath!'

"Mr. Porker, realizing that this is the season when cabbage sprouts are abundant, and visualizing himself potted and peppered, and furthermore seeing that death is inevitable, asks for time and begs of the cook whether it was possible to make a will. This granted, he calls out with a loud voice to his parents to save for them the food that was to have been his own in the future, to wit:

"To my father, Mr. Genuine Bacon-Fat, appointed by me in my last will I give and bequeath: thirty measures of acorns; and to my mother, Mrs. Old-Timer Sow, appointed by me in my last will, I give and bequeath: forty measures of Spartan wheat; and to my sister, Cry-Baby, appointed by me in my last will, whose wedding, alas! I cannot attend, I give and bequeath: thirty measures of barley; and of my nobler parts and property I give and bequeath, to the cobbler: my bristles; to the brawlers, my jaw-bones; to the deaf, my ears; to the shyster lawyers, my tongue; to the cow-herds, my intestines; to the sausage makers, my thighs; to the ladies, my tenderloins; to the boys, my bladder; to the girls, my little pig's tail; to the dancers, my muscles; to the runners and hunters, my knuckles; to the hired man, my hoofs; and to the cook — though not to be named — I give and bequeath and transmit my belly and appendage which I have dragged with me from the rotten oak bottoms to the pig's sty, for him to tie around his neck and to hang himself with.

"I wish to erect a monument to myself, inscribed with golden letters: 'M. Grunter Corocotta Porker lived nine-hundred-and-ninety-nine years, and had he lived another half year, a thousand years would have been nearly completed.'

"I ask of you who love me best, you who live like me, I ask you: will not my name remain to be eulogized in all eternity? if you only will prepare my body properly and flavor it well with good condiments, nuts, pepper and honey!

"My master and my relatives, all of you who have witnessed this execution of my last will and testament, you are requested to sign.

" (Signed) Hard Sausage
            Match Maker
            Fat Bacon
            Bacon Rind
            Celsinus
            Meat Ball
            Sprout Cabbage."

Thus far the story by Petrus Lambecius. The fifth of the signatories of the Porker's Testament is Celsinus; and since the other names are fictitious it is quite possible that Lambecius had a special purpose in pointing out the man for whom the dish, Porcellus Celsinianus, — Suckling Pig à la Celsinus — was named.

Celsinus was councellor for Aurelianus, the emperor.

[377] ROAST PIG *PORCELLUM ASSUM*
CRUSH PEPPER, RUE, SATURY, ONIONS, HARD YOLKS OF EGG, BROTH, WINE, OIL, SPICES; BOIL THESE INGREDIENTS, POUR OVER THE [roast] PIG IN THE SAUCE PAN AND SERVE.

[378] PIG À LA JARDINIÈRE
PORCELLUM HORTOLANUM [1]
THE PIG IS BONED THROUGH THE THROAT AND FILLED WITH QUENELLES OF CHICKEN FORCEMEAT, FINELY CUT

[roast] THRUSHES, FIG-PECKERS, LITTLE SAUSAGE CAKES, MADE OF THE PIG'S MEAT, LUCANIAN SAUSAGE, STONED DATES, EDIBLE BULBS [glazed onions] SNAILS TAKEN OUT OF THE SHELL [and poached] MALLOWS, LEEKS, BEETS, CELERY, COOKED SPROUTS, CORIANDER, WHOLE PEPPER, NUTS, 15 EGGS POURED OVER, BROTH, WHICH IS SPICED WITH PEPPER, AND DILUTED WITH 3 EGGS; THEREUPON SEW IT TIGHT, STIFFEN, AND ROAST IN THE OVEN. WHEN DONE, OPEN THE BACK [of the pig] AND POUR OVER THE FOLLOWING SAUCE: CRUSHED PEPPER, RUE, BROTH, RAISIN WINE, HONEY AND A LITTLE OIL, WHICH WHEN BOILING IS TIED WITH ROUX [2].

[1] Tor. *Hortulanus*; Gardener's style, the French equivalent *Jardinière*, a very common name for all dishes containing young vegetables. However, in the above rich formula there is very little to remind us of the gardener's style, excepting the last part of the formula, enumerating a number of fresh vegetables. It is unthinkable for any gourmet to incorporate these with the rich dressing. The vegetables should be used as a garnish for the finished roast. This leads us to believe that the above is really two distinct formulæ, or that the vegetables were intended for garniture.

[2] This extraordinary and rich dressing, perfectly feasible and admirable when compared with our own "Toulouse," "Financière," "Chipolata," can be palatable only when each component part is cooked separately before being put into the pig. The eggs must be whipped and diluted with broth and poured over the filling to serve as binder. The pig must be parboiled before filling, and the final cooking or roasting must be done very slowly and carefully — procedure not stated by the original which it takes for granted.

[379]   COLD SAUCE FOR BOILED SUCKLING PIG
JUS PORRO [1] *FRIGIDUM IN PORCELLUM ELIXUM*

CRUSH PEPPER, CARRAWAY, DILL, LITTLE ORIGANY, PINE NUTS, MOISTEN WITH VINEGAR, BROTH [2], DATE WINE, HONEY, PREPARED MUSTARD; SPRINKLE WITH A LITTLE OIL, PEPPER, AND SERVE.

[1] Tor. only; *porrò* indicating that the sauce may also be served with the foregoing. Wanting in List. *et al.*

[2] Wanting in Tor.

[380]   SMOKED PIG À LA TRAJANUS
PORCELLUM TRAIANUM [1]

MAKE THUS: BONE THE PIG, TREAT IT AS FOR STEWING

IN WINE [℞ No. 375, i.e. marinate for some time in spices, herbs and wine] THEREUPON HANG IT IN THE SMOKE HOUSE [2] NEXT BOIL IT IN SALT WATER AND SERVE THUS [3] ON A LARGE PLATTER [4].

[1] Tor. and Tac. *traganum.*

[2] *ad fumum suspendes*; G.-V. *et adpendeas, et quantum adpendeas, tantum salis in ollam mittes* — passage wanting in other texts, meaning, probably, that the more pigs are used for smoking the more salt must be used for pickling which is a matter of course, or, the heavier the pig, . . .

[3] Tor. *atque ita in lance efferes*; Tac. *& sic eum* . . .; G.-V. *et siccum in lance inferes.*

[4] Hum. *salso recente*, with fresh salt pork. Tor. *cum salsamento istoc recenti* and Tor. continues without interruption, indicating, perhaps, that the following formula is to be served, or treated (boiled) like the above.

[381] MILK-FED PIG   *IN PORCELLO LACTANTE* [1]

ONE OUNCE OF PEPPER, A PINT OF WINE, A RATHER LARGE GLASS OF THE BEST OIL, A GLASS OF BROTH [2], AND RATHER LESS THAN A GLASS OF VINEGAR [3].

[1] G.-V. *lactans*, suckling, milk-fed; other texts: *lactente*: Dann. wild boar.

[2] wanting in Tac and Tor.

[3] a variant of the foregoing, a mild pickling solution for extremely young suckling pigs, prior to their smoking or boiling, or both, which the original does not state.

Schuch and his disciple Danneil, have inserted here seven more pork formulæ (Sch. p. 179, ℞ Nos. 388-394) taken from the Excerpts of Vinidarius, found at the conclusion of the Apicius formulæ.

VIII

HARE   *LEPOREM*

[382] BRAISED HARE   *LEPOREM MADIDUM*

IS PARBOILED A LITTLE IN WATER, THEREUPON PLACE IT ON A ROASTING PAN WITH OIL, TO BE ROASTED IN THE OVEN. AND WHEN PROPERLY DONE, WITH A CHANGE OF OIL, IMMERSE IT IN THE FOLLOWING GRAVY: CRUSH PEPPER, SATURY, ONION, RUE, CELERY SEED; MOISTEN WITH BROTH, LASER, WINE, AND A LITTLE OIL. WHILE THE ROASTING [of the hare] IS BEING COMPLETED IT IS SEVERAL TIMES BASTED WITH THE GRAVY.

Wanting in Goll.

A difference in the literary style from the foregoing is quite noticeable.

[383]   THE SAME, WITH A DIFFERENT DRESSING
ITEM ALIA AD EUM IMPENSAM

[The hare] MUST BE PROPERLY KEPT [i.e. aged for a few days after killing]. CRUSH PEPPER, DATES, LASER, RAISINS, REDUCED WINE, BROTH AND OIL; DEPOSIT [the hare in this preparation to be cooked] WHEN DONE, SPRINKLE WITH PEPPER AND SERVE.

Wanting in Goll. Tor. continuing without interruption.

[384]   STUFFED HARE   *LEPOREM FARSUM*

WHOLE [pine] NUTS, ALMONDS, CHOPPED NUTS OR BEECHNUTS, WHOLE PEPPER ARE MIXED WITH THE [force] MEAT OF HARE THICKENED WITH EGGS AND WRAPPED IN PIG'S CAUL TO BE ROASTED IN THE OVEN [1]. ANOTHER FORCEMEAT IS MADE WITH RUE, PLENTY OF PEPPER, ONION, SATURY, DATES, BROTH, REDUCED WINE, OR SPICED WINE. THIS IS REDUCED TO THE PROPER CONSISTENCY AND IS LAID UNDER; BUT THE HARE REMAINS IN THE BROTH FLAVORED WITH LASER.

[1] Reminding of the popular meat loaf, made of remnants: *Falscher Hase*, "Imitation Hare," as it is known on the Continent.

The ancients probably used the trimmings of hare and other meat for this forcemeat, or meat loaf, either to stuff the hare with, or to make a meal of the preparation itself, as indicated above.

We also recall that the ancients had ingenious baking moulds of metal in the shape of hares and other animals. These moulds, no doubt, were used for baking or the serving of preparations of this sort. The absence of table forks and cutlery as is used today made such preparations very appropriate and convenient in leisurely dining.

[385]   WHITE SAUCE FOR HARE
IUS ALBUM IN ASSUM LEPOREM

PEPPER, LOVAGE, CUMIN, CELERY SEED, HARD BOILED YOLKS, PROPERLY POUNDED, MADE INTO A PASTE. IN A SAUCE PAN BOIL BROTH, WINE, OIL, A LITTLE VINEGAR AND CHOPPED ONIONS. WHILE BOILING ADD THE PASTE OF SPICES, STIRRING WITH A FAGOT OF ORIGANY OR SATURY [1] AND WHEN THE WORK IS DONE, BIND IT WITH ROUX.

[1] Fagots, or whips made of different herbs and brushes are often employed by Apicius, a very subtle device to impart faint flavors to sauces. The custom

has been in use for ages. With the return of mixed drinks in America it was re-vived by the use of cinnamon sticks with which to stir the drinks.

The above hare formulæ are wanting in Goll.

[386] LIGHTS OF HARE [1]
ALITER IN LEPOREM [2]

A FINE HASH OF HARE'S BLOOD, LIVER AND LUNGS. PUT INTO A SAUCE PAN BROTH AND OIL, AND LET IT BOIL WITH FINELY CHOPPED LEEKS AND CORIANDER; NOW ADD THE LIVERS AND LUNGS, AND, WHEN DONE, CRUSH PEPPER, CUMIN, CORIANDER, LASER ROOT, MINT, RUE, FLEA-BANE, MOISTENED WITH VINEGAR [3].

[1] Wanting in Goll.

[2] Tor. *Condimentum ex visceribus leporinis.*

[3] The various texts combine the above and the following formula; but we are of the opinion that they are two distinct preparations.

[387] LIGHTS OF HARE, ANOTHER WAY   *ALITER*

TO THE HARE'S LIVER ADD THE BLOOD AND POUND IT WITH HONEY AND SOME OF THE HARE'S OWN GRAVY; ADD VINEGAR TO TASTE AND PUT IN A SAUCE PAN, ADD THE LUNGS CHOPPED FINE, MAKE IT BOIL: WHEN DONE BIND WITH ROUX, SPRINKLE WITH PEPPER AND SERVE.

This and the preceding formula resemble closely our purées or forcemeats of livers of game and fowl, which are spread on croutons to accompany the roast.

[388] HARE IN ITS OWN BROTH [1]
ALITER LEPOREM EX SUO IURE

PREPARE THE HARE, BONE IT, GARNISH [2] PUT IT IN A STEW POT [3] AND WHEN HALF DONE ADD A SMALL BUNCH OF LEEKS, CORIANDER, DILL; WHILE THIS IS BEING DONE, PUT IN THE MORTAR PEPPER, LOVAGE, CUMIN, COR-IANDER SEED, LASER ROOT, DRY ONION, MINT, RUE, CEL-ERY SEED; CRUSH, MOISTEN WITH BROTH, ADD HONEY, THE HARE'S OWN GRAVY, REDUCED MUST AND VINEGAR TO TASTE; LET IT BOIL, TIE WITH ROUX, DRESS, GARNISH THE ROAST ON A PLATTER, UNDERLAY THE SAUCE, SPRIN-KLE AND SERVE.

[1] Cf. Goll. ℞ No. 381.

[2] with vegetables for braising, possibly larding.

[3] *braisière*, for this is plainly a "potroast" of hare. The boned carcass should

be tied; this is perhaps meant by or is included in *ornas* — garnish, i.e. getting ready for braising.

[389] HARE À LA PASSENIANUS [1]
LEPOREM PASSENIANUM

THE HARE IS DRESSED, BONED, THE BODY SPREAD OUT [2] GARNISHED [with pickling herbs and spices] AND HUNG INTO THE SMOKE STACK [3] WHEN IT HAS TAKEN ON COLOR, COOK IT HALF DONE, WASH IT, SPRINKLE WITH SALT AND IMMERSE IT IN WINE SAUCE. IN THE MORTAR PUT PEPPER, LOVAGE, AND CRUSH: MOISTEN WITH BROTH, WINE AND A LITTLE OIL, HEAT; WHEN BOILING, BIND WITH ROUX. NOW DETACH THE SADDLE OF THE ROAST HARE, SPRINKLE WITH PEPPER AND SERVE.

[1] This personage, Passenius, or Passenianus, is not identified.

[2] To bone the carcass, it usually is opened in the back, flattened out and all the bones are easily removed. In that state it is easily pickled and thoroughly smoked.

[3] Lan., Tac., and Tor. *suspendes ad furnum*; Hum., List., and G.-V. . . . *ad fumum*. We accept the latter reading, "in the smoke," assuming that *furnum* is a typographical error in Lan. and his successors, Tac. and Tor. Still, roasts have for ages been "hung on chains close to or above the open fire"; Torinus may not be wrong, after all, in this essential direction. However, a boned and flattened-out hare would be better broiled on the grill than hung up over the open fire.

[390] KROMESKIS OF HARE   *LEPOREM ISICIATUM*

THE HARE IS COOKED AND FLAVORED IN THE SAME [above] MANNER; SMALL BITS OF MEAT ARE MIXED WITH SOAKED NUTS; THIS [salpicon] [1] IS WRAPPED IN CAUL OR PARCHMENT, THE ENDS BEING CLOSED BY MEANS OF SKEWERS [and fried].

[1] We call this preparation a salpicon because it closely resembles to our modern salpicons — a fine mince of meats, mushrooms, etc., although the ancient formula fails to state the binder of this mince — either eggs or a thickened sauce, or both.

[391] STUFFED HARE   *LEPOREM FARSILEM*

DRESS THE HARE [as usual] GARNISH [marinate] IT, PLACE IN A SQUARE PAN [1]. IN THE MORTAR PUT PEPPER, LOVAGE, ORIGANY, MOISTEN WITH BROTH, ADD CHICKEN LIVERS [sauté] COOKED BRAINS, FINELY CUT MEAT [2] 3

RAW EGGS, BROTH TO TASTE. WRAP IT IN CAUL OR PARCH-
MENT, FASTEN WITH SKEWERS. HALF ROAST ON A SLOW
FIRE. [Meanwhile] PUT IN THE MORTAR PEPPER, LOVAGE:
CRUSH AND MOISTEN WITH BROTH, WINE, SEASON, MAKE
IT HOT, WHEN BOILING BIND WITH ROUX; THE HALF-
DONE HARE IMMERSE [finish its cooking in this broth] SPRINKLE
WITH PEPPER AND SERVE.

[1] *Quadratum imponis*, which is plain enough. The hare is to be roast therein. Dann. Cut in dice; Goll. Spread it out. Cf. illustration of square roast pan.

[2] Presumably the trimmings of the hare or of pork. This forcemeat is supposed to be used for the stuffing of the hare; it, being boned, is rolled up, the
forcemeat inside, the outside covered with caul or paper, fastened with skewers.
Danneil's interpretation suggests the thought that the raw hare's meat is cut into
squares which are filled with forcemeat, rolled, wrapped, and roast — a roulade
of hare in the regular term.

[392]   BOILED HARE   *ALITER LEPOREM EXLIXUM*

DRESS THE HARE; [boil it]. IN A FLAT SAUCE PAN POUR
OIL, BROTH, VINEGAR, RAISIN WINE, SLICED ONION, GREEN
RUE AND CHOPPED THYME [a sauce which is served on the side]
AND SO SERVE IT.

Tor. continuing without interruption.

[393]   SPICED SAUCE FOR HARE *LEPORIS CONDITURA*

CRUSH PEPPER, RUE, ONIONS, THE HARE'S LIVER, BROTH,
REDUCED WINE, RAISIN WINE, A LITTLE OIL; BIND WITH
RUE WHEN BOILING.

Tor. *id.*

[394]   SPRINKLED HARE
        LEPOREM (PIPERE) SICCO SPARSUM [1]

DRESS THE HARE AS FOR KID À LA TARPEIUS [℞ No. 363].
BEFORE COOKING DECORATE IT NICELY [2]. SEASON WITH
PEPPER, RUE, SATURY, ONION, LITTLE THYME, MOISTEN
WITH BROTH, ROAST IN THE OVEN; AND ALL OVER SPRIN-
KLE HALF AN OUNCE OF PEPPER, RUE, ONIONS, SATURY,
4 DATES, AND RAISINS. THE GRAVY IS GIVEN PLENTY OF
COLOR OVER THE OPEN FIRE, AND IS SEASONED WITH
WINE, OIL, BROTH, REDUCED WINE, FREQUENTLY STIR-
RING IT [basting the hare] SO THAT IT MAY ABSORB ALL THE

FLAVOR. AFTER THAT SERVE IT IN A ROUND DISH WITH
DRY PEPPER.

[1] Tac., Tor. *succo sparsum.*

[2] We have no proof that the ancients used the larding needle as we do (or
did) in our days. "Decorate" may, therefore, also mean "garnish," i.e. marinate
the meat in a generous variety of spices, herbs, roots and wine. It is noteworthy
that this term, "garnish," used here and in the preceding formulæ has survived
in the terminology of the kitchen to this day, in that very sense.

[395] SPICED HARE   *ALITER LEPOREM CONDITUM*

[The well-prepared hare] COOK IN WINE, BROTH, WATER,
WITH A LITTLE MUSTARD [seed], DILL AND LEEKS WITH
THE ROOTS. WHEN ALL IS DONE, SEASON WITH PEPPER,
SATURY, ROUND ONIONS, DAMASCUS PLUMS, WINE,
BROTH, REDUCED WINE AND A LITTLE OIL; TIE WITH
ROUX, LET BOIL A LITTLE LONGER [baste] SO THAT THE
HARE IS PENETRATED BY THE FLAVOR, AND SERVE IT ON
A PLATTER MASKED WITH SAUCE.

IX

DORMICE   *GLIRES*

[396] STUFFED DORMOUSE [1]   *GLIRES*

IS STUFFED WITH A FORCEMEAT OF PORK AND SMALL
PIECES OF DORMOUSE MEAT TRIMMINGS, ALL POUNDED
WITH PEPPER, NUTS, LASER, BROTH. PUT THE DORMOUSE
THUS STUFFED IN AN EARTHEN CASSEROLE, ROAST IT IN
THE OVEN, OR BOIL IT IN THE STOCK POT.

[1] *Glis*, dormouse, a special favorite of the ancients, has nothing to do with
mice. The fat dormouse of the South of Europe is the size of a rat, arboreal
rodent, living in trees.

Galen, III, de Alim.; Plinius, VIII, 57/82; Varro, III, describing the *glirarium*,
place where the dormouse was raised for the table.

Petronius, Cap. 31, describes another way of preparing dormouse. Nonnus,
Diæteticon, p. 194/5, says that Fluvius Hirpinus was the first man to raise dormouse in the *glirarium.*

Dormouse, as an article of diet, should not astonish Americans who relish
squirrel, opossum, muskrat, "coon," etc.

END OF BOOK VIII

EXPLICIT APICII TETRAPUS LIBER OCTAUUS [Tac.]

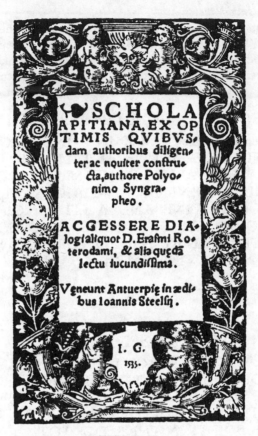

TITLE PAGE

Schola Apitiana, Antwerp, 1535

APICIUS
Book IX

WINE PITCHER, ELABORATELY DECORATED

"Egg and bead" pattern on the rim. The upper end of handle takes the form of a goddess — Scylla, or Diana with two hounds — ending in acanthus leaves below the waist. On the curved back of handle is a long leaf; the lower attachment is in the form of a mask, ivy-crowned maenad (?). Ntl. Mus., Naples, 69171; Field M., 24048.

CACCABUS

Stewpot, marmite, without a base, to fit
into a hole of stove. The flat lid fits into
the mouth of the pot. Found in Pompeii.
Ntl. Mus., Naples, 74806; Field M., 24171.

BOOK IX. SEAFOOD

Lib. IX. Thalassa

CHAP.   I. SHELLFISH.
CHAP.   II. RAY.
CHAP. III. CALAMARY.
CHAP. IV. CUTTLEFISH.
CHAP.   V. POLYPUS.
CHAP. VI. OYSTERS.
CHAP. VII. ALL KINDS OF BIVALVES.
CHAP. VIII. SEA URCHIN.
CHAP. IX. MUSSELS.
CHAP.   X. SARDINES.
CHAP. XI. FISH SAUCES.
CHAP. XII. BAIAN SEAFOOD STEW.

I

SHELLFISH   *IN LOCUSTA*

[397]   SAUCE FOR SHELLFISH
         IUS IN LOCUSTA ET CAPPARI [1]

CHOPPED SCALLIONS FRIED LIGHTLY, CRUSH PEPPER,
LOVAGE, CARRAWAY, CUMIN, FIGDATES, HONEY,
    VINEGAR, WINE, BROTH, OIL, REDUCED MUST; WHILE
BOILING ADD MUSTARD.

[1] *locusta*, spiny lobster; Fr. *langouste*; G.-V. *capparus*; not clear. (*camma-rus*, a crab); List. *carabus* — long-tailed lobster or crab, the *cancer cursor* of Linnæus, according to Beckmann; mentioned by Plinius.

[398]   BROILED LOBSTER   *LOCUSTAS ASSAS*

MAKES THUS: IF BROILED, THEY SHOULD APPEAR IN
THEIR SHELL; [which is opened by splitting the live lobster in two]
SEASON WITH PEPPER SAUCE AND CORIANDER SAUCE [moisten with oil] AND BROIL THEM ON THE GRILL. WHEN THEY
ARE DRY [1] KEEP ON BASTING THEM MORE AND MORE
[with oil or butter] UNTIL THEY ARE PROPERLY BROILED [2].

[1] i.e. when the soft jelly-like meat has congealed.

[2] Same procedure as today.

[399]   BOILED LOBSTER WITH CUMIN SAUCE [1]
LOCUSTAM ELIXAM CUM CUMINATO

REAL BOILED LOBSTER IS COOKED WITH CUMIN SAUCE
[essence] AND, BY RIGHT, THROW IN SOME [whole] [2] PEPPER, LOVAGE, PARSLEY, DRY MINT, A LITTLE MORE WHOLE
CUMIN, HONEY, VINEGAR, BROTH, AND, IF YOU LIKE, ADD
SOME [bay] LEAVES AND MALOBATHRON [3].

[1] Cumin, mustard and other spices similar to the above are used for cooking crawfish today.

[2] Sentence ex Tor. wanting in other texts.

[3] Malabathrum, aromatic leaves of an Indian tree; according to Plinius the
laurus cassia — wild cinnamon.

[400]   ANOTHER LOBSTER DISH — MINCE OF THE
TAIL MEAT
ALITER LOCUSTAM — ISICIA DE CAUDA EIUS
SIC FACIES

HAVE LEAVES READY [in which to wrap the mince croquettes]
BOIL [the lobster] TAKE THE CLUSTER OF SPAWN [from under
the female's tail, and the coral of the male] THEREUPON CUT FINE
THE [boiled] MEAT OF THE TAIL, AND WITH BROTH AND
PEPPER AND THE EGGS MAKE THE CROQUETTES [and fry].

It is understood that hen eggs are added to bind the mince.

[401]   BOILED LOBSTER   *IN LOCUSTA ELIXA*

PEPPER, CUMIN, RUE, HONEY, VINEGAR, BROTH AND OIL.

[402]   ANOTHER LOBSTER PREPARATION
ALITER IN LOCUSTA

FOR LOBSTER LET US PROPERLY EMPLOY [1] PEPPER, LOV-

AGE, CUMIN, MINT, RUE, NUTS, HONEY, VINEGAR, BROTH, AND WINE.

[1] Tor. *rectè adhibemus*, sentence not in the other texts.

II

RAY, SKATE *IN TORPEDINE* [1]

[403] [A Sauce for] RAY *IN TORPEDINE*

CRUSH PEPPER, RUE, SHALLOTS, [adding] HONEY, BROTH, RAISIN WINE, A LITTLE WINE, ALSO A FEW DROPS OF OIL; WHEN IT COMMENCES TO BOIL, BIND WITH ROUX.

[1] *torpedo*; the *raia torpedo* of Linnæus; a ray or skate.

[404] BOILED RAY *IN TORPEDINE ELIXA*

PEPPER, LOVAGE, PARSLEY, MINT, ORIGANY, YOLKS OF EGG, HONEY, BROTH, RAISIN WINE, WINE, AND OIL. IF YOU WISH, ADD MUSTARD AND VINEGAR, OR, IF DESIRED RICHER, ADD RAISINS.

This appears to be a sauce to be poured over the boiled ray.

Today the ray is boiled in water seasoned strongly and with similar ingredients. When done, the fish is allowed to cool in this water; the edible parts are then removed, the water drained from the meat, which is tossed in sizzling brown butter with lemon juice, vinegar and capers. This is *raie au beurre noir*, much esteemed on the French seaboards.

III

CALAMARY *IN LOLIGINE* [1]

[405] CALAMARY IN THE PAN *IN LOLIGINE IN PATINA*

CRUSH PEPPER, RUE, A LITTLE HONEY, BROTH, REDUCED WINE, AND OIL TO TASTE. WHEN COMMENCING TO BOIL, BIND WITH ROUX.

[1] Calamary, ink-fish, cuttlefish. Cf. Chap. IV. G.-V. *Lolligine*.

[405 a] STUFFED CALAMARY [1] *IN LOLIGINE FARSILI*

PEPPER, LOVAGE, CORIANDER, CELERY SEED, YOLKS, HONEY, VINEGAR, BROTH, WINE, OIL, AND BIND [2].

[1] Ex List., Sch., and G.-V. Evidently a sauce or dressing. The formula for the forcemeat of the fish is not given here but is found in ℞ No. 406 — stuffed Sepia, a fish akin to the calamary.

IV

SEPIA, CUTTLEFISH   *IN SEPIIS*

[406]   STUFFED SEPIA   *IN SEPIA FARSILI*

PEPPER, LOVAGE, CELERY SEED, CARRAWAY, HONEY,
BROTH, WINE, BASIC CONDIMENTS [1] HEAT [in water]
THROW IN THE CUTTLEFISH; [when done] SPLIT, THEN
STUFF THE CUTTLEFISH [2] WITH [the following forcemeat]
BOILED BRAINS, THE STRINGS AND SKIN REMOVED, POUND
WITH PEPPER, MIX IN RAW EGGS UNTIL IT IS PLENTY.
WHOLE PEPPER [to be added]. TIE [the filled dish] INTO LITTLE
BUNDLES [of linen] AND IMMERSE IN THE BOILING STOCK
POT UNTIL THE FORCEMEAT IS PROPERLY COOKED.

[1] *Condimenta coctiva* — salt, herbs, roots.
[2] G.-V. treat this as a separate formula.

[407]   BOILED CUTTLEFISH [1]
        SEPIAS ELIXAS AB AHENO [2]

ARE PLACED IN A COPPER KETTLE WITH COLD [WATER]
AND PEPPER, LASER, BROTH, NUTS, EGGS, AND [any other]
SEASONING YOU MAY WISH.

[1] List. connects this article with the foregoing.
[2] Tor. *aheno* for copper kettle; List. *amylo.*

[408]   ANOTHER WAY TO COOK CUTTLEFISH
        ALITER SEPIAS

PEPPER, LOVAGE, CUMIN, GREEN CORIANDER, DRY MINT,
YOLKS, HONEY, BROTH, WINE, VINEGAR, AND A LITTLE
OIL. WHEN BOILING BIND WITH ROUX.

V

POLYPUS [1]   *IN POLYPO*

[409]   POLYPUS   *IN POLYPO*

[cook with] PEPPER, LOVAGE, BROTH, LASER, GINGER [2]
AND SERVE.

[1] The polypus, or eight-armed sepia, has been described by Plinius, Galen,
Cicero, Diocles, Athenæus and other ancient writers. The ancients praise it as a
food and attribute to the polypus the power of restoring lost vitality: *molli
carne pisces, & suaves gustu sunt, & ad venerem conferunt* — Diocles.
Wanting in the Vat. Ms.
[2] Wanting in List. and G.-V. Ex Tor. p. 100.

VI

OYSTERS   *IN OSTREIS*

[410]   OYSTERS [1]   *IN OSTREIS*

TO OYSTERS WHICH WANT TO BE WELL SEASONED ADD [2] PEPPER, LOVAGE, YOLKS, VINEGAR, BROTH, OIL, AND WINE; IF YOU WISH ALSO ADD HONEY [3].

[1] Wanting in the Vat. Ms.

[2] Tor. sentence wanting in the other texts.

[3] Cf. No. 15 for the keeping of oysters. It is not likely that the oysters brought from Great Britain to Rome were in a condition to be enjoyed from the shell — raw.

The above formula appears to be a sort of oyster stew.

VII

[411]   ALL KINDS OF BIVALVES
        IN OMNE GENUS CONCHYLIORUM [1]

FOR ALL KINDS OF SHELLFISH USE PEPPER, LOVAGE, PARSLEY, DRY MINT, A LITTLE MORE OF CUMIN, HONEY, AND BROTH; IF YOU WISH, ADD [bay] LEAVES AND MALOBATHRON [2].

[1] Wanting in the Vat. Ms.

[2] Cf. note to ℞ No. 399.

The shellfish is cooked or steamed with the above ingredients.

VIII

SEA URCHINS   *IN ECHINO*

[412]   SEA URCHIN   *IN ECHINO*

TO PREPARE SEA URCHIN TAKE A NEW EARTHEN POT, A LITTLE OIL, BROTH, SWEET WINE, GROUND PEPPER, AND SET IT TO HEAT; WHEN BOILING PUT THE URCHINS IN SINGLY. SHAKE THEM WELL, LET THEM STEW, AND WHEN DONE SPRINKLE WITH PEPPER AND SERVE.

Plinius states that only a few small parts of the sea urchin are edible.

[413]   ANOTHER METHOD   *ALITER [IN] ECHINO*

PEPPER, A LITTLE COSTMARY, DRY MINT, MEAD, BROTH, INDIAN SPIKENARD, AND [bay or nard] LEAVES.

[414] PLAIN BOILED — *ALITER*

PUT THE SEA URCHINS SINGLY IN BOILING WATER, COOK, RETIRE, AND PLACE ON A PLATTER.

[415] IN CHAFING DISH — *IN THERMOSPODIO* [1]

[To the meat of sea urchins, cooked as above, add a sauce made of bay] LEAVES, PEPPER, HONEY, BROTH, A LITTLE OIL, BIND WITH EGGS IN THE HOT WATER BATH [2] SPRINKLE WITH PEPPER AND SERVE.

[1] This formula is combined with the preceding in the original.

[2] Thermospodium; in this respect resembling seafood à la Newburgh. The thermospodium is an elaborate food and drink heater, used both in the kitchen and in the dining room. Our drawing illustrates an elaborate specimen which was used to prepare dishes such as this one in front of the guests.

[416] SALT SEA URCHIN — *IN ECHINO SALSO*

[The cooked meat of] SALT SEA URCHIN IS SERVED UP WITH THE BEST [fish] BROTH, REDUCED WINE AND PEPPER TO TASTE.

Undoubtedly a commercial article like crabmeat today. The sea urchins were cooked at the fisheries, picked, shells, refuse discarded, the meat salted and marketed. The fish was also salted in the shell as seen in the following:

[417] ANOTHER WAY — *ALITER*

TAKE SALT SEA URCHINS, ADD THE BEST BROTH AND TREAT THEM IN A MANNER AS TO LOOK LIKE FRESH THAT HAVE JUST COME OUT OF THE WATER.

IX

MUSSELS — *IN MITULIS* [1]

[418] MUSSELS — *IN MITULIS*

BEST [2] BROTH, FINELY CUT LEEKS, CUMIN, RAISIN WINE, MUST [3] AND ADD WATER TO MAKE A MIXTURE IN WHICH TO COOK THE MUSSELS.

[1] Variously spelled *mytilus, mitylus, mutulus,* an edible mussel.

Tor. and List. *merula,* merling, whiting, Fr. *merlan. Merula* also is a blackbird, which is out of place here. The Vat. Ms. reads *in metulis.*

[2] Tor.

[3] Tor. *vinum mustum;* List. *v. mixtum.*

X

SARDINES, BABY TUNNY, MULLET
IN SARDA [1] *CORDULA* [2] *MUGILE* [3]

[419]   STUFFED SARDINE   *SARDAM FARSILEM*

PROPERLY, OUGHT TO BE TREATED IN THIS MANNER:
THE SARDINE IS BONED AND FILLED WITH CRUSHED FLEA-
BANE, SEVERAL GRAINS OF PEPPER, MINT, NUTS, DILUTED
WITH HONEY, TIED OR SEWED, WRAPPED IN PARCHMENT
AND PLACED IN A FLAT DISH ABOVE THE STEAM RISING
FROM THE STOVE; SEASON WITH OIL, REDUCED MUST AND
ORIGANY [4].

[1] The freshly caught sardine.
[2] *Cordyla, cordilla*, the young or the fry of tunny.
[3] *Mugil*, sea-mullet.
[4] Tor. origany; List. *alece*, with brine.

[420]   ANOTHER PREPARATION OF SARDINES
**   *SARDA ITA FIT***

COOK AND BONE THE SARDINES; FILL WITH CRUSHED
PEPPER, LOVAGE, THYME, ORIGANY, RUE, MOISTENED
WITH DATE WINE, HONEY; PLACE ON A DISH, GARNISH
WITH CUT HARD EGGS. POUR OVER A LITTLE WINE, VINE-
GAR, REDUCED MUST, AND VIRGIN OIL.

[421]   SAUCE FOR SARDINES   *IUS IN SARDA*

PEPPER, ORIGANY, MINT, ONIONS, A LITTLE VINEGAR,
AND OIL.

Resembling our *vinaigrette*.

[422]   ANOTHER SAUCE FOR SARDINES [1]
**   *IUS ALIUD IN SARDA***

PEPPER, LOVAGE, DRY MINT [2] COOKED, ONION
[chopped], HONEY, VINEGAR, DILUTE WITH OIL, SPRINKLE
WITH CHOPPED HARD EGGS.

[1] Another *Vinaigrette*.
[2] Tac. and Tor. *mentam aridam coctam*, dry mint cooked, which is rea-
sonable, to soften it. Hum., G.-V. dry mint, cooked onion; there is no necessity
to cook the onion. As a matter of fact, it should be chopped raw in this dressing. The onion is wanting in Tac. and Tor.

[423] SAUCE FOR BROILED BABY TUNNY
IUS IN CORDULA ASSA

PEPPER, LOVAGE, CELERY SEED, MINT, RUE, FIGDATE [or its wine] HONEY, VINEGAR, WINE. ALSO SUITABLE FOR SARDINES.

[424] SAUCE FOR SALT SEA-MULLET
IUS IN MUGILE SALSO

PEPPER, LOVAGE, CUMIN, ONION, MINT, RUE, SAGE [1], DATE WINE, HONEY, VINEGAR, MUSTARD AND OIL.

[1] Tor. *calva*; G.-V. *calvam*. Does not exist. Hum. *calva legendum puto salvia*.

[425] ANOTHER SAUCE FOR SALT SEA-MULLET
ALITER IUS IN MUGILE SALSO

PEPPER, ORIGANY, ROCKET, MINT, RUE, SAGE [1], DATE WINE, HONEY, OIL, VINEGAR AND MUSTARD.

[1] Same as above.

XI [1]

[426] SAUCE FOR CATFISH, BABY TUNNY AND TUNNY
IUS IN SILURO [2] *IN PELAMYDE* [3] *ET IN THYNNO* [4]

TO MAKE THEM MORE TASTY USE [5] PEPPER, LOVAGE, CUMIN, ONIONS, MINT, RUE, SAGE [6] DATE WINE, HONEY, VINEGAR, MUSTARD AND OIL.

[1] The twelve chapters of Book IX, as shown in the beginning of the text are here increased to fourteen by G.-V., to wit, XII, *IUS IN MULLO TARICHO* and XIII, *SALSUM SINE SALSO*, but these are more properly included in the above chapter XI, as does Tor. All of the above fish were salt, and probably were important commercial articles. The *silurus*, for instance, is best in the river Danube in the Balkans, while the red mullet, as seen in ℞ No. 427 came from the sea of Galilee. Cf. ℞ Nos. 144, 149.

[2] *Silurus*, probably the sly silurus, or sheatfish, in the U. S. called horn-pout — a large catfish.

[3] *Pelamis*, a tunny before it is a year old.

[4] Tunny, Tunafish.

[5] Tor. wanting in the others.

[6] Cf. note 1 to ℞ No. 424.

XII

[427]   SAUCE FOR SALT RED MULLET
IUS IN MULLO [1] *TARICHO* [2]

IF IN NEED OF CONDIMENTS USE [3] PEPPER, RUE, ON-
IONS, DATES, GROUND MUSTARD; MIX ALL WITH [flaked
meat of] SEA URCHINS, MOISTEN WITH OIL, AND POUR OVER
THE FISH WHICH IS EITHER FRIED OR BROILED, OMITTING
SALT [4].

[1] Tor. *mulo*, the red sur-mullet — a very esteemed fish.

[2] Tarichea, town of Galilee, on the sea of Galilee. Salt mullet as prepared
at Tarichea was known as *Tarichus*. This became finally a generic name for all
kinds of salt fish, whether coming from Tarichea or from elsewhere. We have an
interesting analogy in "Finnan Haddie," smoked Haddock from Findon, Scotland, corrupted into "Finnan," and now used for any kind of smoked Haddock.
Cf. ℞ Nos. 144, 149.

[3] Tor. Quite correctly, he questions the need of condiments for salt fish.

[4] List. uses this last sentence as the title for the next formula, implying
that more salt be added to the salt fish; Tor. is explicit in saying that no salt be
added which of course, is correct.

XIII

ANOTHER WAY, WITHOUT SALT [PORK?]
ALITER, SINE SALSO [1]

[428]   FISH LIVER PUDDING   *SALSUM, SINE SALSO* [2]

COOK THE LIVER [of the mullet] CRUSH [3] AND ADD PEP-
PER, EITHER BROTH OR SALT [4] ADD OIL, LIVER OF HARE,
OR OF LAMB [5] OR OF CHICKEN, AND, IF YOU LIKE, PRESS
INTO A FISH MOULD [6] [unmould, after baking] SPRINKLE
WITH VIRGIN OIL [7].

[1] Tor.

[2] G.-V. plainly, a contradiction. The possible meaning may be, "Salt Fish,
without salt pork" as salt fish is frequently served with bacon.

[3] Dann. Crush the liver, which is probably correct. A paste or forcemeat
of the livers and fish were made.

[4] The addition of salt would be superfluous if the liver of salt meat is used,
excepting if the liver of hare, etc., predominated.

[5] G.-V. or liver of kid, wanting in Tor.

[6] Such fish-shape moulds existed, made of bronze, artistically finished,
same as we possess them today; such moulds were made in various styles and
shapes. Cf. ℞ No. 384.

[7] This is an attempt to make a "fish" of livers, not so much with the intention to deceive as to utilize the livers in an attractive way. A very nutritious dish and a most ingenious device, requiring much skill.

This is another good example of Roman cookery, far from being extravagant as it is reputed to be, it is economical and clever, and shows ingenuity in the utilization of good things which are often discarded as worthless.

[429] ANOTHER WAY, FOR A CHANGE!
ALITER VICEM GERENS SALSI [1]

CUMIN, PEPPER, BROTH, WHICH CRUSH, ADDING A LITTLE RAISIN WINE, OR REDUCED WINE, AND A QUANTITY OF CRUSHED NUTS. MIX EVERYTHING WELL, INCORPORATE WITH THE SALT [2] [fish]; MIX IN A LITTLE OIL AND SERVE.

[1] G.-V. *Alter vice salsi.*

[2] Tor. *& salibus imbue*; List. *& salsa redde.* There is no sense to Lister's version, nor can we accept G.-V. who have *et salari defundes.*

[430] ANOTHER WAY *ALITER SALSUM IN* [1] *SALSO*

TAKE AS MUCH CUMIN AS YOUR FIVE FINGERS WILL HOLD; CRUSH HALF OF THAT QUANTITY OF PEPPER AND ONE PIECE OF PEELED GARLIC, MOISTEN WITH BROTH AND MIX IN A LITTLE OIL. THIS WILL CORRECT AND BENEFIT A SOUR STOMACH AND PROMOTE DIGESTION [2].

[1] Tor., G.-V. *sine.*

[2] The title has reference to salt fish or salt pork; but the formula obviously is of a medicinal character and has no place here.

XII [XIV]

[431] BAIAN SEAFOOD STEW
EMBRACTUM [1] BAIANUM [2]

MINCED [poached] OYSTERS, MUSSELS [3] [or scallops] AND SEA NETTLES PUT IN A SAUCE PAN WITH TOASTED NUTS, RUE, CELERY, PEPPER, CORIANDER, CUMIN, RAISIN WINE, BROTH, REDUCED WINE AND OIL.

[1] List. *emphractum* — a caudle, a stew. Seafood stews of this sort are very popular in the South of Europe, the most famous among them being the *Bouillabaisse* of Marseilles.

[2] Baiæ, a very popular seaside resort of the ancients located in the bay of Naples. The stew was named after the place. Horace liked the place but Seneca warned against it.

[3] Tor. *spondylos*; List. *sphondylos* — scallops. Both terms, if used in connection with the shellfish are correct. Lister in several places confuses this term with *spongiolus* — mushroom. This instance is the final vindication of Torinus, whose correctness was maintained in ℞ Nos. 41, 47, 115, *seq.*; 120, 121, 183, 309, *seq.*

END OF BOOK IX [1]

EXPLICIT APICII THALASSA LIBER NONUS [2]

[1] It appears to us that Book IX and the following, Book X, judging from its recipes, phraseology and from other appearances is by a different author than the preceding books. (Long after having made this observation, we learn from Vollmer, *Studien*, that Books IX and X were missing in the Archetypus Fuldensis.)

[2]. Tac.

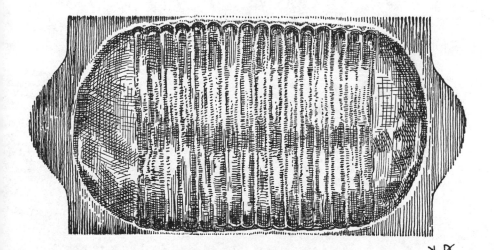

ROAST PLATTER

The indenture is corrugated to receive the juices of the roast. Hildesheim Treas.

(handwritten inscription)

CAELII APITII

SVMMI ADVLATRICIS MEDI-
cinæ artificis DE RE CVLINARIA Libri X. recens è tenebris eruti, & à mendis uindicati,
typisǿ summa diligentia
excusi.

PRAETEREA,

P▸ PLATINAE CREMO

NENSIS VIRI VNDECVNQVE DO
ctissimi, De tuenda ualetudine, Natura rerum, & Popina
scientia Libri X. ad imitationem C. API-
TII ad unguem facti.

AD HAEC,

PAVLI AEGINETAE DE

FACVLTATIBVS ALIMENTORVM TRA
CTATVS, ALBANO TORINO
INTERPRETE.

Cum INDICE copiosissimo.

BASILEAE▸
M. D. XLI.

TITLE PAGE, TORINUS EDITION, BASEL, 1541

Inscribed with comments by Lappius, contemporary scholar. The fly-leaf bears the autograph of M.
Tydeman, 1806, and references to the above Lappius. There are further inscriptions by ancient hands in
Latin and French, referring to the Barnhold [sic] Apicius, to The Diaitetike, to Aulus Cornelius, Celsus,
Hippocrates and Galen. Also complaints about the difficulties to decipher the Apician text.

APICIUS
Book X

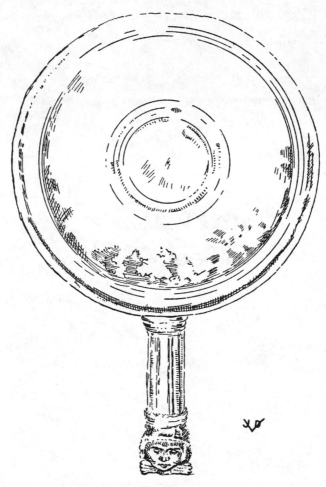

SHALLOW SAUCE PAN

The plain bowl is molded, the fluted handle ends in a head of the young Hercules in a lion's skin, with the paws tied under the neck. This corresponds somewhat to our modern chafing dish pan both in size and in utility. This pan was used in connection with the plain thermospodium for the service of hot foods in the dining room. Ntl. Mus., Naples, 73438; Field M., 24032.

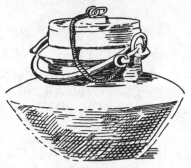

CACCABUS

Stewpot, kettle, marmite. The cover fits
over the mouth. The rings in which the
bail plays are attached by rivets to a sort
of collar encircling the neck of the pot.
Ntl. Mus., Naples, 74775; Field M., 24173.

BOOK X. THE FISHERMAN [1]

Lib. X. Halieus

CHAP. I. DIFFERENT KINDS OF FISH.
CHAP. II. MURENAS.
CHAP. III. EEL.
The numbers of the chapters differ in the various texts.

I

[432] A SAUCE FINES HERBES FOR FRIED FISH
IUS DIABOTANON [2] *PRO* [3] *PISCE FRIXO*

USE ANY KIND OF FISH. PREPARE [clean, salt, turn in flour]
SALT [4] AND FRY IT. CRUSH PEPPER, CUMIN, CORIAN-
DER SEED, LASER ROOT, ORIGANY, AND RUE, ALL
CRUSHED FINE, MOISTENED WITH VINEGAR, DATE WINE,
HONEY, REDUCED MUST, OIL AND BROTH. POUR IN A SAUCE
PAN, PLACE ON FIRE, WHEN SIMMERING POUR OVER THE
FRIED FISH, SPRINKLE WITH PEPPER AND SERVE.

[1] This chapter principally deals with fish sauces. Apparently it is by a
different author than Books I-VIII, which have many formulæ for fish. While
we have no direct proof, we are inclined to believe that Book X is a Roman version of a Greek treatise on fish sauces, a monograph, of which there existed
many, according to Athenæus, which specialized on the various departments of
cookery.

[2] Tor. *Diabotom* (in Greek characters); Greek, relating to herbs.

[3] Tor. G.-V. *in*.

[4] G.-V. *salsas*.

[433]   SAUCE FOR BOILED FISH   *IUS IN PISCE ELIXO*

PEPPER, LOVAGE, CUMIN, SMALL ONIONS, ORIGANY, NUTS, FIGDATES, HONEY, VINEGAR, BROTH, MUSTARD, A LITTLE OIL; HEAT THIS SAUCE, AND IF YOU WISH [it to be richer, add] RAISINS.

[434]   ANOTHER SAUCE FOR BOILED FISH
         ALITER IN PISCE ELIXO [1]

CRUSH PEPPER, LOVAGE, GREEN CORIANDER, SATURY, ONION, [hard] BOILED YOLKS, RAISIN WINE, VINEGAR, OIL AND BROTH.

[1] Tor. *frixo* — fried fish, although his heading reads *elixo*.

[435]   ANOTHER SAUCE FOR BOILED FISH
         ALITER IUS IN PISCE ELIXO

PREPARE THE FISH CAREFULLY; IN THE MORTAR PUT SALT, CORIANDER SEED, CRUSH AND MIX WELL; TURN THE FISH THEREIN, PUT IT IN A PAN, COVER IT AND SEAL IT WITH PLASTER [1] COOK IT IN THE OVEN. WHEN DONE RETIRE [the fish from the pan] SPRINKLE WITH STRONG VINEGAR AND SERVE.

[1] Remarkable culinary ingenuity, resembling in principle the North American Indian method of cooking whitefish wrapped in clay. Today we use flour and water made into a stiff paste to seal a pan hermetically if no "pressure cooker" is available.

This formula cannot be classified under "Sauce for Boiled Fish."

[436]   ANOTHER SAUCE FOR BOILED FISH
         ALITER IUS IN PISCE ELIXO

WHEN THE FISH IS PREPARED, PUT THE SAME IN A FLAT PAN WITH CORIANDER SEED, WATER AND GREEN DILL; WHEN COOKED SPRINKLE WITH VINEGAR AND SERVE [1].

[1] Another fair example of the incompleteness, on the one hand, of the directions, and of the superfluity, on the other hand, of words such as the initial and the closing words, which characterizes so many of the formulæ. This is characteristic of ever so many culinary authors of all ages, who, lacking literary training, assume that the reader is thoroughly versed with the methods indicated. A versatile modern author would have said: "Poach the filleted fish in small water seasoned with coriander seed and green dill; sprinkle with vinegar before serving." He mentioned neither the salt nor the oil which he undoubtedly used.

[437] ALEXANDRINE [1] SAUCE FOR BROILED FISH
IUS ALEXANDRINUM IN PISCE ASSO

PEPPER, DRY ONIONS [shallots] LOVAGE, CUMIN, ORI-GANY, CELERY SEED, STONED DAMASCUS PRUNES [pounded in the mortar] FILLED UP [2] WITH VINEGAR, BROTH, RE-DUCED MUST, AND OIL, AND COOK IT.

[1] Alexandria, Egyptian city, at the mouth of the river Nile, third of the three great cities of antiquity excepting Carthage during Apicius' time a rival of Rome and Athens in splendor and commerce. Most important as a Mediter-ranean port, where fishing and fish eating was (and still is) good.

[2] G.-V. *mulsum*, mead.

[438] ANOTHER ALEXANDRINE SAUCE FOR BROILED FISH
ALITER IUS ALEXANDRINUM IN PISCE ASSO

PEPPER, LOVAGE, GREEN CORIANDER, SEEDLESS RAISINS, WINE, RAISIN WINE, BROTH, OIL, COOKED TOGETHER.

[439] ANOTHER ALEXANDRINE SAUCE FOR BROILED FISH
ALITER IUS ALEXANDRINUM IN PISCE ASSO

PEPPER, LOVAGE, GREEN CORIANDER, ONIONS, STONED DAMASCUS PRUNES, RAISIN WINE, BROTH, OIL AND VINE-GAR, AND COOK.

[440] SAUCE FOR BROILED CONGER
IUS IN CONGRO ASSO

PEPPER, LOVAGE, CRUSHED CUMIN, ORIGANY, DRY ON-IONS, HARD YOLKS, WINE, MEAD, VINEGAR, BROTH, RE-DUCED MUST, AND COOK.

G.-V. *Gongo*.

[441] SAUCE FOR HORNED FISH [1]
IUS IN CORNUTAM [1]

PEPPER, LOVAGE, ORIGANY, ONIONS, SEEDLESS RAISINS, WINE, HONEY, VINEGAR, BROTH, OIL; AND COOK IT [2]

[1] *Cornuta, cornutus* — "horned," "having horns" — an unidentified sea fish.

[2] Goll. collects all succeeding formulæ for sauces into one.

[442]   SAUCE FOR BROILED MULLET
        IUS IN MULLOS ASSOS

PEPPER, LOVAGE, RUE, HONEY, NUTS, VINEGAR, WINE, BROTH, A LITTLE OIL; HEAT AND POUR OVER [1].

[1] List. is of the opinion that this is fresh mullet, while salt mullet was treated in the preceding formulæ.

[443]   ANOTHER SAUCE FOR BROILED MULLET
        ALITER IUS IN MULLOS ASSOS

RUE, MINT, CORIANDER, FENNEL, — ALL OF THEM GREEN — PEPPER, LOVAGE, HONEY, BROTH, AND A LITTLE OIL.

[444]   SEASONING FOR BABY TUNNY
        IUS IN PELAMYDE ASSA

PEPPER, LOVAGE, ORIGANY, GREEN CORIANDER, ONION, SEEDLESS RAISINS [1], RAISIN WINE, VINEGAR, BROTH, REDUCED MUST, OIL, AND COOK.

[1] Wanting in Tor.

[445]
        THIS SAUCE IS ALSO SUITABLE FOR BOILED [tunny]; IF DESIRED ADD HONEY.

[446]   SAUCE FOR PERCH   *IUS IN PERCAM* [1]

PEPPER, LOVAGE, CRUSHED CUMIN, ONIONS, STONED DAMASCUS PRUNES, WINE, MEAD, VINEGAR, OIL, REDUCED MUST; COOK IT.

[1] *Perca*, perch — sea perch or sea bass.

[447]   SEASONING FOR REDSNAPPER
        CONDIMENTUM IN RUBELLIONEM [1]

PEPPER, LOVAGE, CARRAWAY, WILD THYME, CELERY SEED, DRY ONIONS, WINE, RAISIN WINE, VINEGAR, BROTH AND OIL; BIND WITH ROUX.

[1] *Rubellio* — a "reddish" fish; perhaps a species of the red-mullet or redsnapper. Hum. says the Latins called the fish *rubelliones*, *rubellos* and *rubros*; the Greeks *erythrinos* or *erythricos*, because of their reddish color. A fish, according to Athenæus similar to the *pager* or *pagrus*, *phager* or *phagrus*, also called *pagur*, which is not quite identified.

II

[448] SAUCE FOR [BROILED] MURENA
       IUS IN MURENA [ASSA] [1]

PEPPER, LOVAGE, SATURY, SAFFRON [2], ONIONS, STONED
DAMASCUS PRUNES, WINE, MEAD, VINEGAR, REDUCED
MUST AND OIL; COOK IT [3].

[1] V. doubting that this is broiled.

[2] Tor. *Crocomagma*; List. *crocum magnum*; still used today in some fish
preparations, particularly in the Bouillabaisse.

[3] The laconic style in which all these fish preparations are given, is very
confusing to the uninitiated. We assume that most of these ingredients were
used to season the water in which to boil fish; or, to make a *court-bouillon*, a
fish-essence of the bones and the trimmings of the fish, in which to poach the
sliced fish. The liquor thus gained was reduced and in the moment of serving
was bound with roux or with yolks, and the fish was masked with this sauce.
The exceptions from this rule are, of course, in cases where the fish was broiled
or fried.

[449] SAUCE FOR BROILED MURENA
       IUS IN MURENA ASSA

PEPPER, LOVAGE, [stoned] DAMASCUS PRUNES, WINE,
MEAD, VINEGAR, BROTH, REDUCED MUST, OIL; COOK IT.

[450] ANOTHER SAUCE FOR BROILED MURENA
       ALITER IUS IN MURENA ASSA

PEPPER, LOVAGE, CATMINT [1] CORIANDER SEED, ON-
IONS, PINE NUTS, HONEY, VINEGAR, BROTH, OIL; COOK IT.

[1] *Nepeta montana* — nep.

[451] ANOTHER SAUCE FOR BOILED MURENA [1]
       ALITER IUS IN MURENA ELIXA

PEPPER, LOVAGE, DILL, CELERY SEED, CORIANDER, DRY
MINT, PINE NUTS, RUE, HONEY, VINEGAR, WINE [2] BROTH,
A LITTLE OIL, HEAT AND BIND WITH ROUX.

[1] Ex Tac. and Tor.; wanting in List. and G.-V.

[2] Tac.; wanting in Tor.

[452] ANOTHER SAUCE FOR BOILED MURENA
       ALITER IUS IN MURENA ELIXA

PEPPER, LOVAGE, CARRAWAY, CELERY SEED [1] CORIAN-

DER, FIGDATES, MUSTARD, HONEY, VINEGAR, BROTH, OIL, REDUCED WINE.

[1] List., Sch., Dann. add here which is wanting in Tor. *rhus Syriacum* — Syrian Sumach.

The originals are considerably confused on the above and the following formulæ.

[453] ANOTHER SAUCE FOR BOILED MURENA
ALITER IUS IN MURENA ELIXA

PEPPER, LOVAGE, VINEGAR, CELERY SEED, SYRIAN SUMACH [1] FIGDATE WINE, HONEY, VINEGAR, BROTH, OIL, MUSTARD, AND REDUCED MUST. SERVE [2].

[1] See note to ℞ No. 452.

[2] Ex Tor. It appears that this formula is a correction of ℞ No. 452, as this is wanting in the other editions. Tor. also lacks the following formula.

In Tac. the above formula follows the next.

[454] SAUCE FOR BOILED FISH *IUS IN PISCE ELIXO*

PEPPER, LOVAGE, PARSLEY, ORIGANY, DRY ONIONS, HONEY, VINEGAR, BROTH, WINE, A LITTLE OIL, WHEN BOILING, TIE WITH ROUX AND SERVE IN A SMALL SAUCE BOAT [1].

[1] *in lance*; *lanx* may also mean a large oblong platter on which fish would be served. Cf. illustration Oval Dish with Handles.

Horace II Sat. 8 — *in patina porrecta* — a special dish to hold the cooked *murena* and to display it to advantage.

Such special dishes are found in any good table service, to serve special purposes. Not so long ago special forks and knives were used for fish service which have been gradually discarded.

[455] SAUCE FOR BOILED LACERTUS FISH
IUS IN LACERTOS ELIXOS [1]

PEPPER, LOVAGE, CUMIN, GREEN RUE, ONIONS, HONEY, VINEGAR, BROTH, A LITTLE OIL; WHEN BOILING TIE WITH ROUX [2].

[1] *Lacertus*, an unidentified sea fish.

[2] Cf. note 2 to ℞ No. 448.

In G.-V. this formula preceeds the above.

[456] SAUCE FOR BROILED FISH *IUS IN PISCE ASSO*

A SAUCE FOR [this] BROILED FISH MAKE THUS [1] PEPPER,

LOVAGE, THYME, GREEN CORIANDER, HONEY, VINEGAR, BROTH, WINE, OIL, REDUCED MUST; HEAT AND STIR WELL WITH A WHIP OF RUE BRANCHES, AND TIE WITH ROUX.

[1] Tor. wanting in others.

[457]   SAUCE FOR TUNNY   *IUS IN THYNNO*

TUNNY, BY MEANS OF THIS SAUCE WILL BE MORE PALATABLE: [1] PEPPER, CUMIN, THYME, CORIANDER, ONIONS, RAISINS, VINEGAR, HONEY, WINE, AND OIL; HEAT, TIE WITH ROUX, AND SERVE FOR DINNER [2].

[1] and [2] first and last sentences from Tor., wanting in others.

[458]   SAUCE FOR BOILED TUNNY
IUS IN THYNNO ELIXO

PEPPER, LOVAGE, THYME, CRUSHED HERBS [1], ONIONS, FIG DATES [or fig wine] HONEY, VINEGAR, BROTH, OIL, MUSTARD AND TIE [2].

[1] *Condimenta mortaria* — herbs crushed in the "mortar"; also pulverized spices.

[2] "and tie" wanting in List. Leave it out, and you have an acceptable *vinaigrette* — a cold sauce for cold fish.

[459]   SAUCE FOR BROILED TOOTH FISH
IUS IN DENTICE ASSO [1]

SAUCE FOR BROILED TOOTH [1] FISH IS MADE THUS [2] PEPPER, LOVAGE, CORIANDER, MINT, DRY RUE, COOKED QUINCES [3], HONEY, WINE, BROTH, OIL; HEAT AND TIE WITH ROUX.

[1] *Dentex*; Hum. *dentex forma auratæ similis, verum major* — the toothfish is similar to the dory in shape, though larger.

[2] Tor. sentence wanting in other texts.

[3] *Malum Cydonicum.*

[460]   BOILED TOOTHFISH   *IN DENTICE ELIXO* [1]

PEPPER, DILL, CUMIN, THYME, MINT, GREEN RUE, HONEY, VINEGAR, BROTH, WINE, A LITTLE OIL, HEAT AND TIE WITH ROUX.

[1] Ex List.; wanting in Tor.

[461]   SAUCE FOR DORY   *IUS IN PISCE AURATA* [1]

A SEASONING FOR DORY IS MADE THUS [2] PEPPER, LOVAGE, CARRAWAY, ORIGANY, RUE BERRIES, MINT, MYRTLE

BERRIES, YOLKS OF EGG, HONEY, VINEGAR, OIL, WINE, BROTH; HEAT AND USE IT SO.

[1] *Aurata* — the "golden" dory. Very esteemed fish. Martial, III, Ep. 90:
  Non omnis laudem preliúmque aurate meretur:
  Sed cui solus erit concha Lucrina cibus
[2] Tor. wanting in other texts.

[462]   SAUCE FOR BROILED DORY.
        IUS IN PISCE AURATA ASSA

A SAUCE WHICH WILL MAKE BROILED DORY MORE TAS-
TY CONSISTS OF [1] PEPPER, CORIANDER, DRY MINT, CEL-
ERY SEED, ONIONS, RAISINS, HONEY, VINEGAR, WINE,
BROTH AND OIL.

[463]   SAUCE FOR SEA SCORPION [1]
        IUS IN SCORPIONE ELIXO

PEPPER, CARRAWAY, PARSLEY, FIGDATE WINE, HONEY,
VINEGAR, BROTH, MUSTARD, OIL AND REDUCED WINE.

[1] Sea scorpion, boiled like shellfish, with the above ingredients; the cold
meat is separated from the shell and is eaten with *vinaigrette* sauce.

[464]   WINE SAUCE FOR FISH   *IN PISCE ŒNOGARUM*

CRUSH PEPPER, RUE, AND HONEY; MIX IN RAISIN WINE,
BROTH, REDUCED WINE; HEAT ON A VERY SLOW FIRE.

[465]   ANOTHER WAY   *ALITER*
THE ABOVE, WHEN BOILING, MAY BE TIED WITH ROUX.

III

EEL

[466]   SAUCE FOR EEL   *IUS IN ANGUILLAM*
EEL WILL BE MADE MORE PALATABLE BY A SAUCE WHICH
HAS [1] PEPPER, CELERY SEED, LOVAGE [2], ANISE, SYRIAN
SUMACH [3], FIGDATE WINE [4], HONEY, VINEGAR, BROTH,
OIL, MUSTARD, REDUCED MUST.

[1] Tor. sentence wanting in other texts.
[2] Note the position of lovage in this formula. Usually it follows pepper.
We have finally accounted for this peculiarity. Torinus, throughout the original,
treats "pepper" and "lovage" as one spice, whereas we have kept the two separate.
He believed it to be a certain kind of pepper — *piper Ligusticum* —. *Piper*, as a

matter of act, stands for pepper, and *Ligusticum* is the herb, Lovage, an umbelliferous plant, also called *Levisticum*. The fact that the two words are here separated plainly shows that Torinus has been in the dark about this matter almost to the end.

One wonders why he did not change or correct this error in the preceding books. His marginal errata prove that his work was being printed as he wrote it, or furnished copy therefor — namely in installments. Since the printer's type was limited, each sheet was printed in the complete edition, and the type was then used over again for the next sheet.

[3] Tor. *thun.*

[4] Wanting in Tor.

[467] ANOTHER SAUCE FOR EEL
ALITER IUS IN ANGUILLAM

PEPPER, LOVAGE, SYRIAN SUMACH, DRY MINT, RUE BERRIES, HARD YOLKS, MEAD, VINEGAR, BROTH, OIL; COOK IT.

END OF BOOK X THE LAST OF THE BOOKS OF APICIUS

CELII APITII HALIEUS LIBER DECIMUS & ULTIMUS. EXPLICIT [Tac.]

CANTHARUS, WINE BOWL OR CUP

With elaborate ornamentation: Over a sacred fountain the walls of a theatre, with emblems of a theatrical nature and garlands of flowers and fruits, wine skins, tyrsus, torches, masks and musical instruments. Hildesheim Treasure.

Laseratum   Oxyporum   Oxygarum digestibile
Oenogaɤ i tubera Hypotrima   Mortaria
     ¶ Ciminatum in oftrea de conchiliis.
Apicii Celii epimeles Incipit liber primus conditū padoxum.

Onditi Paradoxi compositio:mellis ɡtes.xy.
in æneum uas mittunɛ in præmiſſis inde ſex‑
tariis duobus ut in cocturam mellis uinum de
coques.quod igni lento:& aridis lignis calefa‑
ctum comotum ferula dum coquitur.Si eſſer
uere cœperit uini rore cōpeſcitur preter quod ſub tracto igni
in ſe redit.cum pɟrixerit rurſus accenditur Hoc ſecundo ac ter
tiɋ fiet ac tum demum remotū a foco poſtridie deſpumaɟ cū
p̄peris ūciis iiii.iā triti maſticis ſcrupulo.iii.folii & croci drag‑
mæ ſingulæ.dactiloɤ oſſibus torridis quinɋ hiſdem dactilis
uinomollitis intercedente pri9 ſuffuſione uini de ſuo modo ac
numero:ut tritura lēis habeaɟ:his omnibus paratis ſupmittes
uini lenis ſextaria.xy.ii.carbones perfecto addere duo milia.

       ¶ Conditum meliromum.
Latoɤ conditū meliromum p̄petuū ɋ ſubminiſtraɟ
per uiā pegrinanti.p̄p tritū cū melle deſpumato i cu‑
pellam mittis cōditi loco.& ad mouendū ɋtū ſit bibē
dū tm̄aut mellis proferas:aut uinū inferas:ſed ſua ſerit ñ nihil
uini meliromo mittas adiiciendū propter exitum ſolutiorem.
       ¶ Abſynthium romanum.
Bſynthiū romanū ſic facies. Cōditi camerini præce
ptis utiɋ pro abſynthio ceſſante:in cuius uicē abſyn
thi ponthici purgati terēbitiɋ unciā thebaicā dabis.
maſticis folii.iiii.ſcrupulos ſenos.croci ſcrupulos.iii.uini eiuſ‑
modi ſextarios:xyiii.carbones amaritudo non exigit.

                                 a ii

OPENING CHAPTER, BOOK I, VENICE, 1503

From the Lancilotus edition, printed by Tacuinus in Venice in 1503. Identical with the two previous editions except for very minor variants. The rubrication is not completed here. Fine initials were painted in the vacant spaces by hand; the small letter in the center of the square being the cue for the rubricator. This practice, a remnant from the manuscript books, was very soon abandoned after the printing of books became commercialized.

THE EXCERPTS FROM APICIUS BY VINIDARIUS

BREVSPIMENTORŪ QꞀNDOMO ESSEDEBEANT

VTENDMENTIS NIHILDESIT ;

CROCU PIPER ZINGIBER LASAR FOLIO·BACAMURRE
COSTU· CARIOFILU· SPICAINDICA ADDENA· CARDAMOMU
SPICANARDI DESEMINIBUSHOC·

JAPABER· SEMENRUDE· BACARUTE· BACALAURI· SE
MEN ANETI· SEMEN API· SEMENFENICULI SEMENLIGUS
TICI SEMENERUCE· SEMENCORIANDRI· CUMINU ANESU
PETRO SILENU· CAREU SISAMA

    APICI EXCERPTA·AUINIDARIO UIR INLUT
        DESICCISHOC

LASARIS RADICES MENTA NEPETA· SALUIA· CUPPRESSU
ORICANŪ ZUNIPERUM CEPACENTIMA· BACASTIMMI
CORIANDRUM PIRETRU· CITRI PASTINACA CEPA AS
COLONIA· RADICESIUNCI· ANET PULEIU· OPERUM
ILIU· OSPERA· SAMSUCU· INNULA· SILPIŪ· CARDA
MOMŪ· DELIQUORIB; HOC

MEL DEFRITU CARINU APIPERIU PASSU
        DENUCLEISHOC

NUCES MAIORES NUDOS PINEOS ACMIDULA ABULAN
        DEPOMISSICCISHOC

DAMASCENA·DATILOS· UBAPASSA CRANATA· HEC
OMNIA INLOCOSICCO PONE NEODOREM ETUIR
TUTEM PERDANT BREVIS CYBORŪ
CACCABINA MINORE· lI CACCABINAPUSILE·· lIII OFEL·
LASGARATAS· lIIII OFELLAS ASSAS·· V ALTEROFEL·
· AS· VI OFELLAS GRATON· VII PISCES· SCORPIONES

BREVIS PIMENTORUM

Manuscript of the 8th Century. From the Codex Salmasianus, Excerpts from Apicius by Vinidarius.

THE EXCERPTS FROM APICIUS
BY VINIDARIUS
THE ILLUSTRIOUS MAN

Apici Excerpta A Vinidario Viro Inlustri

FIFTH CENTURY

Vinidarius, a Goth, of noble birth or a scientist, living in Italy. Vinithaharjis is the native name. Of his time and life very little is known. It appears that he was a student of Apicius and that he made certain excerpts from that book which are preserved in the uncial codex of Salmasius, sæc. VIII, Paris, lat. 10318.

Vollmer in his Apicius commentary says that Salmasius and his predecessors have accepted them as genuine. Schuch incorporated these recipes in the Apicius text of his editions, in appropriate places, as he thought. This course cannot be recommended, although the recipes should form an integral part of any Apicius edition.

M. Ihm, who faithfully reprinted the excerpta in the Archiv f. lat. Lex. XV, 64, ff. says distinctly: "These excerpts have nothing to do with the ten books of Apicius, even if some recipes resemble each other . . ." and other researchers have expressed the same opinion. Vollmer, however, does not share this view.

If I may be permitted to concur with Vollmer, I would say that the excerpts are quite Apician in character, and that in a sense they fill certain gaps in the Apicius text, although the language is strongly vulgarized which may be readily expected to be the case in the age of Vinidarius.

The recipes of Anthimus, written around A.D. 511 also confirm the close relation existing between Vinidarius and Apicius. Anthimus was the Greek physician to Theodoric I, (The Great), Frankish king living in Italy. He was not acquainted with Apicius.

SUMMARY OF SPICES   *BREVIS PIMENTORUM* [1]

WHICH SHOULD BE IN THE HOUSE ON HAND SO THAT
THERE MAY BE NOTHING WANTING [in the line of condi-
ments]: SAFFRON, PEPPER, GINGER, LASER, LEAVES [laurel-
bay-nard], MYRTLE BERRIES, COSTMARY, CHERVIL [2], IN-
DIAN SPIKENARD, ADDENA [3], CARDAMON, SPIKENARD.

[1] *Pigmentorum — specierum —* spices. The old *pigmentum* is really any
coloring matter; the word, corrupted to pimento and pimiento is now used for
sweet red pepper and also for allspice.

[2] *Cariofilu — cærefolium — Chærephyllon;* Fr. *Cerfeuille;* Ger. *Kerbel.*
This should be among the herbs.

[3] Not identified.

OF SEEDS [to be on hand]   *DE SEMINIBUS HOC*

POPPY SEED, RUE SEED, RUE BERRIES, LAUREL BERRIES,
ANISE SEED, CELERY SEED, FENNELL SEED, LOVAGE SEED,
ROCKET SEED, CORIANDER SEED, CUMIN, DILL, PARSLEY
SEED, CARRAWAY SEED, SESAM.

OF DRIED [herbs, etc., to be on hand]   *DE SICCIS HOC*

LASER ROOT, MINT, CATNIP, SAGE, CYPRESS, ORIGANY,
JUNIPER, SHALLOTS, BACAS TIMMI [1], CORIANDER, SPAN-
ISH CAMOMILE, CITRON, PARSNIPS, ASCALONIAN SHAL-
LOTS, BULL RUSH ROOTS, DILL, FLEABANE, CYPRIAN RUSH,
GARLIC, LEGUMES [2], MARJORAM [3], INNULA [4] SILPH-
IUM, CARDAMOM.

[1] Not identified. Perhaps the seed of thyme, though the word *bacas* would
be out of place there.

[2] *Ospera,* i.e., *Osperios.*

[3] *Samsucu,* i.e., *sampsuchum* Elderberries?

[4] Not identified; perhaps *laurus innubus,* dried virgin laurel leaves.

OF LIQUIDS [to be on hand]   *DE LIQUORIBUS HOC*

HONEY, REDUCED MUST, REDUCED WINE, APIPERIU [1]
RAISIN WINE.

[1] Not identified. We take it to be honey mead, or some other honey preparation, maybe, *piperatum,* pepper sauce.

OF NUTS [to be on hand]   *DE NUCLEIS HOC*

LARGER NUTS, PINE NUTS, ALMONDS [1] HAZELNUTS
[filberts] [2].

[1] *Acmidula,* i.e., *amygdala.*

[2] *Aballana — abellana — abellinæ — avellana;* Fr. *avelline.*

OF DRIED FRUITS [to be on hand]   *DE POMIS SICCIS HOC*

DAMASCUS PRUNES, DATES, RAISINS, POMEGRANATES. ALL OF THESE THINGS STORE IN A DRY PLACE SO THAT THEY MAY LOSE NEITHER FLAVOR NOR [other] VIRTUES.

SUMMARY OF DISHES [1]   *BREUIS CYBORV* [1]

I. CASSEROLE OF VEGETABLES AND CHICKEN
                              CACCABINA MINORE
II. STUFFED CHARTREUSE   *CACCABINA FUSILE*
III. BRAISED CUTLETS   *OFELLAS GARATAS*
IV. ROAST MEAT BALLS   *OFELLAS ASSAS*
V. GLAZED CUTLETS   *ALITER OFELLAS*
VI. MEAT BALLS WITH LASER   *OFELLAS GRATON*
VII. SEA SCORPION WITH TURNIPS
                 PISCES SCORPIONES RAPULATAS
VIII. ANY KIND OF FISH, FRIED
            PISCES FRIXOS CUIUSCUMQUE GENERIS
IX. FRIED FISH   *ITEM PISCES FRIXOS*
X. ROAST [Grilled] FISH   *PISCES ASSOS*
XI. FRIED FISH AND WINE SAUCE
                         PISCES INOTOGONON
XII. SARDINES, BABY TUNNY, WHITING   *SARDAS*
XIII. FISH STEWED IN WINE *ITEM PISCES INOTOGONON*
XIV. STEWED MULLET WITH DILL   *MULLOS ANETATOS*
XV. MULLET, DIFFERENT STYLE   *ALITER MULLOS*
XVI. MURENA AND EEL   *MURENAS ET ANGUILLAS*
XVII. SPINY LOBSTER AND SQUILL
                 LUCUSTAS ET ISQUILLAS
XVIII. BOILED FISH   *PISCES ELIXOS*
XIX. A DISH OF SOLE AND EGGS   *PATINAS OBORUM*
XX. SUCKLING PIG, CORIANDER SAUCE
                    PORCELLO CORIANDRATU
XXI. SUCKLING PIG, WINE SAUCE
                    PORCELLO IN OCCUCTU
XXII. PORK, PAN GRAVY   *PORCELLO EO IURE*
XXIII. PORK SPRINKLED WITH THYME
                 PORCELLO TYMMO CRAPSU
XXIV. PICKLED PORK   *PORCELLU EXOZOME*
XXV. LASER [sauce for] PORK   *PORCELLU LASARATU*
XXVI. SAUCE FOR PORK   *PORCELLU IUSCELLU*

XXVII. PLAIN LAMB *AGNU SIMPLICE*
XXVIII. KID AND LASER *HEDU LASARATU*
XXIX. THRUSH, HEALTH STYLE *TURDOS APONTOMENUS*
XXX. TURTLEDOVES *TURTURES*
XXXI. SAUCE FOR PARTRIDGE *IUS IN PERDICES*

[1] *Brevis cyboru* could be nicely and appropriately rendered with "Menu," — something minute, short, — but this list is not a menu in our modern sense. It is an enumeration of recipe names, a summary of dishes contained in the excerpts.

There is considerable variation in the spelling of the names here and in the following. Syllables ending with "u" are invariably abbreviations of "um."

I

[468] A CASSEROLE [1] OF VEGETABLE AND CHICK-
EN
CACCABINAM MINOREM

ARRANGE DIFFERENT KINDS OF COOKED VEGETABLES IN A CASSEROLE WITH [cooked] CHICKEN INTERSPERSED, IF YOU LIKE; SEASON WITH BROTH AND OIL, SET TO BOIL. NEXT CRUSH A LITTLE PEPPER AND LEAVES, AND MIX AN EGG IN WITH THE DRESSING [add this to the vegetables] PRESS [into the casserole, eliminating the juice] [2].

[1] The dish resembles a chartreuse.
[2] Juice should be extracted before the addition of the egg, if the dish is to be unmoulded.

Ia

[469] THE SAME, WITH ANOTHER DRESSING
A CABBAGE *CHARTREUSE*
*ALIAS: TRITURA UNDE PERFUNDES CACCA-
BINAM*

CRUSH WHATEVER QUANTITY OF LEAVES IS REQUIRED WITH CHERVIL AND ONE AND A QUARTER PART OF LAUR-EL BERRIES, A MEDIUM-SIZED BOILED CABBAGE, CORIAN-DER LEAVES, DISSOLVE WITH ITS OWN JUICE, STEAM IN THE HOT ASHES, BUT FIRST PLACE IN A MOULD [when stiff unmould on a platter] DECORATE, POUR UNDER A WELL-SEA-SONED SAUCE, AND SO SERVE [1].

[1] Either the vegetables and chicken of ℞ No. 468 are combined with this dressing or a purée of the above cabbage, etc., is made, which will make this an integral dish. The instructions are vague enough to leave room for this choice;

but there can be no doubt but what we have here a formula for a vegetable purée or a pudding, a genuine "Chartreuse," such as were prepared in the fancy moulds so popular in old Rome. The "Chartreuse," then, is not original with the vegetarian monks of the monastery by that name, the Carthusians.

II

[470]   A STUFFED CHARTREUSE
CACCABINAM [1] *FUSILEM*

[Take cooked] MALLOWS, LEEKS, BEETS, OR COOKED CAB-BAGE SPROUTS [shoots or tender strunks] THRUSHES [roast] AND QUENELLES OF CHICKEN, TIDBITS OF PORK OR SQUAB CHICKEN AND OTHER SIMILAR SHREDS OF FINE MEATS THAT MAY BE AVAILABLE; ARRANGE EVERYTHING AL-TERNATELY IN LAYERS [in a mould or in a casserole]. CRUSH PEPPER AND LOVAGE WITH 2 PARTS OF OLD WINE, 1 PART BROTH, 1 PART HONEY AND A LITTLE OIL. TASTE IT; AND WHEN WELL MIXED AND IN DUE PROPORTIONS PUT IN A SAUCE PAN AND ALLOW TO HEAT MODERATELY; WHEN BOILING ADD A PINT OF MILK IN WHICH [about eight] EGGS HAVE BEEN DISSOLVED; [next] POUR [this spiced custard] OVER [the layers of vegetables and meats, heat slowly without allowing to boil] AND WHEN CONGEALED SERVE [either in the casserole, or carefully unmould the dish on a service platter] [2].

[1] It is interesting to note how the generic terms, *salacaccabia* and *caccabina* have degenerated here. In these formulas the terms have lost all resemblance to the former meaning, the original "salt meat boiled in a pot." Such changes are very often observed in the terminology of our modern kitchens, in every language. They make the definition of terms and the classification of subjects extremely difficult. They add much to the confusion among cooks and guests in public dining places and create misunderstandings that only an expert can explain.

[2] This dish affords an opportunity for a decorative scheme by the arrangement of the various vegetables and meats in a pleasing and artistic manner, utilizing the various colors and shapes of the bits of food as one would use pieces of stone in a mosaic. Of course, such a design can be appreciated only if the chartreuse is served unmoulded, i.e. if the cook succeeds in unmoulding it without damaging the structure.

III

[471]   BRAISED CUTLETS   *OFELLAS GARATAS* [1]
PLACE THE MEAT IN A STEW PAN, ADD ONE POUND [2]

OF BROTH, A LIKE QUANTITY OF OIL, A TRIFLE OF HONEY, AND THUS BRAISE [3].

[1] Derived from *garum* or *œnogarum*, the wine sauce. These are supposed to be meat balls or cutlets prepared with garum, but the *garum* is not mentioned in the formula. This also illustrates the interesting etymology of the word. It is not recognized in every-day ancient language because it is a typical technical term, the much complained-of *lingua culinaria*. We find, therefore, that — at least in this instance — *garum* no longer stands for a sauce made from the fish, *garus*, but that *garum* has become a generic term for certain kinds of sauces. Danneil renders *garatus* with *lasaratus*, which is clearly out of place.

[2] In this instance, and in several others, and also according to Sueton. Cæs. fluids were weighed. What idea could be more practical, useful and more "modern" than this? Sheer commercial greed, stubbornness, indolence have thus far made futile all efforts towards more progressive methods in handling food stuffs, particularly in the weighing of them and in selling them by their weight. Present market methods are very chaotic, and are kept purposely so to the detriment of the buyer.

[3] The original: *et sic frigis*. — *Frigo* is equivalent to frying, drying, parching; the word here has taken on a broader meaning, because the "frying" process is clearly out of question here. It appears that the terminology of *frigo* and that of *asso* in the next formula, has not been clearly defined. As a matter of fact, not many modern cooks today are able to give a clear definition of such terms as frying, broiling, roasting, braising, baking, which are thus subject to various interpretations.

IV

[472]   ROAST MEAT BALLS   *OFELLAS ASSAS*

MEATBALLS [previously sauté], CAREFULLY PREPARED, ARRANGE IN A SHALLOW STEW PAN AND BRAISE THEM IN WINE SAUCE; AFTERWARDS SERVE THEM IN THE SAME SAUCE OR GRAVY, SPRINKLED WITH PEPPER.

V

[473]   GLAZED CUTLETS   *ALITER OFELLAS*

THE MEAT PIECES ARE BRAISED [1] IN BROTH AND ARE GLAZED [2] WITH HOT HONEY [3] AND THUS SERVED.

[1] Cf. note 3 to Excerpta III.
[2] *unguantur*.
[3] Dann. oil; G.-V. *melle* — *honey*. It is quite common to use honey for glazing foods. Today we sprinkle meats (ham) with sugar, exposing it to the open heat to melt it; the sugar thus forms a glaze or crust.

VI
[474]   MEAT BALLS WITH LASER
        OFELLAS GARATAS [1]

LASER, GINGER, CARDAMOM, AND A DASH OF BROTH;
CRUSH THIS ALL, MIX WELL, AND COOK THE MEAT BALL
THEREIN [2].

[1] Cf. Summary of Dishes, and note 1 to Excerpta III.

[2] Dann. adds cumin, due perhaps to the faulty reading of the sentence,
misces cum his omnibus tritis, etc.

VII
[475]   SEA-SCORPION WITH TURNIPS
        PISCES SCORPIONES RAPULATOS [1]

COOK [the fish] IN BROTH AND OIL, RETIRE WHEN HALF
DONE: SOAK BOILED TURNIPS, CHOP VERY FINE AND
SQUEEZE THEM IN YOUR HANDS SO THAT THEY HAVE NO
MORE MOISTURE IN THEM; THEN COMBINE THEM WITH
THE FISH AND LET THEM SIMMER WITH PLENTY OF OIL:
AND WHILE THIS COOKS, CRUSH CUMIN, HALF OF THAT
AMOUNT OF LAUREL BERRIES, AND, BECAUSE OF THE COL-
OR, ADD SAFFRON; BIND WITH RICE FLOUR TO GIVE IT THE
RIGHT CONSISTENCY. ADD A DASH OF VINEGAR AND
SERVE.

[1] *rapa, rapum*: white turnip, rape. "turniped."

VIII
[476]   [Sauce for] ANY KIND OF FISH, FRIED MAKE
           THUS:
        PISCES FRIXOS CUIUSCUMQUE GENERIS

CRUSH PEPPER, CORIANDER SEED, LASER ROOT, ORI-
GANY, RUE, FIGDATES, MOISTEN WITH VINEGAR, OIL,
BROTH, ADDING REDUCED MUST, ALL THIS PREPARE AND
MIX CAREFULLY, PLACE IN SMALL CASSEROLE TO HEAT.
WHEN THOROUGHLY HEATED, POUR OVER THE FRIED
FISH, SPRINKLE WITH PEPPER AND SERVE.

IX
[477]   [Sauce for] SAME FRIED FISH MAKE THUS:
        ITEM PISCES FRIXOS

CRUSH PEPPER, LOVAGE [1], LAUREL BERRIES, CORIAN-
DER, AND MOISTEN WITH HONEY, BROTH [2], WINE, RAT

SIN WINE, OR REDUCED SPICED WINE; COOK THIS ON A
SLOW FIRE, BIND WITH RICE FLOUR AND SERVE.

[1] Sch. *ligisticum*.
[2] Wanting in Sch.

X

[478]   [Sauce for] ROAST FISH [1]   *PISCES ASSOS*

CRUSH PEPPER, LOVAGE, SATURY, DRY ONIONS, MOISTEN
WITH VINEGAR, ADD FIGDATES, DILL, YOLKS OF EGG,
HONEY, VINEGAR, BROTH, OIL, REDUCED MUST; ALL THIS
MIX THOROUGHLY AND UNDERLAY [the fish with it].

[1] The fish was probably broiled on the *craticula* (see our illustration).
The nature of this sauce is not quite clear. If properly handled, it might turn
out to be a highly seasoned mayonnaise, or a vinaigrette, depending on the mode
of manipulation; either would be suitable for fried or broiled fish.

XI

[479]   FISH AND WINE SAUCE
        PISCES ŒNOTEGANON [1]

FRY THE FISH; CRUSH PEPPER, LOVAGE, RUE, GREEN
HERBS, DRY ONIONS, ADD OIL [wine] BROTH AND SERVE.

[1] Ihm and G.-V. *œnoteganon; inotogono* and in the Summary of Dishes
inotogonon; Sch. *eleogaro*. Rather an obscure term, owing to the diversity of
spelling. We would call it a dish stewed in or prepared with wine, although wine
is absent in the present formula. However, it is given in XIII, which bears the
same name.
Dann. is obviously mistaken in styling this preparation "oil broth."

XII

[480]   [Cold Sauce for] SARDINES MAKE THUS:
        SARDAS [1] *SIC FACIES*

CRUSH PEPPER, LOVAGE SEED, ORIGANY, DRY ONIONS,
HARD BOILED YOLKS, VINEGAR, OIL; THIS MUST BE COM-
BINED INTO ONE [2] AND UNDERLAID.

[1] A kind of small tunny, which, like our herring, used to be pickled or
salt, corresponding to the anchovy. A "sardine," from the island of Sardinia;
Sardus, the inhabitant of Sardinia.
[2] The absence of detailed instructions as to the manipulation of the yolks,
oil and vinegar is regrettable; upon them depends the certainty or uncertainty
of whether the ancients had our modern mayonnaise.

XIII

[481]   FISH STEWED IN WINE
         PISCES ŒNOTEGANON [1]

RAW FISH ANY KIND YOU PREFER, WASH [prepare, cut into handy size] ARRANGE IN A SAUCE PAN; ADD OIL, BROTH, VINEGAR, A BUNCH OF LEEKS AND [fresh] CORIANDER, AND COOK: [Meanwhile] CRUSH PEPPER, ORIGANY, LOVAGE WITH THE BUNCHES OF LEEKS AND CORIANDER WHICH YOU HAVE COOKED [with the fish] AND POUR [this preparation] IN-TO THE SAUCE PAN. [When the fish is done, retire it and arrange the pieces in the serving dish, casserole, bowl or platter] BRING THE RESI-DUE IN THE SAUCE PAN TO A BOILING POINT, ALLOW IT TO REDUCE SLOWLY TO THE RIGHT CONSISTENCY [Strain the sauce of the fish] SPRINKLE WITH PEPPER AND SERVE.

[1] Cf. note to XI. This *œnoteganon* resembles the *Bouillabaisse*, the famous Marseilles fish chowder. In addition to the above manner it is flavored with saffron. An excellent dish, especially with the judicious addition of onions, parsley, a suspicion of garlic and small sippets of toasted bread.

XIV

[482]   MULLET STEWED WITH DILL MAKE THUS:
         MULLOS ANETHATOS [1] *SIC FACIES*

PREPARE THE FISH [clean, wash, trim, cut into pieces] AND PLACE IN A SAUCE PAN, ADDING OIL, BROTH, WINE, BUNCHES OF LEEKS, [fresh] CORIANDER, [fresh dill]; PLACE ON FIRE TO COOK. [Meanwhile] PUT PEPPER IN THE MORTAR, POUND IT, ADD OIL, AND ONE PART OF VINEGAR AND RAI-SIN WINE TO TASTE. [This preparation] TRANSFER INTO A SAUCE PAN, PLACE ON THE FIRE TO HEAT, TIE WITH ROUX, ADD TO THE FISH IN THE SAUCE PAN. SPRINKLE WITH PEP-PER AND SERVE.

[1] From *anethus* — dill — which is omitted in formula. Sch. *anecatos*, i.e. *submersos*, because the original fails to state the dill in the formula. Such conjecture is not justified.

XV

[483]   MULLET ANOTHER STYLE   *ALITER MULLOS*

SCRAPE, WASH, PLACE [the fish] IN A SAUCE PAN, ADD OIL, BROTH, WINE AND A BUNCH OF LEEKS AND [fresh] CORI-ANDER TO THE MESS, SET ON THE FIRE TO COOK. CRUSH PEPPER, LOVAGE, ORIGANY, MOISTEN WITH SOME OF THE

FISH'S OWN LIQUOR [from the sauce pan] ADD RAISIN WINE TO TASTE, PUT IT INTO A POT AND ON THE FIRE TO HEAT; TIE WITH ROUX AND PRESENTLY ADD IT TO THE CONTENTS IN THE SAUCE PAN [1] SPRINKLE WITH PEPPER AND SERVE.

[1] It appears that the *patina* mentioned in this and in the foregoing formula is either a finely wrought metal sauce pan or chafing dish, or a plainer *cumana*, an earthenware casserole; either of which may be used for service at the table.

It may be noticed how this manner of preparing fish has a tendency to preserve all the savory flavors and juices of the fish, a process in this respect both rational and economical.

XVI

[484] MURENA [1], EEL [2] OR MULLET MAKE THUS: *MURENAM AUT ANGUILLAS VEL MULLOS SIC FACIES*

CLEAN THE FISH AND CAREFULLY PLACE IN A SAUCE PAN. IN THE MORTAR PUT PEPPER, LOVAGE, ORIGANY, MINT, DRY ONIONS, CRUSH, MOISTEN WITH A SMALL GLASS OF WINE, HALF OF THAT OF BROTH, AND OF HONEY ONE THIRD PART, AND A MODERATE AMOUNT OF REDUCED MUST, SAY A SPOONFUL. IT IS NECESSARY THAT THE FISH BE ENTIRELY COVERED BY THIS LIQUOR SO THAT THERE MAY BE SUFFICIENT JUICE DURING THE COOKING.

[1] The ancients considered the murena one of the finest of fish; the best were brought from the straits of Sicily. Rich Romans kept them alive in their fish ponds, often large and elaborate marble basins called, *piscina*, fattened the fish, kept it ready for use. Pollio fattened murenas on human flesh, killing a slave on the slightest provocation and throwing the body into the fish pond; he would eat only the liver of such murenas. This is the only case of such cruelty on record, and it has often been cited and exaggerated.

[2] Perhaps the sea-eel, or conger, according to Dann. Also very much esteemed. The witty Plautus names a cook in one of his comedies "Congrio," because the fellow was "slippery."

XVII

[485] [Dressing for] SPINY LOBSTER (AND SQUILL) *LOCUSTAM (ET SCILLAM)* [1]

CRUSH PEPPER, LOVAGE, CELERY SEED, POUR IN VINEGAR, BROTH, YOLKS OF [hard boiled] EGGS, MIX WELL TO-

GETHER [2] AND DRESS [the boiled shellfish meat with it] AND
SERVE.

[1] Cf. Summary of Dishes.

[2] Another of Apicii hasty and laconic formulæ. No indication as to how to
use the ingredients named. According to our notion of eating, there is only one
way: The shellfish is boiled in aromatic water, allowed to cool off; the meat is
then taken out of the shells; the above named ingredients are combined in a
manner of a mayonnaise or a vinaigrette, although the necessary oil is not mentioned here. The dressing is poured over the shellfish meat, and the result is a
sort of salad or "cocktail" as we have today.

XVIII

[486]   [Sauce] FOR BOILED FISH
IN PISCIBUS ELIXIS

CRUSH PEPPER, LOVAGE, CELERY SEED, ORIGANY WHICH
MOISTEN WITH VINEGAR; ADD PINE NUTS, FIGDATES [1]
IN SUFFICIENT QUANTITY, HONEY, VINEGAR, BROTH, MUS-
TARD, MIX AND COMBINE PROPERLY AND BRING FORTH.

[1] Dann. is undecided as to whether this is dates or date wine; Goll. thinks
it is mustard seed, which is not so bad gastronomically; but the original leaves
no room for any doubt.

XIX

[487]   A DISH OF SOLE WITH EGGS
PATINA SOLEARUM EX OVIS

SCALE [skin] CLEAN [the soles], PLACE IN A [shallow] SAUCE
PAN, ADD BROTH, OIL [white] WINE, A BUNCH OF LEEKS
AND CORIANDER SEED, PLACE ON FIRE TO COOK, GRIND A
LITTLE PEPPER, ORIGANY, MOISTEN WITH THE FISH
LIQUOR [from the sauce pan]. TAKE 10 RAW EGGS, BEAT
THEM AND MIX WITH THE REMAINING LIQUOR; PUT IT
ALL BACK OVER THE FISH, AND ON A SLOW FIRE ALLOW
TO HEAT [without boiling] AND THICKEN TO THE RIGHT
CONSISTENCY; SPRINKLE WITH PEPPER [1].

[1] Very similar to *Sole au vin blanc*. Cf. ℞ No. 155.

XX

[488]   SUCKLING PIG, CORIANDER SAUCE
PORCELLUM CORIANDRATUM

ROAST THE PIG CAREFULLY; MAKE THUS A MORTAR
MIXTURE: POUND PEPPER, DILL, ORIGANY, GREEN CORI-

ANDER, MOISTEN WITH HONEY, WINE, BROTH, OIL, VINE-
GAR, REDUCED MUST. ALL OF THIS WHEN HOT POUR OVER
[the roast] SPRINKLE RAISINS, PINE NUTS AND CHOPPED ON-
IONS OVER AND SO SERVE.

XXI

[489] SUCKLING PIG, WINE SAUCE
       PORCELLUM ÆNOCOCTUM [1]

TAKE THE PIG, GARNISH [with a marinade of herbs, etc.] COOK
[roast] IT WITH OIL AND BROTH. WHEN DONE, PUT IN THE
MORTAR PEPPER, RUE, LAUREL BERRIES, BROTH, RAISIN
WINE OR REDUCED WINE, OLD WINE, CRUSH ALL, MIX AND
PREPARE TO A POINT; DRESS THE PIG ON A SHOWY SERVICE
[2] PLATTER AND SERVE.

[1] i.e. *œnococtum*, cooked or prepared in wine sauce.

[2] Dann. is of the opinion that the pig is cooked in a copper vessel, because
the instructions are to serve it *in patinam aheneam*.

XXII

[490] PIG, PAN GRAVY   *PORCELLUM EO IURE*

ROAST THE PIG IN ITS OWN JUICE; [when done] RETIRE;
BIND THE GRAVY WITH ROUX; [strain] PUT IN A SAUCE
BOAT AND SERVE.

XXIII

[491] PIG SPRINKLED WITH THYME
       PORCELLUM THYMO SPARSUM

MILK-FED PIG, KILLED ON THE PREVIOUS DAY, BOIL WITH
SALT AND DILL; TRANSFER IT INTO COLD WATER, CARE-
FULLY KEEPING IT SUBMERGED, TO PRESERVE ITS WHITE-
NESS. THEREUPON [make a cold dressing of the following] GREEN
SAVORY HERBS, [fresh] THYME, A LITTLE FLEABANE, HARD
BOILED EGGS, ONIONS, [everything] CHOPPED FINE, SPRIN-
KLE EVERYTHING [over the pig which has been taken out of the
water and allowed to drip off] AND SEASON WITH A PINT OF
BROTH, ONE MEASURE OF OIL, ONE OF RAISIN WINE, AND
SO PRESENT IT [1].

[1] We would first mix the liquid components of this dressing with the
chopped ingredients and then spread the finished dressing over the pig. Our
author, no doubt, had this very process in mind.

XXIV

[492] PICKLED SUCKLING PIG
       PORCELLUM OXYZOMUM [1]

GARNISH [prepare and marinate] THE PIG CORRECTLY AND
PLACE IT IN A LIQUOR PREPARED AS FOLLOWS: PUT IN THE
MORTAR 50 GRAINS OF PEPPER, AS MUCH HONEY [2]
AS IS REQUIRED, 3 DRY ONIONS, A LITTLE GREEN OR
DRY CORIANDER, A PINT OF BROTH, 1 SEXTARIUS OF
OIL, 1 PINT OF WATER; [all this] PUT IN A STEW PAN
[braisière] PLACE THE PIG IN IT; WHEN IT COMMENCES TO
BOIL, STIR THE GRAVY QUITE FREQUENTLY [3] SO AS TO
THICKEN IT. SHOULD THE BROTH THUS BE REDUCED [by
evaporation] ADD ANOTHER PINT OF WATER. IN THIS MAN-
NER COOK [braise] THE PIG TO PERFECTION AND SERVE IT.

[1] *exodionum*, and in the Summary of Dishes, *exozome*, i.e. *oxyzomum*. It
is curious to note the various spellings and meanings of *oxyzomum*. This is supposed to be a sour sauce or an acid preparation of some kind, yet this recipe does
not mention acids. In fact, the presence of honey would make it a sweet preparation. We take it, the "garnish" contains the necessary vinegar or other acids
such as lemon juice, wine, etc. *Oxyzomum* is properly rendered "pickle."

[2] Dann. oil, occurring twice in his version.

[3] *sæpius*; Dann. confusing *sæpe* with *cæpa*, renders this "onions sauce." The
same occurs to him in XXVII.

XXV

[493] PIG WITH LASER   *PORCELLUM LASARATUM*

IN THE MORTAR POUND PEPPER, LOVAGE, CARRAWAY,
A LITTLE CUMIN, LIVE LASER, LASER ROOT, MOISTEN WITH
VINEGAR, ADD PINE NUTS, FIGDATES, HONEY, VINEGAR,
BROTH, PREPARED MUSTARD, FINISH WITH OIL TO TASTE,
AND POUR OVER [the roast pig].

XXVI

[494] PIG IN SAUCE   *PORCELLUM IUSCELLATUM*

IN THE MORTAR PUT PEPPER, LOVAGE, OR ANISE, CORI-
ANDER, RUE, A LAUREL BERRY, POUND [all], MOISTENING
WITH BROTH, [add] LEEKS, RAISIN WINE, OR A LITTLE
HONEY, A LITTLE WINE, AND A LIKE AMOUNT OF OIL.
WHEN THIS HAS BEEN COOKED TIE WITH ROUX.

XXVII

[495]   PLAIN LAMB [1]   *AGNUM SIMPLICEM*

OF THE SKINNED LAMB MAKE SMALL CUTLETS WHICH
WASH CAREFULLY AND ARRANGE IN A SAUCE PAN, ADD
OIL, BROTH, WINE, LEEKS, CORIANDER CUT WITH THE
KNIFE; WHEN IT COMMENCES TO BOIL, STIR VERY FRE-
QUENTLY [2] AND SERVE.

[1] Unquestionably the ancient equivalent for "Irish Stew."

[2] Cf. note 3 to ℞ 492, XXIV; the presence of onion, however, would do
no harm here.

XXVIII

[496]   KID WITH LASER   *HÆDUM LASARATUM*

THE WELL-CLEANED GUTS OF A KID FILL WITH [a prepara-
tion of] PEPPER, BROTH, LASER, OIL [1], AND PUT THEM
BACK INTO THE CARCASS WHICH SEW TIGHTLY AND THUS
COOK [roast] THE KID [whole]. WHEN DONE PUT IN THE
MORTAR RUE, LAUREL BERRIES, AND THEN SERVE THE KID
WHICH MEANWHILE HAS BEEN RETIRED FROM THE POT
WITH ITS OWN DRIPPINGS OR GRAVY.

[1] There being only liquids for this filling of the guts, a more solid substance, such as pork forcemeat, eggs, or cereals would be required to make an
acceptable filling for the casings of the kid. Furthermore sausage, for such is
this in fact, must be thoroughly cooked before it can be used for the filling of
the carcass, as not sufficient heat would penetrate the interior during the roasting
to cook any raw dressing.

XXIX

[497]   THRUSH "À LA SANTÉ"
    TURDOS HAPANTAMYNOS [1]

CRUSH PEPPER, LASER, LAUREL BERRY, MIX IN CUMIN [2]
GARUM AND STUFF THE THRUSH [with this preparation, 3]
THROUGH THE THROAT [4], TYING THEM WITH A
STRING. THEREUPON MAKE THIS PREPARATION IN WHICH
THEY ARE COOKED: CONSISTING OF OIL, SALT, WATER [5],
DILL AND HEADS OF LEEKS.

[1] Cf. Summary of Dishes; term not identified, derived from the Greek,
meaning to drive away all stomach ills.

[2] We use juniper berries today instead of cumin.

[3] Cf. note to ℞ 496, XXVIII.

[4] Thrush and other game birds of such small size are not emptied in the usual way: they are cooked with the entrails, or, the intestines are taken out, seasoned, sauté, and are either put back into the carcasses, or are served separately on bread croutons. In this instance, the necessary seasoning is introduced through the throat, a most ingenious idea that can only occur to Apicius.

[5] In other instances we have pointed out where a small amount of water was used to clarify the oil used for frying foods. The presence here of water leads us to believe that the thrush were not "cooked," i.e. "boiled" but that they were fried in a generous amount of oil; this would make the ancient process remarkably similar to the present European way of preparing thrush or fieldfare, or similar game birds.

For water used to clarify oil see note 3 to ℞ No. 250.

XXX

[498]   TURTLEDOVES   *TURTURES*

OPEN THEM, PREPARE [marinate] CAREFULLY; CRUSH PEPPER, LASER, A LITTLE BROTH, IMMERSE THE DOVES IN THIS PREPARATION SO THAT IT WILL BE ABSORBED BY THEM, AND THUS ROAST THEM.

XXXI

[499]   SAUCE FOR PARTRIDGE [1]   *IUS IN PERDICES*

CRUSH IN THE MORTAR PEPPER, CELERY, MINT, AND RUE; MOISTEN WITH VINEGAR, ADD FIGDATE [wine], HONEY, VINEGAR, BROTH, OIL; LET IT BOIL LIKEWISE AND SERVE.

[1] This formula evidently is a fragment.

END OF THE SUMMARY OF DISHES [of the Excerpts of Vinidarius]
EXPLI [cit] BREUIS CIBORUM

[END OF THE RECIPES OF APICIUS]

APICII COELII

DE

OPSONIIS

ET

CONDIMENTIS,

Sive

ARTE COQUINARIA,

LIBRI DECEM.

Cum Annotationibus

MARTINI LISTER,

è Medicis domesticis Serenissimæ Maje-
statis Reginæ Annæ,

E T

Notis selectioribus, variisque lectionibus integris,
HUMELBERGII, BARTHII, REINESII,
A. VAN DER LINDEN, & ALIORUM,
ut & *Variarum Lectionum* Libello.

EDITIO SECUNDA.

Longe auctior atque emendatior.

AMSTELODAMI,
Apud JANSSONIO-WAESBERGIOS

MDCCIX.

TITLE PAGE, LISTER EDITION, AMSTERDAM, 1709

Lister's second edition was printed at Amsterdam, 1709, by very able printers, the Jansson-Wæsbergs.
It is a very worthy book in every respect which, as M. Græsse says in Trésor des livres rares et précieux,
may be included in the collection of the Variorum.

APICIANA

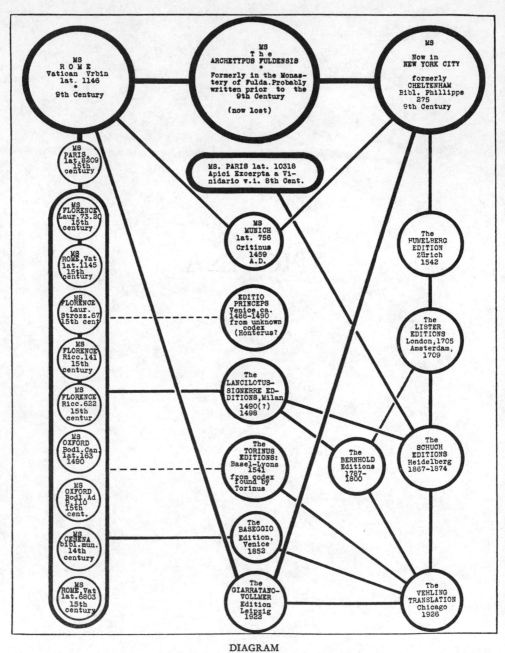

DIAGRAM

of Apicius Manuscripts and Printed Editions, showing relation to each other and indicating the sources of the present translation.

INCIPIT CONDITUM PARADOXUM
Opening recipe No. 1, Book I, Apicius. From the
manuscript of the 9th century in the Library of the
Vatican at Rome.

APICIANA
A Bibliography of Apician Manuscripts and Printed Editions
A. MANUSCRIPTS
SUMMARY OF MANUSCRIPTS

Location	No. of Ms. Books
New York, I	1
Rome, II, IV and XVII	3
Paris, III and V	2
Florence, VI, VII, VIII and IX	4
Oxford, X and XI	2
Cesena, XII	1
Munich, XVII	1
Not accounted for, XIII, XIV, XV, XVI	4
Total of manuscript books	18

(Doubtful as to present location, the Codex Humelbergii, cf. XI, Oxford)

DESCRIPTION OF MANUSCRIPTS
I, 9TH CENTURY

New York, Library of the Academy of Medicine, until 1930 in Cheltenham, Gloucester, Biblioth. Phillipps, 275, in the library of Sir Thomas Phillipps, a codex ca. Ninth century, 4to, parchment, 275 pp., originally bound up with Phill. 386, which is said to have come from the Benedictine Abbey of St. Ghislain, founded at the end of the 7th century in the diocese of Cambrai; partly in Continental, but mostly in Anglo-Saxon minuscle of the 9th century, not unlike the Anglo-Saxon minuscle of Fulda.

Title missing. Cf. Vollmer, Studien, pp. 5-6.

The writer who has hastily inspected the manuscript in 1931 is of the opinion that three different hands wrote this book. Part of the index is gone, too. The book commences with lib. VII of the index. Bound in an 18th century French full leather binding. It was brought to America by Dr. Margaret B. Wilson and presented to the library of the A. of M. in 1931.

II, 9TH CENTURY

Rome, Vatican Library. Vat. Vrbinas, lat. 1146, Ninth century. 58 sheets, 2 blanks in the beginning and 2 at the end. Size 23.75 x 18.75 cm., heavy parchment, 20-21 lines to the page, not numbered. Sheet 1 R, illuminated by square panel in purple and gold letters (capit. quadr.) INC̄P || API || CÆ || — Nothing else. Sheet 1 V — 3 R the title, EPIM e || LES LI || BER I, and the titles of Book I, illuminated with columns, flowers and birds. Sheet 3 R between the foot of the columns EXPLICIVNT CAPITVLA. Sheet 3 V a panel in purple similar to sheet 1 R with inscription, INC̄P || CONDITV̄ || PARADOXV̄. Sheet 4 R commences the text with the title, I, Conditum Paradoxum. Captions, marginal figures and initials in red. The captions are written in good uncials throughout, the first text words usually in half uncials, continuing in an even and beautiful minuscle. The Explicits and Incipits invariably in capitalis rustica. Sheet 58 V end of text with EXPLICIT LIBER X.

Traube, Vollmer and others believe that this manuscript was written in or in the vicinity of Tours in the 9th century.

III, 8TH CENTURY

Paris, lat. 10318. 8th century. Codex Salmasianus, pp. 196-203, Apici excerpta a Vinidario vir. inl. (See illustration.)

Excerpts from Apicius, 31 formulæ not found in the traditional Apicius and quite different in character. Cf. Notes on Vinidarius, preceding the Excerpta which follow the end of Book X of Apicius.

IV, 15TH CENTURY

Rome, Vatican Library, Vat. Vrbinas, lat. 1145, parchment, 15th century. 51 sheets, 20 lines to the page, title, Apicius.

V, 15TH CENTURY

Paris, lat. 8209, paper, 15th century. 131 sheets, 30 lines to the page.

VI, 15TH CENTURY

Florence, Laur. 73, 20. 15th century. 84 sheets, 26 lines to the page.

VII, 15TH CENTURY

Florence, Laur. Strozz. 67, 15th century. 50 sheets, 23 lines to the page. Title, Apicius.

VIII, 15TH CENTURY

Florence, Riccardianus, 141 (L III 29), paper, 179 sheets, irregular number of lines, pp. 123-179, Apicius. 15th century.

IX, 1462

Florence, Riccardianus, 662 (M I 26), finished April 4th, 1462, paper, 79 sheets, 26 lines to the page. Pp. 41-79 Apicius, written by Pascutius Sabinus, Bologna, 1462.

X, 1490

Oxford, Bodl. Canon. lat. 168 4to min. 78 pp. dated May 28th, 1490. (*In fine*) scriptum per me Petrum Antonium Salandum Reginensem die xxviii Maii MCCCCLXXXX.

XI, 15TH CENTURY

Oxford, Bodl. Add. B 110, 15th century, Italian. cf. H. Schenkl, Bibl. Britann. I. p. 79 n. 384 and F. Madan, A Summary Catalogue of Western Mss. in the Bodleian Library, Oxford, 1905, p. 660. Vollmer says that this Ms. belonged to a son of Humelbergius, as proven by P. Lehmann.

XII, 14TH CENTURY

Cesna, bibl. municip., 14th century.

XIII

A manuscript in the library of the Sforza brothers at Pesaro which burned in 1514, known only from the catalogue. Cf. A. Vernarecci, La Libreria di Gio. Sforza in Archivio storico per le Marche e l'Umbria, III, 1886, 518, 790.

XIV

A manuscript used by Bonifaz Amerbach and Joh. Sichardus. Cf. P. Lehman, Joh. Sichardus, Quellen und Untersuchungen, IV, 1, p. 204.

XV-XVI

The two manuscripts mentioned by Albanus Torinus, in his edition of Apicius, Basel, 1541. In 1529 Torinus found an Apicius "codex" on the island of Megalona (Maguellone) which he used for his edition of Apicius. It is almost certain that this was not a very ancient manuscript. The way Torinus speaks of it and of the (first) Venetian printed edition in his *epistola dedicatoria* leaves even doubt as to whether his authority was handwritten or printed. A first edition, printed ca. 1483, may have well been a dilapidated copy such as Torinus describes in 1529. Torinus admits taking some liberties with the text and failed to understand some phases of it. Despite this fact, his text, from a culinary point of view seems to be more authentic than the Humelbergius and Lister versions.

The other codex according to Torinus, was found in Transsylvania by Io. Honterus of Coronea. This codex may have served as authority for the first edition printed ca. 1483 by Bernardinus, of Venice. No other mention is made of this codex anywhere, which according to Torinus, was sent to Venice from Transsylvania. The text of the Editio Princeps, by the way, is thoroughly unreliable.

XVII, 15TH CENTURY

Ms. Rome, Vatican Library, lat. 6803, 15th Century.

XVIII, 15TH CENTURY

Munich, lat. 756. Ex bibl. Petri Victorii 49. 15th century. This codex is particularly valuable and important for the identification of the Apicius text. Cf. Vollmer, Studien, pp. 10 seq.

B. PRINTED EDITIONS

SUMMARY OF PRINTED EDITIONS

No.	YEAR OF PUBLICATION	PLACE OF PUBLICATION	LANGUAGE
1	ca. A.D. 1483 (?)	Venice, Italy	Latin
2	A.D. 1490 (?)	Milan, Italy (doubtful)	Latin
3	A.D. 1498	Milan, Italy	Latin
4	A.D. 1503	Venice, Italy	Latin
5	A.D. 1541	Basel, Switzerland	Latin
6	A.D. 1541	Lyons, France	Latin
7	A.D. 1542	Zürich, Switzerland	Latin
8	A.D. 1705	London, England	Latin
9	A.D. 1709	Amsterdam, Holland	Latin
10	A.D. 1787	Marktbreit, Germany	Latin
11	A.D. 1791	Lübeck, Germany	Latin
12	A.D. 1800	Ansbach, Germany	Latin
13	A.D. 1852	Venice, Italy	Italian
14	A.D. 1867	Heidelberg, Germany	Latin
15	A.D. 1874	Heidelberg, Germany	Latin
16	A.D. 1909	Leipzig, Germany	German
17	A.D. 1911	Leipzig, Germany	German
18	A.D. 1922	Leipzig, Germany	Latin
19	A.D. 1933	Paris, France	French
20	A.D. 1936	Chicago, U. S. A.	English

COMMENTARIES ON APICIUS

No.	YEAR OF PUBLICATION	PLACE OF PUBLICATION	LANGUAGE
21	A.D. 1531*	Frankfurt, Germany	Latin
22	A.D. 1534*	Frankfurt, Germany	Latin

* Excerpts and adaptations have little relation to Apicius.

23	A.D. 1535*	Antwerp, Belgium	Latin
24	A.D. 1831	Heidelberg, Germany	German
25	A.D. 1868	London, England	English
26	A.D. 1912	Naples, Italy	Italian
27	A.D. 1920	Munich, Germany	German
28	A.D. 1921	Rome, Italy	Latin-Italian
29	A.D. 1927	Leipzig Germany	German

Total of Printed Editions, in Latin 15
Total of Printed Editions, in Italian 1
Total of Printed Editions, in German 2
Total of Printed Editions, in French 1
Total of Printed Editions, in English 1
Total of Commentaries in all Languages 9

Editions and Commentaries published in America 1
Editions and Commentaries published in Belgium 1
Editions and Commentaries published in England 2
Editions and Commentaries published in France 2
Editions and Commentaries published in Germany . . . 13
Editions and Commentaries published in Holland 1
Editions and Commentaries published in Italy 7
Editions and Commentaries published in Switzerland 2

BIBLIOGRAPHERS AND COLLECTORS

Albanus Torinus, 1541. describes Mss. XV and XVI.
A. Vernarecci describes Mss. XIII.
P. Lehmann describes Mss. XI and XIV.
F. Vollmer describes Mss I-XVIII.
Dr. Margaret B. Wilson describes Ms. I.
Georges Vicaire describes editions Nos. 1, 3, 4, 5, 6, 7, 8, 9, 11, 14, 15.
Theodor Drexel (Georg) describes editions Nos. 1, 5, 6, 7, 9, 10, 12, 13, 14, 15.
Elizabeth R. Pennell describes editions Nos. 1, 3, 9.
Bernhold describes editions Nos. 2, 10, 11, 12.
Fabricius describes edition No. 2.
Baron Pichon describes editions Nos. 3, 21.
In the author's collection are editions Nos. 4, 5, 6, 7, 8, 9, 10, 15, 16, 17, 18, 19, 20, 23, 27, 28, 29.

DESCRIPTION OF PRINTED EDITIONS

These summaries and descriptions of the known manuscript books and printed editions of Apicius are presented with a desire to afford the students a survey of the field treated in this volume, to illustrate the interest that has existed throughout the past centuries in our ancient book.

Copies of any Apicius edition and commentaries are scarce; famous collectors pride themselves in owning one or several of them. Of the well-known collections of cookery books the most outstanding perhaps is that of Theodor Drexel, of Frankfurt on the Main, who owned nine different editions of Apicius. The Drexel catalogue forms the basis of a bibliography — Verzeichnis der Litteratur über Speise und Trank bis zum Jahre 1887, bearbeitet von Carl Georg, Hannover, 1888, describing some 1700 works.

The Drexel collection, combined with that of Dr. Freund, is now in the Staatsbibliothek in Berlin and is undoubtedly the finest collection of its kind.

Another famous collection of cookery books is described in My Cookery Books, by Elizabeth Robins Pennell, Boston, 1903, listing three of the Apicii.

The Pennel collection was destroyed by a flood in London while being stored away in a warehouse during the world war.

The most important bibliography, well-known to bibliophiles, is the Bibliographie gastronomique par Georges Vicaire, Paris, 1890. Vicaire mentions eleven Apicius editions.

The Baron Pichon and the Georges Vicaire collections are both dispersed.

Despite ardent efforts over a period of many years the writer has been unable to secure either an Apicius manuscript or the editions No. 1 and 2. The existence of No. 2 on our list is doubtful. Therefore, we do not pretend having inspected or read each and every edition described herein, but by combining the efforts of the authorities here cited we have gathered the following titles and descriptions in order to present a complete survey of the Apician literature.

NO. 1 CA. A.D. 1483, VENICE

APITII CELII DE RE COQUINARIA LIBRI DECEM || SUETONIUS TRAQUILLUS DE CLARIS GRAMATICIS. || SUETONIUS TRAQUILLUS DE CLARIS RHETORIBUS || COQUINARIÆ CAPITA GRÆCA AB APITIO POSITA HÆC SUNT || EPIMELELS, (*Etc. In fine*) IMPRESSUM VENETIIS PER BERNARDINUM VENETUM.

No date, but attributed to ca. 1483-6. Given as the earliest edition by most authorities. 4to, old vellum, 30 sheets, the pages not numbered. Georg-Drexel, No. 13; Pennell, p. 111; Vicaire, col. 29.

NO. 2, MILAN, A.D. 1490

APICIUS CULINARIS (*sic*) (CURA BLASII LANCILOTI *In fine*) IMPRESSUM MEDIOLANI PER MAGISTRUM GUILIERUM DE SIGNERRE ROTHOMAGENSEM. ANNO DOMINI M CCCC LXXXX DIE VIII MENSIS JANUARII.

Large 8vo. Edition disputed by bibliographers.

Ex Bernhold, *præfatio*, p. IX, who (we are translating from his Latin text) says, "Here is the exterior of the book as extant in the Nuremberg library, most accurately and neatly described by the very famous and most worthy physician of that illustrious republic, Dr. Preus, a friend of mine for thirty years; whose integrity, of course, is above reproach; these are his own words — The book is made in the size called large octavo. It must be mentioned that the sheets are indeed large, so that the size might be styled an ordinary quarto. Fabricius, in his Bibliotheca, the newest edition, quotes a copy under this name. The entire book consists of five parts [sheets, folded into eight leaves — sixteen printed pages — stitched together] and two leaves. These five parts contain the text proper; these two sheets preceding them, are occupied by the title page, the dedication and a kind of poetic address. The text itself commences with p. 5, I should say, though there is no regular pagination. However, there are nevertheless in the lower ends of the leaves, called the limp parts, some conspicuous letters on the first four leaves of the sheets, while the remaining four leaves though belonging to the respective parts, are blank. For instance aI., aII., aIII., aIIII. Then follows the next sheet or part, signed, bI., II., III., IIII. in the same manner, with the four following leaves blank. And thus in the same manner follows sheet c, d, e. The two leaves preceding the five parts which comprise the text proper, contain the title of the book, Apicius Culinaris [sic] nowhere, to be sure, appears a note of the place or the date where and when the book was made, and on this whole first page, aside from the words already noted, there is nothing else in evidence than the picture of an angel, in the center of which there is the sign, IHS, and around the circle the following words are read, "Joannes de Lagniano M." At the feet of the angel spaces may be seen that are inscribed with the letters, I.O.L. The next page, or the verso of the title page, exhibits the dedication of Blasius Lancilotus, extending to the upper part of the third page. On this very same page occurs the poem by Ludovicus Vopiscus, addressed to Joannes Antonius Riscius, comprising five very beautiful distichs. The remaining part of the third page is finished off with the word, "Finis," while the fourth page is entirely blank. The text of Apicius commences with the fifth, as mentioned above, and from now on the leaves are numbered by letters, as previously described. At the end of the text, on the last page of the book, a poem is conspicuous, entitled, "Antonius Mota to the Public," consisting of four neat distichs, followed by another composition, containing five distichs by Joannes Salandus. And conclusion of the entire work is made with these words, "Printed at Milan by Master Guiliermus de Signerre Rothomagensis, in the year of the Lord 1490, on the 8th day of the month of January."

"From this edition, the oldest as well as the rarest — with no other known earlier edition — all the variants given herewith have been collected by Goezius." Thus far Bernhold.

The existence of this edition is doubted by Brunet, according to Vicaire. This ancient description corresponds substantially to that of Vicaire of the following edition of 1498 which Vicaire proclaims to be the first dated Apicius edition. It is interesting to note, however, what Bernhold has to say of this 1498 edition.

"Without a doubt a repetition of the preceding edition," says he; and he goes on quoting the Bibliotheca Latina Fabricio-Ernestina (Jo. Alberti Fabricii Bibliothec. Latin. edit ab Ernesti 1708) to the effect that two editions were printed at Milan, one of 1490 by Blasius Lancilotus and one of 1498 by Guiliermus de Signerre Rothomagensis.

Our inquiry at the Municipal library of Nürnberg has revealed the fact that this copy of 1490 is no longer in the possession of the library there.

NO. 3, A.D. 1498, MILAN

APICIUS CULINARIUS (*in fine*) IMPRESSUM MEDIOLANI PER MAGISTRUM GUILERUM SIGNERRE ROTHOMAGENSEM, ANNO DNI MCCCCLXXXXVIII, DIE XX, MENSIS IANUARII.

(Ex Pennell, p. 111) First dated edition, 4to, 40 sheets, pages not numbered.

Antonius mota Ad vulgus.

Plaudite fartores: cætari: plaudite ventres
Plaudite myftili tecta per vncta coqui
Pila fit albanis quæcunq; ornata lagænis
Pingue fuum copo limen obefus amet
Occupat infubres altiffimus ille nepotum
Gurges & vndantes auget & vrget aquas
Millia fex ventri qui fixit Apicius alto
Inde timens: fumpfit dira venena: famem.

Ioannes falandus lectori.

Accipe quifquis amas irritamenta palati:
Precepta: & leges: oxigarumq; nouum:
Condiderat caput: & ftygias penitrauerat vndas
Celius: in lucem nec rediturus erat:
Nunc teritur dextra verfatus Apicius omni
Vrbem habet: & tectum qui perigrinus erat:
Acceptum motte noftro debebis: & ipfi
Immortalis erit gratia: laus & honor:
Per quem non licuit celebri caruiffe nepote:
Per quem dehinc fugiet lingua latina fitum.

Impreffum Mediolani per magiftrum Guilermum
Signerre Rothomagenfem Anno dñi . Mcccclxxxx
viii. die. xx. menfis Ianuarii.

COLOPHON, MILAN EDITION, 1498

From the Lancilotus edition of Apicius, printed by Signerre, Milan, 1498, the first dated edition. The poems by Mota and Salandus are identical with the colophon of the 1503 Venice edition.

Note the date of this colophon and observe how easily it can be read for "the 8th day of January, 1490" which date is attributed to our Apiciana No. 2. This edition, as is noted, is doubtful, although several bibliographers speak about it.

This copy has on the fly leaf the book plate of "Georgius Klotz, M.D. Franco-furti ad Mœnum" and the autograph of John S. Blackie, 1862.

Bernhold, p. XI. Not in Georg-Drexel. Vicaire, 28; he reads Appicius [*sic*] Culinarius. Pennell and Vicaire read Guilerum, Bernhold Guilierum.

Vicaire's description of this edition tallies with that of Bernhold's and his collaborator's account of the preceding edition. There are certain copies of this edition, bearing the following titles, Apicius de re coquinaria and Apicivs in re qvoqvinaria. Cf. Vicaire, 28-29.

NOTES TO NOS. 1, 2, AND 3

Gesamtkatalog der Wiegendrucke, Leipzig, 1926, II, p. 510, places as the first printed edition Apicius in re quoquinaria [*sic*] printed by William de Signerre at Milan, on the 20th day of January, 1498. The second place is given Apicius de re coquinaria printed by Bernardinus de Vitalibus at Venice, no date, circa 1500 (our No. 1). This classification follows that of Brunet in 1840. Neither the Gesamtkatalog nor Brunet make any mention whatsoever of the doubtful 1490 Milan edition (our No. 2).

Vicaire, col. 33, mentioning this edition citing Bernhold, quotes Brunet as doubting the existence of this 1490 edition, but we fail to notice this expression of doubt since our Brunet is altogether silent on the subject, same as the other bibliographers.

Vicaire, col. 28-29, quotes Brunet as saying that the undated Apicius (our No. 1) despite its sub-titles of Suetonius, contains only the Apicius text, a statement confirmed by Pennell.

A search of all the available works of Joh. Alb. Fabricius — Bibliotheca Latina [Classics], Hamburg, 1722, Bibliographia Antiquaria, ib. 1760 and the Bibliotheca Latina mediæ et infimæ [middle ages], ib. 1735, has failed to reveal a trace of the 1490 Apicius, displayed by Bernhold, as described by Fabricius and as seen by Preus in the Nürnberg Municipal Library.

Our facsimile of the 1498 colophon shows how easily its date can be mistaken for "the 8th day of January, 1490," Bernhold's very date! Evidently an error of this kind made victims of Preus, Bernhold and Fabricius (if, indeed, he quoted it) and caused us some ardent searching among dusty tomes. We have therefore come to the conclusion that either this 1490 edition disappeared be-tween the year 1787 and our time or else that it never existed.

NO. 4, A.D. 1503, VENICE

Apitii Celii de re Coquinaria libri decem. || Coquinariæ capita Græca ab Apitio posita hæc sunt. || Epimeles: Artoptus: Cepurica: Pandecter: Osprion || Trophetes: Polyteles: Tetrapus: Thalassa: Halieus || Hanc Plato adulatricem medicinæ appellat || [*in fine*] Impressum uenetiis p Iohannem de Cereto de Tridino alias Tacuinum. M.CCCCC.III. die ter-tio mensis Augusti.

4to, 32 sheets, 30 lines to the page, pages not numbered, signed a-h, by 4.

Apitii Celii de re Coquinaria libri decem.

Coquinariæ capita Græca ab Apitio posita hæc sunt.
Epimeles:Artoptus:Cepurica:Pandedter:Ofprion
Trophetes:Polyteles:Tetrapus:Thalaffa:Halicus.
Hanc Plato adulatricem medicina appellat.

TITLE PAGE, VENICE EDITION, 1503

From the Blasius Lancilotus edition, printed by Johannes de Cereto de Tridino alias Tacuinus, Venice,
1503. This is the second dated edition of Apicius, resembling very closely the undated edition and also the
Milan edition, printed by Signerre 1498, the first to bear a date. Same size as the original. This is a first
timid attempt at giving a book a title page. Most books printed before this date have no title pages.

On the last page of our copy are the two poems mentioned in the 1490 Milan
edition (No. 2) "Antonius mota ad uulgus" (4 distichs) and "Iohannes salandi
Lectori" (5 distichs) The verso of this page is blank. The dedication, on the
verso of title page, is likewise by Blasius Lancilotus. It appears that this edition
is closely related to No. 2.

Vicaire, 30; unknown to Georg-Drexel and Pennell.

In the collection of the author.

NO. 5, A.D. 1541, BASEL

CÆLII APITII || SVMMI ADVLATRICIS MEDI || CINÆ ARTIFICIS DE RE CVLINARIA
LIBRI X. RE || CENS È TENEBRIS ERUTI & À MENDIS UINDICATI, || TYPISQVE SVMMA
DILIGENTIA || EXCUSI. || PRÆTEREA, || P. PLATINÆ CREMO || NENSIS VIRI UNDE-
CVNQVE DO || CTISSIMI, DE TUENDA UALETUDINE, NATURA RERUM, & POPINÆ ||
SCIENTIA LIBRI X. AD IMITATIONEM C. API || TII AD UNGUEM FACTI. || AD HÆC, ||
PAVLI ÆGINETÆ DE || FACVLTATIBVS ALIMENTORVM TRA || CTATVS, ALBANO
TORINO || INTERPRETE. || CUM INDICE COPIOSISSIMO. || BASILEÆ || M.D.XLI.
[in fine] BASILEÆ, MENSE MARTIO, ANNO M D X L I.

4to, old calf, 16 pp., containing title, dedication and index, not numbered
but signed in Greek letters. The body of the work commences with p. 1, finishing with p. 366, the sheets are signed first in small Roman letters a-z and numbers 1-3 and then in capital letters A-Z, likewise numbered 1-3. The titles of the
books or chapters, on verso of the title page, under the heading of "Katalogos et
Epigraphè Decem Voluminum De Re Popinali C. Apitii" are both in Greek and
Roman characters. German names and quotations are in Gothic type (black letter). The book is well printed, in the style of the Froschauer or Oporinus press,
but bears no printer's name or device.

The Apicius treatise is concluded on p. 110, and is followed by "Appendicvla De
Conditvris Variis ex Ioanne Damasceno, Albano Torino Paraphraste," not mentioned on the title. This treatise extends from p. 110 to p. 117, comprising fourteen recipes for "condimenta" and "conditvræ"; these are followed on the same
page by "De Facvltatibvs Alimentorvm Ex Pavlo Ægineta, Albano Torino Interprete" which book is concluded on p. 139; but with hardly any interruption nor

with any very conspicuous title on this page there follows the work of Platina:
"P. [*sic*] Platinæ Cremonensis, viri vndecvnqve doctissimi, De tuenda ualetudine
Natura rerum, & Popinæ scientia, ad amplissimum D.D.B. Rouerellam S. Cle-
mentis presbyterum, Cardinalem, Liber I." The ten books of Platina are concluded on p. 366; the type gracefully tapering down with the words: "P. [*sic*]

CAELII

APITII, SVM

MI ADVLATRICIS

MEDICINAE ARTIFICIS,

De re Culinaria libri
Decem.

B. PLATINAE CREMONEN-
ſis De Tuenda ualetudine, Natura rerum, & Popinæ
ſcientia Libri x.

PAVLI AEGINETAE DE FA-
cultatibus alimentorum Tractatus,
Albano Torino Inter-
prete.

VIRTVTE DVCE,

COMITE FORTVNA.

APVD SEB. GRYPHIVM
LVGVDVNI,
1541.

TITLE PAGE, LYONS, 1541

This edition, printed in Lyons, France, in 1541, by Sebastian Gryphius is said to have been pirated from
the Torinus edition given at Basel in the same year. Early printers stole copiously from one another, frequently reproduced books with hundreds of illustrations with startling speed. Gryphius corrected Torinus'
spelling of "P" [Bartholomæus] Platina, but note the spelling of "Lvg[v]dvni" (Lyons). Inscription by a
contemporary reader over the griffin: "This [book] amuses me! Why make fun of me?"

Platinæ libri decimi et vltimi Finis" and the date, as mentioned. The last page blank.

Strange enough, there is another edition of this work, bearing the same editor's name, printed at Lyons, France, in the same year. This edition, printed by Gryphius, bears the abbreviated title as follows:

NO. 6, A.D. 1541, LYONS

CÆLII || APITII SVM || MI ADVLATRICIS || MEDICINÆ ARTIFICIS, || DE RE CULINARIA LIBRI || DECEM || B. PLATINÆ CREMONEN || SIS DE TUENDA UALETU-DINE, NATURA RERUM & POPINÆ || SCIENTIA LIBRI X, || PAULI ÆGINETÆ DE FA CULTATIBUS ALIMENTORUM TRACTATUS, || ALBANO TORINO INTER || PRETE.

The lower center of the title page is occupied by the Gryphius printer's device, a griffin standing on a box-like pedestal, supported by a winged globe. On the left of the device: "virtute duci," on the right: "comite fortuna"; directly underneath: "Apvd Seb. Gryphivm, Lvgvdvni [sic], 1541. Sm. 8vo. Pages numbered, commencing with verso of title from 2-314. Sheets lettered same as Basel edition; on verso of title "Katalogos" etc. exactly like Basel. Page 3 commences with the same epistola dedicatoria. This dedication and the entire corpus of the book is printed in an awkward Italic type, except the captions which are in 6 pt. and 8 pt. Roman. The book is quite an unpleasant contrast with the fine Antiqua type and the generous margins of the Basel edition. Some woodcut initials but of small interest. The index, contrary to Basel, is in the back. The last page shows another printer's device, differing from that on the title, another griffin.

This edition, though bearing Platina's correct initial, B., has the fictitious title given to his work by Torinus, who probably possessed one of the earliest editions of Platina's De honesta Voluptate, printed without a title page.

Altogether, this Lyons edition looks very much like a hurried job, and we would not be surprised to learn that it was pirated from the Basel edition.

The epistola dedicatoria, in which Torinus expresses fear of pirates and asks his patron's protection, is concluded with the date, Basileæ, v. Idus Martias, Anno M. D. XLI., while the copy described by Vicaire appears to be without this date. Vicaire also says that the sheets of his copy are not numbered. He also reads on the title "Lvgdvni, 1541" which is spelled correctly, but not in accordance with the original. Of these two editions Vicaire says:

"Ces deux éditions portent la même date de 1541, mais celle qui a été publiée à Bâle a paru avant celle donnée à Lyon par Seb. Gryphe. Cette dernière, en effet, contient la dédicace datée." The title page of our copy is inscribed by three different old hands, one the characteristic remark: "Mulcens me, gannis?" This copy is bound in the original vellum. Vicaire, 31, G.-Drexel, No. 12.

The work of Torinus has been subjected to a searching analysis, as will be shown throughout the book. An appreciation of Platina will be found in Platina, mæstro nell'arte culinaria Un'interessante studio di Joseph D. Vehling, by Agostino Cavalcabò, Cremona, 1935.

90

IN HOC OPERE CONTENTA

APICII CAELII

DE OPSONIIS ET CONDIMENTIS,
SIVE ARTE COQVINA-
RIA, LIBRI X.

ITEM,

Gabrielis Humelbergij Medici, Physici
Isnensis in Apicij Cælij libros X.
Annotationes.

TIGVRI IN OFFICINA
Froschouiana. Anno,
M. D. XLII.

Votum emptus libros argenteis drach̄is

Johannes Baptista Bassus .

TITLE PAGE, HUMELBERGIUS EDITION, ZÜRICH, 1542

The Gabriel Humelbergius edition is printed by Froschauer, one of the great printers of the Renaissance.
Showing the autograph of Johannes Baptista Bassus. The best of the early Apicius editions.

NO. 7, A.D. 1542, ZÜRICH

In Hoc Opere Contenta. || Apicii Cælii || De Opsoniis et Condimentis, || Sive Arte Coqvina || ria, Libri X. || Item, || Gabrielis Humelbergij Medici, Physici || Isnensis in Apicij Cælij libros X. || Annotationes. || Tigvri in Officina || Froschouiana. Anno, || M.D. XLII.

4to, 123 sheets, pagination commences with title, not numbered. On verso of title a poem by Ioachim Egell, extolling Humelberg. Sheet 2 the dedication, dated "Isnæ Algoiæ, mense Maio, Anno à Christo nato, M.D.XLII." Sheet 3-4 have the preface; on verso of 4 the names of the books of Apicius. On recto of sheet 5 the chapters of Book I; on verso commences the corpus of the work with Apicii Cælii Epimeles Liber I.

The Apicius text is printed in bold Roman, the copious notes by the editor in elegant Italics follow each book. Very instructive notes, fine margins, splendid printing. Altogether preferable to Torinus. Our copy is bound in the original vellum. Inscribed in old hand by Johannes Baptista Bassus on the title.

G.-Drexel, No. 14; Vicaire, 31; not in Pennell.

NO. 8, A.D. 1705, LONDON

Apicii Cælii || De || Opsoniis || Et || Condimentis, || Sive || Arte Coquina- ria, || Libri Decem. || Cum Annotationibus Martini Lister, || è Medicis domesticis serenissimæ Ma || jestatis Reginæ Annæ || Et || Notis selecti- oribus, variisque lectionibus integris, || Humelbergii, Caspari Barthii, || & Variorum. || Londini: || Typis Gulielmi Bowyer. MDCCV.

The first edition by Lister, limited to 120 copies.

8vo. The title in red and black. Original full calf, gilt. Pp. XIV + 231. Index 11 leaves, unnumbered. This scarce book is described by Vicaire, 32, but un- known to the collectors Drexel and Pennell. Our copy has on the inside front cover the label of the Dunnichen library. Above the same in an old hand: "Liber rarissimus Hujus editionis 120 tantum exemplaria impressa sunt." On the fly leaf, in a different old hand a six line note in Latin, quoting the medieval scholar, G. J. Vossius, Aristarch. 1.13. p. 1336, on the authorship of Cœlius. Directly below in still another old hand, the following note, a rather pleasing passage, full of sentiment and affection for our subject, that deserves to be quoted in full: "Alas! that time is wanting to visit the island of Magellone [Megalona-Torinus] where formerly flourished a large town, of which there are now no other re- mains but the cathedral church, where, according to tradition, the beautiful Magellone lies buried by her husband Peter of Province.* Matthison's letters, etc. pag. 269.

"* Jt was in the island of Magellone that Apicius's ten books on cookery were re- discovered." Ibid. — Vide Fabric. Biblioth: Lat: edit. ab Ernesti. vol. 2; p. 365."

On the verso of the title page there is the printed note in Latin to the effect that 120 copies of this edition have been printed at the expense of eigh-

APICII COELII

DE

OPSONIIS

ET   *D- /-*

CONDIMENTIS,

Sive

Arte Coquinaria,

LIBRI DECEM.

Cum Annotationibus MARTINI LISTER,
è Medicis domesticis sereniſſimæ Ma-
jeſtatis Reginæ Annæ.

ET

Notis felectioribus, variiſque lectionibus integris,
HUMELBERGII, CASPARI BARTHII,
& VARIORUM.

LONDINI:

Typis *Gulielmi Bowyer*. MDCCV.

TITLE PAGE, LISTER EDITION, LONDON, 1705

The first Apicius edition by Martin Lister, Court Physician to Queen Anne. Printed in London in 1705
by the famous printer, William Bowyer. This is one of the rarest of the Apician books, the edition being
limited to 120 copies. It has been said that the second edition (Amsterdam, 1709) was limited to 100
copies, but there is no evidence to that effect.

teen gentlemen whose names are given, among them "Isaac Newton, Esq." and
other famous men.

Lister's preface to the reader occupies pp. I-XIV; the same appears in the
1709 (2nd) edition. The ten books of Apicius occupy pp. 1-231; the index
comprises 11 unnumbered leaves; on the verso of the 11th leaf, the errata. One
leaf for the "Catalogus" (not mentioned by Vicaire) a bibliography of the
editor's extensive writings, and works used in this edition principally upon
nature and medical subjects. This list was ridiculed by Dr. King. Cf. Introduction by Frederick Starr to this present work. The last leaf blank. Our copy is in
the original binding, and perfect in every respect.

Hujus Libri centum & viginti *tantùm*
Exemplaria *impreſſa ſunt impenſis in-
fraſcriptorum.*

THo. *Lord A.B. of* Canterbury.
    Ch. *Earl of* Sunderland.
J. *Earl of* Roxborough, *Principal Secretary of State
for* Scotland.
J. *Lord* Sommers.
Charles *Lord* Hallifax.
J. *Lord Bishop of* Norwich
Ge. *Lord Bishop of* Bath *and* Wells.
Robert Harley *Speaker*, *and Principal Secretary of
State.*
Sir Richard Buckley, *Baronet.*
Sir Christopher Wren.
Tho. Foley, *Esq;*
Isaac Newton, *Esq; President of the Royal Society.*
William Gore, *Esq;*
Francis Ashton, *Esq;*
Mr. John Flamstead, *Ast.* Reg.
John Hutton,   ⎫
Tancred Robinson, ⎬ *M. D. D.*
Hans Sloane.   ⎭

VERSO OF TITLE PAGE

of the first Lister edition, London, 1705, giving evidence of the edition being limited to 120 copies. This
edition was done at the expense of the men named in this list. Note particularly "Isaac Newton, Esq.," Sir
Christopher Wren and a few more names famous to this day.

NO. 9, A.D. 1709, AMSTERDAM

APICII CŒLII || DE || OPSONIIS || ET || CONDIMENTIS, || SIVE || ARTE COQUINA-
RIA, || LIBRI DECEM. || CUM ANNOTATIONIBUS || MARTINI LISTER, || è MEDICIS
DOMESTICIS SERENISSIMÆ MAJE || STATIS REGINÆ ANNÆ, || ET || NOTIS SELEC-
TIORIBUS, VARIISQUE LECTIONIBUS INTEGRIS, || HUMELBERGII, BARTHII, REINESII,
|| A. VAN DER LINDEN, & ALIORUM, || UT & VARIARUM LECTIONUM LIBELLO.
|| EDITIO SECUNDA. || LONGE AUCTIOR ATQUE EMENDATIOR. || AMSTELODAMI, ||
APUD JANSSONIO-WÆSBERGIOS. || M D C C I X.

Small 8vo. Title in red and black. Dedication addressed to Martinus Lister
by Theod. Jans. [sonius] of Almeloveen; the preface, M. Lister to the Reader,
and the "Judicia et Testimonia de Apicio" by Olaus Borrichius and Albertus
Fabricius occupy seventeen leaves. The ten books of Apicius, with the many
notes by Lister, Humelberg and others, commence with page 1 and finish on
page 277. Variæ Lectiones, 9 leaves; Index, 12 leaves, none numbered.

Vicaire, 32; Pennell, p. 112; G.-Drexel, No. 164. "Edition assez estimée. On
peut l'annexer à la collection des Variorum" d'après M. Græsse, Trésor des Livres

rares et précieux." — Vicaire. Our copy is in the original full calf gold stamped binding, with the ex libris of James Maidment.

The notes by Lister are more copious in this edition, which is very esteemed and is said to have been printed in 100 copies only, but there is no proof of this.

Typographically an excellent piece of work that would have done justice the Elzevirs.

NO. 10, A.D. 1787, MARKTBREIT

CÆLII APICII || DE || OPSONIIS || ET || CONDIMENTIS || SIVE || ARTE COQUINARIA || LIBRI X || CUM || LECTIONIBUS VARIIS || ATQUE INDICE || EDITIT || JOANNES MICHÆL BERNHOLD || COMES PALATINATUS CÆSAREUS, PHIL. ET || MED. D. SERENISSIMO MARCHIONI BRAN- || DENBURGICO-ONOLDINO-CULBACENSI || A CONSILIIS AULÆ, PHYSICUS SUPREMA || RUM PRÆFECTURARUM VFFENHEMENSIS || ET CREGLINGENSIS, ACADEMIÆ IMPERIALI || NATURÆ SCRUTATORUM ADSCRIPTUS.

The first edition. The title page has a conspicuously blank space for the date etc. of the publication, but this is found at the foot of p. 81, where one reads: Marcobraitæ, Excudebat Joan. Val. Knenlein, M. D. CC. LXXXVII. 8vo. Fine large copy, bound in yellow calf, gilt, with dentelles on edges and inside, by J. Clarke, the binding stamped on back, 1800. Dedication and preface, pp. XIV. The ten books of Apicius commence with p. 1 and finish on p. 81, with the date, as above. Index capitulum, pp. 82-85; Lectiones Variantes collectæ ex Editione Blasii Lanciloti, pp. 86-108, at the end of same: "Sedulo hæ Variantes ex Blasii Lanciloti editione sunt excerpta ab Andrea Gözio Scholæ Sebaldinæ Norimbergiensis Collega." Variantes Lectiones, Lib. I. Epimeles, pp. 109-112, with a note at the head of the same that these variants occur in the Vatican MS. These four pages are repeated in the next chapter, pp. 113-130, "Variæ Lectiones Manuscripti Vaticani," headed by the same note, the text of which is herewith given in full. Bernhold states that these Variæ Lectiones have been taken from the second Lister edition (No. 8) where they are found following p. 277. The first Lister edition does not contain these Variæ, nor does Lister have the Variantes ex Blasii Lanciloti. The following note to the Vatican variants appears in the second Lister edition also:

"Apicii collatio cum antiquissimo codice, literis fere iisdem, quibus Pandectæ Florentinæ, scripto; qui seruatur hodie Romæ in Bibliotheca Vaticana, inter libros MSS., qui fuere Ducis Vrbinatium, sed, nostris temporibus extincta illa familia Ducali, quæ Ducatum istum a Romanis Pontificibus in feudum tenuerat, Vrbino Romam translati, et separato loco in bibliotheca Vaticana respositi sunt. Contulit Henricus Volkmarus [Lister: Volkmas] Scherzerus, Lipsiensis. E bibliotheca Marquardii Gudii ad I. A. Fabricium, et, ex huius dono, ad Theodorum Ianssonium ab Almeloueen transmigrauere; qui illas suæ, Amstelodami 1709 8vo in lucem prolatæ; Apicii editioni inseri curauit."

On pp. 131-154 are found the Lectiones Variantes Humelbergianæ, and on pp. 155-156 the Lectiones differentes etc. On pp. 157-228 the Index Vocabulorum ac Rerum notabiliorum etc.; on pp. 229-30 the Notandum adhuc. One blank leaf.

Described by Vicaire, 33, who has only seen the 1791 edition; G.-Drexel, No. 165; Brunet I. 343. Neither Vicaire nor Georg-Drexel have the date and place of publication, which in our copy is hidden on p. 81.

Georg reads Apicii Cœlii instead of the above. On the fly leaf the autograph of G. L. Fournier, Bayreuth, 1791.

Bernhold has based his edition upon Lister and on the edition by Blasius Lancilotus, Milan, 1490, (our No. 2, which see.) Aside from the preface in which Bernhold names this and other Apicius editions, unknown to the bibliographers, the editor has not added any of his own observations. Being under the influence of Lister, he joins the English editor in the condemnation of Torinus. His work is valuable because of the above mentioned variants.

NO. 11, A.D. 1791, LÜBECK

[Same as above] The Second Edition. Vicaire, 33. not in G.-Drexel nor Pennell.

NO. 12, A.D. 1800, ANSBACH

Apitius Cœlius de re culinaria. Ed. Bernhold. 8vo. Ansbachii, 1800.

Ex Georg, No. 1076; not in Vicaire nor in Pennell. Though listed by Georg, it is not in the Drexel collection.

NO. 13, A.D. 1852, VENICE

Apitius Cælius Delle vivande e condimenti ovvero dell' arte de la cucina. Volgarizzamento con annotationi di G. Baseggio.

8vo, pp. 238. With the original Latin text. Venezia, 1852, Antonelli.

Ex Georg-Drexel, No. 1077.

NO. 14, A.D. 1867, HEIDELBERG

Apici Cæli || De || Re Coquinaria Libri Decem. || Novem codicum ope adiutus, auxit, resti || tuit, emendavit, et correxit, variarum || lectionum parte potissima ornavit, stric || tim et interim explanavit || Chr. Theophil. Schuch. || Heidelbergæ, 1867.

8vo. pp. 202.

Ex Vicaire, 33; Not in G.-Drexel, not in Pennell.

NO. 15, A.D. 1874

[The same] Editio Secunda Heidelbergæ, 1874, [Winter].

Although G.-Drexel, No. 1075, reads Apitius Cœlius, our copy agrees with the reading of Vicaire, col. 889, appendix. Not in Pennell. Brandt (Untersuchungen [No. 29] p. 6) calls Schuch *Wunderlicher Querkopf*. He is correct. The Schuch editions are eccentric, worthless.

NO. 16, A.D. 1909, LEIPZIG

DAS APICIUS-KOCHBUCH AUS DER ALTRÖMISCHEN KAISERZEIT. Ins Deutsche übersetzt und bearbeitet von Richard Gollmer. Mit Nachbildungen alter Kunstblätter, Kopfleisten und Schlusstücke. Breslau und Leipzig bei Alfred Langewort, 1909. 8vo. pp. 154.

NO. 17, A.D. 1911, LEIPZIG

APICIUS CÆLIUS: ALTRÖMISCHE KOCHKUNST IN ZEHN BÜCHERN. Bearbeitet und ins Deutsche übersetzt von Eduard Danneil, Herzoglich Altenburgischer Hoftraiteur. Leipzig: 1911: Herausgabe und Verlag: Kurt Däweritz, Herzoglich Altenburgischer Hoftraiteur Obermeister der Innung der Köche zu Leipzig und Umgebung. 8vo, pp. XV + 127.

NO. 18, A.D. 1922, LEIPZIG

APICII || LIBRORVM X QVI DICVNTVR || DE RE COQVINARIA || QVÆ EXTANT || EDIDERVNT || C. GIARRATANO ET FR. VOLLMER || LIPSIÆ IN ÆDIBVS B. G. TEVBNERI MCMXXII.

NO. 19, A.D. 1933, PARIS

LES DIX LIVRES DE CUISINE D'APICIUS traduits du latin pour la Première fois et commentés par Bertrand Guégan. Paris René Bonnel Éditeur rue Blanche, No. 8.

No date (*in fine* October 16th, 1933). Three blank leaves, false title; on verso, facing the title page (!) "*du même auteur*" — a full-page advertisement of the author's many-sided publications, past and future. Title page, verso blank. On p. ix *Introduction*, a lengthy discourse on dining in ancient times, including a mention of Apician manuscripts and editions. This commences on p. Li with *Les Manuscrits d'Apicius*. The *Introduction* finishes on p. Lxxviii. On p. 1 *Les Dix Livres d'Apicius*, on p. 2 a facsimile in black of the *incipit* of the Vatican manuscript, Apiciana II. On p. 3 commences the translation into French of the Apician text, finishing on p. 308. *Table Analytique* (index) pp. 309-322. Follow three unnumbered sheets, on the first page of which is the *Justification du tirage*, with the date of printing and the printer's name, Durand of Chartres. The copies printed are numbered from 1 to 679. The copy before us is No. 2; copies 1 to 4 are printed on Montval vellum, 5 to 29 on Dutch Pannekoek vellum, the rest, 30 to 679 on Vidalon vellum paper.

Unfortunately, the present work did not reach us until after ours had gone to press. The text of this edition, the first to appear in the French language, could not be considered in our work, for this reason.

However, a few casual remarks about it may be in order here.

A hasty perusal reveals the disconcerting fact that the editor has been influenced by and has followed the example of Schuch by the adoption of his system of numbering the recipes. We do not approve of his inclusion of the excerpts of Vinidarius in the Apician text.

The observations presented in this edition are rich and varied. The material, comprising the *Introduction* and also the explanatory notes to the recipes are interesting, copious and well-authenticated. The editor reveals himself to be a better scholar, well-read in the classics, than a practical cook, well-versed in kitchen practice. Frequently, for instance, he confounds *liquamen* with *garum*, the age-old shortcoming of the Apician scholars.

The advertisement facing the title page of this work is misplaced, disturbing.

Nevertheless, we welcome this French version which merits a thorough study; this we hope to publish at some future date. Any serious and new information on Apicius is welcome and much needed to clear up the mysteries. The advent of a few additional cooks on the scene doesn't matter. Let them give lie to the old proverb that too many cooks spoil the broth. Apicius has been so thoroughly scrambled during the sixteen-hundred years preceding his first printing which started the scholars after him. So far, with the exception of a few minor instances, they have done remarkably well. The complete unscrambling can be done only by many new cooks, willing to devote much pain and unremunerative, careful, patient work in discovering new evidence and adding it to what there is already, to arrive at the truth of the matter.

NO. 20, A.D. 1926-1936, CHICAGO

Apicius, J. D. Vehling, the present edition.

DESCRIPTION OF COMMENTARIES

NO. 21, A.D. 1531, FRANKFORT

DE RE COQUINARIA. VON SPEISEN. Natürlichen und Kreuterwein, aller Verstandt. Vber den Zusatz viler bewerter Künst, insonders fleissig gebessert und corrigirt aus Apitio, Platina, Varrone, Bapt.Fiera cet.'; Francofurti, apud Egenolfum, 1531, 4to.

Ex Bernhold, p. XIV, unknown to the bibliographers. The above is related to the following two works. Apparently, all three have little bearing on Apicius.

NO. 22, A.D. 1534, FRANKFORT

POLYONYMI SYNGRAPHEI SCHOLA APICIANA. Ibid. 1534, 4to.

Ex Bernhold, p. XIV., unknown to the bibliographers. Copy in the Baron Pichon collection, No. 569.

NO. 23, A.D. 1535, ANTWERP

SCHOLA || APITIANA, EX OP || TIMIS QVIBVS || DAM AUTHORIBUS DILIGEN || TER AC NOUITER CONSTRU || CTA, AUTHORE POLYO || NIMO SYNGRA || PHEO. || A C GESSERE DIA || LOGI ALIQUOT D. ERASMI RO || TERODAMI, & ALIA QUÆDAM || LECTU IUCUNDISSIMA. || VÆNEUNT ANTUERPIÆ IN ÆDI || BUS IOANNIS STEELSIJ. || I. G. 1535. Small 8vo. Title in beautiful woodcut border. [*in fine*] TYPIS IOAN. GRAPHEI. M.D.XXXV.

Pagination A-I 4, on verso of I 4, device of Io. Steels, Concordia, with doves on square and astronomical globe. On verso of title, In Scholam Apitianam Præfatio. Sheet A3 Mensam Amititiæ Sacram esse, etc. On sheet A6 The dialogue by Erasmus of Rotterdam between Apitivs and Spvdvs to verso of sheet A8; follows: Conviviarvm qvis nvmervs esse debeat [etc.] ex Aulo Gellio; Præcepta Cœnarvm by Horace; De Ciborvm Ratione by Michæle Savonarola [Grandfather of the great Girolamo S.]; on sheet C5 De Cibis Secvndæ Mensæ, by Paulus Aegineta; and a number of other quotations from ancient and medieval authors, partly very amusing. The Apician matter seems to be entirely fictitious.

In the collection of the author. Vicaire, 701, who also describes in detail the 1534 edition printed by Egenolph but which is not the same as the above in text.

NO. 24, A.D. 1831, HEIDELBERG

FLORA APICIANA. Dierbach, J. H. Ein Beitrag zur näheren Kenntniss der Nahrungsmittel der alten Römer. Heidelberg, 1831, Groos. 8vo.

NO. 25, A.D. 1868, LONDON

H. C. COOTE: THE CUISINE BOURGEOISE OF ANCIENT ROME. Archæologia, vol. XLI.

Ex Bibliotheca A. Shircliffe.

NO. 26, A.D. 1912, NAPLES

CESARE GIARRATANO: I CODICI DEI LIBRI DE RE COQUINARIA DI CELIO. Naples, 1912, Detken & Rocholl.

NO. 27, A.D. 1920

FRIEDRICH VOLLMER: STUDIEN ZU DEM RÖMISCHEN KOCHBUCHE VON APICIUS. Vorgetragen am 7. Februar 1920. Sitzungsberichte der Bayerischen Akademie der Wissenschaften Philosophisch-philologische und historische Klasse Jahrgang, 1920, 6. Abhandlung. München, 1920. Verlag der Bayerischen Akademie der Wissenschaften in Kommission des G. Franzschen Verlags (J. Roth).

NO. 28, A.D. 1921

G. STERNAJOLO: CODICES VRBINATI LATINI.

NO. 29, A.D. 1927

UNTERSUCHUNGEN ZUM RÖMISCHEN KOCHBUCHE Versuch einer Lösung der Apicius-Frage von Edward Brandt, Leipzig, Dietrich'sche Verlagsbuchhandlung, 1927. Philologus, Supplementband XIX, Heft III. 164 pp.

Dr. Edward Brandt, the philologist of Munich, is the latest of the Apician commentators. His researches are quite exhaustive. While not conclusive (as some of the problems will perhaps never be solved) he has shed much new light on the vexatious questions of the origin and the authors of our old Roman cookery book.

APICIANÆ FINIS

CANTHARUS, WINE CUP WITH HANDLES

Elaborate decoration of Bacchic motifs: wine leaves and masks of satyrs. Hildesheim Treasure.

INDEX and VOCABULARY

INDEX and VOCABULARY

A

ABALANA, Abellana, hazelnut, see Avellana

Abbreviations, explanation of, p. xv

ABDOMEN, sow's udder, belly, fat of lower part of belly, figur. Gluttony, intemperance

ABROTANUM, — ONUM, — ONUS the herb lad's love; or, according to most Southerwood. ABROTONUM is also a town in Africa

Absinth. ABSINTHIUM, the herb wormwood. The Romans used A. from several parts of the world. ℞ 3, also APSINTHIUM

ABSINTHIATUS, — UM, flavored with wormwood, ℞ 3

ABSINTHITES, wine tempered or mixed with wormwood; modern absinth or Vermouth, cf. ℞ 3

ABSINTHIUM ROMANUM, ℞ 3

ABUA, a small fish; see APUA, ℞ 138, 139, 147

ACER, ACEO, ACIDUM, to be or to make sour, tart

ACETABULUM, a "vinegar" cruet: a small measure, equivalent to 15 Attich drachms; see Measures

ACETUM, vinegar
— MULSUM, mead

ACICULA, ACUS, the needle fish, or horn-back, or horn-beak; a long fish with a snout sharp like a needle; the gar-fish, or sea-needle

ACIDUM, sour; same as ACER

ACINATICIUS, a costly raisin wine

ACINOSUS, full of kernels or stones

ACINUS, — UM, a grain, or grape raisin berry or kernel

ACIPENSER, a large fish, sturgeon, ℞ 145; also see STYRIO

ACOR, — UM, sourness, tartness; the herb sweet-cane, gardenflag, galangale

ACRIMONIA, acidity, tartness, sourness; harshness of taste

ACUS, same as ACICULA

Adjustable Table, illustration, p. 138

ADULTERAM, "tempting" dish, ℞ 192

Adulterations of food in antiquity, pp. 33, 39, seq. 147; ℞ 6, 7, 9, 15, 17, 18. Also see Cookery, deceptive

Advertising cooked ham, ℞ 287

Advertising ancient hotels, p. 6

Aegineta, Paulus, writer on medicine and cookery, see Apiciana, No. 5-6

AENEUM, a "metal" cooking utensil, a CACCA-BUS, which see AENEUM VAS, a mixing bowl; AENEA PATELLA, a pewter, bronze or silver service platter. Aeno Coctus, braised, sometimes confused with oenococtum, stewed in wine

AËROPTES, fowl, birds; the correct title of Book VI, see p. 141

Aethiopian Cumin ℞ 35

"AFFE" (Ger.) Monkey; ℞ 55; also see Caramel Coloring

AGITARE (OVA), to stir, to beat (eggs)

AGNUS, IN AGNO, lamb; AGNINUS, pertaining to L. ℞ 291 seq., 355, 364, 495
— COPADIA AGNINA, ℞ 355 seq.
— AGNI COCTURA, ℞ 358
— ASSUS, ℞ 359
— AGNUM SIMPLICEM, ℞ 495
— TARPEIANUS, ℞ 363

AGONIA, cattle sacrificed at the festivals: only little of the victims was wasted at religious ceremonies. The priests, after predicting the future from the intestines, burned them but sold the carcass to the innkeeper and cooks of the POPINA, hence the name. These eating places of a low order did a thriving business with cheaply bought meats which, however, usually were of the best quality. In Pompeii such steaks were exhibited in windows behind magnifying glasses to attract the rural customer

Albino, writer, p. 10

ALBUM, ALBUMEN, white; — OVORUM, the "whites" of egg; — PIPER, white pepper, etc.

ALEX, (ALEC, HALEC), salt water, pickle, brine, fish brine. Finally, the fish itself when cured in A. cf. MURIA

Alexandria, the city founded by Alexander the Great, important Mediterranean harbor. A. was a rival of Rome and Athens in Antiquity, famous for its luxury

Alexandrine dishes ℞ 75, 348, seq.

ALICA, spelt. ℞ 200

ALICATUM, any food treated with ALEX, which see

ALLIATUM, a garlic sauce, consisting of a purée of pounded garlic whipped up with oil into a paste of a consistency of mayonnaise, a preparation still popular in the Provence today; finally, anything flavored with garlic or leeks.

ALLIUM, garlic; also leek. Fr. AILLE

Almonds, AMYGDALA, peeling and bleaching of A. ℞ 57

AMACARUS, sweet-marjoram, fewerfew

AMBIGA, a small vessel in the shape of a pyramid

AMBOLATUS, unidentified term; p. 172; ℞ 57, 59

Amerbach Manuscript, Apiciana XIV

AMMI, (AMMIUM, AMI, AMIUM), cumin

AMURCA (AMUREA), the lees of oil

AMYGDALA (-UM) Almonds, ℞ 57; OLEUM AMYGDALIUM, almond oil

AMYLARE (AMULARE), to thicken with flour. AMYLATUM (AMULATUM) that which is thickened with flour. Wheat or rice flour and fats or oil usually were used for this purpose, corresponding to our present roux. However, the term was also extended to the use of eggs for the purpose of thickening fluids, thus becoming equivalent to the present liaison, used for soups and sauces. Hence AMYLUM and AMULUM, which is also a sort of frumenty

Anacharsis, the Scythian, writer. He described a banquet at Athens during the Periclean age. pp. 3, 7

ANAS, a duck or drake; ℞ 212-17. ANATEM, ℞ 212; ANATEM EX RAPIS, ℞ 214

Anchovy, a small fish; ℞ 147; cf. APUA — forcemeat, ℞ 138; — sauce and GARUM (which see) ℞ 37. — omelette ℞ 147

ANET(H)ATUM, flavored with dill; ANET(H)-UM, dill, also anise

ANGUILLA, eel, ℞ 466-7, 484. cf. CONGRIO

ANGULARUS, a "square" dish or pan

ANISUM, anise, pimpinella

ANSER, goose, gander; IN ANSERE, ℞ 234; — JUS CANDIDUM ℞ 228

ANTIPASTO, "Before the Meal," modern Italian appetizer; the prepared article usually comes in cans or glasses, consisting of tunny, artichokes, olives, etc., preserved in oil

APER, see APRUS

APEXABO, a blood sausage; cf. LONGANO

Aphricocks, ℞ 295

APHROS, ℞ 295

APHYA, see APUA

Apician Cheesecakes, p. 9
— cookery, influence, p. 16, 23
— Archetypus, p. 19
— manuscripts, p. 19, p. 253, seq.
— Terminology, p. 22
— dishes, compared with modern dishes, p. 23
— sauces, p. 24
— Style of writing, p. 26
— research, p. 34 seq.

Apiciana, Diagram of, p. 252

Apicius, pp. 7, 9
— The man, p. 9
— Athenaeus on, p. 9
— and Platina, p. 9
— Expedition to find crawfish, p. 9
— ships oysters, p. 10

— school, p. 10
— death, pp. 10, 11
— reflecting Roman conditions, pp. 14, 15
— authenticity of, pp. 18, 19
— writer, p. 26, ℞ 176, 436
— confirmed by modern science, p. 33
— editors as cooks, p. 34 seq.

Apion, writer, quoted by Athenaeus, p. 9

APIUM, celery, smallage, parsley. ℞ 104

APOTHERMA (-UM, APODERMUM) hot porridge, gruel, pudding. ℞ 57; cf. TISANA

APPARATUS, preparation; — MENSAE, getting dinner ready

Appetizers. ℞ 174 and others. According to Horace, eggs were the first dishes served. The "moveable appetizer" of Apicius is very elaborate, p. 210

Appert, François, ℞ 24, father of the modern canning methods

Apples, ℞ 22, 171

APRUS, APRUGNUS, wild boar. ℞ 329-38. APRINA, PERNA, ℞ 338, also APER

APUA (ABUA, APHYA), a small kind of fish, anchovy, sprat, whiting, white bait, or minnow. ℞ 138-9, 146. cf. Pliny. Apua is also a town in Liguria; its inhabitants APUANI

AQUA, water; — CALIDA, hot w.; — CISTERNINA, well w.; — MARINA, sea w.; — NITRATA, soda w. for the cooking of vegetables; RECENS; fresh, i.e., not stale w.; — PLUVIALE, rain w.

AQUALICUS lower part of belly, paunch, ventricle, stomach, maw

Archetypus Fuldensis, manuscript, see Apiciana Diagram

ARCHIMAGIRUS, principal cook, chef, cf. Cooks' names

ARIDA (-US, -UM) dry, — MENTHA, dry mint

ARTEMISIA, the herb mugwort, motherwort, tarragon

ARTOCREAS, meat pie

ARTOPTES, Torinus' title of Book II; better: SARCOPTES, minces, minced meats

ARTYMA, spice; cf. CONDIMENTUM

Asa foetida, use of — ℞ 15, p. 23

ASARUM, the Herb foalbit, foalfoot, coltsfoot, wild spikenard

ASCALONICA CEPA, "scallion," young onion

Asparagus, ASPARAGUS, p. 188, ℞ 72, — and figpecker, ℞ 132; — custard pie, ℞ 133

ASSATURA, a roast, also the process of roasting. ℞ 266-270

ASSUS, roast

ASTACUS, a crab or lobster

Athenaeus, writer, pp. 3, seq.
— on Apicius, p. 10

Athene, Dish illustration, p. 158

ATRIPLEX, the herb orage, or orach

ATRIUM, living room in a Roman residence, formerly used for kitchen purposes, hence the name, "black room," because of the smoky walls. Like all simple things then and now, the Atrium often developed into a magnificently decorated court, with fountains and marble statues, and became a sort of parlor to receive the guests of the house

ATTAGENA (ATAGENA), heath cock, a game bird. ℞ 218, seq.

AURATA, a fish, "golden" dory, red snapper. ℞ 157, 461, 462

AVELLANA, hazelnut, filbert, Fr. AVELLINE; — NUX, — NUCLEUS, kernel of f. ℞ 297 and in the list of the Excerpta

AVENA, a species of bearded grass, haver-grass, oats, wild oats

AVIBUS, IN- ℞ 220, 21, 24, 27

AVICULARIUS, bird keeper, poulterer

AVIS, bird, fowl; AVES ESCULENTAE, edible birds. — HIRCOSAE, ill-smelling birds, ℞ 229-30, — NE LIQUESCANT, ℞ 233

B

BACCA, berry, seed. — MYRTHEA, myrtle berry; — RUTAE, rue berry; — LAUREA, laurel berry, etc.

Bacon, ℞ 285-90; see also SALSUM

BAIAE, a town, watering place of the ancients, for which many dishes are named. ℞ 205. BAIANUM pertaining to BAIAE; hence EMPHRACTUM —, FABAE, etc. ℞ 202, 205, 432, Baian Seafood Stew, ℞ 431

Bakery in Pompeii, illustration, p. 2

Bantam Chicken, ℞ 237

Baracuda, a fish, ℞ 158

Barley Broth, ℞ 172, 200, 247

BARRICA, ℞ 173

Barthélemy, J. J., writer, translator of Anacharsis, p. 8

Baseggio, G., editor, Apiciana, No. 13, p. 270

BASILICUM, basil

Bavarian Cabbage, ℞ 87

Beans, ℞ 96, 189, 194-8, 247; Green — ℞ 247; — sauté, ℞ 203; — in mustard, ℞ 204 — Baian style, ℞ 202 — "Egyptian," see COLOSASIUM

Beauvilliers, A., French cook; cf. Styrio

Beef, p. 30; shortage of — diet, p. 30 — "Beef Eaters," p. 30 — dishes, ℞ 351, seq.

Beets, ℞ 70, 97, 98, 183 — named for Varro, ℞ 70, 97, 98

Bernardinus, of Venice, printer, p. 258

Bernhold, J. M., editor, Apiciana, Nos. 2-3, 12-14, pp. 258, seq.

BETA, beet, which see BETACEOS VARRONES, ℞ 70

Bibliographers of Apicius, see Apiciana

Birds, Book VI, ℞ 210-227; treatment of strong-smelling — ℞ 229, 230

BLITUM, a pot herb, the arrack or orrage, also spinach, according to some interpreters

Boar, wild, ℞ 329-38, p. 314

Boiled Dinners, ℞ 125

BOLETAR, a dish for mushrooms, ℞ 183

BOLETUS, mushroom, ℞ 309-14

Bordelaise, ℞ 351

Borrichius, Olaus, p. 268

BOTELLUS, (dim. of BOTULUS) small sausage, ℞ 60. BOTULUS, a sausage, meat pudding, black pudding, ℞ 60, 61, 172

BOUILLABAISSE, a fish stew of Marseilles, ℞ 431, 481

Bouquet garni, ℞ 138

BOVES, Beef cattle; cf. BUBULA

Bowls for mixing wine, etc., see Crater — for fruit or dessert, illustration, p. 61

Brain Sausage, ℞ 45 — Custard, ℞ 128 — and bacon, ℞ 148 — and chicken with peas, ℞ 198

Brandt, Edward, Editor, Commentator, ℞ 29, 170, p. 273

BRASSICA, cabbage, kale; — CAMPESTRA, turnip; — OLERACEA, cabbage and kale; — MARINA, sea kale (?)

Bread, Alexandrine, ℞ 126; Picentian —, ℞ 125. The methods of grinding flour and baking is illustrated with our illustrations of the Casa di forno of Pompeii and the Slaves grinding flour, which see, pp. 142, 149. Apicius has no directions for baking, an art that was as highly developed in his days as was cookery

BREVIS PIMENTORUM, facsimile, p. 234

Brissonius, writer, quoting Lambecius, ℞ 376

Broiler and Stove, illustration, p. 182

Broth, see LIQUAMEN; Barley —, ℞ 172, 200, 201 — How to redeem a spoiled, ℞ 9

BUBULA, Beef, flesh of oxen, p. 30, 351, 352

BUBULUS CASEUS, cow's cheese

BUCCA, BUCCEA, mouth, cheek; also a bite, a morsel, a mouth-full; Fr. BOUCHÉE; BUCELLA (dim.) a small bite, a dainty bit, delicate morsel; hence probably, Ger. "Buss'l" a little kiss and "busseln," to spoon, to kiss, in the Southern German dialect

BUCCELLATUM, a biscuit, Zwieback, soldier's bread, hard tack

BULBUS, a bulbous root, a bulb, onion, ℞ 285, 304-8

BULBI FRICTI, ℞ 308

BULLIRE, to boil; Fr. BOUILLIR

BUTYRUM, butter. Was little used in ancient households, except for cosmetics. Cows were expensive, climate and sanitary conditions interfered with its use in the Southern kitchen. The Latin butyrum is said to derive from the German Butter.

C

CABBAGE, ℞ 87-92, 103; p.188. Bavarian, ℞ 87. Ingenious way of cooking, ℞ 88. Chartreuse, ℞ 469

CACABUS, CACCABUS, a cook pot, marmite; see OLLA. Illustrations, pp. 183, 209, 223, 235. Hence: CACCABINA, dish cooked in a caccabus. See also SALACACCABIA, ℞ 468. I Exc. 470

CAELIUS, see Coelius

CAEPA, CEPA, onion; — ARIDA, fresh onion; — ROTUNDA, round onion; — SICCA, dry o.; — ASCALONICA, young o. "scallion;" — PALLACANA or PALLICANA, a shallot, a special Roman variety

Calamary, cuttlefish, ℞ 405, p. 343

CALAMENTHUM, cress, watercress

CALLUM, CALLUS (— PORCINUM) tough skin, bacon skin, cracklings. ℞ 9, 251, 255

CAMERINUM, town in Umbria, ℞ 3, where Vermouth was made

CAMMARUS MARINUS, a kind of crab-fish, ℞ 43

CANABINUM, CANNABINUM, hemp, hempen

CANCER, crab

Canning, ℞ 23-24

CANTHARUS, illustrations, p. 231; p. 274

CAPON, ℞ 166, 249; CAPONUM TESTICULI, ℞ 166

CAPPAR, caper

CAPPARA, purslane, portulaca

CAPPARUS, CARABUS, ℞ 397

CAPRA, she-goat, also mountain goat, chamois; Ger. GEMSE; ℞ 346-8

Caramel coloring, ℞ 55, 73, 119, 124, 146

CARDAMOMUM, cardamom, aromatic seed

CARDAMUM, nasturtium, cress

Cardoons, ℞ 112-4

CARDUS, CARDUUS, cardoon, edible thistle, ℞ 112-3

Carême, Antonin, The most talented French cook of the post-revolution period; his chartreuses compared, ℞ 186, p. 35

CARENUM, CAROENUM, wine or must boiled down one third of its volume to keep it. ℞ 35

CAREUM, CARUM, Carraway

CARICA (-FICUS) a dried fig from Caria, a reduction made of the fig wine was used for coloring sauce, similar to our caramel color, which see

CARIOTA, CARYOTA, a kind of large date, fig-date; also a wine, a date wine; ℞ 35

CARO, flesh of animals, ℞ 10; — SALSA, pickled meat

CAROTA, CAROETA, carrot; ℞ 121-3

Carthusian monks, inventors of the CHARTREUSE, ℞ 68, see also Carême

CARTILAGO, gristle, tendon, cartilage

CARYOPHYLLUS, clove

Casa di Forno, Pompeii, "House of the Oven," illustration, p. 2

CASEUS, cheese; ℞ 125, 303; — BUBULUS, cow's cheese; — VESTINUS, ℞ 126

CASTANEA, chestnut, ℞ 183 seq.

Catesby, writer, ℞ 322

Catfish, ℞ 426

CATTABIA, see Salacaccabia

Caul Sausage, Kromeski, ℞ 45

CAULICULOS, ℞ 87-92; also Col — cul — and coliclus

Cauliflower, ℞ 87

Caviar, see STYRIO

Celery, ℞ 104

Celsinus, a Roman, ℞ 376-7

CENA, COENA, a meal, a repast; CENULA, a light luncheon; — RECTA, a "regular" meal, a formal dinner, usually consisting of GUSTUS, appetizers and light ENTRÉES, the CENA proper which is the PIÈCE DE RESISTANCE and the MENSÆ SECUNDAE, or desserts. The main dish was the CAPUT CENAE; the desserts were also called BELLARIA or MENSAE POMORUM, because they usually finished with fruit. Hence Horace's saying "AB OVO USQUE AD MALA" which freely translated and modernized means, "Everything from soup to nuts."

— AUGURALIS, — PONTIFICALIS, — CAPITOLINA, — PERSICA, — SYBARITICA, — CAMPANAE, — CEREALIS, — SALIARIS, — TRIUMPHALIS, — POLINCTURA are all names for state dinners, official banquets, refined private parties each with its special significance which is hard to render properly into our language except by making a long story of it

— PHILOSOPHICA, — PLATONICA, — LACONICA, — RUSTICA, — CYNICA are all more or less skimpy affairs, while the — ICCI is that of a downright miser. — HECATES is a hectic meal, — TERRESTRIS a vegetarian dinner, — DEUM, a home-cooked meal, and a — SATURNIA is one without imported dishes or delicacies, a national dinner

— NOVENDIALIS is the feast given on the ninth day after the burial of a dead man when his ashes were scattered while yet warm and fresh. — DUBIA, ℞ 139, is the "doubtful meal" which causes the conscientious physician Lister so much worry

The CENA, to be sure, was an evening meal, the PRANDIUM, a noon-day meal, a luncheon, any kind of meal; the JENTACULUM, a breakfast, an early luncheon; the MERENDA was a snack in the afternoon between the meals for those who had "earned" a bite

There are further CENAE, such as — DAPSILIS, — PELLOCIBILIS, — UNCTA, — EPULARIS, — REGALIS, all more or less generous affairs, and our list of classical and sonorous dinner names is by no means exhausted herewith. The variety of these names is the best proof of how seriously a meal was considered by the ancients, how much thought was devoted to its character and arrangements

CEPA, same as CAEPA, onion

CEPAEA, purslane, sea-purslane, portulaca

CEPUROS, Gr., gardener; title of Book III

CERASUM, cherry, Fr. CERISE; Cerasus is a city of Pontus (Black Sea) whence Lucullus imported the cherry to Rome

CEREBRUM, CEREBELLUM, brains, ℞ 46

CEREFOLIUM, CAEREFOLIUM, chervil, Ger. KERBEL, Fr. CERFEUILLE

Cereto de Tridino, printer, see Tacuinus

CERVUS, stag, venison, ℞ 339-45

Cesena, a town in Italy where there is an Apicius Ms.; Apiciana XII

CHAMAE, cockles

Chamois, ℞ 346 seq.

Charcoal used for filtering, ℞ 1

CHARTREUSE, ℞ 68, 131, 145a, 186, 469-70; also see Carthusian monks and Carême

"Chasseur," ℞ 263

Cheese, cottage, ℞ 303; also see CASEUS

Cheltenham codex, Apiciana I

Cherries, ℞ 22, see CERASUS

Chestnuts, ℞ 183-84a

Chicken, PULLUS
— forcemeat, ℞ 50; — broth, 51; — fricassé, 56; — boiled, 235, 236, 242; — and dasheens, 244; — creamed, with paste, 247; — stuffed, 248, 199, 213-17, 235; — in cream, 250; — disjointed, 139, note 1; — Bantam, 237; — cold, in its own gravy, 237; — fried or sauté, 236; — Guinea hen, 239; — Fricassé Varius, 245; — à la Fronto, 246; — Parthian style, 237; — and leeks, 238; — with laser, 240; — roast, 241; — and pumpkin, 243; — galantine, 249; — fried with cream sauce, 250; — Maryland, Wiener Backhähndl, 250

Chick-peas, ℞ 207-9; p. 247

Chimneys on pies, ℞ 141

Chipolata garniture, ℞ 378

CHOENIX, a measure, — 2 SEXTARII, ℞ 52

Chops, ℞ 261

CHOUX DE BRUXELLES AUX MARRONS, ℞ 92

Christina, Queen of Sweden, eating Apician dishes, pp. 37, 38

CHRYSOMELUM, CHRYSOMALUM, a sort of quince

CIBARIA, victuals, provisions, food; same as CIBUS. Hence CIBARIAE LEGES, sumptuary laws; CIBARIUM VAS, a vessel or container for food; CIBARIUS, relating to food; also CIBATIO, victualling, feeding, meal, repast

CIBARIUM ALBUM, white repast, white dish, blancmange. Fr. BLANC MANGER, "white eating." A very old dish. Platina gives a fine recipe for it; in Apicius it is not yet developed. The body of this dish is ground almonds and milk, thickened with meat jelly. Modern cornstarch puddings have no longer a resemblance to it; to speak of "chocolate" blancmange as we do, is a barbarism. Platina is proud of his C.A. He prefers it to any Apician dessert. We agree with him; the incomplete Apicius in Platina's and in our days has no desserts worth mentioning. A German recipe of the 13th century (in "Ein Buch von guter Spise") calls C.A. "Blamansier," plainly a corruption of the French. By the translation of C.A. into the French, the origin of the dish was obliterated, a quite frequent occurrence in French kitchen terminology.

CIBORIUM, a drinking vessel

CIBUS, food, victuals, provender

CICER, chick-pea, small pulse, ℞ 207-209

Cicero, famous Roman, ℞ 409

CICONIA, stork. Although there is no direct mention of the C. as an article of diet it has undoubtedly been eaten same as crane, egrets, flamingo and similar birds

CINARA, CYNARA, artichoke

CINNAMONUM, cinnamon

CIRCELLOS ISICATOS, a sausage, ℞ 65

CITREA MALA, citron; see CITRUM

CITREUS, citron tree

CITRUM, CITRIUM, the fruit of the CITREUS, citron, citrus, ℞ 23, 81, 168. The citron tree is also MALUS MEDICA. "MALUS QUAE CITRIA VOCANTUR"; CONDITURA MALORUM MEDICORUM, Ap. Book I.; Lister thinks this is a cucumber

CITRUS, orange or lemon tree and their fruits. It is remarkable that Apicius does not speak of lemons, one of the most indispensable fruits in modern cookery which grow so profusely in Italy today. These were imported into Italy probably later. The ancients called a number of other trees CITRUS also, including the cedar, the very name of which is a corruption of CITRUS

Classic Cookery, pp. 16-17

CNECON, ℞ 16

COCHLEAE, snails, also sea-snails, "cockles," periwinkles, ℞ 323-25. — LACTE PASTAE, milk-fed snails. COCHLEARIUM, a snail "farm," place where snails were raised and fattened for the table. Also a "spoonful," a measure of the capacity of a small shell, more properly, however, COCHLEAR, a spoon, a spoon-full, ¼ cyathus, the capacity of a small shell, also, properly, a spoon for drawing snails out of the shells. COCHLEOLA, a small snail

COCOLOBIS, basil, basilica

COCTANA, COTANA, COTTANA, COTONA, a small dried fig from Syria

COCTIO, the act of cooking or boiling

COCTIVA CONDIMENTA, easy of digestion, not edible without cooking. COCTIVUS, soon boiled or roasted

COCTOR, cook, which see; same as COQUUS

COCULA, same as COQUA, a female cook

COCULUM, a cooking vessel

COCUS, COQUUS, cook, which see

Coelius, name of a person, erroneously attached to that of Apicius; also Caelius, p. 13

COLADIUM, — EDIUM, — ESIUM, — OESIUM, variations of COLOCASIUM, which see

Colander, illustration of a, p. 58

COLICULUS, CAULICULUS, a tender shoot, a small stalk or stem, ℞ 87-92

COLO, to strain, to filter, cf. ℞ 73

COLOCASIA, COLOCASIUM, the dasheen, or taro, or tanyah tuber, of which there are many varieties; the root of a plant known to the ancients as Egyptian Bean. Descriptions in the notes to the ℞ 74, 154, 172, 200, 244 and 322

COLUM NIVARIUM, a strainer or colander for wine and other liquids. See illustration, p. 58

COLUMBA, female pigeon; COLUMBUS, the male; COLUMBULUS, — A, squab, ℞ 220 Also used as an endearing term

Columella, writer on agriculture; — on bulbs, ℞ 307; — mentioning Matius, ℞ 167

COLYMBADES (OLIVAE), olives "swimming" in the brine; from COLYMBUS, swimming pool

Combination of dishes, ℞ 46

Commentaries on Apicius, p. 272

Commodus, a Roman, ℞ 197

Compôte of early fruit, ℞ 177

CONCHA, shellfish muscle, cockle scallop, pearl oyster; also the pearl itself, or mother-of-pearl; also any hollow vessel resembling a mussle shell (cf. illustration, p. 125) hence CONCHA SALIS PURI, a salt cellar. Hence also CONCHIS, beans or peas cooked "in the shell" or in the pod; and diminutives and variations: CONCHICLA FABA, (bean in the pod) for CONCHICULA, which is the same as CONCHIS and CONCICLA; ℞ 194-98, 411. — APICIANA, ℞ 195; — DE PISA, ℞ 196; — COMMODIANA, ℞ 197; — FARSILIS, ℞ 199

CONCHICLATUS, ℞ 199

CONCRESCO, grow together, run together, thicken, congeal, also curdle, etc., same as CONCRETIO, CONCRETUM

CONDIO, to salt, to season, to flavor; to give relish or zest, to spice, to prepare with honey or pepper, and also (since spicing does this very thing) to preserve

CONDITIO, laying up, preserving. CONDITIVUS, that which is laid up or preserved, same as CONDITUM

CONDITOR, one who spices. Ger. Konditor, a pastry maker

CONDIMENTARIUS, spice merchant, grocer

CONDIMENTUM, condiment, sauce, dressing, seasoning, pickle, anything used for flavoring, seasoning, pickling; — VIRIDE green herbs, pot herbs; cf. CONDITURA. — PRO PELAMIDE, ℞ 445; — PRO THYNNO, ℞ 446; — IN PERCAM, ℞ 447; — IN RUBELLIONEM, ℞ 448; — RATIO CONDIENDI MURENAS, ℞ 449; — LACERTOS, ℞ 456; — PRO LACERTO ASSO, ℞ 457; — THYNNUM ET DENTICEM, ℞ 458; — DENTICIS, ℞ 460; — IN DENTICE ELIXO, ℞ 461; — AURATA, ℞ 462; — IN AURATAM ASSAM, ℞ 463; — SCORPIONES, ℞ 464; — ANGUILLAM, ℞ 466; — ALIUD — ANGUILLAE, ℞ 467

CONDITUM, preserved, a preserve; cf. CONDIO; — MELIRHOMUM, ℞ 2; — ABSINTHIUM ROMANUM, ℞ 3; — PARADOXUM, ℞ 1; — VIOLARUM, ℞ 5

— Paradoxum, facsimile of Vat. Ms., p. 253

CONDITURA, a pickle, a preserve, sauce, seasoning, marinade; the three terms, C., CONDITUM and CONDIMENTUM are much the same in meaning, and are used indiscriminately. They also designate sweet dishes and desserts of different kinds, including many articles known to us as confections. Hence the German, KONDITOR, for confectioner, pastry cook. Nevertheless, a general outline of the specific meanings of these terms may be gathered from observing the nature of the several preparations listed under these headings, particularly as follows: — ROSATUM, ℞ 4; (cf. No. 5) — MELLIS, ℞ 17; — UVARUM, ℞ 20; — MALORUM PUNICORUM, ℞ 21; — COTONIORUM, ℞ 19; — FICUUM, PRUNORUM, PIRORUM, ℞ 20; — MALORUM MEDICORUM, ℞ 21; — MORORUM, ℞ 25; — OLERUM, ℞ 26; — RUMICIS, ℞ 27; — LAPAE, ℞ 27; — DURACINORUM, ℞ 29; — PRUNORUM, etc., ℞ 30

— in most of these instances corresponds to our modern "preserving"

CONGER, CONGRIO, CONGRUS, sea-eel, conger. CONGRUM QUEM ANTIATES BRUNCHUM APPELLANT, — Platina, cf. ANGUILLA. Plautus uses this fish name to characterize a very cunning person, a "slippery" fellow. A cook is thus called CONGRIO in one of his plays

CONILA, CUNILA, a species of the plant ORIGA-NUM, origany, wild marjoram. See SATUREIA

CONYZA, the viscous elecampane

Cook, COCUS, COQUUS is the most frequent form used, COCTOR, infrequent. COQUA, COCULA, female cook; though female cooks were few. The word is derived from COQUERE, to cook, which seems to be an imitation of the sound, produced by a bubbling mess

The cook's work place (formerly ATRIUM, the "black" smoky room) was the CULINA, the kitchen, hence in the modern Romance tongues CUISINE, CUCINA, COCINA. Those who work there are CUISINIERS, COCINEROS, the female a CUISINIÈRE, and so forth

The German and Swedish for "kitchen" are KÜCHE and KÖKET, but the words "cook" and "KOCH" are directly related to COQUUS

A self-respecting Roman cook, especially a master of the art, having charge of a crew, would assume the title of MAGIRUS, or ARCHI-MAGIRUS, chief cook. This Greek — "MAG-EIROS" plainly shows the high regard in which Greek cookery stood in Rome. No American CHEF would think of calling himself "chief cook," although CHEF means just that. The foreign word sounds ever so much better both in old Rome and in new New York. MAGEIROS is derived from the Greek equivalent of the verb "to knead," which leads us to the art of baking. Titles and distinctions were plentiful in the ancient bakeshops, which plainly indicates departmentisation and division of labor

The PISTOR was the baker of loaves, the DULCIARIUS the cake baker, using honey for sweetening. Martial says of the PISTOR DUL-CIARIUS, "that hand will construct for you a thousand sweet figures of art; for it the frugal bee principally labors." The PANCHESTRA-RIUS, mentioned in Arnobius, is another confectioner. The LIBARIUS still another of the sweet craft. The CRUSTULARIUS and BOTULARIUS were a cookie baker and a sausage maker respectively

The LACTARIUS is the milkman; the PLA-CENTARIUS he who makes the PLACENTA, a certain pancake, also a kind of cheese cake, often presented during the Saturnalia. The SCRIB-LITARIUS belongs here, too: in our modern parlance we would perhaps call these two "ENTRE-METIERS." The SCRIBLITA must have been a sort of hot cake, perhaps an omelet, a pancake, a dessert of some kind, served hot; maybe just a griddle cake, baked on a hot stone, a TORTIL-LA — what's the use of guessing! but SCRIB-LITAE were good, for Plautus, in one of his plays, Poenulus, shouts, "Now, then, the SCRIB-LITAE are piping hot! Come hither, fellows!" Not all of them did eat, however, all the time, for Posidippus derides a cook, saying, CUM SIS

COQUUS, PROFECTUS EXTRA LIMEN ES, CUM NON PRIUS COENAVERIS, "What? Thou art a cook, and hast gone, without dinner, over the threshold?"

From the FOCARIUS, the scullion, the FOR-NACARIUS, the fireman, or furnace tender, and the CULINARIUS, the general kitchen helper to the OBSONATOR, the steward, the FARTOR to the PRINCEPS COQUORUM, the "maitre d'hôtel" of the establishment we see an organization very much similar to our own in any well-conducted kitchen

The Roman cooks, formerly slaves in the frugal days of the nation, rose to great heights of civic importance with the spread of civilization and the advance of luxury in the empire. Cf. "The Rôle of the Mageiroi in the Life of the Ancient Greeks" by E. M. Rankin, Chic., 1907, and "Roman Cooks" by C. G. Harcum, Baltimore, 1914, two monographs on this subject

Cookery, Apician, as well as modern c., discussed in the critical review of the Apicius book

— examples of deceptive c. in Apicius, ℞ 6, 7, 9, 17, 229, 230, 384, 429

— of flavoring and spicing, ℞ 15, 277, 281, 369

— deserving special mention for ingenuity and excellence, ℞ 15, 21, 22, 72, 88, 177, 186, 212, 213, 214, 250, 287, 315, 428

— modern Jewish, resembling Apicius, ℞ 204 seq.

— examples of attempts to remove disagreeable odors, ℞ 212-14, 229, 230, 292

— removing sinews from fowl, ℞ 213

— utensils, p. 15

Coote, C. T., commentator, pp. 19, 273

COPA, a woman employed in eating places and taverns, a bar maid, a waitress, an entertainer, may be all that in one person. One of the caricatures drawn on a tavern wall in Pompeii depicts a COPA energetically demanding payment for a drink from a reluctant customer, p. 7

COPADIA, dainties, delicate bits, ℞ 125, 179, 180, 271, 276, seq., 355

Copper in Vegetable Cookery, ℞ 66

Copyists and their work, p. 14

COQUINA, cooking, kitchen. COQUINARIS, — IUS, relating to the kitchen. COQUO, — IS, COXI, COCTUM, COQUERE, to cook, to dress food, to function in the kitchen, to prepare food for the table. See cook

COR, heart

CORDYLA, CORDILLA, ℞ 419, 423

CORIANDRUM, the herb coriander; CORIAN-DRATUM, flavored with c.; LIQUAMEN EX CORIANDRO, coriander essence or extract

Corn, green, ℞ 99

CORNUM, cornel berry; "CORNA QUAE VER-GILIUS LAPIDOSA VOCAT" — Platina

CORNUTUS, horn-fish, ℞ 442

CORRUDA, the herb wild sparrage, or wild asparagus

CORVUS, a kind of sea-fish, according to some the sea-swallow. Platina describes it as a black fish of the color of the raven (hence the name), and ranks it among the best of fish, cf. STURNUS

COTANA, see COCTANA

COTICULA (CAUDA?), minor cuts of pork, either spareribs, pork chops, or pig's tails

COTONEA, a herb of the CUNILA family, wallwort, comfrey or black bryony

COTONEUM, COTONEUS, COTONIUS, CYDONIUS, quince-apple, ℞ 163

COTULA, COTYLA, a small measure, ½ sextarius

COTURNIX, quail

COSTUM, COSTUS, costmary; fragrant Indian shrub, the root of burning taste but excellent flavor

Court-bouillon, ℞ 37, 138

Cow-parsnips, p. 188, ℞ 115-122, 183

COXA, ℞ 288

CLIBANUS, portable oven; also a broad vessel for bread-making, a dough trough

CNICOS, CNICUS, CNECUS, bastard saffron; also the blessed thistle

CNISSA, smoke or steam arising from fat or meat while roasting

Crabs, ℞ 485; crabmeat croquettes, ℞ 44

Cracklings, p. 285, ℞ 255

Crane, ℞ 212, 213, p. 265. Crane with turnips, ℞ 214-17

CRATER, CRATERA, a bowl or vessel to mix wine and water; also a mixing bowl and oil container — see illustrations, p. 140

CRATICULA, grill, gridiron; illustration, p. 182

Crème renversée, ℞ 129, 143

CREMORE, DE-, ℞ 172

CRETICUM HYSOPUM, ℞ 29, Cretan hyssop

CROCUS, —OS, — ON, — UM, saffron; hence CROCEUS, saffron-flavored, saffron sauce or saffron essence. CROCIS, a certain herb or flavor, perhaps saffron

Croquettes, ℞ 42, seq.

Cucumber, CUCUMIS, ℞ 82-84

CUCURBITA, pumpkin, gourd, ℞ 73-80, 136

CULINA, kitchen; CULINARIUS, man employed in the kitchen; pertaining to the kitchen

CULTER, a knife for carving or killing; the blade from 9 to 13 inches long

CUMANA, earthen pot or dish; casserole, ℞ 237

Cumberland sauce, ℞ 345

CUMINUM, CYMINUM, cumin; CUMINATUM, — US, sauce or dish seasoned with cumin, ℞ 39, 40. Aethiopian, Libyan, and Syriac cumin are named, ℞ 178

CUNICULUS, rabbit, cony

CUNILAGO, a species of origany, flea-bane, wild marjoram, basilica

CUPELLUM, CUPELLA, dim., of CUPA, a small cask or tun. Ger. KUFE; a "cooper" is a man who makes them

CURCUMA ZEODARIA, tumeric

Custard, brain, ℞ 27; — nut, ℞ 128, 142; — of vegetables and brain, ℞ 130; — of elderberries, ℞ 134; — rose, ℞ 135; see also ℞ 301

Cutlets, ℞ 261, 471-3

Cuttle-fish, ℞ 42, 406-8

CYAMUS, Egyptian bean

CYATHUS, a measure, for both things liquid and things dry, which according to Pliny 21.109, amounted to 10 drachms, and, according to Rhem. Fann. 80., was the 12th part of a SEXTARIUS, roughly one twelfth pint. Also a goblet, and a vessel for mixing wine, ℞ 131

CYDONIIS, PATINA DE, ℞ 163, see also Malus

CYMA, young sprout, of colewort or any other herb; also cauliflower, ℞ 87-9-92

CYPERUS, CYPIRUS, a sort of rush with roots like ginger, see MEDIUM

CYRENE, a city of Africa, famous for its Laser Cyrenaicum, the best kind of laser, which see. Also Kyrene

D

DACTYLIS, long, "finger-like" grape or raisin; — US, long date, fruit of a date tree, ℞ 30

DAMA, a doe, deer, also a gazelle, antelope (DORCAS). In some places the chamois of the Alps is called DAMA

DAMASCENA [PRUNA], plum or prune from Damascus, ℞ 30. Either fresh or dried

Danneil, E., editor, pp. 33-34, 35, 271

Dasheen, ℞ 74, 152, 172, 216, 244, 322

Dates, stuffed, ℞ 294

DAUCUM, — US, — ON, a carrot

DE CHINE, see Dasheen

"Decline of the West," p. 17

DECOQUO, to boil down

DEFRUTARIUS, one who boils wine; CELLA DEFRUTARIA, a cellar where this is done, or where such wine is kept

DEFRUTUM, DEFRICTUM, DEFRITUM, new wine boiled down to one half of its volume with sweet herbs and spices to make it keep. Used to flavor sauces, etc., see also Caramel color

DENTEX, a sparoid marine fish, "Tooth-Fish," ℞ 157, 459-60

Dessert Dishes, illustrations, pp. 61, 125

Desserts, absent, p. 43

Desserts, Apician, ℞ 143, 294, seq.

Destillation, see Vinum

DIABOTANON PRO PISCE FRIXO, ℞ 432

Diagram of Apician editions, p. 252

Didius Julianus, ℞ 178

Dierbach, H. J., commentator, p. 273

Dining in Apician style, modern, p. 37
— in Rome, compared with today, pp. 17, 18

Diocles, writer, ℞ 409

Dionysos Cup, illustration, p. 141

Dipper, illustrated, p. 3

DISCUS, round dish, plate or platter
Disguising foods, ℞ 133, pp. 33-4
Dormouse, ℞ 396
Dory, ℞ 157, 462-5
Doves, p. 265
Drexel, Theodor, collector, pp. 257-8
Dubois, Urbain, chef, p. 16
Duck, p. 265, ℞ 212-3; — with turnips, ℞ 214-7
DULCIA, sweets, cookies, confections, ℞ 16, 216, 294-6
— RIUS, pastry cook, ℞ 294
Dumas, Alexandre, cooking, p. 24
Dumpling of pheasant, ℞ 48; — and HYDROGA-RUM, ℞ 49; — with broth, plain, ℞ 52, 181
DURACINUS, hard-skinned, rough-skinned fruit; — PERSICA, the best sort of peach, according to some, nectarines, ℞ 28

E

EARLY fruit, stewed, ℞ 177
ECHINUS, sea-urchin, ℞ 412-17
Economical methods: flavoring, ℞ 15
EDO, to eat; great eater, gormandizer, glutton
EDULA, chitterlings
Eel, ℞ 466-7
Egg Dish, illustration, p. 93
Eggs, ℞ 326-28; — fried, ℞ 336; — boiled, ℞ 327; — poached, ℞ 328; — scrambled with fish and oysters, ℞ 159
Eglantine, ℞ 171
Egyptian Bean, ℞ 322; also see CYAMUS
EIERKÄSE, ℞ 125, 301
ELAEOGARUM, ℞ 33
Elderberry custard, ℞ 135
ELIXO, to boil, boil down, reduce. -US, -UM, boiled down, sodden, reduced. According to Platina an ELIXUM simply is a meat bouillon as it is made today. ELIXATIO, a court-bouillon, liquid boiled down; ELIXATURA, a reduction
EMBAMMA, a marinade, a pickle or sauce to preserve food, to give it additional flavor; same as INTINCTUS, ℞ 344
EMBRACTUM, EMPHRACTUM, a dish "covered over"; a casserole of some kind. E. BAIANUM, ℞ 431
Endives, ℞ 109
Enoche of Ascoli, medieval scholar, cf. Apiciana
Entrées, potted , ℞ 54, 55; — sauces, ℞ 56; — of fish, poultry and sausage, ℞ 139; — of fowl and livers, ℞ 175
EPIMELES, careful, accurate; choice things. Title of Book I
Erasmus of Rotterdam, Dialogue, p. 273
ERUCA, the herb rocket, a colewort, a salad plant, a mustard plant
ERVUM, a kind of pulse like vetches or tares
ESCA, meat, food, victuals; ESCO, to eat
Escoffier, A. modern chef, writer, ℞ 338
ESCULENTES, things good to eat
ESTRIX, she-glutton

ESUS, eating
Every Day Dishes, ℞ 128, 142
EXCERPTA A VINIDARIO, p. 235
Excerpts from Apicius by Vinidarius, pp. 21, 234
EXCOQUO, to boil out, to melt, to render (fats)

F

FABA, bean, pulse. — AEGYPTIACA, ℞ 322; — IN FRIXORIO, string beans in the frying pan, Fr.: HARICOTS VERTS SAUTÉS; — VITEL-LIANA, ℞ 189, 193
FABACIAE VIRIDES, green bean, ℞ 202; — FRICTAE, ℞ 203; — EX SINAPI, ℞ 204
Fabricius, Albertus, bibliographer, pp. 258, seq., 268
"Fakers" of manuscripts, p. 13
FALSCHER HASE, ℞ 384
FAR, corn or grain of any kind, also spelt; also a sort of coarse meal
Farce, forcemeat, ℞ 131
FARCIMEN, sausage, ℞ 62-64
FARCIO, to fill, to stuff; also to feed by force, cram, fatten
FARINA, meal, flour, ℞ 173; — OSUS, mealy
FARNEI FUNGI, ℞ 309
FARRICA, ℞ 173
FASEOLUS, PHASEOLUS, a bean; Ger.: Fisole, ℞ 207
FARSILIS, FARTILIS, a rich dish, something crammed or fattened, ℞ 131
FARTOR, sausage maker; keeper of animals to be fattened, ℞ 166, 366
FARTURA, the fattening of animals; also the dressing used to stuff the bodies in roasting, forcemeat, ℞ 166, 366
FATTENING FOWL, ℞ 166, 366
FENICOPTERO, IN, ℞ 220, 231
FENICULUM, FOENI — fennel
FENUM GRAECUM, FOEN — ; the herb fenu-greek, also SILICIA, ℞ 206
FERCULUM, a frame or tray on which several dishes were brought in at once, hence a course of dishes
FERULA, a rod or branch, fennel-giant; — ASA FOETIDA, same as LASERPITIUM
FICATUM, fed or stuffed with figs, ℞ 259-60
FICEDULA, small bird, figpecker, ℞ 132
FICUS, fig, fig tree, FICULA, small fig
Field herbs, ℞ 107; Field salad, ℞ 110; a dish of field vegetables, ℞ 134
Fieldfare, a bird, ℞ 497
Fig-fed pork, p. 285, ℞ 259
Figpecker, a bird, ℞ 132
Figs, to preserve, ℞ 22
Filets Mignons ℞ 262
Filtering liquors, ℞ 1
Financière garniture, ℞ 166, 378
Fine ragout of brains and bacon, ℞ 147
Fine spiced wine, ℞ 1
Fish cookery, "The Fisherman," title of Book X; — boiled, ℞ 432, 4, 5, 6, 455; — fried, herb

sauce, ℞ 433; — to preserve fried fish, ℞ 13; — with cold dressing, ℞ 486; — baked, ℞ 476-7; — balls in wine sauce, ℞ 145, 164; — fond, ℞ 155; a dish of any kind of —, ℞ 149, 150, 156; — au gratin, ℞ 143; — loaf, ℞ 429; — liver pudding, ℞ 429; — pickled, spiced, marinated, ℞ 480; — oysters and eggs, ℞ 157; — salt, any style, ℞ 430, 431; stew, ℞ 153, 432; — sauce, acid, ℞ 38-9

FISKE BOLLER, ℞ 145, 41, seq.

Flaccus, a Roman, ℞ 372

Flamingo, ℞ 220, 231-2

Flavors and spices, often referred to, especially in text; instances of careful flavoring, ℞ 15, 276-77. Flavoring with faggots, ℞ 385, seq.

Florence Mss. Apiciana VI, VII, VIII, IX

FLORES SAMBUCI, elder blossoms

Fluvius Hirpinus, Roman, ℞ 323, 396; a man interested in raising snails, dormice, etc., for the table

FOCUS, hearth, range; unusually built of brick, on which the CRATICULA stood. Cf. illustratios, p. 182 ,

FOLIUM, leaf, aromatic leaves such as laurel, etc. — NARDI, several kinds, nard leaf. The Indian nard furnishes nard oil, the Italian lavender

FONDULI, see SPHONDULI, ℞ 114, 121

Food adulterations, pp. 33, 34

Food disguising and adulteration, p. 33, ℞ 6, 7, 134, 147
— displayed in Pompeii, p. 7

Forcemeats, ℞ 42, 172

Fowl, p. 265; a dish of, ℞ 470; — and livers, ℞ 174; various dishes and sauce, ℞ 218, seq. Picking —, ℞ 233; Removing disagreeable odors from —, ℞ 229-30

French Dressing, ℞ 112

French Toast, ℞ 296

FRETALE, FRIXORIUM, FRICTORIUM, frying pan, illustrations, pp. 355, 366; cf. SARTAGO

FRICTELLA, fritter; "A FRICTO DICI NULLA RATIO OBSTAT" — Platina. Ger. "Frikadellen" for meat balls fried in the pan. "De OFFELLIS, QUAS VEL FRICTELLAS LICET APPELLARE" — Platina

FRICTORIUM, FRIXORIUM, same as FRETALE, frying pan

FRISILIS, FRICTILIS, FUSILIS, ℞ 131

FRITTO MISTO (It.), ℞ 46

Friture, (Fr.) frying fat, ℞ 42, seq.

FRIXUS, roast, fried, also dried or parched, term which causes some confusion in the several editions

Frontispice, 2nd Lister Edition, illustration, p. 156

Fronto, a Roman, ℞ 246, 374

FRUGES, farinaceous dishes

Fruit dishes, ℞ 64, 72; Fruits, p. 210; — dried, Summary, p. 370
— Bowl illustration, pp. 61, 125

FRUMENTUM, grain, wheat or barley

Frying, ℞ 42, seq.

Frying pans, illustrated, cf. FRETALE and SARTAGO

Fulda Ms., cf. Apiciana

FUNGUS, mushroom; — ULUS, small m.; see BOLETUS — FARNEI, ℞ 309, seq.

FURCA, a two-pronged fork; — ULA, — ILLA, (dim.) a small fork. FUSCINA, — ULA, a three-pronged fork. Cf. "Forks and Fingerbowls as Milestones in Human Progress," by the author, Hotel Bulletin and The Nation's Chefs, Chicago, Aug., 1933, pp. 84-87

FURNUS, oven, bake oven. See illustration, p. 2

G

GALEN, writer, ℞ 396, 410

GALLINA, hen; — ULA, little hen; — ARIUS, poulterer

GALLUS, cock

Game of all kinds, sauce for, ℞ 349
— birds, ℞ 218, seq.

GANONAS CRUDAS, fish, ℞ 153

GARATUM, prepared with GARUM, which see

Gardener, The — Title of Book III, ℞ 377

GARUM (Gr.: GARON) a popular fish sauce made chiefly of the scomber or mackerel, but formerly from the GARUS, hence the name, cf. p. 22, ℞ 10, 33, 471

Mackerel is the oiliest fish, and plentiful, very well suited for the making of G.

G. was also a pickle made of the blood and the gills of the tunny and of the intestines of mackerel and other fish. The intestines were exposed to the sun and fermented. This has stirred up controversies; the ancients have been denounced for the "vile concoctions," but garum has been vindicated by modern science as to its rational preparation and nutritive qualities. Codfish oil, for instance, has long been known for its medicinal properties, principally Vitamin D; this is being increased today by exposure to ultraviolet rays (just what the ancients did). The intestines are the most nutritious portions of fish

G. still remains a sort of mystery. Its exact mode of preparation is not known. It was very popular and expensive, therefore was subject to a great number of variations in quality and in price, and to adulteration. For all these reasons GARUM has been the subject of much speculation. It appears that the original meaning of G. became entirely lost in the subsequent variations

In 1933 Dr. Margaret B. Wilson sent the author a bottle of GARUM ROMANUM which she had compounded according to the formulae at her disposal. This was a syrupy brown liquid, smelled like glue and had to be dissolved in water or wine, a few drops of the G. to a glass of liquid, of which, in turn, only a few drops were used to flavor a fish sauce, etc.

— SOCIORUM, the best kind of G.; ALEX

GARI VITIUM, the cheap kind of G., cf. ALEX, HALEC. OENOGARUM, G. mixed with wine; HYDROGARUM G. mixed with water; OLEOGARUM, G. mixed with oil; OXYGARUM, G. mixed with vinegar

GARUS, small fish from which the real GARUM was made

GELO, cause to freeze, to congeal; GELU, jelly GELU IN PATINA, gelatine: "QUOD VULGO GELATINAM VOCAMUS" — Platina

Georg, Carl, Bibliographer, p. 257

Gesamt-Katalog, bibliography, p. 261

Gesner, Conrad, Swiss scientist, bibliographer, polyhistor, see Schola Apitiana, p. 206

GETHYUM, -ON, same as PALLACANA, an onion

Giarratano, C., editor, Apiciana, pp. 18, 19, 26, 271, 273

GINGIBER, ginger; also ZINGIBER, faulty reading of the "G" by medieval scribes

GINGIDON, — IUM, a plant of Syria; according to Spengel the French carrot. Paulus Aegineta says: "BISACUTUM (SIC ENIM ROMANI GINGIDION APPELLANT) OLUS EST SCANDICI NON ABSIMILE," hence a chervil root, or parsnip, or oysterplant

GLANDES, any kernel fruit, a date, a nut, etc.

Glasse, Mrs. Hannah, writer, ℞ 127

GLIS, pl. GLIRES, dormouse, a small rodent, very much esteemed as food. GLIRARIUM, cage or place where they were kept or raised, ℞ 396

Gluttons, p. 11

Goat, wild, ℞ 346, seq. — liver, ℞ 291-3

Gollmer, R., editor, Apiciana, pp. 18, 35, 270

GONG for slaves, illustration, p. 151

Goose, p. 265; white sauce for, ℞ 228

Grapes, to keep, ℞ 19

Greek influence on Roman cookery, p. 12, seq. — Banquet, by Anacharsis, p. 8

Greek monographs, p. 43

Green beans, p. 247, ℞ 202, 206

Greens, green vegetables, ℞ 99

Grimod de la Reynière, writer, p. 4, cf. Mappa

Gruel, p. 210; ℞ 172, 200-1, seq. — and wine, ℞ 179-80

GRUS, crane; GRUEM, ℞ 212-3; — EX RAPIS, ℞ 215-6

Gryphius, S., printer, Apiciana No. 6, facsimile of title, p. 263

Guégan, Bertrand, editor, p. 271, seq.

Guinea Hen, ℞ 239, cf. "Turkey Origin," by the author, Hotel Bulletin and The Nation's Chefs, for February and March, 1935, Chicago

GULA, gluttony

GUSTUS, taste; also appetizers and relishes and certain entrées of a meal, Hors d'oeuvres. Cf. CENA, ℞ 174-77

H

HABS, R., writer, p. 18

HAEDUS, HAEDINUS, kid, ℞ 291-3, 355, seq. — SYRINGIATUS, ℞ 360;—PARTHICUM, ℞ 364; — TARPEIANUM, ℞ 363; — LAUREATUM EX LACTE, ℞ 365; — LASARATUM, ℞ 496

HALEC, see ALEC

HALIEUS, HALIEUTICUS, pertaining to fish; title of Book X, p. 356

Ham, fresh, p. 285, ℞ 287-9

HAND-MILL, operated by Slaves, illustration, p. 60

HAPANTAMYNOS, ℞ 497

Harcum, C. G., writer, see COQUUS

Hard-skinned peaches, to keep, ℞ 28

Hare, B. VIII, ℞ 382, seq. — imitation, ℞ 384; — braised, ℞ 382-3; — different dressings, ℞ 383; — Stuffed, ℞ 384, 91; — white sauce for, ℞ 385; — lights of, ℞ 386-7; — liver, ℞ 170; — in its own broth, ℞ 388; — smoked Passianus, ℞ 389; — tidbits. kromeskis, ℞ 390; — boiled, ℞ 393; — spiced sauce, ℞ 393; — sumptuous style, ℞ 394; — spiced, ℞ 395

Haricot of lamb, ℞ 355

HARPAGO, a meat hook for taking boiled meat out of the pot, with five or more prongs; hence "harpoon." Cf. FURCA

"Haut-goût" in birds, to overcome it, ℞ 229-30

Headcheese, ℞ 125

Heathcock, ℞ 218, seq.

HELENIUM, plant similar to thyme(?); the herb elecampane or starwort

Heliogabalus, emperor, p. 11

HEMINA, a measure, about half a pint

Henry VIII, of England, edict on kitchens, p. 156

HERBAE RUSTICAE, ℞ 107

Herbs, pot herbs, to keep, ℞ 25

Hildesheim Treasure, found in 1868, a great collection of Roman silverware, now in the Kaiser Friedrich Museum, Berlin, our illustrations show a number of these pieces, p. 43

Hip dog-briar, ℞ 171

HIRCOSIS AVIBUS, DE, ℞ 229-30

Hirpinus, Fluvius, Roman, ℞ 323, 396, who raised animals for the table

HISPANUM, see Oleum

HOEDUS, see HAEDUS

HOLERA, pot herbs, ℞ 25, 66; also OLERA and HOLISERA, from HOLUS

HOLUS, OLUS, kitchen vegetables, particularly cabbage, ℞ 99

Home-made sweets, ℞ 294

Honey cakes, ℞ 16

Honey Refresher, ℞ 2; — cake, ℞ 16; — to renew spoiled, ℞ 17; testing quality of, ℞ 18; — pap, ℞ 181; see also Chap. XIII, Book VII

Horace, writer, pp. 3, 4, 273, ℞ 455

HORDEUM, barley

Horned fish, ℞ 442

Hors d'oeuvres, ℞ 174; cf. GUSTUS

HORTULANUS, gardener, Hortolanus, pork, ℞ 378

Horseradish, ℞ 102

House of the Oven in Pompeii, illustration, p. 2

Humelbergius, Gabriel, editor, ℞ 307; title page of his 1542 edition, p. 265

Hunter style, ℞ 263

HYDROGARATA, foods, sauces prepared with GARUM (which see) and water, ℞ 172

HYDROMELI, rain water and honey boiled down one third

HYPOTRIMA, — IMMA, a liquid dish, soup, sauce, ragout, composed of many spiced things, ℞ 35

HYSITIUM, ISICIUM, a mince, a hash, a sausage, forcemeat, croquette, ℞ 41-56. The term "croquette" used by Gollmer does not fully cover H.; some indeed, resemble modern croquettes and kromeskis very closely. The ancients, having no table forks and only a few knives (which were for the servants' use in carving) were fond of such preparations as could be partaken of without table ware. The reclining position at table made it almost necessary for them to eat H.; such dishes gave the cooks an opportunity for the display of their skill, inventive ability, their decorative and artistic sense. As "predigested" food, such dishes are decided preferable to the "grosses-pièces," which besides energetic mastication require skillful manipulation of fork and knife; such exercise was unwelcome on the Roman couches. Modern nations, featuring "grosses-pièces" do this at the expense of high-class cookery. The word, H., is probably a medieval graecification of INSICIUM. Cf. ISICIA

HYSSOPUS, the herb hyssop; H. CRETICUS, marjoram. Also Hysopum creticum, hyssop from the island of Creta, ℞ 29

I

IECUR, JECUR, liver; ℞ 291-3. IECUSCULUM, small (poultry, etc.) liver

Ihm, Max, writer, p. 19

Ill-smelling fish sauce, ℞ 9; ditto birds, ℞ 229-30

Indian peas, ℞ 187

Ink-fish, ℞ 405

INSICIA, chopped meat, sausage, forcemeat, dressing, stuffing for roasts, ℞ 42; see Hysitia and Isicia; — ARIUS, sausage maker

INTINCTUS, a sauce, seasoning, brine or pickle in which meat, etc., is dipped. See EMBAMMA, ℞ 344

INTUBUS, INTYBUS, -UM, chicory, succory, endive, ℞ 109

INULA HELENIUM, the herb elecampane or starwort

ISICIA, see HYSITIA, ℞ 41-54, 145

— AMULATA AB AHENO, ℞ 54; — DE CAMMARIS, ℞ 43; — DE CEREBELLIS, ℞ 45; DE LOLLIGINE, ℞ 42; — DE SPONDYLIS, ℞ 46; DE PULLO, ℞ 50; — DE SCILLIS, ℞ 43; — HYDROGARATA, ℞ 49;

— PLENA, ℞ 48; — SIMPLEX, ℞ 52; — DE TURSIONE, ℞ 145

Italian Salad, ℞ 123

IUS, JUS, any juice or liquid, or liquor derived from food, a broth, soup, sauce. IUSCELLUM, more frequently and affectionately, IUSCULUM, the diminutive of I

— DE SUO SIBI, pan-gravy; such latinity as this proves the genuineness of the Apicius text, ℞ 153; — IN DIVERSIS AVIBUS, ℞ 210-228; — IN ELIXAM, ℞ 271-7; — IN VENATIONIBUS, ℞ 349, seq.; — DIABOTANON, ℞ 432; — IN PISCE ELIXO, ℞ 433-6; — ALEXANDRINUM, ℞ 437-9; — CONGRO, ℞ 440; — IN CORNUTAM, ℞ 441; IN MULLOS, ℞ 442-3; — PELAMYDE, ℞ 444; — IN PERCAM,.℞ 446; IN MURENA, ℞ 448, 449-52; — IN PISCE ELIXO, ℞ 454; — IN LACERTOS ELIXOS, ℞ 455; — PISCE ASSO, ℞ 456; — THYNNO, ℞ 457; — ELIXO, ℞ 458; IN DENTICE ASSO, ℞ 459-60; — IN PISCE AURATA, ℞ 461-2; — IN SCORPIONE, ℞ 463; — PISCE OENOGARUM, ℞ 464-5; — ANGUILLAM, ℞ 466-7

J

Jardinière, ℞ 378

JECINORA, ℞ 291

Jewish Cookery, compared with Apician, ℞ 205

Johannes de Cereto de Tridino, Venetian printer, p. 261

John of Damascus, see Torinus edition of 1541, Basel

Julian Meal Mush, ℞ 178

K

KEEPING meat and fish, ℞ 10-14, seq.

Kettner, writer, p. 38

Kid, p. 314, ℞ 355, seq. — liver, ℞ 291-93; — stew, ℞ 355-8; — roast, ℞ 359-62; — boned, ℞ 360-1; — Tarpeius, ℞ 363-4; — Prize, ℞ 365; — plain, ℞ 366; — laser, ℞ 496

Kidney beans, ℞ 207-8

King, Dr. W., writer, quoted: Introduction, pp. 38, 267

Kromeskis, ℞ 44, 47, 60; cf. ISICIA and HYSITIA

Kyrene, Cyrene, City of Northern Africa, see Laser

L

LABOR item in cookery, pp. 18, 24

LAC, milk; — FISSILE, cottage cheese

LACERTUS, a sea-fish, not identified, ℞ 147, 152, 455-7

LACTARIS, having milk, made of milk; — IUS, dairyman

LACTES, small guts, chitterlings

LACTUA, LACTUCULA, lettuce, ℞ 105, 109-11

LAGANUM, a certain farinaceous dish; small cake made of flour and oil, a pan cake

LAGENA, -ONA, -OENA, -UNA, flask, bottle

Lamb, ℞ 291-3, 355-65, 495-6; preparations same as Kid, which see

Lambecius, Petrus, writer, on "The Porker's Last Will," ℞ 376

Lanciani, Rodolfo, writer, pp. 29, 30

Lancilotus, Blasius, co-editor, 1498-1503 editions, pp. 27-30, 41

— see also Tacuinus

— facsimile of opening chapter, 1503, p. 232

Langoust, ℞ 485

LANX, broad platter, dish, charger, ℞ 455

LAPA, LAPATHUM, LAPADON, same as RUMEX, ℞ 26

Larding, ℞ 394

LARIDUM, LARDUM, ℞ 147, 290; cf. SALSUM

LASER, LASERPITIUM, — ICIUM, the juice or destillate of the herb by that name, also known as SILPHIUM, SYLPHIUM, Greek, SYLPHION. Some agree that this is our present asa foetida, while other authorities deny this. Some claim its home is in Persia, while others say the best LASER came from Cyrene (Kyrene), Northern Africa. The center picture of the so-called Arkesilas-Bowl of Vulci at Paris, Cab. d. Méd. 189, represents a picture as seen by the artist in Kyrene how King Arkesilas (VI. saec.) watches the weighing and the stowing away in the hold of a sailing vessel of a costly cargo of sylphium. It was an expensive and very much esteemed flavoring agent, and, for that reason, the plant which grew only in the wild state, was probably exterminated.

There is much speculation, but its true nature will not be revealed without additional information

℞ 15, 31, 32, 34, 100; p. 22

Method of flavoring with laser-impregnated nuts, ℞ 15

LASERATUS, LASARATUS, prepared or seasoned with LASER, or SILPHIUM

Latin title of Vehling translation, opposite title page

LAUREATUM, prepared with LAURUS; also in the sense of excellence in quality, ℞ 365, 373

LAURUS CINNAMOMUM, cinnamon; — NOBILIS, laurel leaf, bay leaf

La Varenne, French cook, p. 16

Laws, sumptuary, p. 25, ℞ 166

Laxatives, ℞ 4, 5, 6, 29, 34

Leeks, p. 188, ℞ 93-6; — and beans, ℞ 96

LEGUMEN, leguminous plants; all kinds of pulse-peas, beans lentils, etc., Book V

LENS, LENTICULA, lentils, ℞ 183-4

LEPIDIUM SATIVUM, watercress

LEPOREM MADIDUM, ℞ 382, seq.; — FARSUM, ℞ 384; — PASSENIANUM, ℞ 389; — ISICIATUM, ℞ 390; — FARSILEM, ℞ 391; — ELIXIUM, ℞ 392; — SICCO SPARSUM, ℞

394; — LEPORIS CONDITURA, ℞ 393-5

LEPUS, hare; LEPUSCULUM, young hare; LEPORARIUM, a place for keeping hare; LEPORINUM MINUTAL, minced hare, Hasenpfeffer, ℞ 382-395

Lettuce, B. V, ℞ 105, 109-111; — and endives, ℞ 109; — purée of, ℞ 130

LEUCANTHEMIS, camomile

LEUCOZOMUS, "creamed," prepared with milk, ℞ 250

Lex Fannia, ℞ 166

Liaison, lié, ℞ 54; cf. AMYLARE

LIBELLI, little ribs, spare ribs, also loin of pork, ℞ 251

LIBRA, weight, 1 pound (abb. "lb," still in use); LIBRAE, balances, scales

LIBURNICUM, see oil, oleum

LIGUSTICUM, lovage (from Liguria); also LEVISTICUM; identical with garden lovage, savory, basilica, satury, etc.

LIQORIBUS, DE, p. 370

LIQUAMEN, any kind of culinary liquid, depending upon the occasion. It may be interpreted as brine, stock, gravy, jus, sauce, drippings, marinade, natural juice; it must be interpreted in the broadest sense, as the particular instance requires. This much disputed term has been illustrated also in page 22. Also see ℞ 9, 42

Liquids, Summary of, p. 370

— thickening of, by means of flour, eggs, etc., called Liaison, cf. AMYLARE

Lister, Dr. Martinus, editor, edition of 1705, title page, ditto, verso of, ditto of 1709, p. 38; frontispiece

— quoted in many foot notes, ℞ 8, seq.

— assailing Torinus, p. 13, ℞ 15, 26, 100, 205

— edition, 1709, facsimile, p. 250

Liver kromeskis, ℞ 44; fig-fed, of pig, ℞ 259-60; — and lungs, ℞ 291-3; — hash, ℞ 293; — of fish, see GARUM and Pollio

Lobster, ℞ 398, 399, 400, 401, 2; in various ways

LOCUSTA, a langoust, spiny lobster, large lobster without claws; ℞ 397-402, 485; — ASSAE, ℞ 398; — ELIXAE, ℞ 399, 401-2

Loins, p. 285, ℞ 286

LOLIGO, LOLLIGO, calamary, cuttle-fish, ℞ 42, 405

LOLIUM, LOLA, darnel, rye-grass, ray-grass, meal. The seeds of this grass were milled, the flour or meal believed to possess some narcotic properties, as stated by Ovid and Plautus, but recent researches have cast some doubt upon its reported deleterious qualities. Apicius, ℞ 50, reads LOLAE FLORIS

LONGANO, a blood sausage, ℞ 61. The LONGANONES PORCINOS EX IURE TARENTINO in ℞ 140 is a part of the PATINA EX LACTE; a pork sausage made in Tarent of the straight gut, the rectum. Lister says they are cooked in Tarentinian sauce and are not unlike the sausage

called APEXABO and HILLA. These sausages
were in vogue before the Italians learned to make
them; it was in Epirus, Greece, that they were
highly developed. Their importation into Rome
caused quite a stir, politically. Lister, ℞ 50, p.
119, describes the sausage and calls the inhabitants of Tarent "most voluptuous, soft and delicate" because Juvenal, Sat. VI, v. 297, takes a
shot at Tarent

This part of Italy, and especially Sicily, because
in close contact with Greece was for many years
much farther advanced in art of cookery than
the North

Lucania, district of lower Italy whence came the
Lucanian sausage, p. 172, ℞ 61; see also LON-
GANO

LUCIUS FLUVIALIS, a river fish, perch, or pike,
according to some; Platina also calls it LICIUS.
Cf. MERULA

Lucretian Dish, ℞ 151

Lucullus, Roman general, proverbial glutton, has a
place here because of his importation into Rome
of the cherry, which he discovered in Asia
Minor. He cannot be expected to be represented
in the Apicius book because he died 57 B.C.

LUCUSTA, see LOCUSTA

LUMBUS, loin, (Ger. LUMMEL), ℞ 286; LUM-
BELLI, ℞ 255

Lung, ℞ 291-2

LUPINUS, lupine

LUPUS, fish, ℞ 158

M

MACELLARIUS, MACELLINUS, market man,
butcher

MACELLUM, market

MACERO, to soak, soften, steep in liquor, mace-
rate; MACERATUM, food thus treated

MACTRA, trough for kneading dough

MAGIRUS, MAGEIROS, cook, see COQUUS

MALABATHRUM — THRON, ℞ 32, 399

Mallows, ℞ 86

MALUS, fruit tree, apple tree; — PUNICORUM,
pomegranate; — ASSYRIA, — CITRUS DECU-
MANA, one of the larger citrus fruits; — MED-
ICA, citron tree; — CYDONIA, quince tree

MALUM, fruit, an apple, but quinces, pomegranates, peaches, oranges, lemons, and other
fruits were likewise designated by this name.
℞ 18, 20. See also CITRUM

It is remarkable that Apicius does not spe-
cifically speak of lemons and oranges, fruits that
must have grown in Italy at his time, that are so
indispensible to modern cookery

MALUM PUNICUM, ℞ 20, 21; — CYDON-
IUM, ℞ 21; — GRANATUM, ℞ 20; — MED-
ICUM, ℞ 24; — ROSEUM, ℞ 178, 171. This
name, which according to Schuch simply stands
for a rose-colored apple, has led to the belief
that the ancients made pies, etc., of roses. To-

day a certain red-colored apple is known as
"Roman Beauty." We concur in Schuch's opinion, remembering, however, that the fruit of the
rose tree, namely the hip, dog-brier, or eglantine,
is made into dainty confections on the Continent
today. It is therefore quite possible that MALUM
ROSEUM stands for the fruit of the rose

MANDUCO, to chew, to munch, to enjoy food by
munching; a glutton

MAPPA, table napkin (Fr. nappe). M. is a Punic
word, according to Quintil. 1, 5, 57

Each banquet guest brought with him from
his own home such a napkin or cloth which he
used during the banquet to wipe his mouth and
hands. The ancients, evidently, were conscious
of the danger of infection through the common
use of napkins and table ware. Sometimes they
used their napkins to wrap up part of the meal
and to give it to their slaves to carry home in.
Horace, Martial, Petronius attest to this fact. The
banquet guests also employed their own slaves
to wait on them at their Host's party. This custom and the individual napkin habit have survived until after the French revolution. Grimod
de la Reynière, in his Almanach des Gourmands,
Paris, 1803, seq., describes how guests furnished
their own napkins and servants for their own
use at parties to which they were invited

This rather sensible custom relieved the host
of much responsibility and greatly assisted him
in defraying the expenses of the dinner. On the
other hand it reveals the restrictions placed upon
any host by the general shortage of table ware,
table linen, laundering facilities in the days prior
to the mechanical age

Marcellus, a Roman physician, ℞ 29

Marinade, pickle; a composition of spices, vegetables, herbs, and liquids, such as vinegar, wine,
to preserve meats for several days and to impart
to it a special flavor, ℞ 11, 236, 244, 394; cf.
EMBAMMA

MARJORANA, marjoram

Marmites, illustrated, pp. 264, 284, 312, 342

MARRUBIUM, the plant horehound

Martial, writer, p. 10, ℞ 307, 461 (on bulbs)

Martino, Maestro, p. 3, cf. Vehling: Martino and
Platina, Exponents of Renaissance Cookery, Hotel
Bulletin and The Nation's Chefs, Chicago, October, 1932, and Platina, Maestro nell'arte culinaria Un'interessante studio di Joseph D. Vehling, Cremona, 1935

Mason, Mrs., a writer, ℞ 126

MASTIX, MASTICE, MASTICHE, the sweet-scent-
ed gum of the mastiche-tree; hence MASTICA-
TUS, MASTICINUS for foods treated with M.

Matius, a writer, was a friend of Julius Caesar. His
work is lost, ℞ 167; apples named after him, *ibid.*

MAYONNAISE DE VOLAILLE EN ASPIC, ℞
126, 480

Meal mush, Book V, ℞ 178

Measures, liquid. The following list is confined to terms used in Apicius

PARTES XV equal 1 CONGIUS

CONGIUS I equal 6 SEXTARII (1 S. equals about 1½ pt. English)

SEXTARII II equal 1 CHOENIX

SEXTARIUS I equal 2 HEMINAS

HEMINA I equal 4 ACETABULA

ACETABULUM I equal 12 CYATHI (15 Attic drachms)

CYATHUS I equal 1/12 SEXTARIUS (a cup)

COCHLEAR I equal ¼ CYATHUS (a spoonful)

COTULA, COTYLA, same as HEMINA, same as ½ SEXTARIUS

QUARTARIUS I equal ¼ pint

Meat ball, ℞ 261, seq. — with laser, ℞ 472-3; meat, boiled, stewed, ℞ 271; keeping of, ℞ 10, 13; how to make pickled meat sweet, ℞ 12; to decorate or garnish, ℞ 394, (see marinade; meat pudding, ℞ 42; — loaf, ℞ 384, 172

Meat displayed in windows, p. 73; ancient — diet, p. 31, ancient — supply, p. 31

Meat diet, ancient, pp. 30, 31

Meat supply, ancient and modern, p. 31

Medicinal formulae in Apicius, ℞ 4, 5, 6, 29, 34, 67, 68, 68, 70, 71, 108, 111, 307

MEDIUM, an iris or lily root which was preserved (candied) with honey, same as ginger, or fruit glacé

Medlar, ℞ 159; see MESPILA

Megalone, place where Torinus found the Apicius codex, p. 266

MEL, honey; MELLITUM, sweetened with honey — PRAVUM, ℞ 15; — PROBANDUM, ℞ 16; — ET CASEUM, ℞ 303

MELCAE, ℞ 294, 303

MELEAGRIS, Turkey; cf. Vehling: "Turkey Origin," Hotel Bulletin and The Nation's Chefs, Chicago, February-March, 1935

MELIRHOMUM, MELIZOMUM, ℞ 2

MELO, small melon, B. III, ℞ 85; MELOPEPO, muskmelon

Melon, ℞ 85

MENSA, repast, see CENA

MENTHA, MINTHA, mint; — PIPERITA, peppermint

"Menu," cf. Brevis Ciborum, Excerpts of Vinidarius, p. 235

Merling, see MERULA

MERULA, MERLUCIUS, cf. LUCIUS, a fish called merling, whiting, also smelt; Fr. MERLAN; also blackbird. Platina discussed MERULA, the blackbird, the eating of which he disapproves. "There is little food value in the meat of blackbirds and it increases melancholia," says he. Perhaps because the bird is "black," ℞ 419

MERUS, MERUM, pure, unmixed, "mere," "merely"; hence MERUM VINUM, — OLEUM, pure wine, oil, etc.

MESPILA, medlar; Ger. MISPEL

Milan edition, Colophon, p. 260

Milk Toast, ℞ 171

Mill operated by slaves, illustration, p. 60

Minced dishes, Book II

Mineral salts in vegetables, ℞ 71, 96

MINUTAL, a "small" dish, a "minutely" cut mince; — MARINUM, ℞ 164; — TARENTINUM, ℞ 165; — APICIANUM, ℞ 166; — MATIANUM, ℞ 167; — DULCE, ℞ 168; — EX PRAECOQUIS, ℞ 169; — LEPORINUM, ℞ 170; — EX ROSIS, ℞ 171; — of large fruits, ℞ 169

MITULIS, IN, ℞ 418

Mixing bowls, see Crater

Monk's Rhubarb, ℞ 26

"Monkey," ℞ 55

Moralists, ancient, see Review

MORETUM, salad, salad dressing of oil, vinegar, garlic, parsley, etc., cf. ℞ 38

Morsels, ℞ 261, seq., 309, seq.

MORTARIA, foods prepared in the mortar, MORTARIUM, ℞ 38, 221

MORUS, mulberry; — ALBA, white m.; — NIGRA, black m. Platina, DE MORIS, has a very pretty simile, comparing the various stages of ripening and colors of the mulberry to the blushing of Thysbes, the Egyptian girl, ℞ 24

Moulds, ℞ 384, 126

MUGIL, sea-mullet, ℞ 159, 419, 424, 425

Mulberries, ℞ 24

MULLUS, the fish mullet, ℞ 148, 427, 442, 443, 482-4

MULSUM, mead, honey-wine; — ACETUM, honey-vinegar

Munich Ms. XVIII Apiciana

MURENA, MURAENA, the sea fish murena, p. 356, ℞ 448-53, 484

MUREX, shellfish, purple-fish

MURIA, brine, salt liquor, p. 22, ℞ 30; cf. ALEC

Mush, ℞ 178

Mushrooms, B. III, ℞ 121, 309-14 — Omelette, ℞ 314

Muskrat, ℞ 396

Mussels, ℞ 418

MUSTEIS PETASONEM, ℞ 289

MUSTEOS AFROS, ℞ 295

MUSTUM, fresh, young, new; — VINUM, must, new wine; — OLEI, new oil

Mullet, see MULLUS, ℞ 148, 428, 443-4

MYRISTICA, nutmeg

MYRRHIS ODORATA, myrrh, used for flavoring wine

MYRTUS, myrtle berry, often called "pepper" and so used instead of pepper

MYRTUS PIMENTA, allspice

N

Napkins, individual, see MAPPA

NAPUS, p. 188, a turnip, navew, ℞ 100-1

NARDUS, nard, odoriferous plant; see FOLIUM

NASTURTIUM, the herb cress

NECHON, ℞ 16

Neck, roast, ℞ 270

NEPATA, cat-mint; — MONTANA, mountain mint; see MENTHA

Nero, emperor, p. 11

Nettles, ℞ 108

New York codex, No. 1, Apiciana

Newton, Sir Isaac, scientist, Apiciana No. 8, p. 268

NITRIUM, ℞ 66

Nonnus, writer, ℞ 307, 396

NOVENDIALES, see CENA

NUCEA LASERIS, ℞ 16; also see LASER

NUCLEUS, nut, kernel, ℞ 92

NUCULA, dim. of NUX, small nut; also a certain muscular piece of meat from the hind leg of animals, Fr. NOIX DE VEAU, as of veal, Ger. KALBSNUSS, and a certain small part of the loin of animals, Fr. NOISETTE

NUMIDICUS, PULLUS, guinea hen, which see

Nut custard, turn-over, ℞ 129, 143; — porridge, ℞ 297-9; — pudding, ℞ 298, 299, 230; — meal mush, ℞ 300

Nuts, Summary of, p. 236

NUX, p. 236, a nut, both hazel nut and walnut; — JUGLANDIS, walnut; — PINEIS, — PINEA, pine nuts, pignolia; — MUSCATA, nutmeg

O

OBLIGABIS, ℞ 83; also see AMYLARE

OBSONARE, to provide, to buy for the table; to prepare or to give a dinner; from the Greek, OPSON

OBSONATOR, steward

OBSONIUM, OP-, a dish, a meal, anything eaten with bread

OCIMUM, -YMUM, -UMUM, OCINUM, basil, basilica; also a sort of clover

OENOGARUM, wine and GARUM (which see), a wine sauce, ℞ 33, 146, 465; OENOGARA-TUM, a dish prepared with O.

OENOMELI, wine and honey

OENOPOLIUM, wine shop; a wine dealer's place, who, however, did a retail business. The TABER-NA VINARIA seems to have been the regular wine restaurant, while the THERMOPOLIUM specialized in hot spiced wines. Like today in our complicated civilization, there were in antiquity a number of different refreshment places, each with its specialties and an appropriate name for the establishment

OENOTEGANON, ℞ 479-81

OFFA, OFFELLA, OFELLA, a lump or ball of meat, a "Hamburger Steak," a meat dumpling, any bit of meat, a morsel, chop, small steak, collop, also various other "dainty" dishes, consisting principally of meat.
  "INTER OS ET OFFAM MULTA INTER-VENIUNT" — Cato; the ancient equivalent

for our "'twixt cup and lip there is many a slip"
  ℞ 261; — APICIANA, ℞ 262; — APRUG-NEA MORE, ℞ 263; — ALIAE, ℞ 264-5; — LASERATA, ℞ 271; — GARATAS, ℞ 471-74; — ASSAS, ℞ 472, 473

Oil substitute, ℞ 9; — oil, to clarify for frying, ℞ 250

—Liburnian, ℞ 7

OLEUM, oil, olive oil; — LIBURNICUM, ℞ 7; HISPANUM, Spanish olive oil

OLEATUS, moistened, mixed, dressed with oil 103; — MOLLE, vegetables strained, a purée, ℞ 103-106; also HOLUS, etc.

OLIFERA, OLYRA, a kind of corn, spelt, ℞ 99; see OLUS

OLIVA, olive, ℞ 30, 91; to keep olives green, ℞ 30

OLLA, a cook pot, a terra-cotta bowl; see also CACCABUS. OLLULA, a small O., a casserole, or cassolette. Sp. OLLA PODRIDA, "rotten pot"

OLUS, OLUSATRUM, OLUSTRUM, OLUSCU-LUM, OLERA, OLISERA, OLIFERA, OLISA-TRA, any herb, kitchen greens, pot herbs, sometimes cabbage, from OLITOR, the truck farmer, ℞ 25, 67, 99, 103
  OLUS ET CAULUS, cabbage and cale, ℞

OLUSATRUM, see OLUS

Omelette with sardines, ℞ 146; — with mush-rooms, ℞ 314; — Soufflée, ℞ 302

OMENTUM, caul, the abdominal membrane, used for sausage-making or to wrap croquettes (kro-meskis) which then were OMENTATA, ℞ 43, 47

Onions, ℞ 304-8

OPERCULUM, a cover, lid, or dish with a cover

Opossum, ℞ 396

ORIGANUM MARJORANA, marjoram; — ori-gany; — VINUM, wine flavored with O.

ORYZA, rice, rice flour; see RISUM

OSPREON, OSPREOS, OSPRION, legumes, Title of Book V

Ostia, town, harbor of Rome; the OFFELLAE OS-TIENSIS, ℞ 261, are the ancient "Hamburg-ers"; this seems to confirm the assumption that the population of sea-port towns have a prefer-ence for meat balls

OSTREA, oyster, ℞ 15, 410; — RIUM, oyster bed or pit, or place for keeping oysters

Ostrich, ℞ 210-11

Oval pan, illustration, p.

Oval service dish, p. 43

Oven, ancient bakery in Pompeii, illustration, p. 2

OVIS SYLVATICA, OVIFERO, wild sheep, ℞ 348-50

OVUM, egg; OVA SPHONGIA EX LACTE, ℞ 302

OXALIS, sorrel

OXALME, acid pickle, vinegar and brine

Oxford Mss., Apiciana X, XI

OXYCOMIUM, pickled olive

OXYGALA, curdled with curds

OXYGARUM, vinegar and GARUM, which see, ℞ 36, 37

OXYPORUS, easily digested, ℞ 34

OXYZOMUM, seasoned with acid, vinegar, lemon, etc.

Oyster sauce, CUMINATUM, ℞ 41

Oysters, how to keep, ℞ 14, 410, 411
— shipped by Apicius, p. 10

P

PALLACANA CEPA, shallot, young onion; cf. CEPA

Pallas Athene Dish, The Great, illustration, p. 158

PALMA, PALMITA, palm shoots

PALUMBA, wood pigeon, ℞ 220

PAN with decorated handle, p. 73

Panada, ℞ 127

PANAX, PANACEA, the herb all-heal; it contains a savory juice like LASER and FERULA

PANDECTES, -ER, a book on all sorts of subjects; Title of Book IV

PANIS, bread, PICENTINUS, ℞ 126

Pans, kitchen, see illustrations, pp. 155, 159

Pap, ℞ 172-3, 182

PAPAVER, poppy-seed; — FICI, fig-seed

PARADOXON, CONDITUM, ℞ 1

Parboiling, ℞ 119

Paris Mss., Apiciana III, IV

Parrot, ℞ 231-2

Parsnips, ℞ 121-3

PARTHIA, ℞ 191, 237, 364; a country of Asia

Partridge, ℞ 218, seq., 499

Passenius — anus, an unidentified Roman, ℞ 389

PASSER, a sea-fish, turbot; also a sparrow which Platina does not recommend for the table

PASSUM, raisin wine

PASTINACA, -CEA, parsnip, carrot, ℞ 121-3; also a fish, the sting-ray

Pastry, absent, p. 43

PATELLA, a platter or dish on which food was cooked and served, corresponding to our gratin dishes; a dish in general. In this sense it is often confused with PATINA, which see, so that it has become difficult to distinguish between the two terms
— THIROTARICA, ℞ 144; — ARIDA, ℞ 145; — EX OLISATRO, ℞ 145a; — SICCA, ℞ 145

PATELLARIUS, pertaining to a PATELLA; also one who makes or sells dishes, and, in the kitchen, also a dishwasher; cf. PATINARIUS

PATINA, PATENA, a pot, pan, dish, plate; also food, eating, a dish, or cookery in general in which sense it corresponds to our "cuisine"
PATINARIUS, a glutton, gormandizer, also a pile of dishes, also the craftsman who makes and the merchant who sells dishes as well as the scullion who washes them.

PATINA APICIANA, ℞ 141; — APUA, ℞ 138-9, 146; — DE ASPARAGIS, ℞ 132-33; — DE CYDONIIS, ℞ 163; — EX LACTE, ℞ 140; — EX LARIDIS ET CEREBELLIS, ℞ 147; — FRISILIS, ℞ 131; — EX RUSTICIS, ℞ 134; — DE ROSIS, ℞ 136; — DE LACERTIS, ℞ 152; — DE LUPO, ℞ 158; — DE PERSICIS, ℞ 160; — EX URTICA, ℞ 162; — EX SOLEIS, ℞ 154; — EX PISCIBUS, ℞ 155-7, 486; — MULLIS, ℞ 148; — QUIBUSLIBET, ℞ 149; — ALIA PISCIUM, ℞ 150; — SOLEARUM EX OVIS, ℞ 487; — QUOTIDIANA, ℞ 122, 142; — VERSATILIS, ℞ 129, 143; — ZOMORE, ℞ 153; — DE PIRIS, ℞ 161; — DE SORBIS, ℞ 159; — DE SAMBUCO, ℞ 135; — DE CUCURBITIS, ℞ 137

PAVO, peacock, ℞ 54

Peaches, a dish of, ℞ 160

Peacock, Book VI, ℞ 54

Pears, ℞ 22, 161

Peas, p. 247, ℞ 185-6, 190-2; — a tempting dish of, ℞ 192; — Indian, ℞ 187; — purée of peas, cold, ℞ 188; — or beans à la Vitellius, ℞ 189, 193; — in the pod, Apician style, ℞ 194-6; — in the pod à la Commodus, ℞ 197; purée of peas with brains and chicken, ℞ 198

PECTINE, scallop, ℞ 52

Peeling young vegetables, ℞ 69

PELAMIS, young tunny, ℞ 426, 444

Pennell, Elizabeth R., writer, pp. 17, 18, 257-58

PEPON, a kind of gourd, melon or pumpkin, ℞ 85

Pepper, ℞ 1; — for other spices, ℞ 143, 177, 295, seq.

PERCA, perch, ℞ 446

Perch, ℞ 446

PERDICE, IN, ℞ 218

PERDRIX, partridge, ℞ 218, seq., 499

PERNA, ham; pork forequarter or hindquarter, ℞ 287, 288
— APRUGNA, ℞ 338

PERSICUM, peach, ℞ 29, 160; — US, peach-tree

Persons named in recipes, pp. 11, 21

PETASO, fresh ham, hind leg of pork, ℞ 289

Petits pois à la française, ℞ 185

Petits salés, ℞ 41, 147, 149, 150, 151

Petronius Arbiter, writer, pp. 3, 7, 11, 15

PETROSELINUM, parsley

PHARIAM, UVAM PASSAM, ℞ 197

PHASEOLUS, FASEOLUS, green string beans, kidney bean, young bean and pod, both green and wax bean varieties. Ger. FISOLE and FASOLE, ℞ 207

PHASIANUS, pheasant; — ARIUS, one who has care of or who raises pheasants, game-keeper, ℞ 49, p. 265

Pheasant, dumplings of, ℞ 48; — plumage as decoration, ℞ 213

Phillipps, bibl. Apiciana I

PHOENICOPTERUS, Flamingo, ℞ 220, 231-2

Picentinian bread, ℞ 126

Pichon, Baron J., collector, pp. 257-8, Apiciana, Nos. 21-22, p. 272

Picking birds, ℞ 233

Pie chimneys, ℞ 141

Pig, see PORCELLUM

PIPER, pepper; — NIGRUM, black p.; — VIRIDUM, green p., ℞ 134; "pepper" for other spices, ℞ 143, 177, 295, seq., — ATUS, prepared with p.

PIPERITIS, pepperwort, Indian pepper, capsicum

PIPIO, a young bird, a squab; from the chirping or "peeping" sounds made by them, — EXOSSATUS, boned squab

PIRUM, pear, ℞ 160-1

PISA, -UM, peas, pea, ℞ 185, seq., 190-2, 195-8; — FARSILIS, ℞ 186; — INDICAM, ℞ 187; — FRIGIDA, ℞ 188; — M VITELLIANAM, ℞ 189, 193; — ADULTERAM, ℞ 192

PISCINA, fish pond, fish tank, which was found in every large Roman household to keep a supply of fresh fish on hand

PISCIS, fish; PISCES FRIXOS, ℞ 476-7; — SCORPIONES RAPULATOS, ℞ 475; — ASSOS, ℞ 478; OENOTEGANON, ℞ 479, 81; — IN PISCIBUS ELIXIS, ℞ 486; — IN PISCE ELIXO, ℞ 433, 434, 435, 436, 454; — AURATA, ℞ 461; — ASSA, ℞ 462; — OENOGARUM, ℞ 464-5

PISTACIUM, -EUM, pistache

PISTOR, baker, pastry cook, confectioner, see COQUUS

Pitch, for sealing of vessels, ℞ 25

PLACENTA, a certain cake, a cheese cake

Plaster in bread, p. 39
— for sealing of pots, ℞ 23

Platina, Bartolomeo, humanist, writer, pp. 8, 9, 19, Apiciana No. 6, and often quoted in this index. Author of first printed Cookery book. Cf. Martino and Platina Exponents of Renaissance Cookery, by J. D. Vehling. Cf. Cibarium, Cornum, Corvus, Frictella, Merula, Morus, Passer, Ranae, Risum, Sturnus, Styrio, Thinca, Thymus, Zanzerella

Plato, writer, p. 12

Platters, Roast, p. 219; Athene, p. 158

Plautus, writer, p. 147, — naming cooks, ℞ 484; Plautian Latinity, ℞ 153

Pliny, writer, p. 31, ℞ 307, 396, 410

Plumage of birds as a decoration, ℞ 213

Plums, ℞ 22

Plutarch, writer, pp. 3, 66, 128

Poggio, medieval scholar, at Fulda, p. 20

POLEI, POLEGIUM, PULEIUM, penny-royal, fleabane, flea-wort

POLENTA, peeled or pearled barley, ℞ 178

Pollio, Roman, feeding human flesh to fish, ℞ 484

POLYPODIUM, the herb fern or polypody

POLYPUS, the fish polypus, ℞ 410

POLYTELES, POLI-, fine dishes, trimmed, set off; "Recherché" food; Title of Book VII

Pomegranates, to keep, ℞ 20

Pompeii: Casa di Forno. See p. 2
— destroyed, p. 3, seq.
— Wine Room, illustration, p. 124

Pompeii, city, description of, see Review. Innkeeper at — advertising ham, ℞ 287; objects, table ware, etc., found at P., see list of illustrations

POMUM, fruit of any tree, as apples, pears, peaches, cherries, figs, dates, nuts, also mulberries and truffles. Cf. MALUM, p. 370

PONTUS, Black Sea Region

PORCA, PORCUS, female and male swine; PORCELLUS, PORCELLINUS, young s., pig, ℞ 336-81, 488-94; — PORCELLUM FARSILEM, ℞ 366, 367; — ASSUM, ℞ 369; — ELIXUM, ℞ 368; — APICIANUM, ℞ 370; — VITELLIANUM, ℞ 371; — LAUREATUM, ℞ 373; — FRONTINIANUM, ℞ 374; — CELSINIANUM, ℞ 376, 377; — HORTULANUM, ℞ 378; — ELIXUM IUS FRIGIDUM, ℞ 379; — TRAIANUM, ℞ 380; — CORIANDRATUM, ℞ 488; — FLACCIANUM, ℞ 372; — OENOCOCTUM, ℞ 489; — EO IURE, ℞ 490; — THYMO SPARSUM, ℞ 491; OXYZOMUM, ℞ 492; — LASARATUM, ℞ 493; — IUSCELLATUM, ℞ 494; — ASSUM TRACTOMELINUM, ℞ 369; — LACTE PASTUM, ℞ 370; — IN PORCELLO LACTANTE, ℞ 381

Pork, p. 285; — and onions à la Lucretius, ℞ 151; — skin, cracklings, ℞ 251-55; — udder, ℞ 251; — tenderloin, ℞ 251-255; — tails and feet, ℞ 251; — fig-fed, ℞ 259; — cutlets, Hunter Style, ℞ 263; — paunch, ℞ 285; — loin and kidneys, ℞ 286; — shoulder, ℞ 287-88; — fresh ham, ℞ 289; — bacon, ℞ 290; — Salt — ℞ 290; — forcement, ℞ 366

Porker, The -'s Last Will and Testament, ℞ 376

Porridge, Books IV, V, ℞ 172, 178; — and wine sauce, ℞ 179; — another, ℞ 180

PORRUM, -US, leek, ℞ 93, 96; "SECTILE —" -Martial

PORTULACA, PORCILACA, purslane

POSCA, originally water and vinegar or lemon juice. It became an acid drink of several variations, made with wine, fruit juice, eggs and water

Pot Roast, ℞ 270

Potherbs, to keep, ℞ 25, 188, see OLUS

Potted Entrées, ℞ 54

POTUS, drink

PRAECOQUO, -OCTUS, -OCIA, "cooked beforehand," also ripened too early, but the present kitchen term is "blanching," or "parboiling." Cf. PRAEDURO

PRAEDURO, to harden by boiling, to blanch, ℞ 119

Preserves, several in Book I

Preserving (keeping of) meats, ℞ 10-12; — fried fish, ℞ 13 — fruit, figs, prunes, pears, etc., ℞ 19-24, 28, 29, 30; — grapes, ℞ 19; — honey cakes, 16; — mulberries, ℞ 24; — oysters, ℞ 14; — pomegranates, ℞ 20; — pot herbs, ℞ 25; — quinces, ℞ 21; — sorrel, sour dock, ℞ 26; — citron, ℞ 23; — truffles, ℞ 27; — vegetable purée, ℞ 106

Press, wine illustration, p. 92

Processing, ℞ 19-24

PRUNA, live, burning coal

PRUNUM, plum; — DAMASCENUM, p. from Damascus, ℞ 22; this variety came dried, resembling our large prunes. — SILVESTRIS, sloe berry, which by culture and pruning has become the ancestor of plums, etc.

PTISANA, (better) TISANA, barley broth, rice broth, a gruel, ℞ 173-3, 200-1; — TARICHA, ℞ 173

Pudding, ℞ 60

PULLUS, PULLULUS, young animal of any kind but principally a pullet, chicken, ℞ 51, 2-7, 213, 235-6, seq. — RAPTUS, note 1, ℞ 140
PULLUM PARTHICUM, ℞ 237; OXYZOMUM, ℞ 238; — NUMIDICUM, ℞ 239; — LASERATUM, ℞ 240; — ELIXUM, ℞ 242; — CUM CUCURBITIS, ℞ 243; — CUM COLOCASIIS, ℞ 244; — VARDANUM, ℞ 245; — FRONTONIANUM, ℞ 246; — TRACTOGALATUM, ℞ 247; — FARSILIS, ℞ 248; LEUCOZOMUM, ℞ 250

PULMENTARIUM, any food eaten with vegetables, pulse or bread, or a dish composed of these ingredients, ℞ 67-71

PULMO, lung, ℞ 29

PULPA, -MENTUM, ℞ 42, 134; also PULMENTUM

PULS, -E, PULTICULUM, Books IV, V, a porridge, polenta, ℞ 178, seq.; PULTES JULIANAE, ℞ 178; — OENOCOCTI, ℞ 179; — TRACTOGALATAE, ℞ 181

PULTARIUS, a bowl, a "cereal" dish, ℞ 104

Pumpkin, B. III, ℞ 73-80; — pie, ℞ 137; — fritters, ℞ 176; — like dasheens, ℞ 74; — Alexandrine Style, ℞ 75; — boiled, ℞ 76; — fried, ℞ 77; — 78; — mashed, ℞ 79; — and chicken, ℞ 80

Purée of lettuce, ℞ 130

PYRETHRUM, -ON, Spanish camomile, pellitory

Q

QUARTARIUS, a measure (which see), ¼ pint

Quenelles, ℞ 131

Quinces, ℞ 21, 162

R

RABBIT, ℞ 54

Radishes, ℞ 102

Ragoût of brains and bacon, ℞ 147 — financière, ℞ 166

RAIA, the sea-fish ray, or skate; also whip-ray; p. 343, ℞ 403-4; Raie au beurre noir, ℞ 404

Raisins, ℞ 30

RANAE, frogs, have been an article of diet for ages. Platina gives fine directions for their preparation. He recommends only frogs living in the water. RUBETAS ET SUB TERRA VIVENTES, UT NOXIAS REJICIO! AQUATILAS HAE SUNT DE QUIBUS LOQUOR
Platina skins the frogs, turns them in flour and fries them in oil; he adds fennel flower garnish and SALSA VIRIDA (green sauce, our ravigote or remoulade) on the side. No modern chef could do different or improve upon it. The fennel blossom garnish is a startling stroke of genius

Rankin, E. M., writer, see COQUUS

RAPA, RAPUM, rape, turnip, navew, ℞ 26, 100-1

RAPHANUS SATIVUS, Horseradish, ℞ 102

Ray, fish, ℞ 403-4

RECOQUO, RECOCTUM, re-heated, warmed-up

Redsnapper, ℞ 448

Réduction, ℞ 145, 168

Reference to other parts of the book by Apicius, ℞ 170, 166

Relishes, ℞ 174-5

RENES, ℞ 286

Reynière, Grimod de la — writer, p. 3, see MAPPA

RHOMBUS, fish, turbot

RHUS, a shrub called SUMACH, seed of which is used instead of salt

RISUM, rice, also ORYZA. The word RISUM is used by Platina who says: "RISUM, QUOD EGO ANTIQUO VOCABULO ORIZAM APPELLATUM PUTO." This is one of the many philologically interesting instances found in Platina and Aegineta of the evolution of a term from the antique to the medieval Latin and finally emerging into modern Italian. What better proof, if necessary, could be desired than this etymology for the authenticity of the Apicius book? Its age could be proven by a philologist if no other proof were at hand

Roasts, Roasting, p. 285, ℞ 266-70

Roman Beauty Apple, ℞ 136
— excesses, p. 15

Roman Cook Stove, illustration, p. 182
— economic conditions, p. 15

Roman Vermouth, ℞ 3

ROSATUM, ROSATIUM, flavored with roses; — VINUM, rose wine, ℞ 4-6; — without roses, ℞ 6

Rose pie, see MALUM ROSEUM, also ℞ 136, 171
— custard, ℞ 136; — pudding, ℞ 136; — apple, ℞ 136

Rose wine, ℞ 4-6

ROSMARINUS, rosemary

Round sausage, ℞ 65
Roux, ℞ 172, see AMYLARE
RUBELLIO, fish, ℞ 447
RUBRA TESTA, red earthen pot
RUMEX, sorrel, sour dock, monk's rhubard, ℞ 24
Rumohr, B., writer, pp. 3, 18
Rumpolt, Marx, cook, cf. Styrio
RUTA, rue; — HORTENSIS, garden r.;
SYLVESTRIS, wild r.; RUTATUS, prepared
with r. Rue was very much esteemed because
of its stimulating properties
Rye, ℞ 99

S

SABUCO, see SAMBUCO
SACCARUM, SACCHARUM, sugar; destillate from
the joints of the bamboo or sugar cane, coming
from India, hence called "Indian Salt." It was
very scarce in ancient cookery. Honey was generally used in place of sugar. Only occasionally
a shipment of sugar would arrive in Rome from
India, supposed to have been cane sugar; other-
wise cane and beet sugar was unknown in ancient
times. Any kind of sweets, therefore, was considered a luxury
SAL, salt. Laxative salt, ℞ 29; "For many ills,"
ibid.
Sala, George Augustus, writer, p. 38
SALACACCABIA, SALACATTABIA, "salt" food
boiled in the "caccabus," ℞ 125-7, 468-70
Salad, ℞ 109-11; — dressing, ℞ 112-3; Italian —
℞ 122
Salcisse, ℞ 41
SALINUM, salt cellar
Salmasius, Codex of —, see Apiciana, III
SALPA, a sea-fish like stock-fish
SALSAMENTUM IN PORCELLO, ℞ 381
Salsicium, ℞ 41
SALSUM, pickled or salt meat, especially bacon;
℞ 10, 41, 147, 149, 150, 428, seq. — CRUDUM,
℞ 151, cf. petits salés
Salt, laxative, ℞ 29; "for many ills," ibid.; —
meat, to make sweet, ℞ 12; — fish, ℞ 144,
seq., 427, seq. — balls, ℞ 145
SALVIA, SALVUS, sage
SAMBUCUS, elder-tree, or e.-berry; ℞ 135
Sanitary measures, see MAPPA
SAPA, new wine boiled down
SAPOR, taste, savor, relish; — ROSELLINUS, rose
extract, prepared rose flavor
SARCOPTES, title of Book II
SARDA, SARDELLA, small fish, sardine, anchovy, ℞ 146, 419, 420, 480; — CONDITAE,
℞ 480; SARDAM FARSILEM, ℞ 419; — Sar-
dine omelette, ℞ 146
Sarinus, Pompeiian innkeeper, p. 7
SARTAGO, frying pan, flat and round or oblong,
of bronze or of iron; some were equipped with
hinged handles, to facilitate packing or storing

away in small places, in soldiers' knapsack, or
to save space in the pantry. This, as well as the
extension handle of some ancient dippers are ingenious features of ancient kitchen utensils. See
also FRICTORIUM, and the illustrations of pans,
pp. 155, 159
SATUREIA, savory, satury
Sauce pans, illustrations, pp. 155, 159, 73, 231
Sauces, ancient compared with modern, pp. 22, 24,
26, 27; — for roasts, ℞ 267-70; — for partridge, ℞ 499; — crane and duck, ℞ 215; —
for fowl, ℞ 218-28
Sauces. Bread Sauce, ℞ 274; Brine, ℞ 284; — for
broiled fish, Alexandrine style, ℞ 437-39; —
for boiled fish, ℞ 433-6, 454; — for broiled
mullet, ℞ 442-3; — boiled meats, ℞ 271-3; —
for roasts, ℞ 267, seq.; English —, ℞ 267; —
for broiled murenas, ℞ 448-51; Dill —, ℞
283; Herb — for fried fish, ℞ 432; — for
Horned fish, ℞ 441; — for lacertus, ℞ 455-
7; — perch, ℞ 446; — redsnapper, ℞ 447;
— dory, ℞ 461-2; — for suckling pig, ℞
379; — young tunny, ℞ 444-5, 459; — for
tooth-fish, ℞ 460-1, 486; — shellfish, ℞ 397;
— for venison, ℞ 339, 349; — for wild sheep
or lamb, ℞ 350; White —, ℞ 276, 277; Wine
— for fish, ℞ 464; Tasty — for conger, ℞
441 — for tidbits, ℞ 276-82; — for sea-scorpion, ℞ 463; — for eel, ℞ 440, 466-7
Saucisse, ℞ 41
Sauerbraten-Einlage, ℞ 11
Sausage, p. 172, ℞ 41, 45, 60-65, 139, 165
Savonarola, Michaele, p. 273
Scalding poultry, ℞ 233
Scallops, ℞ 46
SCANDIUS, chervil
SCARUS, a certain sea-fish esteemed as a delicacy,
a parrot-fish
SCHOLA APITIANA, Apiciana, Nos. 21, 22, 23,
facsimile, p. 206
Schuch, C. Th. editor, Apiciana, Nos. 16-17, p.
34, 25, 270 seq.
Science confirming ancient methods, p. 32
SCILLA, SCYLLA, SQUILLA, a shell-fish, a sea-
onion, ℞ 43, 485
SCORPIO, a sea-scorpion, ℞ 463, 475
SCRIBLITA, SCRIBILITA, pastry, some kind of
pancake, extra hot. Plautus and Martial, hence
Scriblitarius, cake baker, cf. Coquus
SCRUPULUM, SCRI —, a weight, which see
Sealing vessels to prevent air from entering, ℞
23, 25
Sea Barb, ℞ 482-3; — Bass, ℞ 158, 447; — Eel,
℞ 484; — food, p. 343, — stew, Baian style,
℞ 432; — mullet, ℞ 157; nettles, ℞ 162; —
perch, ℞ 447; — pike, ℞ 158; — urchin, ℞
413-4; — scorpion, ℞ 475
Sea-scorpion with turnips, ℞ 475
Sea water, ℞ 8
Seasoning, see flavoring

Secrecy in recipes, pp. 29, 30

Seeds, Summary of, p. 236

SEL, see SIL

SEMINIBUS, DE, p. 236

Seneca, Roman philosopher, pp. 3, 11, 15

SEPIA, cuttle-fish, ℞ 406-9

SERPYLLUM, wild thyme

Service berry, ℞ 159
— pan with decorated handle, illustration, p. 73
— dish for eggs, p. 93

SESAMUM, sesame herb or corn

SESESIL, SEL, SIL, hartwort, kind of cumin

SETANIA, a kind of medlar, also a certain onion or bulb

SEXTARIUS, a measure, which see, ℞ 1

Sforza Ms. Apiciana XIII

Shellfish, ℞ 397, 412

Shell-shaped Dessert Dish, p. 125

Shircliffe, Arnold, Dedication, p. 273

Shore Dinner, ℞ 46

Sicardus Ms. Apiciana XIV

Signerre Rothomag., editor, pp. 258, seq., also see Tacuinus

Signerre, Colophon, p. 260.

SIL, see SESELIS

SILIGO, winter wheat, very hard wheat

SILIQUA, shell, pod, husk

SILPHIUM, SYLPHIUM, same as LASERPITIUM, which see, ℞ 32

SILURUS, supposed to be the river fish sly silurus, or sheat-fish, also called the horn-pout, or cat-fish, ℞ 426

SIMILA, — AGO, fine wheat flour

SINAPIS, mustard

"Singe," ℞ 55

SION, -UM, plant growing in the marshes or on meadows, water-parsnip

SITULA, hot water kettle

SISYMBRUM, water cress

Skate, ℞ 403-4

Slang in ancient text, p. 19

Slaughter, cruel methods of, ℞ 259, 260

Slaves grinding flour, illustration, p. 60

Sloe, see PRUNUM

Smelts, ℞ 138-39

SMYRNION, -UM, a kind of herb, common Alexander

Snails, ℞ 323-5

Soda, use of — to keep vegetables green, ℞ 66

Soft cabbage, ℞ 103-6

SOLEA, flat fish, the sole, ℞ 154, 487; SOLEARUM PATINA, ibid.

SORBITIO, from SORBEO, supping up, sipping, drinking, drought; any liquid food that may be sipped, a drink, a potion, a broth, a sherbet, Fr. SORBET

Sorrel, ℞ 26

Sour Dock, ℞ 26

Soups, ℞ 178, seq.

Sow's womb, matrix, udder, belly, ℞ 59, 172, 251-8

Soyer, Alexis, chef, 35

Sparrow, see PASSER

Spätzli, ℞ 247

Spelt, ℞ 58-9

Spengler, O., writer, p. 17

SPICA, a "spike," ear of corn, top of plants, the plant spikenard, SPICA NARDI

Spiced Fruit, ℞ 177

Spices, Summary of, pp. 234-5; spicing, ancient and modern, ℞ 15, 276-77, 385, seq.

Spiny lobster, ℞ 54, 485

Spoiling, to prevent food from — see Book I, and Preserving, to prevent birds from spoiling, ℞ 229-30, 233

SPONDYLIUM, -ION, a kind of plant, cow-parsnip, or all-heal. Also called SPHONDYLIUM and FONDULUM. It is quite evident that this term is very easily confused with the foregoing, a mistake which was made by Humelbergius and upheld by Lister and others. For comparison see ℞ 46, 115-21, 183, 309, 431

SPONDYLUS, the muscular part of an oyster or other shellfish, scallop, for instance; also a species of bivalves, perhaps the scallop, ℞ 46

SPONGIOLA, rose gall, also the roots of asparagus, clottered and grown close together

SPONGIOLUS, fungus growing in the meadows, a mushroom, cf. SPONDYLIUM and notes pertaining thereto

Sprats, ℞ 138-9

Sprouts, cabbage —, ℞ 89-92

Squab, ℞ 218-27, cf. Pipio

Squash, ℞ 73-80

Squill, ℞ 485

Squirrel, ℞ 396

Stag, ℞ 339-45

Starch, in forcemeats, sausage, etc., ℞ 50

Starr, Frederick, see introduction

STATERAE, steelyards for measuring

Sternajola, writer, Apiciana, No. 28, p. 273

Stewed Lacertus, ℞ 152; — meats, p. 285, ℞ 356, seq.

Stewpots, illustrated, pp. 183, 209, 223, 235

String beans and chick-peas, ℞ 209

STRUTHIO, ostrich, ℞ 210-11

Studemund, W., writer, p. 19

Stuffed pumpkin fritters, ℞ 176; — chicken or pig, ℞ 199; — boned kid or lamb, ℞ 360

STURNUS, a starling, stare; Platina condemns its meat as unfit, likewise that of the blackbird (cf. MERULA); he pronounces their flesh to be "devilish." "STURNI, QUOS VULGO DIABOLICAM CARNEM HABERE DICIMUS." Yet three-hundred years later, French authorities recommend this sort of food. Viger, La Nouvelle Maison Rustique, Paris, 1798, Vol. iii, p. 613, tells how to catch and fatten STURNI. "After a month [of forced feeding] they will be nice and fat and good to eat and to sell; there are persons who live of this trade." He praises the crow similarly.

These instances are cited not only as a commentary upon the taste of the Southern people and their habits which have endured to this day but also to illustrate the singular genius of Platina. Also the following notes to STYRIO tend to show how far advanced was Platina in the matter of food as compared with the masters of the 18th century in France

STYRIO STIRIO STURIO, ℞ 145, sturgeon; probably the same fish as known to the ancients as ACIPENSER or STURIO. (A. SIVE S. OBLONGO TEREDEQUE — Stephanus à Schonevelde, in Ichthyologia, Hamburg, 1624). There can be no doubt that the sturgeon or sterlet is meant by this term, for Platina calls the eggs of the fish "caviare." "OVA STIRIONIS CONDITUM QUOD CAUARE UOCANT." Eloquently he describes his struggle with the changing language. The efforts of this conscientious man, Platina, to get at the bottom of things no matter how trivial they may appear, are highly praiseworthy.

He writes "DE STIRIONE. TRAHI PER TENEBRAS NŪC MIHI VIDEOR, QUANDO HORŪ, DE QUIBUS, DEINCEPS DICTURUS SUM, PISCIŪ, NULLUS CERTUS UEL NOMINIS, UEL NATURAE EXISTAT AUTOR. NEGLIGENTIAE MAIORUM & INSCITIAE ID MAGIS, QUÀM MIHI ASCRIBENDUM EST. VTAR EGO NOUIS NOMINIBUS NE DELICATORUM GULAE PER ME DICANT STETISSE, QUO MINUS INTEGRA UTERENTUR UOLUPTATE."

As for the rest, Platina cooks the sturgeon precisely in our own modern way: namely in water, white wine and vinegar. And: SALEM INDERE MEMENTO! — don't forget the salt!"

Compare him with France 350 years later. As for caviare, A. Beauvilliers, in his L'Art du cuisinier, Paris, 1814, treats this "ragoût" as something entirely new; yet Beauvilliers was the leading restaurateur of his time and a very capable cook, save Carême, the best. Beauvilliers has no use for caviare which he calls "Kavia." Says he: "LES RUSSES EN FONT UN GRAND CAS ET L'ACHETENT FORT CHER [The Russians make a big thing of this and buy it very dearly] CE RAGOUT, SELON MOI, NE CONVIENT QU' AUX RUSSES — this stew, according to my notion, suits only the Russians or those who have traveled thereabouts."

Shakespeare, in speaking about "Caviare to the General" apparently was more up-to-date in culinary matters than this Parisian authority. A search of the eight volumes (Vol. I, 1803) of the famous Almanach des Gourmands by Grimod

de la Reynière, Paris, 1803, seq., fails to reveal a trace of caviare

A German cook, a hundred years after Platina, Marx Rumpolt in "Ein new Kochbuch, Franckfort am Mayn, bey Johan Feyrabendt, 1587" on verso of folio XCVII, No. 9, gives an exact description of caviare and its mode of preparation. He calls it ROGEN VOM HAUSEN. The HAUSEN is the real large sturgeon, the Russian Beluga from which the best caviare is obtained. Rumpolt, whose book is the finest and most thorough of its kind in the middle ages, and a great work in every respect, remarks that caviare is good eating, especially for Hungarian gentlemen

'". . . SO ISSET MAN JN ROH / IST EIN GUT ESSEN / SONDERLICH FÜR EINEN VNGERISCHEN HERRN."

SUCCIDIA a side of bacon or salt pork

SUCCUM, SUCUM, ℞ 172, 200

Suckling Pig, see PORCELLUS

Sugar and pork, ℞ 151; use of — in ancient Rome, see SACCARUM

Suidas, writer, p. 11

SUMEN, ℞ 257; — PLENUM, ℞ 258

Sumptuary laws, p. 25, ℞ 166

Sumptuous dishes, ℞ 285

Sweet dishes, home-made, ℞ 294-6

Sweet MINUTAL, ℞ 168

SYRINGIATUS, ℞ 360

T

TABLE, adjustable, illustration, p. 138; — round, id., p. 122

Tacuinus, editor-printer, p. 258; quoted in recipes 8 seq.; Facs. of Title Page, 1503, p. 262; Facs. of opening chapter, p. 232

TAMNIS, -US, TAMINIUS, wild grape

TANACETUM, tansy

Taranto, Tarentum, city, ℞ 165; -ian sausage, ℞ 140; — Minutal, ℞ 165; see also LONGANO

Taricho, Tarichea, town, ℞ 427, seq.

Taro, dasheen, ℞ 74, 154, 172, 200, 244, 322; see COLOCASIA

Tarpeius, a Roman, ℞ 363

TEGULA, tile for a roof, also a pan, a plate of marble or of copper; Ger. TIEGEL

Tempting Dish of Peas, A —, ℞ 192

TERENTINA, ℞ 338

Tertullian, writer, p. 3

TESTA, -U, -UM, an earthen pot with a lid, a casserole

TESTICULA CAPONUM, ℞ 166

TESTUDO, TESTA, turtle, tortoise. Platina praises the sea-turtle as good eating

TETRAPES, -US, four-footed animals; title of Book VIII

TETRAPHARMACUM, a course of four dishes, or a dish consisting of four meats. In modern language, a "Mixed Grill," a "Fritto Misto," a "Shore-Dinner"

THALASSA, the sea; title of Book IX, treating of fish

Theban ounce, ℞ 3

THERMOPOLIUM, a tavern, specializing in hot drinks

THERMOSPODIUM, a hot-plate, a hot dish carrier, a BAIN-MARIS, illustrations, pp. 72, 90

THINCA, a fish, moonfish (?) "OLIM MENAM APPELLATAM CREDIDERIM" — Platina

Thudichum, Dr., writer, p. 18

THUS, TUS, frankincense, or the juice producing incense, Rosemary (?); also the herb groundpine, CHAMAEPITYS, ℞ 60

Thrush, p. 265, ℞ 497

THYMBRIA, savory; see SISYMBRIUM, SATUREIA and CUNILA; also see THYMUS

THYMUS, thyme. Platina describes THYMUS and THYMBRIA with such a love and beauty that we cannot help but bestow upon him the laurels worn by the more well-known poets who became justly famous for extolling the fragrance of less useful plants such as roses and violets

THYNNUS, tunny-fish, ℞ 426, 457-8

Tidbits, p. 285, ℞ 261, seq. — of lamb or kid, ℞ 355

TISANA, see PTISANA, ℞ 172-3, 200-1

Title pages, Venice, 1503, 262; Lyons, p. 263; Zürich, p. 265; London, p. 267

Toasting, ℞ 129

Tooth-fish, ℞ 157

Torinus, Albanus, editor of the Apicius and Platina editions of 1541, text, p. 14

— quoted, ℞ 1, 2, 8, seq., assailed by Lister, see L.

— facsimile of Title page 1541, p. 220

TORPEDO, -IN, -INE, ℞ 403-4

TORTA, cake, tart; — ALBA, cheese cake

Toulouse garnish, compared, ℞ 378

TRACTOGALATUS, a dish prepared with milk and paste (noodles, spätzli, etc.) — PULLUS, a young chicken pie

TRACTOMELITUS, a dish prepared with honey paste; a gingerbread or honeybread composition

TRACTUM, ℞ 181

Traianus, a Roman, ℞ 380, also Traganus, Trajanus

Traube, writer, p. 19

Trimalchio, fictitious character by Petronius, whose "Banquet" is the only surviving description of a Roman dinner, unfortunately exaggerated because it was a satire on Nero, pp. 8, 11

Tripod, illustration, p. 40

TRITICUM, -EUS, -INUS, wheat, of wheat

TROPHETES, erroneously for AËROPTES, Gr. for fowl, title of Book VI

Truffles, ℞ 27, 33, 315-321, 333, cf. TUBERA

TRULLA, any small deep vessel, also a dipper, ladle

TUBERA, "tubers"; TUBER CIBARIUM, — TERRAE, truffle, a fungus, mushroom growing underground, ℞ 27, 35, 315, seq., 321; T. CYCLAMINOS, "sow-bread," because swine, being very fond of T. dig them up. The truffle defies cultivation, grows wild and today is still being "hunted" by the aid of swine and dogs that are guided by its matchless aroma

TUCETUM, a delicate dish; particularly a dessert made of prunes

Tunny, fish, ℞ 427, 458, 459; Baby, ℞ 420, 424, 425, 426; Salt, ℞ 427

TURDUS, thrush, ℞ 497

Turkey, probably known to the ancients. See Guinea Hen and Meleagris

Turnips, ℞ 100, 101

Turnover dish, ℞ 129

TURTUR, "turtle" dove, ℞ 218, seq., 498; — ILLA, young t., an endearing term

TURSIO, TH, ℞ 145

TYROPATINA, ℞ 301

TYROTARICUS, a dish made of cheese, salt fish, eggs, spices — ingredients resembling our "Long Island Rabbit," ℞ 137, 143, 180, 439; see TARICA, ℞ 144, 428

U

UDDER, ℞ 251

UNCIA, ounce, equals 1/12 lb.; also inch, -/12

UNGELLAE, ℞ 251-5 foot

Urbino, Duke of, p. 269

URNA, urn, pitcher, water bucket; — ULA, small vessel; also a liquid measure, containing half of an AMPHORA, of four CONGII, or twelve SEXTARII; see measures

URTICA, nettle; also sea-nettle, ℞ 108, 162

U. S. Dept. of Agr. on Dasheens, ℞ 322

UVA, grape, ℞ 19; Uvam passam Phariam, ℞ 97

V

VAERST, Baron von, a writer, pp. 3, 8

Vanilla, ℞ 15

VARIANTES LECTIONES, Apiciana No. 12

Varianus, Varius, Varus, Vardanus, Roman family name, ℞ 245

Varro, a writer, ℞ 70, 307, 396, p. 21

VAS, a vase, vat, vessel, dish, plate; — CULUM, a small v.; — VITREUM, glass v., ℞ 23

Vasavarayeyam, ancient Sanscrit book, p. 13

Vatican Mss. Apiciana, p. 254, seq., Incipit facsimile, p. 253

Veal Steak, p. 314, ℞ 351, 2; — Fricassée, ℞ 353, 4

Vegetable Dinner, ℞ 67-9; 71, 145, 188; — purée, ℞ 103-6; — peeling of young v., ℞ 66; to keep v. green, ℞ 67, 188; — and brain pudding, ℞ 131

Vehling, J. D., see Introduction V. collection, p. 257

VENERIS OSTIUM, ℞ 307

Venison, ℞ 339-45

VENTREM, AD —, ℞ 68, 69, 70, 71; — ICU-LUM, ℞ 285

VERMICULI, "little worms," noodles, vermicelli

Vermouth, Roman, French, and Black Sea, different kinds of, ℞ 3, seq.

VERVEX, a wether-sheep, mutton

VESTINUS, see Caseus, ℞ 126

Vicaire, Georges, bibliographer, p. 18

VICIA, a kind of pulse, vetch

VICTUS, way of life, diet; — TENUIS, reduced diet

Vinaigrette, ℞ 113, 336, 341

Vinidarius, Excerpts of, pp. 12, 21, 234

VINUM, wine; — CANDIDUM FACIES, ℞ 8; many technical terms are given to wines, according to their qualities, such as ALBUM, CONDITUM, FUSCUM, NIGRUM, LIMPIDUM, ATRUM, DURUM, FULVUM, SANGUINEM, RUBENS, FIERI, BONUM, DULCE SUAVUM, FIRMUM, SALUBRE, DILUTUM, VAPIDUM, etc. These, as our modern terms, are employed to designate the "bouquet," color and other characteristics of wine. Then there are the names of the different brands coming from different parts, too numerous to mention. Furthermore there are wines of grapes, old and new, plain or distilled, raw or cooked, pure and diluted, natural or flavored, and the many different drinks made of grape wine with herbs and spices.

V. NIGRUM, "black wine," may be muddy wine in need of clarification; there is some slight doubt about this point. It appears that the vintner of old was much more tempted to foist unworthy stuff upon his customers than his colleague of today who is very much restricted by law and guided by his reputation

VINUM also is any drink or liquor resembling grape wine, any home-made wine fermented or fresh. There is a V. EX NAPIS, — PALMEUM, — EX CAROTIS, — EX MILII SEMINE, — EX LOTO, — EX FICO, — EX PUNCICIS, — EX CORNIS, — EX MESPILIS, — EX SORBIS, — EX MORIS, — EX NUCLEIS PINEIS, — EX PIRIS, — EX MALIS, (cf. Pliny), resembling our cider, perry, berry wines and other drink or liquor made of fruit, berries, vegetables or seeds

VIOLATIUM and ROSATIUM, ℞ 5, are laxatives; — ORIGANUM is wine flavored with origany; etc., etc.

It is doubtful, however, that the Romans knew the art of distillation to the extent as perfected by the Arabs centuries later and brought to higher perfection by the medical men and alchymists of the middle ages

Violet Wine, ℞ 5

Virility, supposed stimulants for, ℞ 307, 410

VITELLINA, VITULINA, calf, veal, ℞ 351-4

Vitellius, emperor, p. 11, ℞ 189, 193, 317

VITELLUS OVI, yolk of egg; also very young calf. "Calf's sweetbreads" — Danneil

Vollmer, F., editor, commentator, Apiciana No. 21, 23, 27, pp. 13, 18, 19, 273

Vossius, G. J., philologist, on Coelius, p. 266

VULVA, sow's matrix, womb; — ULA, small v., ℞ 59, 251-54, 256. Was considered a delicacy. Pliny, Martial and Plutarch wrote at length on the subject. The humane Plutarch tells of revolting detail in connection with the slaughter of swine in order to obtain just the kind of V. that was considered the best

Cf. Pliny, Hist. Nat., VIII, 51; XI, 37, 84, 54; Plutarch's essay on flesh eating, Martial, Ep. XII, 56 and VII, 19

W

WEIGHTS. LIBRAE, scale, balance. LIBRA — pound — lb — 12 ounces, equivalent to one AS

UNCIA, an ounce, properly the twelfth part of any unit, also any small bit

SCRIPULUM, or SCRU —, 1 scruple, 288 to 1 lb.

SELIBRA for SEMILIBRA, half a pound Theban ounce, cf. ℞ 3

Weighing fluids, ℞ 471

Welsh rabbit, see ZANZERELLA

Whiting, ℞ 419

Wild Boar, ℞ 329, seq., 338; — sheep, ℞ 348; — goat, ℞ 346, seq.

Wilson, Dr. Margaret B., collector, cf. Preface, p. 37; cf. Apiciana I, pp. 254, 257; cf. Garum

Wine, fine spiced, ℞ 1; Rose, ℞ 4; — without roses, ℞ 6; — Violet, ℞ 5; — To clarify muddy, ℞ 8; — New — boiled down, DEFRITUM, ℞ 21; — sauce for truffles, ℞ 33; — Palm, ℞ 35; — of Carica figs, ℞ 55; — sauce for fig-fed pork, ℞ 259, 260; — fish, ℞ 479; cf. VINUM

Wine pitcher, illustration, p. 208; — press, illustration, p. 92; — storage room in Pompeii, illustration, p. 124; — Dipper, p. 3; — Crater, p. 140

Wolf, Rebecca, writer, ℞ 205, seq.

Woodcock, ℞ 218, seq.

Wood-pigeon, ℞ 218, seq.

Wooley, Mrs. Hannah, writer, ℞ 52

Writers, ancient, on food, pp. 3, 4

Y

YEAST, ℞ 16

Young cabbage, p. 188, ℞ 87

Z

ZAMPINO, ℞ 338

ZANZERELLA, a "Welsh rabbit." "CIBARIUM QUOD VULGO ZANZERELLAS UOCANT" — Platina

ZEMA, ZU-, ZY-, a cook pot for general use

ZINZIGER, GINGIBER, ginger; the latter is the better spelling

ZOMORE, ZOMOTEGANON, ZOMORE GANONA, ZOMOTEGANITE, — a dish of fish boiled in their own liquor, resembling the modern bouil-labaisse, ℞ 153. The GANON, — A, — ITE, is the name of an unidentified fish, the supposed principal ingredient of this fish stew. Cf. Oenoteganon

[End of Index and Vocabulary]
[INDICIS FINIS]

ADDENDA

Description of Commentaries

APICIANA NOS. 30-31, A.D., 1935-36

J. SVENNUNG: UNTERSUCHUNGEN ZU PALLADIUS UND ZUR LATEINISCHEN FACH- UND VOLKSSPRACHE.

"Skrifter utgivna med understöd av Vilhelm Ekmans universitets-fond, Uppsala," tom. 44, (Uppsala, 1935)

and

DE LOCIS NON NULLIS APICIANIS SCRIPSIT J. SVENNUNG.

(Särtryck ur Eranos vol. XXXIV) Gotoburgi 1936. Typis descr. Elanders Boktr. A. –B.

[Through the good offices of Dr. Edwardt Brandt, of Munich, the above two commentaries on Apicius were received in the last moment, thanks to the courtesy of the author, Lekto J. Svennung, of Uppsala, Sweden. The first study is a critique of technical terms and colloquialisms as found in Palladius, touching frequently upon Apicius, published in 1935 at Uppsala by the Vilhelm Ekman University Foundation and the other is a reprint of an article on a number of Apician formulae from Eranos, Vol. XXXIV, published at Gothenburg, 1936, by Elander, Ltd.

J. D. V., Chicago, November 30th, 1936.]

LIBRO COMPLETO···
SALTAT SCRIPTOR
PEDE LAETO ······

(Squib on the margin of an ancient manuscript in the Monastery of St. Gallen, Switzerland)